John Owen, Edward Williams

An Exposition of the Epistle to the Hebrews

with the preliminary exercitations - Vol. 1

John Owen, Edward Williams

An Exposition of the Epistle to the Hebrews
with the preliminary exercitations - Vol. 1

ISBN/EAN: 9783337316587

Printed in Europe, USA, Canada, Australia, Japan

Cover: Foto ©Lupo / pixelio.de

More available books at **www.hansebooks.com**

AN
EXPOSITION

OF THE

EPISTLE TO THE HEBREWS;

WITH THE

PRELIMINARY EXERCITATIONS.

By JOHN OWEN, D. D.

REVISED AND ABRIDGED;

WITH A FULL AND INTERESTING

LIFE OF THE AUTHOR,

A COPIOUS INDEX, &c.

By EDWARD WILLIAMS.

Search the Scriptures.—John v. 39.

IN FOUR VOLUMES.
VOL. I.

LONDON:

Printed for T. PITCHER, No. 44, Barbican;
sold also by C. DILLY, Poultry; T. PARSONS, Paternoster
Row; and T. MATHEWS, Strand.
M.DCC.XC.

[Entered at Stationer's-Hall.]

CONTENTS.

VOL. I.

	Page.
THE Editor's Preface	1—8
Memoirs of Dr. Owen	9—42

EXERCITATIONS.

PART I.

Concerning the Epistle to the Hebrews.

EXER. 1. The Epistle to the Hebrews proved to be strictly canonical — 43—60
EXER. 2. St. Paul the Author of the Epistle to the Hebrews — 61—78
EXER. 3. Of the Time when, and Language in which the Epistle to the Hebrews was written — 78—85
EXER. 4. Of the Oneness of the Church — 85—90
EXER. 5. Of the Jewish Writings — 90—104

PART II.

Concerning the Messiah.

EXER. 1. Messiah, the Deliverer from Evil, promised of old — 104—

CONTENTS

	Page
Exer. 2. Appearances of the Son of God under the Old Testament	141—152
Exer. 3. The Faith of the Jews concerning the Messiah	152—170
Exer. 4. The promised Messiah is long since come	170—188
Exer. 5. Daniel's Prophecy explained and vindicated	189—213
Exer. 6. The Evasions of the modern Jews answered	214—223
Exer. 7. Jesus of Nazareth the only true and promised Messiah	224—245
Exer. 8. The Jews' Objections against the Christian Religion answered	245—257

PART III.

Concerning the Priesthood of Christ.

Exer. 1. Of the Origin of Christ's Priesthood	258—293
Exer. 2. The Necessity of the Priesthood of Christ	293—310
Exer. 3. Of the Kingdom or Lordship of Christ	310—329

APPENDIX.

The Editor's Letter to Dr. Priestley	333—350
The Editor's Letter to Mr. David Levi	353—362

VOL. II.

Exposition of the Epistle to the Hebrews.

Chap. I.	1—117
Chap. II.	117—241

CONTENTS.

	Page.
Chap. III. - - -	242—402
Chap. IV. - -	402—513

VOL. III.

Exposition of the Epistle to the Hebrews.

Chap. V. - - -	1—93
Chap. VI. - -	94—235
Chap. VII. - - -	236—378
Chap. VIII. - -	378—463
Chap. IX. - - -	464—583

VOL. IV.

Exposition of the Epistle to the Hebrews.

Chap. X. - -	1—102
Chap. XI. - - -	103—259
Chap. XII. - -	259—432

Index to the whole.
A Table of the **Texts more** or less illustrated in this Work.
Advertisement and Errata.

THE

EDITOR's PREFACE.

THE many encomiums that have been paſſed upon Dr. OWEN's theological works, by the beſt judges in the laſt and preſent century; and the high eſteem in which they are held by orthodox, judicious, and truly ſpiritual Chriſtians in the preſent day, are an inconteſtable proof of their intrinſic value. He often diſcovers, beyond diſpute, great acuteneſs of thought, profound ſentiments, and eſpecially a ſolid judgement, in reference to the unadulterated Goſpel; and, in the more practical and experimental parts of his writings, an uncommon degree of devotion, an alarming or melting animation, and ſpiritual fervour; qualities in an author, it muſt be owned, equally rare and invaluable!

We find, however, that frequently theſe excellent materials, (the ſubſtance and ſpirit of his writings,) are negligently dreſſed; or, at leaſt, when art is employed, it is employed according to the faſhion of the times in which he lived; the effect of which may be juſtly termed a "cumbrous drapery," when compared with the "*ſimplex munditiis*," the neatneſs and taſte in ſtile and compoſition, on which modern authors pique themſelves: owing to this revolution in the mode of dreſſing thought, the innumerable ſcholaſtic diviſions, the long ſentences and involved parentheſes, the numerous quotations of Latin

THE EDITOR's PREFACE.

Latin and Greek in the body of a work, often cause a modern eye to turn away in disgust, and to neglect a precious pearl that is lodged in so unfashionable a cabinet; while, perhaps, the same eye is charmed with another prettier casket, which contains only gewgaws and trifles.

Impartiality must also confess, that Dr. OWEN was what we may a call a *voluminous* writer; and in the present day, the very *idea* of an expository work, consisting of four volumes folio, on a single epistle, is enough to frighten the fashionable class of readers, who are never better pleased, as one observes, than when they peruse a book " brief, gaudy, and superficial." The difference between the taste of the last and present age, in this respect, is very striking. As a specimen of the former, we might mention, beside the work under immediate notice, " CARYL on Job;" and as a portrait of the latter, the following remarks of a shrewd anonymous observer, " Μεγα βιβλιον μεγα κακον, *A great book is a great evil*," is a maxim which was perhaps never more universally assented to than at present. With all the fondness for reading, now so observable in every class of the community, few are to be met with who will enter on laborious discussions, or peruse *voluminous* performances. Unambitious of possessing those genuine pearls of science, which must be sought by diving to the bottom of the ocean which produces them, the *generality of readers* content themselves with the shells that are to be gathered from its sands and its shallows.—Many writers *now* employ themselves in dealing out learning, as innkeepers do their liquors—in " *small quantities*." This is *satyrical*.

On the other hand, the art of reducing the *bulk* of books, when it avoids the fault of being superficial and desultory, is not to be condemned. If a large work, abounding with excellent thoughts, and a truly evangelical spirit, a work comparatively but little known, too dear for the pockets, too voluminous for the courage and patience, and too unfashionable for the taste of the generality of religious readers; if, I say, such a work may be fairly compressed into about *one third* of the original size, and exhibited in a form more modern, perspicuous, and correct; it may be presumed that such a present might not be unacceptable, but received with gladness by the religious public, as calculated to promote the real interest of evangelical piety. Such is the design of this publication.—" The world," says an ingenious writer, " becomes every day more and more convinced of the utility of *abridgements*. For so great is the increase of all kinds of knowledge, that the human mind finds herself incapable of taking in the whole ; and becomes sensible of the necessity of being assisted in her choice of essential and valuable things."* Hence the Cyclopædias and Encyclopædias, for which modern times are noted, and with which the more enlightened countries (in point of science and arts) abound; which yet are only *abridgements* of voluminous, inconvenient, or inaccessible works. And though the public is often grossly imposed upon by pompous titles prefixed to superficial contents, yet the very attempt to impose is a presumptive argument, that such a plan well executed is valuable. To which we may add, that the method of publishing large and valuable works *abridged*, tends perhaps to avoid what might be thought a growing evil—the multiplication of modern authors, who but barely stand on the list of mediocrity ; while the most valuable sentiments obtain a fresh and more vigorous circulation.

But as the author just mentioned farther observes, " The same cause makes a *good abridgement* very difficult to compile. To omit nothing which is *essential*, and to insert nothing which is *superfluous*, requires a thorough knowledge of the subject, and a great discernment; for to reduce much into little, is far more difficult than to enlarge little into much."† And, indeed, the task becomes more difficult in proportion as the bulk of the original is reduced in the abridgement. The difficulty lies, in avoiding on the one hand, a mere *extract*, which deserves not the name of an abridgement ; and, on the

* FORMEY's Ecclesiastical History. Preface.
† Ut supra.

other, the injudicious crowding of too many ideas into a small compass, which instead of enlightening dazzle the mind, appearing like a number of sparks in the midst of smoke, rather than a bright and pleasant flame; instead of engaging distracts, and instead of alluring fatigues the attention. In such a case the affections, which ought to be consulted by every writer who expects to profit by pleasing (and he must have an extraordinary invention, and no small share of assurance, who expects to profit by any other way) are prevented from operating, they have no room to play, their elasticity and expansive force are either weakened or destroyed.

It may probably occur to some, that, seeing four volumes *octavo* must needs contain much less matter than the original work, which consists of so many small *folios*, much valuable matter is left out. To which I answer, that though this be granted, we have no need to regret the loss, when we observe, that nothing is left out but what appeared either tautological, redundant, digressive, and unnecessarily prolix; or else what was so plain to most intelligent readers, as by no means requiring a formal and long proof. The reader, who has no opportunity to compare this edition with the original work, may depend upon it, that all the valuable, useful, and pertinent *criticisms*; the most forcible *arguments* in proof of any important point; the most evangelical and sublime *sentiments* and *doctrines*; the most close, convincing, and edifying *improvements*; the most animating and pathetic addresses and exhortations, contained in the other, are preserved in this. And this, I presume, will be deemed a sufficient apology for reducing the size. But after all, I wish it may not be deemed by most still too long, as I suppose there is not another exposition on this epistle, the original excepted, so full and large as this abridgement will be found. And I cannot help thinking that, with the exercitations, it may be reckoned one of the most valuable systems of doctrinal, practical, and experimental divinity, that is to be met with in the English language.

It

THE EDITOR's PREFACE.

It is hardly needful to observe, that it is the incumbent duty of every faithful abridger, as well as a faithful translator, to adhere scrupulously to the *sense* of his author, except the reason to the contrary be universally obvious, nor even then without apprizing the reader of it. This is what I have endeavoured throughout to pay the strictest regard to. The reader of the ensuing pages will find in them the genuine thoughts and sentiments of Dr. Owen, to the best of my knowledge, and no other. Sometimes, indeed, the abridger thought it absolutely necessary, in discharging his duty to his readers, to exchange an expression, or to alter a phraseology, for others that appear now more expressive, or better understood. And now and then he has taken the liberty, for a similar reason, of inserting an expressive or animating epithet, justified by the connection, or turned a sentence merely declarative into an awakening interrogation. Some may think that these liberties are after all *too seldom* used, while others are ready to entertain a jealousy, when they apprehend that any freedom is taken with an author whom they so much revere. To please all is impossible, while men's ideas of propriety and utility are so various; and, therefore, to attempt it would be a fruitless toil, the offspring of folly, and the parent of disappointment. Suffice it to say, that in the present undertaking the Editor has proposed as the end, the greatest and most general good, and with dependance on the head of all gifts and graces—the blessed and adorable person, whose glory in the salvation of his people is the sublime and delightful subject of these volumes—he has pursued that end according to the best of his judgement. And he cannot help indulging a pleasing hope, that the cause of truth, the profitable knowledge of God our Saviour, the edification of believers, and the increase of fervent love among brethren, will be promoted by the present attempt.

Every one knows, that in all kinds of composition, the article of *method* is of considerable moment; and there appears to me two extremes into which we are apt to run. The one is the dry, scholastic mode of dividing and

and subdividing a discourse into bits and crumbs, and often for no other reason than because the subject is *capable* of being so much divided, or merely because the ideas cloathed have some *dependance* among themselves! And the other, which is at present much more in vogue, is that which affects to discard all signs of order and division, and is content with a cryptic or hidden method. And here it must be granted, that where the only or principal design of an Author is to amuse and please, the last mode is well adapted to it; but where the judgement, reason, and memory are addressed, as well as the imagination and passions, a moderate use of that method which is open and avowed seems necessary, and more especially is it indispensably so, in such a work as the ensuing exposition. I have, therefore, attempted to avoid both extremes, by adopting a reconciling medium. He who is regardless of the heads and divisions, may pass on, as a traveller who is regardless of the mile-stones on his road, without any inconvenience; while another, who is more observant, is gratified by marking his progress. The judicious and inquisitive will be pleased, I presume, with having the contents of each discourse at the head of it, as a curious traveller is pleased with viewing a well proportioned map of a road which he has not travelled. And through the use of *sections*, that serve as marks and distances on a map, any head of discussion may be found out with a glance, with the general design and connection of the whole.

After all, my principal endeavour has been, as undoubtedly it *ought* to have been, to preserve as much as possible the excellent spirit and unction of the original; that no part of its light or heat be lost, but rather collected, and, as it were, brought into a focus. To succeed in such a design *effectually*, requires no small preparation. I am convinced, that nothing short of a just, consistent, and comprehensive acquaintance with the gospel;—a disinterested and earnest regard to the glory of God;—a fervent love to the Redeemer, and the souls of men for his sake;—the continual teaching and influences of the Spirit of all grace;—a moſt ſteady faith in the divine promiſes;—deep humility and diligent attention in learning the whole revealed will of God;—the ſpirit of prayer and ſublime devotion;—an experimental foretaſte of heavenly bliſs and glory;—with a delightful mixture of patient hope, ſubmiſſive longing after the end of faith, and an unwearied proſecution of that end in the uſe of appointed means: nothing but theſe qualifications appear neceſſary to *keep pace,* if I may ſo expreſs myſelf, with the ſpirit and unction of Dr. OWEN. Alas! how ſhort am I of ſuch a ſtature! However, according to the talent and meaſure of faith received, the Lord be praiſed, it is my ſincere deſire to ſerve the beſt intereſts of immortal ſouls, to edify the body of Chriſt in knowledge and faith, holy love and obedience, as the inſtituted preparatives to the promiſed everlaſting reſt and glory.

It has been well obſerved, that " ſentiments of eſteem and veneration, combining with natural curioſity, prompt us to inquire into the *hiſtory* of thoſe men by whoſe writings we have been improved in wiſdom and virtue." Therefore, the prefixing an account of the moſt memorable particulars in the life and character of Dr. OWEN, will no doubt be acceptable to all intelligent and inquiſitive readers of this performance. Though the Editor has availed himſelf of other ſources and hints (which he thought it unneceſſary to refer to) yet, in compariſon, he has done little more than abridge the memoirs already drawn up, prefixed to the Doctor's poſthumous ſermons and tracts; reduced them to a method a little more diſtinct and perſpicuous, with the addition of a few obvious reflections, which he thought had a tendency to diverſify, to enliven, and to improve the narrative.

I have only to add, that from a conviction of the utility of an abridged edition of Dr. OWEN " on the Hebrews," with the " preliminary diſſertations," I have had the work in contemplation for ſome years, (and I bleſs the God of all grace for the pleaſure and improvement the undertaking has been the means of affording me;) that after I had made ſome progreſs therein, with a view

to

to publish it by subscription, I was applied to by the publisher of the *Evangelical Library* about its being sent into the world through the medium of that repository of valuable and scarce divinity. And I own I was not averse to send it abroad in company with that venerable band of worthies, who, though dead, it is hoped will yet speak, with increasing force, not only to the present, but also to future generations. But, like the other publications in the *Evangelical Library*, the present work stands entirely detached from all preceding or future volumes, by the judicious mode adopted by the publisher of having double title pages.

This performance is now launched into the world, with earnest prayer to the God of all grace, that both it and every other of the same tendency, may be abundantly owned by him as a means of grace and salvation.

Oswestry,
March 18, 1789.

EDWARD WILLIAMS.

MEMOIRS

OF THE LIFE OF

JOHN OWEN, D.D.

§ 1. *Introduction.* § 2. *His pedigree and parentage.* § 3. *His birth, education, and uncommon application to studies.* § 4. *His youthful vanity.* § 5. *How supported at College.* § 6. *Forced to leave it. Ordained.* § 7. *His great convictions and distress.* § 8. *Disowned of his Uncle, he removes to London.* § 9. *How relieved.* § 10. *His afflictions useful.* § 11. *Settles at Fordham and is married there.* § 12. *Removes to Coggeshall.* § 13. *Becomes more popular.* § 14. *His first acquaintance with Fairfax and Cromwell. Goes to Ireland.* § 15. *To Scotland.* § 16. *Made Vice-chancellor.* § 17. *His prudent and moderate conduct.* § 18. *With due authority.* § 19. *Is hospitable and generous.* § 20. *His exemplary diligence.* § 21. *Retires to Stadham.* § 22. *Is offered preferment.* § 23. *Yet persecuted.* § 24. *Calumniated.* § 25. *Improves his liberty.* § 26. *Opposes the conventicle bill.* § 27. *Noticed by King Charles II.* § 28. *Sickness and death.* § 29. *Character.* § 30. *Epitaph.*

§ 1. DOCTOR JOHN OWEN, the celebrated Author of the following expository work, was a person confessedly of superior talents, erudition, and piety. This is abundantly witnessed by his cotemporaries, and corroborated by the concessions of those who were enemies to his theological principles. It is to be lamented that the materials requisite to fill up his just character are not more ample; particularly those parts of his private conduct, which could be known but to a few; but which, nevertheless, are the truest indications of those motives that reflect a lustre on actions, which otherwise may appear common. However, we are furnished with as many facts and circumstances, of undoubted authenticity, in connection with his writings, as prove him to be an extraordinary person, whether we consider him as the profound scholar and divine, or the experienced humble Christian.

§ 2. He derived his pedigree from LEWIS OWEN, of *Llwyn*, near *Dolgelle*, Merionethshire, Esquire.* GRIFFITH, the fifth son of this gentleman, had a daughter named SUSAN, who was married to HUMPHREY, a branch of the same family in another line. This HUMPHREY

---

* This gentleman, who was heir to an estate of about 300l. *per annum*, was lineally descended (according to LEWIS DYNN's book of records relating to the antiquities of Wales) from a younger son of Llewelyn [not Kewelyn, I presume, as some have written it] ap GWRGAN, Prince of *Glamorgan*, and Lord of *Cardiffe*, which was the last family of the five royal tribes of Wales. He was Vice-chamberlain, and Baron of the Exchequer in North Wales, about the middle of the reign of HENRY the Eighth; and continued in those honourable stations through the reigns of EDWARD the Sixth, and Queen MARY, and until the eighth year of Queen ELIZABETH, in great credit and authority. This appears by the letters of these three royal personages to him and John WYNNE ap MEREDITH, of GWYDIR, Esq. in whose family those letters are kept, who both jointly employed their power in apprehending felons and outlaws; of whom there was a great number in those parts during the wars betwixt the houses of *York* and *Lancaster*. When LEWIS OWEN was High Sheriff of the county of Merioneth, he had to attend *Montgomery* assizes, (which opportunity he embraced of treating with the Lord of *Mouthrey* for his daughter in marriage with JOHN his eldest son) but in his return he fell among some outlaws, being several brothers called *gwillied cochion*, i. e. the *red robbers*, at a place called *Dugöed*, near *Mowthy*, and was shot through the head with an arrow. A plain cross was erected to the Baron's memory, upon the place where he was murdered, of which there are now no remains to be seen; but the gate which the assassins had made fast to obstruct his free passage, is to this day called *Llidiart crôes y Baron*, i. e. *The gate of the Baron's cross.*

had

had fifteen sons, and the youngest, whose name was HENRY, was our author's father. *

§ 3. JOHN was his second son, and was born at *Stadham*, in Oxfordshire, *Anno Domini* 1616. He had his school learning at Oxford, and being a boy of such extraordinary genius and parts, he made so quick a proficiency, that he was admitted into Queen's College, under the learned Dr. BARLOW, afterwards Bishop of *Lincoln*, at about twelve years of age; and commenced Master of Arts when he was but nineteen. † He pursued his studies with incredible diligence, allowing himself, for several years, only about four hours sleep in a night (which is a clear proof of his constitutional strength, as well as thirst for literature), so that he soon had made a considerable progress in learning. His youthful recreations were chiefly of the violent kind, as leaping, throwing the bar, ringing of bells, and the like; which, though in him expressive of more than ordinary vigour, are not to be recommended for imitation, especially to candidates for the sacred ministry; for as, to most constitutions, such exertions are too violent to answer the purpose of recreation, so they are not the most decent and inoffensive to serious minds; which consideration ought, undoubtedly, to have

---

* HENRY OWEN was bred a scholar, and having passed through his academical studies at Oxford, was, after some time, chosen minister at *Stadham* in that county. He was reckoned a strict puritan for his more than ordinary zeal in those early days of reformation. He married a pious woman, had several children, and, after many years of reputation and service, died in a good old age.

† Literis natus, literis innutritus, totusque deditus;
   Donec animata plane evasit bibliotheca:
   Authoribus classicis, qua Græcis, qua Latinis,
 Sub. EDV. SYLVESTRO, scholæ privatæ Oxonii moderatore,
   Operam navavit satis felicem:
   Feliciorem adhuc studiis philosophicis,
 Magno sub BARLOVIO, coll. reginalis, id tempus, socio.

These lines are taken from the Rev. Mr. T. GILBERT's *larger* epitaph, (for that which is intire at the close of these memoirs, was composed also by him) and for the sake of the learned reader, will be occasionally referred to when it conveys any peculiar information relative to our Author's history or character.

no small influence in regulating even our recreative exercises.

§ 4. During nearly all the time he continued at college, being as yet in the days of his vanity, his whole aim and ambition was, in his indefatigable application to study, to raise himself to some eminence in church or state, to either of which he was then indifferent; and he was ready to confess after, with shame and sorrow, that then, being totally under the influence of an aspiring mind, the love of popular applause, and the desire of secular honour and preferment, the honour of God, or serving his country, otherwise than he might thereby serve himself, were most remote from his intentions. And happy were it for seminaries of learning, if these motives in pursuit of literature were less prevalent in them every day! How desirable for the interest of true religion, that the constraining love of Christ, and a concern for precious souls, reigned in the heart of every candidate for the sacred function! Then self-applause, and other sinister and base motives, that disgrace the Christian ministry, would be kept under, the love of learning and science would be duly regulated, and all the furniture acquired devoted to God, in serving the immortal interests of mankind. However, we may observe and admire the wisdom of divine Providence, that often over-rules the natural genius and inclination, as in the present case, for while our young student was actuated by no higher motive than self gratification, he was accumulating such a stock of learning and knowledge, as was afterwards consecrated to the very important and extensive service of the church of God.

§ 5. His father, being the youngest of fifteen brothers, and having a large family, could not afford him any considerable maintenance at the university; but he was liberally supplied by an uncle, one of his father's brothers, a gentleman of a fair estate in Wales; who having no children of his own, intended to have made him his heir. He lived in the college until he was twenty-one years
of

of age, from which time he met with extraordinary changes.

§ 6. About A. D. 1636, Dr. LAUD, Archbishop of *Canterbury*, and Chancellor of *Oxford*, imposed several superstitious rites on the university, upon pain of expulsion But Mr. OWEN had then received such light to discover the rights of men and Christians, and to distinguish between real and spurious authority, that his conscience would not submit to those arbitrary impositions. However temporal interest might have pleaded for his compliance, yet other more weighty considerations of a religious nature prevailed; for by this time such gracious impressions were made upon his mind, as inspired him with ardent zeal for the purity of divine worship, and greater reformation in the church. This change of judgement soon discovered itself; his former friends forsook him as one infected with puritanism; and, in short, he was become so much the object of resentment from the *Laudensian* party, that he was forced to leave the college. Soon after this, it is supposed, he took orders, and became chaplain to Sir ROBERT DORMER, of *Ascott*, in Oxfordshire, being tutor at the same time to his eldest son.

§ 7. But we must here take a more particular survey of his spiritual exercises, a scene which at first appears very dark and gloomy, but afterwards grows bright and pleasant. It may be previously remarked, that when we observe the several steps of Divine conduct towards him, through that remarkable part of his life, wherein the great and gracious change upon his soul was taking place, how he was supported and carried on through amazing steps of dejection and temptations; it might be naturally expected that he was destined in the order of Providence (as LUTHER and many others were after the severest exercises of mind) for some eminent services; as we find in fact he afterwards proved one of the most useful instruments and brightest ornaments in the church of God. We must then know *that as the source of his troubles* he was exercised with many perplexing thoughts about his

spiritual

spiritual state, which, joined with outward discouragements, threw him into a deep melancholy for three months; during which time he could hardly be induced to speak a word, and when he did, it was with much observable disorder. And even when the violence of his distress was in some measure abated, he underwent no small trouble of mind, and grievous temptations, for near *five years*. But the all-wise and gracious God at last brought forth " judgement unto victory;" for this long night of trouble and mourning was afterwards succeeded with lasting light, serenity, and joy. Thus, like Job, after " being tried, he came forth as gold," [Job xxiii. 10.]

§ 8. When the civil war commenced, he openly avowed the Parliament's cause, which his uncle, who had supported him at college, being a zealous royalist, so vehemently resented, that he turned him at once out of his favour, settled his estate upon another person, and left him nothing in his will. He now lived as chaplain with John Lord LOVELACE, of *Hurley*, in Berkshire, who, though a royalist, used him with great civility; but his honourable friend going at length to the King's army, Mr. OWEN went to *London*, where he was a perfect stranger, and took lodgings in *Charter-House Yard*.

§ 9. He still laboured under his melancholy and spiritual troubles; but the Lord's time was now come. And seeing the circumstances attending his recovery, and establishment in solid comfort, were somewhat singular, they deserve insertion. He went one Lord's day with Mr. OWEN, a cousin of his, to *Aldermanbury* church, with a view to hear Mr. CALAMY; but after waiting a long time, it was known that Mr. CALAMY was prevented from attending service by some extraordinary occasion, upon which many went out of the church. But Mr. OWEN being well seated, and too much indisposed for a farther walk, resolved to abide there, though his cousin would fain have persuaded him to go and hear Mr. JACKSON, then an eminent preacher in the city. At last there came a country minister, a stranger not only to

Mr. Owen, but to the parish; who, having fervently prayed, took for his text these words, 'Why are ye fearful, O ye of little faith?' [Matt. viii. 26.] The very reading of the words surprised him, upon which he secretly put up a prayer, that God would be pleased by this discourse, to speak to his condition; and his prayer was heard. For in that sermon, though a plain familiar discourse, the minister was directed to answer those very objections which Mr. Owen had commonly formed against himself: and though he had formerly given the same replies to his own scruples without any effect, yet now the time was come, for God to speak comfort to his soul, to remove all his doubts, and to lay the foundation of that solid peace which he afterwards enjoyed as long as he lived. And it is somewhat remarkable that Mr. Owen could never come to the knowledge of this minister, though he made the most diligent inquiry. But it was a circumstance of no great moment that he should continue ignorant of the instruments of the blessing, while he had so indubitable and substantial an evidence, that the work was of the Lord. And we are hence furnished with an obvious reflection, that faithful gospel ministers may sometimes be of essential use in the church of Christ, when they themselves are not aware of it, and therefore enjoy neither the honour nor the pleasure of that usefulness, until they are surprised with the intelligence in glory, when those perhaps they little thought of will appear as their crown and joy.

§ 10. These being his troubles, and his happy deliverance, is it not worth our while to admire the gracious conduct of divine Wisdom in thus preparing him for that eminent service in the church, wherein he was a burning and shining light to the end of his days. The foundation of his experience was laid deep. His Divine deliverer from so great a peril became infinitely precious to him. Having, like the mariner, escaped the storms and dangers of a long voyage, and safely landed, he could not easily forget the skill and compassion of his pilot. Here was a rich treasure of experience laid up, which furnished nifhed him with a peculiar ability to inftruct others. He was particularly happy in giving proper advice and comfort to fouls under fpiritual diftrefs, " an interpreter, one among a thoufand, to fhew unto man his uprightnefs;" fkilful to publifh to the fallen race of Adam, the riches of the glory of that myftery contained in the gofpel, which he found fo precious to his own foul. We may farther obferve, that by the uncommon diftreffes, and humiliations he paffed through, his natural vanity and ambition, of which he complained, were happily fubdued: whereby he was brought to preach the gofpel in all plainnefs and fimplicity, which is the peculiar excellency of an evangelical minifter. And having thus enjoyed peace in believing, his bodily health alfo was reftored, which had been impaired by his deep diftrefs; though till then he fcarce knew what ficknefs was, being of a ftrong conftitution.

§ 11. Soon after this, and during his abode at the *Charter-Houfe*, he wrote his book entitled, " *A Difplay of Arminianifm*." It came out at a very feafonable time, (A. D. 1643.) when the errors he attacked had fpread themfelves pretty much in this nation; fo that the book was the more taken notice of, and highly approved by many good judges. And, no doubt, a juft obfervation on the ftate of religious opinions, with the dangerous tendency of thofe he oppofed in this work, muft have been a prevailing motive to undertake it. Through the whole performance, he has acquitted himfelf as a champion in the caufe of truth, cutting in pieces the finews of Arminianifm, and eftablifhing the pure gofpel doctrine with great force of argument. There were fome confiderable perfons who entertained a juft fenfe of the value of this work, and did not fail to give real and particular marks of their refpect to fo learned an author. For, foon after its publication, the committee for ejecting fcandalous minifters, paid fuch a regard to him on account of it, that Mr. WHITE, chairman of the committee, fent a fpecial meffenger to prefent him with the living of *Fordham* in Effex; which offer he the more readily
em-

embraced, as it gave him a favourable opportunity for the stated exercise of his ministerial gifts. He continued at this place about a year and a half; where his preaching was so acceptable, that people resorted to his ministry from other parishes; and visibly great was the success of his labours. Soon after he came to *Fordham*, he married * and had several children, all which survived. It was now he published his discourse, " Of the duty of pastors and people," in which he attempts to secure to the sacred calling its antient dignity, and to assert the just liberties of the people.

§ 12. Upon a report that the sequestered incumbent of *Fordham* was dead, the patron, who had no kindness for Mr. Owen, presented another to the living; upon which the people at *Coggeshall*, a market town about five miles from thence, earnestly invited him to be their minister; and the Earl of Warwick, the patron, very readily gave him the living; which favour he thankfully acknowledged, as he had great reason; for here he preached to a congregation more judicious and far more numerous, seldom fewer than two thousand. A very fervent affection was cultivated between minister and people to their mutual satisfaction and joy; and here also he met with great success in his ministerial labours, with the universal approbation of the country round about. Hitherto Mr. Owen had followed the presbyterian way; but he was now put upon a more diligent inquiry into the nature of church government and discipline, and the result was, that he was fully convinced the *congregational* plan was most agreeable to the rule of the New Testament. And were his writings on this subject consulted without partiality, they may give to many a better opinion of this order of the gospel churches than they perhaps entertain, and teach others not to slight, or, at least, not to revile what

---

* Prima ætatis virilis consors MARIA,
   Rei domesticæ perite studiosa,
   Rebus Dei domus se totum addicendi;
      Copiam illi fecit gratissimam.
                                    GILB. Epit.

they do not underſtand. He formed a church at *Cog-geſhall* upon theſe congregational principles, which continued long a flouriſhing church, and ſubſiſts to this very day.

§ 13. So eminent a light could not be concealed; his reputation ſpread through city and country. He was now ſent for to preach before the Parliament; which he did April 29, 1646, and ſeveral times afterwards; where he diſtinguiſhed himſelf by pleading for liberty of conſcience, and moderation towards men of different perſuaſions. Particularly his diſcourſe on Jer. xv. 19, 20, preached the very day after the death of CHARLES I. deſerves to be recorded as a perpetual monument of his integrity, modeſty, and wiſdom. In the year 1648, he publiſhed his book intitled " *Salus Electorum, Sanguis Jeſu,*" or, " The Death of Death, in the Death of Chriſt," which he dedicated to Robert Earl of *Warwick*. In his preface to the reader he tells us, " That this performance was the reſult of *ſeven years* ſerious inquiry into the mind of God about theſe things, with a peruſal of all which he could attain, that the wit of men in former or latter days hath publiſhed in oppoſition to the truth." It is a noble undertaking, carried on with all the vigour of argument and learning; and, indeed, of this he himſelf ſeemed to be fully conſcious, though one of the moſt humble and modeſt of all writers; for he ſcrupled not to declare, that " He did not believe he ſhould live to ſee a ſolid anſwer given to it." And may we not add, that the event has more than verified the conjecture? Does it not remain to *our* day without a ſolid anſwer?

§ 14. About this time *Colcheſter* was beſieged; and Lord FAIRFAX, General of the Parliament forces, quartering at *Coggeſhall* ſome days, became acquainted there with Mr. OWEN. Soon after, alſo, he became known to CROMWELL, who, having heard him preach, ſolicited his friendſhip. The ſermon that CROMWELL was ſo much pleaſed with, was that preached before the Houſe of Commons on the 28th of February 1649, being the day of humiliation for the intended expedition to Ireland.

Our preacher designed to go to his cure at COGGESHALL within two days, but thought himself obliged to make his compliments to General FAIRFAX first. While he was waiting for admission, in comes Lieutenant CROMWELL, who at sight of him came directly up to him; and laying his hand familiarly on his shoulder, said, " Sir, you are the person that I must be acquainted with." Mr. OWEN modestly replied, " That will be more to my advantage than yours, Sir." " We shall soon see that," says CROMWELL; and, taking him by the hand, led him into FAIRFAX's garden, and from that time held a most intimate friendship with him as long as he lived. He now acquainted Mr. OWEN with his intended expedition into Ireland, and desired his company there, to reside in the College of *Dublin*; but he answered, that the charge of the church at *Coggeshall* would not permit him to comply with his request. But CROMWELL was not satisfied with the objection, nor would he take a denial; and at last, proceeding from desires to commands, he *insisted* upon his company; at the same time telling him, that his younger brother was to go as standard-bearer in the same army. He not only engaged his brother to persuade him to a compliance; but also wrote to the church at *Coggeshall*, to desire *leave* that he might go; which letter was read publicly amongst them. They were utterly unwilling to part with him on this occasion; but at length CROMWELL told them plainly, " He must and should go." With great reluctance, and after much deliberation, Mr. OWEN complied. He went to *Dublin*, (not with the army, but in a more private way) and continued there about half a year, preaching and observing the affairs of the college. Then with CROMWELL's leave he returned into England, and went to his beloved charge at *Coggeshall*, where he was joyfully received.

§ 15. He scarcely had time to breathe there, before he was called to preach at *Whitehall*, which order he obeyed. And in September 1650, CROMWELL requested Mr. OWEN to go with him into Scotland, but he being averse to this journey also, the General procured an order of

Parliament, which left no room for objections. He staid at *Edinburgh* about half a year, and then returning into England, he went once more to his people at *Coggeshall*, where he hoped to have spent the remainder of his days: but God had prepared for him other work.

§ 16. He must now leave his beloved flock in the country, to superintend a college in *Oxford*. The first intelligence he had of this matter, was by one of the weekly newspapers at *Coggeshall*, where he read words to this effect; " The House taking into consideration the worth and usefulness of Mr. JOHN OWEN, student of Queen's College, Master of Arts, has ordered that he be settled in the Deanery of Christ's College in *Oxford*, in the room of, &c." And soon after he received a letter from the principal students of that college, signifying their desire of his coming, and their great satisfaction in the choice the House had made of him to be their Dean. With the consent of his church he went to *Oxford*, and settled there A. D. 1651; and in the following year (when also he was diplomated D. D.) he was chosen Vice-chancellor of that university, in which office he continued about five years.—This is the man—who, for his non-conformity, was deserted by his friends, disappointed of a good estate, exercised with spiritual troubles, and had to grapple with many other difficulties and hardships—that is now chosen to preside over that university, which, for conscience sake, he had been forced to quit.

§ 17. It would be an inexcusable defect in this history, not to take notice of that singular prudence with which the Doctor (for so we must now call him) managed this honourable trust. He took care to restrain the vicious, to encourage the pious, and to prefer men of industry and learning. Under his administration the whole body of that university was visibly reduced to good order, and flourished with a number of excellent scholars and persons of distinguished piety. When men are advanced to places of power and authority, they often discover a magisterial air and a severity of temper towards inferiors,

and

and generally incline to be partial in the diftribution of their favours; but we find a very different temper and conduct in Doctor Owen, while he fat in this chair of honour. Though himfelf an Independent, he difcovered great moderation both towards Prefbyterians and Epifcopalians; to the former of whom he gave many vacant livings at his difpofal, and the latter he was very ready to oblige. A large congregation of *thefe* ftatedly celebrated divine fervice very near him according to the liturgy of the church of England; and though he was often urged to it, yet he would never give them the leaft difturbance; and if at any time they met with oppofition or trouble on that account, it was from other hands, and always againft his mind.

§ 18. This moderation and goodnefs in the exercife of power gained him great love and refpect. Yet we muft obferve alfo, that he would not fuffer authority to be flighted when there was occafion to affert it, of which we may take the following anecdote as an inftance. When one of Trinity College, at an act, declaimed in a very unbecoming and profane manner, contrary to ftrict orders, the Doctor feveral times defired him to forbear what reflected fuch difhonour on the univerfity; but notwithftanding this he went on in the fame manner. At length the Doctor feeing him obftinate, fent his beadles to pull him down, upon which the fcholars interpofed, and would not fuffer them to come near. Then the Doctor refolved to pull him down himfelf; and while his friends diffuaded him from it, for fear any of the fcholars (for there were fome of them fons of Belial) would do him fome mifchief; he replied, "I will not fee authority thus trampled on;" and hereupon he pulled him down, and fent him to *Bocardo,* * the fcholars ftanding at a diftance amazed to fee his courage and refolution.

§ 19. But while he reftrained the loofe and diforderly, he failed not to fhew kindnefs to the fober and ingenious.

---

* The name of a prifon in *Oxford.*

He was hospitable in his house, generous in his favours, charitable to the poor, and especially to poor scholars; some of whom he took into his family, and maintained at his own charge, giving them academical education. One time, for instance, a poor scholar presented to him a Latin epistle, which the Doctor highly approving, he sent for him in, and asked him, if he wrote that letter? he affirmed he did; "Well, said he, go into the next room and write me another as good, and I will not be wanting to encourage you;" which he did to his great satisfaction; whereupon he took him into his house to teach his children; and afterwards he became an excellent schoolmaster and bred up several good scholars. At another time, as he was hearing the scholars disputing for their degrees, he took special notice of one of Queen's College, who disputed very accurately, and discovered more than ordinary parts and learning, with which the Doctor was very much pleased; and making inquiry, he understood his circumstances were very low (though he made a considerable figure afterwards in the world) and gave him a handsome present by way of encouragement, which that gentleman ever after gratefully acknowledged.

§ 20. The government of a Vice-chancellor took up a great part of the Doctor's time, together with other avocations which daily attended him in that station; yet notwithstanding all, he redeemed time for his studies, preached every other Lord's day at St. Mary's, and often at *Stadham*, and other places in the country, and wrote some excellent books. In 1654, he published his book, "Of the Saints Perseverance," in answer to Mr. JOHN GOODWIN's book, entitled, "Redemption Redeemed." It is a masterly piece, full of close and strong reasoning, whereby he has enervated all the subtle arguments, and answered all the objections of his opponent, and confirmed the truth by scripture evidence. And in the whole of this performance, he exhibits to religious polemics an excellent example of a Christian temper in the management of controversy. In 1656, he published his "*Vindiciæ Evangelicæ*;" or, "The Mystery of the Gospel

"Vin-

Vindicated," which was chiefly defigned againſt JOHN
BIDDLE, a Socinian, who had publiſhed two Socinian
catechiſms of the ſame nature with the *Racovian*, written
by VALENTINUS SMALCIUS, which alſo the Doctor
takes into examination, being willing to give a full con-
futation to Socinian errors. It is an elaborate work, in
which he has cut the ſinews of the cauſe he oppoſes,
and (as his memorialiſt expreſſes it) " ſtabbed it to the
heart." Soon after this he alſo publiſhed that excellent
book, entitled, " Communion with God," which has
ever ſince recommended itſelf to the ſpiritual taſte of judicious readers, and in which the author has given ſuf-
ficient evidence, that he was himſelf very intimately acquainted with a life of communion with Father, Son,
and Spirit.

§ 21. He continued Vice-chancellor of the univer-
ſity till 1657, when he gave place to Doctor CONANT,
and in 1659, he was caſt out of his deanery, not long
after Richard's being made protector, and ſucceeded by
Dr. EDWARD REYNOLDS, afterwards Biſhop of *Norwich*.
Nor can we wonder at theſe changes happening to an individual, when we conſider the great alterations that took
place in the whole government. Quitting his public
ſtation at *Oxford*, he retired to *Stadham*, the place of his
birth, where he poſſeſſed a good eſtate and lived privately,
till the perſecution grew ſo hot that he was obliged to
move from place to place, and at length came to *London*.
All which time he was not idle, but employed every moment like a faithful ſervant of Chriſt, in preaching as he
had opportunity, and in writing ſeveral valuable and uſeful books, to ſerve the common intereſt of religion and
learning. In the year 1661, he publiſhed that elaborate
and learned treatiſe, entitled, Θεολογουμενα: " *De natura, ortu, progreſſu, et ſtudio veræ Theologiæ*," " Concerning the nature, riſe, progreſs, and ſtudy of true Theology," which was afterwards reprinted at *Bremen* in Ger-
many. This work muſt have coſt him no ſmall time and
pains, as it evidently beſpeaks a vaſt compaſs and variety
of reading and learning.

§ 22.

§ 22. The next year (1660) came out a book, called "*Fiat Lux*," written by JOHN VINCENT LANE, a Franciscan friar; wherein, under the pretence of recommending moderation and charity, he with a great deal of subtility invites men over to the church of *Rome*, as the only infallible cure of all church divisions. Two impressions of this book were printed off before the Doctor had seen it; at length it was sent him by a person of honour, who desired him to write an answer to it; which he did in a very short time: the answer bears the title of " Animadversions on *Fiat Lux*, by a Protestant ;" which being generally accepted, made the friar very angry, so that he published a sheet or two by way of reply, which produced the Doctor's answer, intitled, " A Vindication of Animadversions on *Fiat Lux*," to which no reply was given. There was some difficulty in obtaining a licence for this last book, when the bishops who were appointed by act of parliament to be the principal licencers of divinity books had examined it: at last Sir E. NICHOLAS procured the Bishop of *London*'s licence. This work recommended him to the esteem of Lord Chancellor HYDE; who by Sir BULSTRODE WHITLOCK sent for him, and assured him, that " he had deserved the best of any English protestant of late years, and that the church was bound to own and advance him ;" at the same time offering him preferment, if he would accept it; but he expressed his surprise that so learned a man should embrace the *novel* opinion of *independency*. The Doctor offered to prove that it was practised for several hundred years after Christ, against any bishop his lordship should please to appoint. " Say you so ?" said the chancellor, " then I am much mistaken." They had some further discourse, and particularly about liberty of conscience ; and to the Doctor's honour be it mentioned, he ever held it a sacred principle, whether in or out of power, that no peaceable persons, holding the foundation of the Christian faith, ought by the rule of scripture, or right reason, to have any violence offered them for their profession of religion,

and

and their worshipping of God according to the dictates of their consciences.

§ 23. But notwithstanding all the good service he had done the church of England, and notwithstanding " he had deserved the best of any English protestant of late years," he was still persecuted from place to place; which perpetual trouble inclined him to think of leaving his native country, having received an invitation from his brethren in New England to the government of their university; but he was stopped by particular orders from the King. He was afterwards invited to be professor of divinity in the United Provinces, but he felt such a love for his native country, that he could not quit it so long as there was any opportunity of being serviceable in it. About the time of his receiving these invitations from abroad, the nation was alarmed by the plague, that swept away above one hundred thousand persons, and the lamentable fire that consumed so great a part of the metropolis. On account of these awful visitations, there was a cessation for some time from prosecuting the dissenters, but the impressions they made soon wore off; the temporary indulgence alarmed the high church party, who instantly fled to Parliament for aid, lest the dæmon of persecution should be suffered to sleep too long. Nor were they disappointed. About this time the Doctor, who had lived privately in *London* for some years, went to visit his old friends at *Oxford*, and to attend some affairs of his own estate not far from thence; but, notwithstanding all his privacy, he was observed, and intelligence was given of the very house where he lay: upon which some troopers came and knocked at the door; the mistress of the house came down, and boldly opened the door, asking, " What they would have?" Who thereupon inquired of her, " Whether she had any lodgers in her house?" Instead of giving a direct answer to the question, she asked, " Whether they were seeking for Doctor OWEN?" " Yes," said they; she told them, " He went from my house this morning betimes." Then they immediately went off: in the mean time the Doctor, who she really thought had been gone, (as he told her he intended) arose and went into a field near the house, whither he ordered his horse to be brought, and so rode off immediately to *London.*

§ 24. Nor did he escape the tongues and pens of calumny and false innuendos. His baffled antagonist, the author of "Fiat Lux," had charged the Doctor with having had a hand in the late troubles of the nation; to this he replies, "Let me inform you that the author of the "Animadversions" is a person that never had a hand in, nor gave consent to the raising of any war in these nations, nor to any political alteration in them; no, not to any one that was amongst us during our revolutions: but he acknowledges that he lived and acted under them the things wherein he thought his duty consisted, and challenges all men to charge him with doing the least personal injury to any man, professing himself ready to give satisfaction to any one that can justly claim it." It had also been insinuated, that it was through his influence, or rather by his *doing*, the synod at the *Savoy* consented to have these articles—"That it is not faith but Christ's righteousness that we are justified by—and that Christ's righteousness imputed is our sole righteousness" —inserted in their confession. But this has been sufficiently confuted by Mr. JOHN GRIFFITH, who was scribe to the synod, by a solemn declaration made but a few weeks before his death, under his own hand, part of which follows: " I declare upon my own certain knowledge, having been a member of the Savoy meeting, and thoroughly acquainted with all matters of moment that passed in it, from first to last, that what Mr. —— says about the two aforesaid articles being put into the Savoy confession by Dr. OWEN's " doing," is altogether false, and that whoever made this report to him, has done a great injury to that assembly, wherein nothing was laid down as any part of their confession, which was not first debated, duly weighed, and approved, and agreed to by all, and more especially in the great and important doctrine of justification. I thought it my duty to leave this

attesta-

attestation, under my own hand, to clear the aforesaid meeting of worthy ministers, and faithful brethren, from such a foul aspersion. And this I do with the greatest regard to truth, as one daily expecting my change, and to stand before my Judge; and, therefore, I hope, under no temptation to favour any party or persuasion of men through sinful partiality."—To this we may add, that it ought to be mentioned (as one of his successors observes) to Doctor Owen's honour, that he seems to be one of the first of our countrymen, who entertained just and liberal notions of the right of private judgement and toleration; which he was honest and zealous enough to maintain in his writings, when the times were the least encouraging, for he not only published two pleas for indulgence and toleration in 1667, when the dissenters were suffering persecution under Charles II. but took the same side much earlier, pleading very cogently against intolerance, in an Essay for the Practice of Church Government, and a Discourse of Toleration, both which are printed in the Collection of his Sermons and Tracts; and clearly appear to have been written, and were probably first published, about the beginning of the year 1647, when the Parliament was arrived at full power, and he was much in repute.

§ 25. The Lord Chancellor Hyde having been impeached and discarded in 1667, and the Duke of *Buckingham* succeeding him as chief favourite, the dæmon of persecution was suffered once more to take a nap, or at least a momentary slumber. The nonconformists in *London* were connived at, and people went openly to their meetings without fear. This encouraged the country ministers to do the like in most parts of England, and crowds of the most religious people were their auditors. Now the Doctor had opportunity of preaching publicly and setting up a lecture, to which, among others, many persons of quality and eminent citizens resorted; and his time was filled up with other useful studies, which produced several books both learned and practical. In the year 1668 he published his excellent "Exposition of the cxxxth

cxxxth Psalm." This book is admirably calculated for the service of those who of all persons in the world stand most in need of compassion, poor distressed souls in the depths of spiritual trouble; and contains as good an exemplification of the doctrine of repentance and gospel forgiveness as is any where to be met with. In this year also he published the first volume of his " Exposition on the Epistle to the *Hebrews*," and the three other followed in their order, the last coming out in 1684. This is the work, together with the exercitations, which is now presented to the public, and it is hoped, with regard to most readers, at least, in a more acceptable and useful form. Of this work, the largest and most elaborate he ever published, he speaks in the following terms: " It is now sundry years since I purposed in myself, if God gave life and opportunity, to endeavour, according to the measure of the gift received, an Exposition of the Epistle to the Hebrews; and in the whole course of my studies have not been without some regard thereunto: but yet I must now say, that after all searching and reading, prayer and assiduous meditations on the text have been my only reserve; careful I have been, as of my life and soul, to bring no prejudicate sense to the words, to impose no meaning of my own, or other men's upon them, nor to be imposed on by the reasonings, pretences, or curiosities of any; but always went nakedly to the word itself, to learn humbly the mind of God in it, and to express it as he shall enable me." To this I shall only subjoin the following account of it, drawn up by the publishers of his sermons and tracts, in their " Memoirs of his Life" prefixed to that volume: " It is not easy for us to give a full account of the value and usefulness of this work; it is filled with a great variety of learning, particularly rabbinical, which he has made serviceable to give light unto the subject matter chiefly treated of in this Epistle: with all he has taken care to adapt his Exposition to the service of the faith and comfort of Christians, and to recommend the practice of the substantial duties of religion; so that it is hard to say, whether the scholar or divine shine

brightest

brighteſt through this excellent work. Beſides the Expoſition itſelf, there are very learned exercitations, which ſerve to illuſtrate many difficult parts of ſcripture, and to anſwer the deſign of the whole work; we ſhall only farther obſerve, that here the Doctor has enumerated all the arguments, and anſwered all the main objections of the Socinians, overthrown entirely their whole ſcheme, and driven them out of the field; ſo that whoever reads this work needs ſcarce any other for the aſſailing of their pernicious errors."

§ 26. When the Bill againſt conventicles, drawn up in 1670 with the moſt rigorous ſeverity, was ſent up to the Houſe of Lords, and debates aroſe upon it, the Doctor was deſired to draw up ſome reaſons againſt it, which he did; and it was laid before the Lords by ſeveral eminent citizens and gentlemen of diſtinction. This paper is called " The State of the Kingdom, with reſpect to the preſent Bill againſt Conventicles;" but it did not prevail: the bill was carried, and paſſed into an act; all the Biſhops were for it but two, viz. Dr. WILKINS, Biſhop of *Cheſter*, and Dr. RAINBOW, Biſhop of *Carliſle*, whoſe names ought to be mentioned with honour for their great moderation. This was executed with ſeverity to the utter ruin of many perſons and families. To this period we may refer, among other learned and religious publications, his " Diſcourſe of the Holy Spirit." At that time the oppoſition to the Deity and Perſonality of the Holy Spirit, and all his gracious operations, roſe to a very great height; and happy it was for the church of God, that this excellent perſon was raiſed to explain and defend this doctrine in ſo able a manner. One great objection againſt the work of the Spirit in his illumination, ſanctification, and ſpiritual gifts, was, that thoſe who plead for thoſe operations are enemies to *reaſon*, and impugn the *uſe* of it in religion. Hence ſome peeviſhly affirmed, that it was caſt on them as a reproach, " that they were *rational divines.*" On which the Doctor obſerves: " As far as I can diſcern, if it be ſo, it is as HEIROM was beaten by an angel for being a *Ciceronian* (in the judgement of some) very undeservedly." To follow our author through all his publications would require a moderate volume; for one while we find him writing—a primmer for children, and catechisms for youth; another while rules for church fellowship, and an investigation of the origin and nature of evangelical churches; at one time assisting the weakest in the faith, and at another developing the sublime mysteries of Christianity; one while he turns his learned weapons against the various troops of heretics that surround him, another while he contends for liberty and toleration, in opposition to the persecuting zeal of bigots. The following treatises, however, in addition to those already mentioned, must not be left unnoticed as highly deserving the warm esteem of the evangelical world, viz. " The Doctrine of Justification by Faith through the Imputation of the Righteousness of Christ, explained, confirmed, and vindicated," Χριστολογια: Or, " A Declaration of the Glorious Mystery of the Person of Christ, God, and Man." Such a strain of piety, zeal, and learning runs through the whole of this work, as renders it worthy of the most serious perusal of all, and especially ministers, and will endear his memory to all that love our Lord Jesus Christ in sincerity. Φρονημα του πνευματος: Or, " The Grace and Duty of being spiritually minded." It was composed out of his own deep and spiritual meditations, originally designed for his own use, not long before his death; and in it he breathes out the sentiments and devotion of a mind full of heaven. He observed and bewailed the carnal frames and lives of professors, and the prevalence of the world over their minds and affections, which, as it were, corrode the very vitals of true religion. This discourse, which has been judiciously abridged by the Rev. Dr. Mayo, is designed as an antidote against this growing evil, and calculated to promote a spiritual and heavenly frame of mind, and it is earnestly recommended to the diligent perusal of all Christians of the present day, wherein this dangerous disease of worldly mindedness so evidently abounds. In his " Meditations on the Glory of Christ,

Chrift, in two Parts," we have an ample teftimony of that pious and heavenly frame, that clear and intimate knowledge of the glory of Chrift, and that fervent love to his divine Perfon, by which the Doctor's experience was eminently diftinguifhed; there he thinks and writes like one that was in a full and near view of unveiled glory.*

§ 27. The writings which he thus continually produced, drew upon him the admiration and refpect of feveral perfons of honour, who were much delighted in his converfation; particularly the Earl of ORRERY, the Earl of ANGLESEA, Lord WILLOUGHBY, of *Parham*, Lord

---

* The excellent Mr. HERVEY fpeaks of this piece in the following terms: " *To fee the Glory of Chrift*, is the grand bleffing which our Lord folicits and demands for his difciples, in his laft folemn interceffion, [John xvii. 24.]—Should the reader defire affiftance in this important work, I would refer him to a little Treatife of Dr. OWEN's, intituled, " Meditations on the Glory of Chrift:" it is little in fize, not fo in value. Was I to fpeak of it, in the claffical ftile, I fhould call it, *aureus, gemmeus, mellitus*. But I would rather fay, it is richly replenifhed with that unction from the Holy One, which tends to enlighten the eyes, and cheer the heart; which fweetens the enjoyments of life, foftens the horrors of death, and prepares for the fruitions of eternity. THER. and ASPASIO, vol. iii. p. 75. Lond. 1767.— The fame writer, fpeaking of the *Puritan* Divines, places with propriety our Author as *foremoft*; and as the *other* names he mentions are accompanied with fhort characters, beautifully expreffive of their refpective peculiar excellencies, the reader will be pleafed with them: " Dr. OWEN, with his correct judgement, and an immenfe fund of learning.—Mr. CHARNOCK, with his mafculine ftile, and an inexhauftible vein of thought.—Dr. GOODWIN, with fentiments eminently evangelical, and a moft happy talent at opening, fifting, and difplaying the hidden riches of fcripture.—Thefe, I think, are the *firft three:*—Then comes Mr. HOWE, nervous and majeftic; with all the powers of imagery at his command.—Dr. BATES, fluent and polifhed; with a never-ceafing ftore of beautiful fimilitudes.—Mr. FLAVEL, fervent and affectionate; with a mafterly hand at probing the confcience, and ftriking the paffions.—Mr. CARYL, Dr. MANTON, Mr. POOL, with many others; whofe works will fpeak for them ten thoufand times better than the tongue of panegyric, or the pen of Biography.—Id. vol. i. p. 206.

Wharton, Lord Berkley, and Sir John Trevor. When he was at *Tunbridge* the Duke of York sent for him, and several times discoursed with him concerning the Dissenters, &c. and after his return to *London* he was sent for by King Charles himself, who discoursed with him two hours, assuring him of his favour and respect, telling him that he might have access to him when he would: at the same time he assured the Doctor he was for liberty of conscience, and was sensible of the wrong that had been done to Dissenters, as a testimony of which he gave him a thousand guineas to distribute among those who had suffered the most. This he thankfully accepted, and faithfully applied. The Doctor had some friends also among the Bishops, particularly Dr. Wilkins, Bishop of *Chester*, and Dr. Barlow, Bishop of *Lincoln*, formerly his tutor, who (when he had applied to him on behalf of John Bunyan) promised to " deny him nothing that he could legally do;" though, in this particular, he hardly fulfilled his word. The case was this; Mr. Bunyan had been confined to gaol for twelve years, upon excommunication for non-conformity, and Dr. Owen was applied to on this occasion, in virtue of a law that admitted of a cautionary bond to be offered to the Bishop of the diocese, and which admitted that the Bishop may release the prisoner upon that bond; and though Bishop Barlow was so obliging as to say that he would strain a point to serve Dr. Owen, yet he could not be prevailed upon to accept it. And, after all, they were obliged to move the Lord Chancellor to issue forth an order to the Bishop to take the cautionary bond before Mr. Bunyan was released. This Bishop once asked the Doctor, " What can you object to our liturgical worship which I cannot answer?" The Doctor's answer occasioned the Bishop to make a pause; on which the Doctor said, " Don't answer suddenly, but take time till our next meeting," which never happened. His great worth procured him the esteem of many strangers who resorted to him from foreign parts; and many foreign divines having read his *Latin* works, learned *English* for the benefit

nefit of the rest. His correspondence with the learned abroad was great, among whom we may particularly mention that prodigy of genius and learning, ANNA MARIA A SCHURCHMAN; and several travelled into England to see and converse with him. It is a loss to the public, much to be regretted, that none of those letters can be found.

§. 28. His many labours brought upon him, as might be expected, frequent infirmities, the weight of which daily increased, whereby he was taken off from his public service, though not rendered useless, for he was continually writing whenever he was able to sit up. At length he retired to *Kensington*. As he was once coming from thence to *London*, two informers seized upon his carriage, but he was discharged upon the interposition of Sir EDM. GODFREY, a justice of peace who happened to come by at that instant. The Doctor afterwards removed to a house of his own at *Ealing*, where he finished his course. He there employed his thoughts on the other world as one who was drawing near it in full prospect, which produced his " Meditations on the Glory of Christ," already mentioned, in which he breathed out the devotion of a soul continually growing in the temper of the heavenly state. Two days before his death he dictated a letter to a particular friend (CHARLES FLEETWOOD, Esq.) in which are the following words: " I am going to him whom my soul has loved, or rather who has loved me with an everlasting love, which is the whole ground of all my consolations. The passage is very irksome and wearisome, through strong pains of various sorts, which are all issued in an intermitting fever. All things were provided to carry me to *London* to-day, according to the advice of my physicians; but we were all disappointed, by my utter disability to undertake the journey. I am leaving the ship of the church in a storm, but whilst the great pilot is in it, the loss of a poor under-rower will be inconsiderable. Live and pray, and hope and wait patiently, and do not despond: the promise stands invincible that he will never " leave us or forsake us," &c. Mr.

PAYNE, who for several years kept an academy at *Saffron Walden* (at which several eminent dissenting ministers were educated) being intrusted by the Doctor to put his last performance to the press, came in to see the Doctor the morning of that day on which he died, and told him, Doctor, I have been just putting your book " On the Glory of Christ" to the press; to which he answered, " I am glad to hear, that that performance is put to the press ;" and then lifting up both his hands and his eyes, as in a kind of rapture, he said, " But, O Brother PAYNE, the long looked-for day is come at last, in which I shall see that glory in another manner than I have ever done yet, or was capable of doing in this world." He died August 24th 1683, aged 67. He was carried from *Ealing* to the burying ground in *Bunhill Fields*, his herse being attended by a very great number of noblemen's and gentlemen's coaches, and many gentlemen on horseback. He was interred in a new vault towards the east end of that burying place, with a monument of free stone erected over it, and a Latin Epitaph.* He left

---

* Though, in my opinion, the best eulogium, and most lasting monument, by which Dr. OWEN's just merit is exhibited to posterity, are his own writings ; yet, lest it should be deemed a deficiency in this memoir to omit his epitaph, it is here subjoined ; and Dr. GIBBONS' translation of it, as a summary conclusion of his character :

        JOHANNES OWEN, S. T. P.
         Agro Oxoniensi Oriundus ;
Patre insigni Theologo, Theologus Ipse Insignior ;
Et Seculi hujus Insignissimis annumerandus :
Communibus Humaniorum Literarum Suppetiis,
    Mensura parum Communi, Instructus ;
Omnibus, quasi bene Ordinata Ancillarum Serie,
    Ab illo jussis Suæ Famulari Theologiæ ;
Theologiæ Polemicæ, Practicæ, et quam vocant Casuum ;
  (Harum enim omnium quæ magis Sua habenda erat,
       ambigitur)
In illa, Viribus plusquam Herculeis, Serpentibus tribus,
  Arminio, Socino, Cano, Venenosa, strinxit Guttura :
In ista Suo prior, ad verbi amussim, Expertus Pectore,
  Universam Sp. Scti. Oeconomiam Alliis tradidit :
    Et Missis Cæteris, Coluit ipse Sensitque,
                                Beatam,

left behind him a mournful widow who had lived with him about seven years: a gentlewoman of a considerable family, being the daughter of ——— Michael, Esq. of *Kingston Russel*, Dorsetshire; she was a person of very good sense, truly religious, very tender and affectionate to the Doctor; she survived him many years, and was interred in the same vault which she had erected for him.†

§. 29. His character may be briefly summed up as follows:

As to his person, his stature was tall; his visage grave, majestic and comely; his aspect and deportment, genteel; his mental abilities incomparable; his temper affable and courteous; his common discourse moderately facetious. He was a great master of his passions, especially that of anger: and possessed great serenity of mind, neither elated with honour or estate, nor depressed with difficulties; of great moderation in his judgements, and of a charitable spirit, willing to think the best of all men he could, not confining Christianity to a party. A friend of

> Beatam, quam Scripsit, cum Deo Communionem:
> In Terris Viator comprehensori in Cœlis proximus:
> In Casuum Theologia, Singulis Oraculi instar habitus;
> Quibus opus erat, et Copia Consulendi:
> Scriba ad Regnum Cœlorum usquequoque institutus;
> Multis privatos iufra Parietes, a Suggesto Pluribus,
> A Prelo Omnibus, ad eundem Scopum collineantibus,
> Pura Doctrinæ Evangelicæ Lampas Præluxit;
> Et sensim, non sine Aliorum, suoque sensu,
> Sic prælucendo Periit,
> Assiduis Infirmitatibus Obsiti,
> Morbis Creberrimis Impetiti,
> Durisque Laboribus potissimum Attriti Corporis
> (Fabricæ, donec ita Quassatæ, Spectabilis) Ruinas,
> Deo ultra Serviendo inhabiles, Sancta Anima,
> Deo ultra Fruendi Cupida, Deseruit;
> Die, a Terrenis Potestatibus, Plurimis facto fatali;
> Illi, a Cœlesti Numine, Felici reddito;
> Mensis Scilicet Augusti XXIV°, Anno a Partu Virginea
> MDCLXXXIII°, Ætat. LXVII°.

† Dorothea Vice, non Ortu, Opibus, Officiisve, Secunda, Laboribus, Morbis, Senioque ipso Elanguenti Indulgentissimam etiam se Nutricem præstitit.

GILBERT's *smaller* Epit.

peace and a diligent promoter of it among Christians.* In point of learning he was one of the brightest ornaments of the University of Oxford. Even Mr. Ant. Wood, who seldom could drop any thing favourable of a pious non-conformist, thinks fit to own, that " He was a person well skilled in the tongues, rabbinical learning, and Jewish rites; that he had a great command of his English pen, and was one of the fairest and genteelest writers that appeared against the church of England." His Christian temper in managing controversy was admirable. He was well acquainted with men and things, and would shrewdly guess a man's temper and designs on the first acquaintance. His labours, as a minister of the gospel, were incredible. He was an excellent preacher, having a good elocution, graceful and affectionate: and could on all occasions, without any premeditation, express himself pertinently on any subject; yet the sermons were mostly well studied and digested, though he generally used no notes in the pulpit. His piety and devotion were eminent; his experimental knowledge of spiritual things very uncommon. In every department, and in all relations of life, he conducted himself like a great Chris-

* The following letter to a friend, which was never published, tending in a measure to illustrate this part of our author's character, is deemed not unworthy of insertion here.

" SIR,

" I AM very sorry to find that there is a difference arisen between Mr. C—— and yourself. Since the receipt of yours, I received one from him, with an account of the difference, and his thoughts upon it at large. I do not therefore judge it meet to write any thing at present about it, until I am ready to give unto you both an account of my thoughts, which by reason of many avocations I cannot now do. All that I shall therefore say at present, is, That without mutual love and condescension no interposition of advice will issue the business to the glory of Christ and the gospel. I pray God guide you both by that spirit which is promised to lead us into all truth. Upon the first opportunity you will have a farther account of his sense who is your

Affectionate brother," &c.

January 2*d* 1678-9.

tian,* a faithful and loving hufband, a tender father, a good mafter, a prudent governor in places of honour and truft, and a very dutiful peaceable fubject.—The following extracts from Mr. CLARKSON's funeral fermon for Dr. OWEN may be here fubjoined, in juftice to his character: " A great light is fallen; one of eminency for holinefs, learning, parts and abilities; a paftor, a fcholar, a divine of the firft magnitude: holinefs gave a divine luftre to his other accomplifhments, it fhined in his whole courfe, and was diffufed through his whole converfation. It was his great defign to promote holinefs in the power, life, and exercife of it.—It was his great complaint that the power of it declined among profeffors. It was his care and endeavour to prevent or cure fpiritual decays, in his own flock: he was a burning and fhining light.

" He was mafter of all parts of learning requifite to an accomplifhed divine; thofe that underftood him, and will be juft, cannot deny him the reputation and honour of being a great fcholar; and thofe that detract from him in this, feem to be led by a fpirit of envy, that would not fuffer them willingly to fee fo great an ornament among thofe that are of another perfuafion. Indeed he had parts able to mafter any thing he applied himfelf unto, though he reftrained himfelf to thofe ftudies which might

---

* The following extract from a letter to Sir JOHN HARTOPP, which is not in print, may not be unacceptable, as a fpecimen of the Doctor's friendly correfpondence:—" My duty, my obligations, and my inclinations, do all concur in the efteem I have for you both; [Sir John and his Lady] and I do make mention of you daily in my poor fupplications—and that with particular refpect unto the prefent condition of your Lady. That God who hath revealed himfelf unto us, as the God that heareth prayer, will yet glorify his name and be a prefent help unto her, in the time of trouble. In the mean time, let her, and you, and me, ftrive to love Chrift more, to abide more with him, and to be lefs in ourfelves. He is our beft friend. I pray God with all my heart that I may be weary of every thing elfe but converfe and communion with him; yea, of the beft of my mercies, fo far as at any time they may be hindrances thereof.—My wife prefents her humble fervice unto your Lady and yourfelf, as fo doth alfo, Sir, your moft affectionate friend and fervant in our dear Lord,

" JOHN OWEN."

render him most serviceable to Christ, and the souls of men.—He was a passionate lover of *light* and *truth*, of *divine* truth especially; he pursued it unweariedly, through painful and wasting studies.—He was ready to spend and he spent for Christ; he did not bury his talent, with which he was richly furnished, but still laid it out for the Lord who had intrusted him. He preached while his strength and liberty would serve, then by discourse and writing. That he was an excellent preacher, none will deny who knew him, and knew what preaching was, and think it not the worse because it is spiritual and evangelical.*—If holiness, learning and a masculine unaffected style can commend any thing, his practical discourses cannot but find much acceptation with those who are sensible of their soul concerns, and can relish that which is divine, and value that which is not common or trivial. His excellent " Comment upon the Hebrews"† gained him a name and esteem, not only at home but in foreign countries. When he had finished it (and it was a merciful providence that he lived to finish it) he said, Now his work was done, it was time for him to die."

§. 30. The late Rev. Doctor GIBBONS has given us, through the vehicle of the " Nonconformist's Memorial," an English translation of the Latin epitaph above-men-

---

* Tam in Palæstra, quam Pulpito, Dominatus est:
In *Pulpito*, maxime Infirmi Corporis
 Præsentia minime infirma;
Gestu, Theatrica procul Gesticulatione,
 Ad optimas Decori Regulas composito:
Sermone, a Contemptibili remotissimo; Canoro,
 Sed non Stridulo: Suavi, sed prorsus virili;
 Et Authoritatis quiddam Sonante:
 Pari, si non & Superiore, Animi Præsentia;
Concionum, quas, ad verbum, totas Chartis commisit,
Ne verbum quidem, vel carptim & stringente Oculo,
 Inter Prædicandum Lectitavit:
Sed Omnia, Suo primum Impressa altius Pectori,
Auditorum Animis, Cordibusque potentius Ingessit:
GILB. Epit.
† Cujus Præluftri e multis unum Sufficiat Epitaphio:
AUTHOR QUADRIPARTITI IN EP. AD HEBR. COMMENTARII.

tioned,

tioned, which, as it may gratify the curiosity and pleasure of those in a peculiar manner who are not possessed of that work, or may not be versed in the Latin language, so the inserting of it here is highly proper as a just tribute to the Doctor's memory, and a suitable recapitulation of these memoirs:

JOHN OWEN, D. D.

Born in the county of *Oxford*,
The son of an eminent minister,
Himself more eminent,
And worthy to be enrolled
Among the first divines of the age.
Furnished with human literature
In all its kinds,
And in its highest degrees,
He called forth all his knowledge
In an orderly train
To serve the interests of religion,
And minister in the sanctuary of his God.
In divinity, practic, polemic, and casuistical,
He excelled others, and was in all equal to himself.
The *Arminian*, *Socinian*, and *Popish* errors,
Those *Hydras*, whose contaminated breath
And deadly poison, infested the Church,
He, with more than *Herculean* labour,
Repulsed, vanquished, and destroyed.
The whole œconomy of redeeming grace,
Revealed and applied by the Holy Spirit,
He deeply investigated, and communicated to others,
Having first felt its divine energy,
According to its draught in the holy scriptures,
Transfused into his own bosom.
Superior to all terrene pursuits,
He constantly cherished, and largely experienced,
That blissful communion with Deity
He so admirably describes in his writings.
While on the road to heaven
His elevated mind

Almost

Almoſt comprehended
Its full glories and joys.
When he was conſulted
On caſes of conſcience
His reſolutions contained
The wiſdom of an oracle.
He was a ſcribe every way inſtructed
In the myſteries of the Kingdom of God.
In converſation he held up to *many*,
In his public diſcourſes to *more*,
In his publications from the preſs to *all*,*

Ema-

---

* A complete CATALOGUE of the DOCTOR's Works.

FOLIO.   *When publiſhed.*

1. An Expoſition of the Epiſtle to the Hebrews
 —— Vol. I.   —— London 1668
 —— Vol. II.   ——   —— 1674
 —— Vol. III.   ——   —— 1680
 —— Vol. IV.   ——   —— 1684
2. Of the Saints Perſeverance   —— 1654
3. A Diſcourſe of the Holy Spirit   —— 1674
4. A complete Collection of his Sermons and Tracts 1721

QUARTO.

1. A Diſplay of Arminianiſm   ——   —— 1643
2. The Duty of Paſtors and People diſtinguiſhed - 1644
3. *Salus Electorum, Sanguis Jeſu*: Or, The Death of Death in the Death of Chriſt   —— 1648
4. Of the Death of Chriſt
5. *Vindiciæ Evangelicæ*: Or, The Myſtery of the Goſpel vindicated, in anſwer to J. BIDDLE - 1655
6. Of Communion with God; Father, Son, and Holy Spirit   —— 1657
7. Θεολογουμενα: Sive de Natura, Ortu, Progreſſu, et Studio Veræ Theologiæ   —— 1661
8. An Expoſition of the cxxxth Pſalm   —— 1668
9. The Doctrine of Juſtification by Faith, &c.   — 1677
10. The Glorious Myſtery of the Perſon of Chriſt 1679
11. The Grace and Duty of being Spiritually Minded 1681
12. An Enquiry into the Original, &c. of Evan. Churches 1681
13. The True Nature of a Goſpel Church - 1689
14. A Review of the Annotations of Grotius — 1656
15. A Diſcourſe concerning Liturgies   —— 1662
16. Indulgence and Toleration conſidered in a Letter 1667
17. A Peace Offering, or Plea for Indulgence   — 1667

18. The

Who were set out for the celestial *Zion*,
The effulgent lamp of evangelical truth
To guide their steps to immortal glory.
While he was thus diffusing his divine light,
With his own inward sensations,
And the observations of his afflicted friends,
His earthly tabernacle gradually decayed,

18. The Church of Rome no Safe Guide	——	1679
19. Some Consideration about Union among Protestants		1680
20. Vindication of the Nonconformists	——	1680
21. An Account of the Nature of the Protestant Religion		1682

OCTAVO.

1. Two Catechisms	——	1645
2. Esheol: Or, Rules for Church Fellowship	—	1648
3. Diatriba de Justitia divina	——	1653
4. Of the Mortification of Sin in Believers	——	1656
5. A Discovery of the True Nature of Schism		1657
6. A Reveiw of the True Nature of Schism, &c.		1657
7. Of the Nature and Power of Temptation	—	1658
8. A Defence of Cotton against Cawdry	——	1658
9. Exercitationes quatuor pro sacris Scripturis	—	1658
10. The Divine Original and Authority of the Scriptures		1659
11. A Primmer for Children	——	1660
12. Animadversions on Fiat Lux	——	1662
13. Vindication of those Animadversions	——	1664
14. A Brief Instruction in the Worship of God	——	1667
15. The Nature of Indwelling Sin	—	1668
16. Truth and Innocence Vindicated	——	1669
17. A Brief Vindication of the Doctrine of the Trinity		1669
18. Dissertations on the Sabbath and Lord's-Day	—	1674
19. Of Evangelical Love, Church-Peace, and Unity		1673
20. A Vindication of his Book of Communion with God from the Exceptions of Dr. Sherlock	——	1674
21. The Nature of Apostacy from the Profession of the Gospel	——	1676
22. The Reason of Faith in the Scriptures	——	1677
23. Of Understanding the Mind of God in the Scriptures		1678
24. An Humble Testimony to the Goodness and Severity of God in his Dealing with Sinful Churches and Nations		1681
25. The Work of the Holy Spirit in Prayer	——	1682
26. Meditations on the Glory of Christ. Part I.		1684
27. —— —— Part II.		1691
28. Of the Dominion of Sin and Grace	——	1688
29. Two Discourses of the Work of the Spirit	—	1693
30. Evidences of the Faith of God's Elect	——	1695

Till at length his deeply-sanctified soul,
Longing for the fruition of its God,
Quitted the body: in younger age
A most comely and majestic form;
But in the latter stages of life,
Depressed by constant infirmities,
Emaciated with frequent diseases,
And, above all, crushed under the weight
Of intense and unremitting studies,
It became an incommodious mansion
For the vigorous exertion of the Spirit
In the service of its God.
He left the world on a day
Dreadful to the Church
By the cruelties of men,*
But blissful to himself
By the plaudits of his God,
August 24, 1683, aged 67.

* The ever-memorable Bartholomew day, 1662, when the good ministers, to the number of 2000, were ejected from their livings, or silenced, for non-compliance with the Act of Uniformity.

EXERCITATIONS

ON THE

EPISTLE TO THE HEBREWS;

ALSO, CONCERNING THE

MESSIAH,

AND THE

PRIESTHOOD OF CHRIST.

EXERCITATIONS, &c.

PART I.

Concerning the Epistle to the Hebrews.

EXERCIT. I.

THE EPISTLE TO THE HEBREWS PROVED TO BE STRICTLY CANONICAL.

§ 1. *Of the term canonical.* § 2. *The marks of canonical authority.* § 3. *The Epistle to the Hebrews strictly canonical.* § 4. (I.) *By whom opposed.* § 5. *The judgement of the Latin church concerning it.* § 6. (II.) *Objections answered.* § 7. (III.) *Its canonical authority proved from,* 1. *Its general argument.* § 8. 2. *The particular subject matter of it.* § 9. 3. *Its end and design.* § 10—13. 4. *The style of it.* § 14. 5. *The authority of its principal author.* § 15. 6. *Its divine efficacy.* § 16. 7. *Catholic tradition.* § 17—21. 8. *Its not being liable to any solid exceptions.*

§ 1. THE canonical authority of the Epistle to the Hebrews having been by some called into question, we must previously shew what we intend by such authority, and then prove, that this Epistle is clearly interested therein.

The Greek word (κανων) which gives rife to the term 'canonical,' feems to be derived from the Hebrew (קנה) *Kaneh*, which, in general, fignifies any *reed* whatever, [I. Kings, xiv. 15. Ifa. xlii. 3.] and particularly, a reed made into an inftrument, wherewith they meafured their buildings, containing fix cubits in length, [Ezek. xl. 7. xlii. 16.) and hence indefinitely it is taken for a *rule* or meafure. Befides, it fignifies the beam and tongue of a balance, [Ifa. xlvi. 6.] 'They weighed filver on the *cane*;' that is, faith the *Targum*, 'In the balance.' This alfo is the primary and proper fignification of the Greek word.* Hence its metaphorical ufe, which is moft common, wherein it fignifies a *moral rule*. Ariftotle calls the law (Κανονα της πολιτειας) 'the *rule* of the adminiftration.†' And hence it is, that the written word of God, being in itfelf abfolutely *right*, and appointed to be the *rule* of faith and obedience, is eminently called ' canonical.'

This appellation is of ancient ufe in the church. The fynod of Laodicea makes mention of it, as what was generally admitted; for the fathers of it decree, "That no private pfalms ought to be ufed in the church, nor any *uncanonical* books; but only the canonical ones of the Old and New Teftaments."‡ And thus Aquinas himfelf confeffeth, that the fcripture is called canonical; "becaufe it is the rule of our underftanding in the things of God."‖

§ 2. Moreover; as the fcripture is faid to be canonical; fo there is alfo a canon, or rule, to determine what books in particular are fuch. Two things are included in that expreffion:

1. That any writing be (Θεοπνευστος) "given by immediate infpiration from God." Without this, it can by no means have any intereft in that *authority*, which lays a foundation for receiving it into the canon.

---

* Vid Schol. in Aristoph. in Ran. Act III. Sc. 1. Aristot. de Anim. Lib. Cap. ult.
† Polit. Lib. II. Cap. viii.
‡ Concil. Laod. Can. 59.
‖ Aquin. in I. Tim. VI. Lect. I.

2. It is requisite, that any writing, or book, be *designed* by the Holy Ghost, for the Catholic standing use of the church.—In giving out the whole, ' holy men of ' God spake as they were moved by the Holy Ghost.' [II. Pet. i. 21.] So that whatever different means God might make use of, in the communication of his mind and will to any of the sacred penmen, it was this " inspiration of God," that rendered them infallible revealers thereof to the church.

Some of the ancients, indeed, used the term " canonical" ambiguously; and, therefore, sometimes call books by this term, that absolutely are not so; as not being written by Divine inspiration, nor given by the Holy Ghost as a *rule*. But this does not affect our point; for, according to our definition, if any book, or writing, have not the above-mentioned properties, it differs in the *whole kind*, and not in degrees only, from all those that have them; so, that it can be truth, at best, only materially, by virtue of its analogy, to that which is absolutely, universally, and perfectly, so. And this was well observed by LINDANUS: " They defile themselves (faith he) with the impiety of sacrilege, who endeavour to bring in, as it were, divers *degrees* into the body of the scriptures; for by the impious discretion of human folly, they would cast the one voice of the Holy Ghost into various forms of unequal authority."* As then, whatever difference there may be, as to the subject, matter, manner of writing, and present usefulness, between any of the inspired books, they are all *equal* as to their canonical authority, being equally interested in that which is the formal reason of it; so, whatever usefulness or respect in the church, any other writings may claim, they can no way be interested in that distinguishing formal reason.

§ 3. In the sense explained, we affirm the *Epistle to the Hebrews* to be canonical; that is, properly and strictly so. In confirmation of which, we shall

* Panopl. Evang. Lib. III. Cap. iv.

I. Obferve by whom it hath been oppofed or queftioned.

II. Confider what reafon they pretend, or *objections* urge, for fo doing; which being removed out of our way, we fhall

III. Infift on the arguments whereby the truth of our affertion is evinced.

§ 4. (I.) By whom oppofed.—We need not much infift on their madnefs who of old with a facrilegious licentioufnefs rejected what portions of fcripture they pleafed. The *Ebronites* not only rejected all the epiftles of Paul, but alfo reviled his perfon as a Greek, and an apoftate.* Their folly and blafphemy were alfo imitated by the Helefcheitæ.† MARCION rejected in particular this Epiftle to the Hebrews, and thofe alfo to Timothy and Titus.‡ And to thefe, with refpect to the epiftle to the Hebrews, fome of the *Arians* alfo may be joined, according to THEODORET.‖ Now through the folly of thefe perfons may be eafily repelled, as it is effectually done by PETRUS CLUNIÆNSIS,** yet JEROME hath given us a fufficient reafon why we fhould not fpend time therein: "They did not fo much as plead or pretend any *caufe* or *reafon* for the rejection of thefe epiftles, but did it upon their own authority; fo they deferve neither anfwer nor confideration."††

§ 5. It is of more importance to obferve, that it was four hundred years at leaft, after the writing of this epiftle, before it was *publicly received* by the church of Rome;‡‡

---

* Vid. IREN. Lib. I. Cap. ii. EPIPHAN. Hæref. XXX. Cap. xxv.
† EUSEB. Lib. VI. Cap. xxxi.
‡ EPIPHAN. Hæref. XLII. Cap. ix. HIERON. Præf. in Com. ad Titum.
‖ Præf. in Epif. ad Heb.
** Epif. ad Petrob.
†† HIERON. ut fupra.
‡‡ EUSEB. Lib. II. Cap. xxiv. Lib. III. Cap. iii. Lib. VI. Cap. xiv. PHOT. Biblioth. Cod. xlviii. cxx. HIERON. Epif. cxxix. ad DARDAN. Comment. in Ifa. Cap. viii. in Zechar. Cap. viii. in Matt. Cap. xxvi.

and

and BARONIUS in vain labours to take off this failure.* Nor does it appear that the Latin church did ever *reject* this epistle; yea, we find that many amongst them, even in those early days, reckoned it canonical, and owned St. Paul as the penman of it.† And this undeniably evinceth the injustice of some men's pretensions, that the Roman church is the *only proposer* of canonical scripture; and that upon the authority of her proposal alone it is to be admitted. Four hundred years elapsed before she herself publicly received it, or read it in her assemblies; so far was she from having proposed it to others! And yet all this while was it received by all other churches in the world, as JEROME testifies, and that from the days of the apostles—to whose judgement the Roman church itself at length *submitted!*

Nor are the *occasions* of this hesitation of the western church obscure. The epistle was written probably in Rome; at least in some part of Italy, [chap. xiii. 24.] There, no doubt, it was seen, and it may be, copied out before it was sent, by some who used to accompany the apostle, as CLEMENS, who not long after mentions divers things contained in it.‡ The *original* was without question speedily sent into Judea, being directed to the Hebrews; and that copies of it were by them, also, communicated to their brethren in the East, equally concerned in it with themselves, cannot be doubted, unless we suppose them grossly negligent in their duty towards God and man, which we have no reason to do. But the churches of the Hebrews, at that time, by reason of some peculiar observances, living in a manner separate from those of the Gentiles, were not, probably, very forward in communicating this epistle; being written, as they supposed, about an especial concern of their own. By this means, it seems to have been kept much within the compass of the Hebrew churches, until after the destruction

---

* Annal. Eccles. ad ann. CLX.
† EUSEB. Ecclef. Hist. Lib. III. Cap. xxxvii.
‡ Epist. ad Corinth.

of the temple; when by their difperfion, and their coalefcing with other churches in the Eaft, it came to be generally received amongft them.* But the Latin church, having loft that advantage of receiving it when firft written, was fomewhat flow in inquiring after it. Thofe that fucceeded in that church, it is not unlikely, had their fcruples increafed; becaufe they found in not in common ufe among their predeceffors, like the reft of St. Paul's epiftles; not confidering the *occafion* of it. To which we may add, that, by the time it had gradually made its progrefs in its *return* to the Weft, it began to evince its own authority, by the conqueft it obtained over the *Novatians*, and other oppofers.

Some among the *moderns*, particularly CAJETAN, ERASMUS, ENIEDINUS, and a few more, have *fcrupled* its authority; and the reafons they make ufe of in fupport of their conjectures, are amaffed together by ERASMUS. [Annot. in Heb. xiii. 24.] We fhall, therefore,

§ 6. Confider what reafons they pretend, or objections urge, for fo doing.

1. The firft thing generally pleaded is, the uncertainty of its penman. How groundlefs this pretence is, we fhall hereafter fully demonftrate; but at prefent I fhall only fhew, that, in general, it is of no importance in this caufe. The author being certainly known, may indeed afford fome light to its nature and authority. Thus when it is confeffed, that the penman of any book was divinely infpired, and that it was written for the ufe of the church, its authority is unqueftionable; but when it is doubtful who the author was, nothing fatisfactory can then be concluded on either fide; and, therefore, it hath pleafed the Holy Ghoft to keep the names of many of the facred penmen in everlafting obfcurity. There is not, then, the leaft ftrength in this exception, unlefs it could be proved, that he *was not* divinely infpired; which yet cannot be done, as we fhall abundantly prove.

* Vid. HIERON. Epif. ad DARDAN.

2. It is objected, that the author of this epistle cites various things out of the Old Testament, which are not therein contained; as many of the *stories* referred to chap. xi. and that in particular chap. xii. 21. where he affirms, that Moses, terrified at the sight that appeared to him, said, ' I exceedingly fear and quake.' But the author quotes no book of the Old Testament; he only relates a matter of *fact*, and one circumstance of it, which he doubtless had by Divine revelation. It is an *uncouth* way of proving an author not to have written by Divine inspiration, because he writeth truths which he could no *otherwise* be acquainted with !

3. It is an objection of more importance, that the writer citeth testimonies out of the Old Testament, *that are not to his purpose.* Now, two things must be supposed to give countenance to this objection: *First*, that those who make it, do better understand the meaning of the testimonies so produced, than he did, by whom they are alledged. How vain and presumptuous this supposition is, needs little labour to demonstrate. Nay, it may much more rationally be supposed, that we are rather ignorant of God's utmost intention in *every* place of scripture, than that we know it in *all*. There is a depth in the word of God, *because his*, which we are not able to fathom. One says, well : " The holy scriptures are as a rich overflowing fountain, which the deeper you dig, the more you find it abounds with water: in like manner, the more carefully you search the sacred volume, the fuller you will find, are the veins of living water."* *Secondly*, they who object must take it for granted, that they are, beforehand, fully acquainted with the particular intention of the author, in producing these testimonies. Neither is this supposition less rash and presumptuous than the former; for those only, who bring their hypothesis and pre-concerted notions to the scripture, with a wish to have them confirmed, are apt to make such conclusions. But those that come with humility and reverence, to learn of

* BRENT. Hom. XXXVI. in I. Sam. xi.

the

the Supreme Majesty, his mind and will therein, will have other thoughts and apprehensions.

§ 7. Having removed these objections out of our way, we shall now proceed

(III.) To demonstrate the canonical authority of this epistle, taken in the strict and proper sense, before declared.—Now the sum of what we shall plead in this cause, amounts to this: that—whereas there are many (τεκμήρια) *infallible evidences* of any writings being given by Divine inspiration; and sundry arguments whereby, books, vainly pretending to that original, may be disproved—of the *former*, there is no one that is not applicable to this epistle; nor is it obnoxious to any one of the *latter* sort: so that it stands on the same basis with the whole, which, at present, we suppose firm and immoveable. And,

1. The *general argument* of it is the same with that of the whole scriptures. It treats of things which eye hath not seen, nor ear heard; nor have they, by any natural means, ever entered into the heart of man; and yet, in absolute harmony with all other unquestionable revelations of the will of God. Human diligence, regulated by what is revealed elsewhere, is *human* still; and can never free itself from those inseparable attendances, that manifest it to be such. The truth of this consideration is demonstrable from every one of those books, commonly called *apocryphal*; not one of which is there, wherein human diligence doth not discover itself to be its fountain and spring.

§ 8. 2. To the general argument, we may add the *particular subject matter*, as farther confirming its Divine original; wherein we have eminently four things:

(1.) The principal things treated of are matters of the greatest importance, and such as concern the very foundation of faith. Such are the doctrines about the person, offices, and sacrifice of Christ; the nature of gospel worship, and our communion with God therein. In these consist the very vitals of our profession; and they are all opened in a most excellent and heavenly manner in this epistle, in absolute harmony with what is taught concerning them in other parts of holy writ.

(2.) Some things of great moment to the faith and consolation of the church, which are but obscurely and sparingly taught elsewhere, are here plainly, fully, and excellently taught and improved. Such, in particular, are the doctrines of the priesthood of Christ, his sacrifice, and intercession; and how these were typically represented under the Old Testament œconomy. He that understands aright the importance of these things, their use and influence and the support they afford under temptations and trials, will be ready to conclude—that the world may as well want the sun in the firmament, as the church this epistle.

(3.) God's way, in teaching the Old Testament church, with the operose pedagogy of Moses, is here fully revealed, and shewn to be full of wisdom, grace, and love. Here we see, that the whole Aaronical priesthood, with its duties and offices, are transferred to the use of believers under the gospel. How dark Mosaical institutions were in themselves, is evident from the whole state of the church in the days of Christ and his apostles, when they could not see to the end of the things to be abolished. In their nature, they were *carnal*; in their number, *many*; as to their reason, *hidden*; in their observance, *burdensome*; and in their external appearance, *pompous*. By all which they so possessed the minds of the church, that very few saw clearly into their use, intention, and end; but in this epistle the veil is taken off from Moses; the mystery of his designs laid open; and a perfect clew is given to believers, to pass safely through all the turnings and windings of them, to rest and truth in Jesus Christ.

(4.) The grounds and manner of that great alteration which God caused in his worship, are here laid open; and the greatest controversy that ever the church of God was exercised with, is here fully determined. There was nothing in the first propagation of the gospel, and the planting of Christian churches, that so much divided and perplexed the professors of the truth, as the difference
about

about the continuation of Mosaical rites and ceremonies. The will of God, in this matter, before the writing of this epistle, could only be collected from the nature and state of things in the church, upon the coming of the Messiah; and conclusions, from that consideration, the believing Jews were very slow to admit. Now who was fit, who was able, to determine upon these various institutions, but God himself? to declare *positively*, that all obligation from his former positive commands had now ceased; that the time allotted for their observance was expired? Surely, this was no otherwise to be effected, but by an immediate revelation from himself. And this we have here done; not by a bare declaration of God's authoritative interposition, but by a method marked with singular wisdom. The whole nature and design of them are evidenced to be such, as that, having received their full end and accomplishment, they of themselves naturally expired. For my part, I can truly say, that I know not any portion of holy writ, that will more effectually raise up the heart of an intelligent reader to an holy admiration of the goodness, love, and wisdom of God, than this epistle. Such, I say, is the *subject matter* of it; so divine, so excellent, so singular!

§ 9. 3. Consonant to its general argument, and peculiar subject matter, is the *design and end* of it. That the whole scripture hath a special end, peculiar to itself, and wherein no other writing shares, but by way of conformity, is evident to all who seriously consider; and this end is supremely and absolutely the glory of that God, who is the author of it. This is the centre where all the lines of it meet; the scope and mark towards which all its contents are directed. It is true, God's works of power and providence all declare his glory—the glory of his eternal perfections and excellencies; but the end of holy scripture is the glory of *God in Christ*, as he hath revealed himself, and " gathered all things into an head in him," to the manifestation of that glory. The more clearly any *portion* of scripture discovers this end, and the more *parts* it manifesteth of the *series* and orders of things, in their mutual

mutual connection, dependence and subferviency, whereby the laſt end of God's glory is produced, the more fully doth it expreſs this *general end* of the whole, and thereby evince its own intereſt therein. Now herein doth this epiſtle come behind no other portion of ſcripture whatever; nor does it betray the leaſt alloy or mixture of any *by end* of the writer; nothing of his honour, reputation, advantage, or ſelf-pleaſing, in any thing; but all runs evenly and ſmoothly, to the general end propoſed. And this alſo hath deſervedly a place among the ($\tau\varepsilon\varkappa\mu\eta\rho\iota\alpha$) *infallible evidences* of writings by Divine inſpiration.

§ 10. 4. The *ſtyle* alſo of the ſacred ſcripture is of deſerved conſideration. By the ſtyle of any writing, we underſtand both the propriety of the words, with their grammatical conſtruction, and that compoſition of the whole, which renders it fit and decorous to effect the end propoſed. I know ſome have, with atheiſtical boldneſs, deſpiſed the ſtyle of the holy writers, as ſimple and barbarous; among whom was Petrus Bembus, who could ſcarce touch the ſcriptures; when his own epiſtles, not one of them excepted, are not free from ſoleciſms in grammar. But be it obſerved, that wherever there appears to us an irregularity in the original languages, when compared with the arbitrary rules or uſages of other men, it much more becomes us to ſuſpect our own apprehenſions and judgement, than to reflect the leaſt failure or miſtake on the inſpired writers. The cenſure of Heinsius, in this matter, is ſevere, but true: "To rail at any thing in them, or to find fault therewith, as defective, is to act the part, not of a learned man, but of a blaſphemer, and an idler, who never conſiders what is the condition of man, or how great the reverence and reſpect which are due to God, who diſpoſeth all things, and who does not require a *judge*, but a humble petitioner."*

§ 11. Eloquence and propriety of ſpeech, for their proper ends, are the gift of God, [Exod. iv. 10, 11.] and, therefore, it may well be expected, that they ſhould

* Prolegom. Ariſtarch. Sacr.

not be wanting, if neceffary, in books written by his own infpiration. Nor, indeed, are they; yet he who shall expect to find in the heavenly oracles a flourish of painted words, artificial ornaments of fpeech, language calculated to entice, and to work upon weak and carnal affections, or fophiftical and captious ways of reafoning to deceive, or a fmooth harmonious ftructure of periods, will be miftaken in his aim. Such things become not the authority, the majefty, the greatnefs and holinefs of the Divine Speaker. Even an earthly monarch, who fhould make ufe of them in his edicts, laws, or proclamation, would but proftitute his authority to contempt, and invite his fubjects to difobedience, by fo doing; how much more unbecoming the declaration of His mind and will, who is the great Poffeffor of heaven and earth! Therefore, the apoftle tells us, [I. Cor. ii. 5—7.] that the rejecting of *this* kind of oratory, in his preaching and writings, was indifpenfably neceffary, that it might appear the effects were the genuine productions of the things themfelves, which he delivered.

§. 12. That the proper excellency of fpeech, or ftyle, confifteth in (το πρηπον) the meet accommodation of words to things; confidering the *perfon* ufing them, and the *end* to which they are applied, all competent judges will confefs. And the ftyle of the holy fcripture, we affirm, is every way anfwerable to what may be rationally expected from it. Hence it is, that, by its fimplicity without corruption, gravity without affectation, and plainnefs without alluring ornaments, it does not fo much entice, move, or perfuade, as conftrain, prefs, and pierce, into the mind and affections, transforming them into a likenefs of the things delivered. "I dare affert (faith St. Austin, fpeaking of the holy penmen) that whofoever rightly underftands what they fpeak, will alfo underftand, that they ought not to have fpoken otherwife."* Bodies poffeffed of native beauty, and fymmetry of parts, have more advantage by being cloathed in fit gar-

---

* De Doctr. Chrift. Lib. IV. Cap. vi.

ments, than by the ornaments of gay attire; and the garb of plainnefs and fimplicity is beft adapted to the fpiritual *native beauty* of heavenly truths. Therefore, we fay with Austin, that " nothing is delivered in fcripture, but *juft as it ought to be.*"* The ftyle of the facred penmen difcovers, in a manner peculiar to itfelf, a gracious condefcenfion, fuited to the capacity of thofe for whom principally their writings were defigned.† Befides, there is in it, as all who read it with faith and reverence, can witnefs, a fecret efficacious energy, fubjecting the mind of the humble reader to its grand defign in all things.

§ 13. What we have faid concerning the ftyle of the facred fcripture in general, is eminently applicable to *this epiftle* in particular, as containing, in the moft confpicuous manner, the fame fimplicity, gravity, unaffectednefs, and fuitablenefs to its author, matter, and end, which recommends the *whole*. If any where, as in the beginning of the firft chapter, the ftyle feems to fwell in its current, above the ordinary banks of the New Teftament writings, it is from the greatnefs and fublimity of the matter treated of, which was not capable of any other kind of expreffion. Does the author, for inftance, any where ufe words or phrafes in any uncommon fenfe? It is becaufe his matter is peculiar. Does he often fpeak in an Old Teftament dialect, after it had been manumitted, as it were, from its *typical* import? It is from the confideration of their ftate and condition, with whom, in an efpecial manner, he had to do; which is perfectly agreeable to the wifdom of the Holy Ghoft in other portions of fcripture. Moreover,

§ 14 .5. The *authority* of its principal author exerts itfelf in the whole of it. Now this authority, as it refpects the minds of men, confifts, partly, in an exurgency, or forcible influence of the holy matter contained in it, and the heavenly manner wherein it is declared; and, partly, in the ineffable emanation of Divine excellency, which is

---

* Vid. Origen. contr. Cels. Lib. V.
† Hilar. in Pfal. cxxvi.

communicated to the word, as a diftinguifhing property of its *relation* to God. And this authority do all they who have their minds fpiritually exercifed, find and acknowledge in this epiftle.

§ 15. 6. From this authority procceds a *divine efficacy*; a powerful operation upon the foul and confcience; a reverence and awe of God. And humble readers find their minds effectually brought into the pleafing captivity of unreferved obedience. ' Is not my word as fire, faith the ' Lord, and like a hammer, that breaketh the rocks in ' pieces?' [Jer. xxiii. 29.] It is ' quick and powerful, ' and fharper than any two-edged fword, piercing even to ' the dividing afunder of the foul and fpirit, and of the ' joints and marrow, and is a difcerner of thoughts and ' intents of the heart,' [Heb. iv. 12.] A learned man faid, well, " The holy fcriptures do not fo much admonifh, or perfuade, as *compel*, agitate, and forcibly influence. You read therein plain and countrified words; but they are *living* words; they animate, they inflame, they fting, they penetrate into the inmoft foul, and transform the whole man, by their wonderful power."*

Such is the nature, power, and efficacy of this epiftle towards believers. It fearches their hearts, difcovers their thoughts, judges their actions, fupports their fpirits, comforts their fouls, enlightens their minds, guides them in their hopes, directs them in all their communion with God, and finally leads them to enjoy him. When once they have obtained this experience of its Divine power, it is in vain for men or devils to oppofe its canonical authority, with their frivolous cavils and objections. Neither is the experience merely fatisfactory to themfelves alone, but is alfo fairly pleadable even to *others*; though not to atheiftical fcoffers, yet to humble inquirers after facred truths.

§ 16. 7. To thefe things we may add, that the canonical authority of this epiftle is confirmed by *Catholic tradition*. But by this tradition I intend a general *uninterrupted fame*, conveyed and confirmed by particular inftances, records

* PICUS MIRANDUS ad Hermol. Barbar.

records and testimonies in all ages; which is undoubtedly of great importance. And how clearly this may be pleaded in our present case, shall be manifested in our investigation of the penman of this epistle.

§ 17. 8. Thus I hope we have made it evident, that it is not destitute of any one of those (τεκμηρια) *infallible proofs* and arguments, whereby any particular book of scripture evinceth itself to the consciences of men, to be written by inspiration of God. It remaineth now to shew, that it is not liable to any of those *exceptions*, or arguments, whereby any book, pretending a claim to a divine original, and canonical authority, may be convicted, and manifested to be of another extract; whereby, at length, its just privilege will be on *both sides* secured.

(1.) The first consideration of this nature is taken from the author, or *penman* of any such writing. The books of the Old Testament were all of them written by *prophets*, or holy men inspired of God. Hence Peter calls the whole of it '*prophecy*,' [II. Pet. i. 21.] delivered by men *acted* or moved therein by the Holy Ghost. And though there be a distribution made of the several books from their subject matter, into the *law*, *prophets*, and *psalms*, [Luke xxiv. 44.] and often into the *law* and *prophets*, on the same account, [Acts xxvi. 22. Rom. iii. 21.] yet their penmen being all equally prophets, the whole, in general, is ascribed to them and called '*prophecy*,' [Rom. xvi. 26. Luke xxiv. 25. II. Peter i. 19.]

So were the books of the *New Testament* written by *apostles*, or men endowed with an apostolical spirit, and in their work *equally inspired* by the Holy Ghost; whence the church is said to be ' built on the foundation of the pro-
' phets and apostles; Jesus Christ himself being the chief
' corner stone,' [Ephes. ii. 20.] If then the author of any writing acknowledgeth himself to be, or may otherwise be convinced to have been neither prophet, nor apostle; nor, indued, with the same infallible spirit with them, his work, how excellent soever in other respects, must needs be esteemed a mere fruit of his own skill, diligence,

and wisdom, and not any way to belong to the canon of scripture.

Now *this epistle* is free from this exception : the penman of it doth no where intimate, directly or indirectly, that he wrote by his own ability; which, if he had done so, it must have been incumbent on him to have declared, that he might not lead the church into a pernicious error, in embracing that as given by inspiration from God, which was but a fruit of his diligence and fallible endeavours. But on the contrary, he speaks as in the name of God, referring to *him* all that he delivers; nor can he, even in any minute instance, be convicted to have wanted his assistance.

§ 18. (2.) *Circumstances* of the general argument of a book may also convince it to be of an human, or fallible original. But our epistle is no way obnoxious to any exception of this nature. Yea, the *state* of things in the churches of God, and among the Hebrews in particular, did at that time administer so just and full an occasion for a writing of this kind, as gives countenance to its being ascribed to the wisdom and care of the Holy Ghost. For, if the corruption of the poisonous brood of hereticks, particularly CIRINTHUS, gave occasion to the writing of the gospel, by St. John; and if the dissentions in the church of Corinth deserved *two epistles*, and if the *lesser* differences between believers of the Jews and Gentiles had a remedy provided for them in the epistles of St. Paul to them, is it not at least *probable*, that the same spirit who moved the penmen of those books to write, and directed them in their so doing, did also provide for removing the prejudices, and healing the distempers of the *Hebrews*, which were so great, and of so great importance to all the churches of God!

§ 19. (3.) The most manifest eviction of any writing, pretending to the privilege of Divine inspiration, may be taken from the *subject matter* of it. God himself being the first, and only essential *truth*, nothing can proceed from him, but what is absolutely so; and truth being but *one*, every way uniform and consonant to itself, there can be be no discrepancy in the branches of it, nor contrariety in the streams that flow from that one fountain. God is also *holy*, ' glorious in holiness,' and nothing proceeds immediately from him, but what bears a stamp of his holiness, as well as his greatness and wisdom. If then, any thing in the subject matter of any writing be *untrue, impious, light*, or any way contradictory to the *ascertained* writings of Divine inspiration, all pleas and pretences to that privilege must cease for ever. We need no other proof to evince its *original*, than what itself affords. And by this means do those books commonly called *apocryphal*, to which the Romanists ascribe canonical authority, destroy their own pretensions. They have, *all of them*, on *this* account among others, long since been cast out of the limits of any tolerable defence. Now, that no one portion of scripture is less obnoxious to any exception of this kind, from the matter treated of, and doctrines delivered in it, than this epistle, we shall, by God's assistance, manifest in our exposition of the whole.

§ 20. (4.) The *style and method* of a writing may be such, as to lay a *just prejudice* against its claim of canonical authority. For though the matter may be good in the main, and generally suited to the analogy of faith; yet there may be in the *manner* of its composure, such an *ostentation* of wit, learning, or eloquence; such an *affectation* of words and phrases; such rhetorical paintings of things inconsiderable, as may sufficiently demonstrate *human* ambition, ignorance, pride, or desire of applause, to have been mixt in the forming of it. Much of this JEROME observes in particular, concerning the book intitled the " *Wisdom of Solomon* ;" written, as it is supposed, by PHILO, an eloquent and learned Jew, (*redolet Græcam eloquentiam*) *it savours of Græcian eloquence.*[*] When, therefore, these human failings and sinful infirmities manifest themselves, they cast out the writings where they are, from that harmony and consent, which in general appears amongst all the books of Divine inspiration. Of the style

* Præf. in Prov. Solom.

of this epistle we have spoken before. Its gravity, simplicity, majesty, and absolute suitableness to the high, holy, and heavenly mysteries treated of in it, are, as far as I can find, not only very *evident*, but also *acknowledged* to be so by all who are able to judge of them.

§ 21. (5.) Want of *catholic tradition* in all ages of the church, from the first giving forth of any writing, testifying to its Divine original, is another impeachment of its pretence to canonical authority. And this argument ariseth fatally against the *apocryphal* books before-mentioned. The suffrage of this kind given to our epistle, we have mentioned before; but we shall give a farther confirmation of its Divine original, by proving it undeniably to be written by the apostle St. Paul, that eminent penman of the Holy Ghost.

Thus clear stands the canonical authority of this epistle. It is *destitute* of no evidence needful for the manifestation of it; nor is it *obnoxious* to any just exception against its claim of that privilege. And hence it comes to pass, that whatever have been the *fears*, doubts, and scruples of some; the *rash* objections, conjectures and censures of others; the provident care of God over it, as a part of his most holy word, co-operating with the prevailing evidence of its original implanted in it, and its spiritual efficacy to all the ends of holy scripture, hath obtained an *absolute conquest* over the hearts and minds of all that believe, and settled it in full possession of *canonical authority* in all the churches of Christ throughout the world.

Exercit. II.

Saint Paul the Author of the Epistle to the Hebrews.

§ 1. *Knowledge of the penman not abſolutely neceſſary, yet of ſome uſe.* § 2.—4. *That St. Paul was the author of this epiſtle appears,* (I.) *From the uncertainty of other ſuppoſitions.* § 5. (II.) *From the inſufficiency of the argument inſiſted on to the contrary,* (1.) *Diſſimilitude of ſtyle.* § 6, 7. (2.) *Its being unſubſcribed.* § 8, 9. (III.) *From the teſtimony given it in other ſcriptures.* § 10. (IV.) *From conſiderations taken from the writing itſelf, compared with St. Paul's writings.* § 11. (V.) *From the teſtimony of the firſt churches.* § 12. (VI.) *From reaſons and circumſtances relating to the epiſtle itſelf.*

§ 1. THE divine authority of the epiſtle having been vindicated, it is of no *great* moment to inquire ſcrupulouſly after its *penman*. Writings that proceed from divine inſpiration, receive no addition of *authority* from the reputation or eſteem of them by whom they were written; and this the Holy Ghoſt hath ſufficiently manifeſted, by ſhutting up the *names* of many of them from the knowledge of the church in all ages. Had any prejudice to their authority enſued, this had not been. Nor were any eſteemed to be given by prophecy, becauſe their authors were prophets; but they were known to be prophets by the word which they delivered. If not, they were ſome other way known to be divinely inſpired, as by the working of *miracles;* or that they were in their days received as *ſuch* by the church. But neither of theſe can be aſſerted: for as it is not known that any one penman of the Old Teſtament, Moſes only excepted, ever wrought any miracles, ſo it is certain that moſt of them

them were rejected and condemned by the *church* in their days. The only way, therefore, whereby they were proved to be *prophets*, was by the *word* itself which they delivered and wrought; and thereon depended the evidence and certainty of their being divinely inspired. [See Amos vii. 14—16. Jer. xxiii. 25—31.]

But whereas there are not wanting *evidences* sufficient to discover who was the *writer* of this epistle, whereby also the remaining exceptions made to its divine original may be finally obviated, they also shall be taken into consideration.—We affirm, then, that the epistle was written by St. Paul. And what I shall offer in proof of the position may be reduced to these heads;— The manifest *failure* of all of them who have endeavoured to assign it to any other penman—the *insufficiency* of the arguments insisted on to disprove our assertion—the *testimony* given it in other scriptures—*considerations* taken from the writing itself, compared with other acknowledged writings of Paul—the general suffrage of *antiquity*, or ececlesiastical tradition—and, finally, reasons taken from sundry *circumstances* relating to the epistle itself.

§ 2. (I.) The *uncertainty* of them who question whether Paul was the writer of this epistle, and their want of probable grounds in assigning it to any other, hath some *inducement*, or presumptive reason, why we should ascribe it to him, whose of old it was esteemed to be.

Origen, in Eusebius,[*] affirms, that some supposed Luke to have been the author of it. But neither doth he *approve* their opinion, nor mention what *reasons* they pretend for it. He adds also, that *some* esteemed it to be written by Clemens of Rome. Clemens of Alexandria allows St. Paul to be its *author*; but supposes it might be *translated* by Luke, because, as he saith, the *style* of it is not unlike his in the Acts of the Apostles. Grotius, of late, contends for Luke to be the *author*, on the same account;[†] but the instance he gives rather

[*] Hist. Eccles. Lib. VI. Chap. xxvi.
[†] Præfat. in Annot. ad Epist. ad Heb.

argues

argues a coincidence of some words and *phrases*, than a similitude of *style*, which things are very different. JEROME also tells us, " that it was supposed by some to be written by Luke;" * which he undoubtedly took from CLEMENS, ORIGEN, and EUSEBIUS. But none of them acquaint us who were the authors or approvers of this *conjecture*, nor do they give any credit to it themselves. This opinion, then, may be well rejected as a groundless *guess* of an obscure, unknown original, and not *tolerably* confirmed either by testimony or circumstances. GROTIUS alone, in reality, *contends* for Luke; and with this only argument, that sundry words are used in the same sense, by St. Luke and the writer of this epistle. But I shall add one consideration, that will cast this opinion quite out of the limits of probability, viz.

By general consent this epistle was written, whilst James was yet alive, and presided in the church of Jerusalem. These were the *Hebrews*, whose instruction in this epistle is principally intended, and, by their means, that of their brethren in the *eastern dispersion*. Now is it reasonable to imagine, that any one, who was not an *apostle*, but only a *scholar* and follower of them, should be employed to write to that church, wherein so great an apostle, a *pillar* among them, [Gal. ii. 9.] had his special residence, and did actually preside; and that in an argument of such importance, which reasons against a a practice wherein they were all engaged? Incredible.

§ 3. Some have assigned the writing of this epistle to BARNABAS. TERTULLIAN was the author of this opinion; and it is reported as his by JEROME. † But CLEMENS, ORIGEN, and EUSEBIUS, make no mention of him. It is of late defended by CAMERO, (as the former concerning *Luke* by GROTIUS,) whose conjectural rea-

---

* Scrip. Ecclef. in Paul.

† TERTULL. de Pudicit. Chap. xx. HIRON. Cat. Scrip. in Paul et Barnab.

fons are confuted by SPANHEMIUS.* We add, the reason before mentioned is of the same validity against this opinion as the other concerning Luke; for Barnabas was not an apostle, properly and strictly so called, nor had he an *apostolical* mission or authority.†

Many *circumstances* also concur to the removal of this conjecture. The epistle now written in Italy, [chap. xiii. 24.] where it doth not appear that Barnabas ever was. Again, Timothy was the companion of the writer of this epistle, [chap. xiii. 23.] a person, as far as appears, unknown to Barnabas; being taken into St. Paul's company after their difference and separation, [Acts xv. 39. xvi. 1.] This writer had also been in *bonds* or imprisonment, [Heb. x. 34.] whereof we cannot learn any thing concerning Barnabas, at that time; but those of Paul are well known. And lastly, not long before the writing of this epistle, Barnabas was so far from that light into the nature, use, and expiration of Judaical rites, that he was easily misled into a practical miscarriage in the observance of them, [Gal. ii. 13.] and shall we suppose that he, who but a little before, upon the coming of some few brethren of the church of Jerusalem, from James, durst not avouch and abide by his own *personal liberty*, without some blameable dissimulation; [Gal. ii. 13.] that he, I say, should now with so much authority write an epistle to that church (with St. James at the head of it) and all the Hebrews in the world concurring with them in judgement and practice, about that very thing in which himself, out of respect to them, had particularly miscarried? This, certainly, was rather the office of St. Paul; whose light and constancy in the doctrine delivered in this epistle, with his engagements in the defence of it, above all the rest of the apostles, is well known from the History of the Acts and his other invaluable writings.

* CAMER. Quæf. in Epift. ad Heb. SPANHEM. de Auth. Epift. ad Heb.
† Vid. EPIPHAN. Hær. Lib. I. Cap. x. EUSEB. Ecclef. Hift. Lib. I. Cap. xiii.

§ 4.

§ 4. *Apollos* hath been thought by some to be the penman; because it answers the character given of him, that he was an *eloquent* man, *mighty* in the scripture, fervent in spirit, and one that mightily convinced the Jews out of the scripture itself, [Acts xviii. 24. 28.] all which things appear throughout this epistle. But this conjecture hath no countenance from antiquity; no mention being made of any epistle written by Apollos, or indeed any other literary production, so that he is not reckoned by JEROME amongst the ecclesiastical writers; nor is he reported by CLEMENS, ORIGEN, or EUSEBIUS, to have been by any esteemed the author of it. However, were not these qualifications found in St. Paul in a more eminent manner and degree than in the other? And therefore this conjecture is groundless.

ERASMUS, after some others, hath taken up a report, concerning some who ascribed it to CLEMENS ROMANUS; but he hath not advanced any thing of *reason* or *testimony* to confirm it; and no ancient writer of any learning or judgement ever laid any weight on this conjecture. For what had he, who was a *convert* from among the GENTILES, to do with the churches of the HEBREWS? What authority had he to interpose himself in that which was *their* peculiar concernment? Whence may it appear, that he had that *skill* in the nature, use, and end, of Mosaical rites and institutions, which the writer of this epistle discovers? Neither doth that epistle of CLEMENS to the church of Corinth, which is yet extant, though excellent in its kind, permit us to think that he wrote by divine inspiration. Besides, the author of *this epistle* had a desire and purpose to go to the *Hebrews*; [chap. xiii. 23.] Yea, he desires to be *restored* to them as one that had been with them before. But as it doth not appear that this CLEMENS was ever in *Palestine*, so, what reason he should have to leave his own *charge* now to go thither, no man can imagine.

From the *uncertainty* of these conjectures, with the evidence of reason and circumstances, whereby they are disproved, *two* things we seem to have obtained:—*First*, that

that no objection on their account can arise against our *assertions*; and—*Secondly*, that if St. Paul be not acknowledged to be the writer, the whole church of God is, and ever was, at a total loss whom to ascribe it to.

§ 5. (II.) The *objections* that are laid by some against our assignation of it to Paul, are, according to the order proposed, next to be considered.

1. *Dissimilitude of style* and manner of writing from that used by him in his other epistles, is principally insisted on; and indeed it is the whole of what, with any colour of reason, is made use of in this cause. The elegance, propriety, and sometimes loftiness of speech that occur in the epistle, distinguish it, they say, from St. Paul's writings, (Δοκει μεν εκ ειναι Παυλε δια τον χαρακ]ηρα) " it seems not to be Paul's, because of the style, or character of the speech," saith OECUMENIUS. For this cause, CLEMENS of ALEXANDRIA supposed it to be written in *Hebrew*, and to be translated to *Greek* by St. Luke, the evangelist; the style of it, as he says, being like to that which is used in the Acts of the Apostles. And yet, the latter is acknowledged by all to be *purely Greek*, whereas the former is accused of being full of *Hebraisms*; so little weight is to be laid on these critical censures, wherein learned men perpetually contradict one another!

The sum of this *objection* is, That St. Paul was " rude in speech," which is manifest from his other epistles; but the style of this is pure, elegant, florid, such as hath no affinity with his, so that he cannot be esteemed the penman of it. But this is of little force; for Paul in that place is dealing with the Corinthians about the false teachers who seduced them from the simplicity of the gospel, by their vain, affected eloquence, and strains of rhetoric utterly unbecoming the work they pretended to be engaged in. Puffed up with this singularity, they contemned St. Paul as a rude, unskilful person, unable to rival them in their fine pompous declamations. In answer to this, he first tells them, that it became not him to use (σοφιας λογε, I. Cor. i. 7.) *wisdom of words*, or that kind

kind of speech with which *orators* flourish; or (διδακτες ανθρωπινης σοφιας λογες, I. Cor. ii. 13.) *the words that man's wisdom teacheth*, an *artificial* composition of words to *entice* thereby; which he calls (υπεροχην λογε, chap. ii. 1.) *excellency of speech*; and which, for many reasons, it did not become him to use for the same ostentatious design, as the seducers and false apostles did. Again; he answers only by *concession*, (ει δε και ιδιωτης τω λογω) '*suppose I were rude or unskilful in speech*,' doth the matter in question depend upon that? Is it not manifest to you that I am not so in the knowledge and mystery of the gospel? " He doth not confess *that he is* so, faith Austin, but *grants* it for their conviction." And in this sense concur Oecumenius, Aquinas, Lyra, Catharinus, Clarius, and Capellus, with many others on the place. If, then, by (λογος) *speech* be intended that enticing *rhetoric* wherewith the false teachers entangled the affections of their unskilful hearers, we may grant that St. Paul was unskilful in it, and are sure that he would make no use of it; and it is denied that any footsteps of it appear in this *epistle*; but if any thing of solid, convincing, unpainted eloquence be intended, it is evident that he neither did, nor justly could confess himself unacquainted with it. He therefore only made a concession of the objection made against him by the *false teachers*, to manifest, that they could gain no manner of advantage thereby.

Neither are his other epistles written in so low and homely a style as is pretended. I shall now only add the words of a person who was no incompetent judge in things of this nature: " When I well consider," says he, speaking of St. Paul, " the genius and character of his style, I confess I never found that grandeur in Plato himself, which I find in him, when he thundereth out the mysteries of God; nor that gravity and vehemence in Demosthenes which I find in him, when he intends to terrify our minds with a dread of the divine judgement; or when he would solemnly warn them, or draw them to the contemplation of his goodness, or exhort to

the

the performance of the duties of piety and mercy. Nor do I find a more exact method of teaching in those great and excellent masters, ARISTOTLE, and GALEN, than in him."* Upon the whole, I shall confidently assert, that there is no manner of defect in any of his writings; and that every thing (considering the matter and nature of it, in whose name, and to whom he wrote) is expressed *as it ought to be* for the end proposed. And hence it is, that there is such a *variety* in his way and manner of expressing himself in sundry of his epistles.

It may then be granted (though it be not proved) that there is some *dissimilitude* of style between this and the rest of Paul's epistles, since the *argument* treated of is diverse from that of most of the others; many *circumstances* in those to whom he wrote were singular; to which we may add, that the spring and mode of his reasonings are peculiarly suited to the condition of those to whom he wrote. Besides, in the writing of this epistle there was in him an especial frame and incitation of spirit, occasioned by many occurrences relating to it. His *intense love* to them to whom he wrote (being his kinsmen according to the flesh) affectionately remembered by himself, and inimitably expressed, [Rom. ix. 1, 3.] did undoubtedly exert itself in his treating about their greatest and nearest concernment. The *prejudices* and enmity of some of them against him, recorded in several places of 'the Acts,' and remembered by himself in some of his other epistles) lay also under his consideration. Much of the *subject* he treated about was a matter of controversy, which was to be debated from *scripture*, and according to which those with whom he dealt thought they might dissent from him, without any prejudice to their faith or obedience. Their *condition* also must needs greatly affect him; for they were now not only under present troubles, dangers, and fears, but (*positi inter sacrum et saxum*) at the very door of ruin, if not delivered from the snare of obstinate adherence to *Mosaical institutions*. Now they who know not what

* Poz. Annot. in II. Cor. xi. 6.

what alterations in *style*, and manner of writing, these things will produce, in those who have ability to express their conceptions, and the affections wherewith they are attended, know nothing of this matter. Neither is it to be omitted, that there is such a coincidence in many *phrases* in this *epistle*, compared with the rest of St. Paul's, as will not allow us to grant such a *discrepancy in style*, as some imagine. Many of them have been gathered by *others*; and, therefore, I shall only point to the place from whence they are taken below.*

§ 6. 2. It is objected, that the epistle is (ανεπιγραφος) *unsubscribed*; and, indeed, this being once taken notice of, and admitted as an *objection*, the rest were but men's needless diligence to give countenance to it. And the strength of it lies—not in its being *without inscription*; for so is the epistle of St. John, concerning which it was never doubted, that he was the author of it; but—in the constant usage of Paul, prefixing his name to all his other epistles; so, that unless a *just reason* can be given, why he should divert from that custom, it may be supposed to be none of his.

Now, by the *title* which is wanting, must be intended, either the mere *titular superscription*, ' the epistle of Paul ' to the *Hebrews*,' or the inscription of his *name*, joined with an *apostolical salutation*, in the epistle itself. For the *first*, it is uncertain of what antiquity the titular super-

---

* See chap. i. 1, compared with II. Cor. xiii. 3. chap. ii. 14. Gal. i. 16. Ephes. vi. 12. chap. ii. 2. with Ephes. v. 26. chap. iii. 1. with Phil. iii. 14. II. Tim. i. 9. chap. iii. 16. with Rom. v. 2. chap. v. 14. with I. Cor. xi. 6. Phil. iii. 15. Ephes. iv. 13. chap. v. 13. with I. Cor. iii. 2. chap. vi. 2. with Col. ii. 2. I. Thes. i. 5. chap. vii. 18. with Rom. viii. 3. Gal. iv. 9. chap. viii. 6. 9. with Gal. iii. 19, 20. I. Tim. ii. 5. chap. x. 1. with Col. ii. 17. chap. x. 22. with II. Cor. vii. 1. chap. x. 23. a phrase peculiar to St. PAUL, and common with him, chap. x. 33. with I. Cor. iv. 9. chap. x. 36. with Gal. iii. 22. chap. x. 39. with I. Thes. v. 9. II. Thes. ii. 14. chap. xii. 1. with I. Cor. ix. 24. chap. xiii. 10. with Ephes. iv. 14. I. Cor. ix. 13. I. Cor. x. 18. chap. xiii. 15, 16. with Rom. xii. I. Phil. iv. 8. chap. xiii. 20. with Rom. xv. 33. Rom. xvi. 20. II. Cor. xiii. 2. Phil. iv. 9. I. Thes. v. 23.

scription of *any* of the epistles are; but most certain, that they did not *originally* belong to them, and are, therefore, destitute of all authority. The transcribers, it may be, have at pleasure made bold with them, as with the *subscription* also of some of them, as to the *place* from whence they were sent, and the *persons* by whom. Though this, therefore, should be wanting, (and yet there is some variety about it, both in ancient copies of the *original*, and *translations*, the most owning and retaining it); yet it would be of no moment, seeing we know not whence *any* of them are. The remainder of the objection, then, is taken from the want of the usual *apostolical salutation*, as a part of the epistle.

Some of the *ancients*, and principally THEODORET, insist, that, if in writing to the *Hebrews*, Paul had prefixed his name, he might have seemed to transgress the *line of his allotment*, as the apostle of the Gentiles. But on this supposition it seems he did what was not meet for him to do; he entered on the charge of another, only he conceals his name, that he might not appear to be doing what was unwarrantable and unjustifiable!

Others insist on the *prejudices* that many of the Hebrews had against him. The *persecuting* party of the nation looked on him as an *apostate*, a *deserter* of the cause wherein he was once engaged, and one that taught apostacy from the law of Moses; yea, as they thought, that set the whole world against them and all that they *gloried in*, [Acts xxi. 28.] and what enmity is usually stirred up on such occasions all know, and his example is a sufficient instance of it. To which it has been justly *added*, that he was no *ordinary* person, but a man of great and extraordinary abilities, which mightily increased the provocation. This being the state of things in reference to St. Paul, and not of any other, the defect of *inscription*, as BEZA well observes, proves the epistle to be his, rather than any other person's whatever.

§ 7. But if we would know the *true* and just cause of the *omissions* in question, we must consider what were the *just reasons* of prefixing them to his other epistles. The real

real cause, then, of prefixing the names of *any* of the apostles to their writings, was merely for the introduction of their titles, as the *apostles of Jesus Christ*, and therein an intimation of that *authority* by which they wrote. This was the true and only reason, why the apostle Paul in particular prefixed his name to his epistles. And hence it was, that—when something he had taught was called in question and opposed, and he wrote in vindication of it, for establishing in the truth those whom before he had instructed—he, at the *entrance* of his writings, singularly and *emphatically* mentions his *apostolical authority*, [Gal. i. 1.] ' Paul, an apostle, not of men, neither by man, ' but by *Jesus Christ*; and God, the Father, had raised ' him from the dead;' thus intimating the absolute obedience that was due to the doctrine by him revealed.

In this dealing with the Hebrews, the case was far otherwise; they who believed amongst them, never changed the *old foundation*, or church state, grounded on the scriptures, though they had a new addition of privileges by their faith in *Christ Jesus*, as the Messiah now exhibited; and, therefore, he deals not with them as with those whose faith was built absolutely on *apostolical* authority and revelation, but upon the common principles of the *Old Testament*, on which they still stood, and out of which *evangelical* faith was educed. Hence the beginning of the epistle, wherein he appeals to the *scripture*, as the foundation he intended to build upon, and the *authority* with which he would press them, supplies the room of the usual intimation of his *apostolical authority*, and serves to the very same purpose, *viz*. as the immediate reason of their assent and obedience. This is the true and *proper* cause, that renders the prefixing his *apostolical authority* needless.

§ 8. (III.) 1. Amongst the *arguments* usually insisted on, to prove this epistle to have been written by St. Paul, the testimony given to it by St. Peter deserves consideration in the first place, and is indeed itself sufficient to determine the inquiry about it. His words are, [II. Pet. iii. 15, 16.] ' And account that the long-suffering of our ' Lord is salvation; even as our beloved brother Paul

' also, according to the wisdom given unto him, hath
' *written* unto *you*; as also in all his epistles speaking in
' them of these things, in which are some things hard to
' be understood, which they that are unlearned and unsta-
' ble wrest, as they do also the other scriptures, unto their
' own destruction.' To clear this testimony, some few
things must be observed.

(1.) That Peter wrote his *second* epistle to the same
churches and people to whom he wrote his *first*, [chap.
iii. 1.]

(2.) That *his first epistle* was written to the *Jews*, or
Hebrews in the *Asian* dispersion. Now it is plainly asserted
in this *testimony*, that Paul wrote a peculiar epistle to them,
to whom he wrote this; that is, to the *Hebrews*; ' he hath
' *written to you*, as also in all his epistles.' Besides his *other
epistles* to *other* churches and persons, he hath also written
to you. So, that if St. Peter's testimony may be received,
St. Paul undoubtedly wrote an epistle to the *Hebrews*. But
this may be, say some, *another* epistle, and not *this*. And
they may as well say, it is true, *Moses* wrote five books,
but they are lost, and those we have under his name were
written by another!

St. Peter declares, that St. Paul, in that epistle which
he wrote to the *Hebrews*, had declared the *long-suffering
of God* (whereof he had minded them) *to be salvation*.
There was no reason why Peter should direct the Jews to
the epistles of Paul in particular, to learn ' the long-suf-
' fering of God *in general*,' which is so plentifully revealed
in the whole scriptures of the Old and New Testament,
and which is only *occasionally* at any time mentioned by
him. There was, therefore, an *especial long-suffering* of
God, which, at that time, he exercised towards the *Jews*,
and by which he waited for the conversion and gathering
of his elect before that total and final destruction, which
they had deserved, should come upon them. This he
compares to the ' long-suffering of God in the days of
' Noah,' whilst he preached repentance to the world,
[I. Pet. iii. 20.] For, as those that were *obedient* to his
preaching, his own family, were saved in the ark, from
the

the general deſtruction that came upon the world by water; ſo, they that became *obedient* upon the preaching of the goſpel, during this new ſeaſon of God's eſpecial long-ſuffering, were to be ſaved by *baptiſm*, or profeſſional *ſeparation* from the unbelieving Jews, from that deſtruction which was to come upon them by fire. This long-ſuffering of God, the unbelieving Jews, not underſtanding to be *particular*, ſcoffed at, [II. Pet. iii. 4.] which cauſeth the apoſtle to declare the *nature* and *end* of this long-ſuffering, which they were ignorant of, [ver. 9.]

And thus was this *particular long-ſuffering* of God towards the Jews, whilſt the goſpel was preached to them before their final deſolation, ' *ſalvation*,' in that God ſpared them, and allowed them to abide for a while in the obſervance of their *old worſhip* and *ceremonies*, granting them in the mean time bleſſed means of light and inſtruction, to bring them to ſalvation. ' Even as our beloved ' brother Paul alſo,' [ver. 15.] Not that this is formally, and in terms, the main doctrine of our epiſtle; but that he effectually acquaints them with the *intention* of the Lord, in his long-ſuffering towards them, and peculiarly ſubſerves that intention of Chriſt, in his inſtruction of them. And, therefore—after he hath taught them the true nature, uſe, and end of all the Moſaical inſtitutions, which they were, as yet, permitted to uſe by the ſpecial patience of God, intimated by St. Peter; and convinced them of the neceſſity of faith in Chriſt, and the profeſſion of his goſpel—he winds up all his reaſonings, in minding them of the *end* which was to be put ſhortly to that long-ſuffering, [Heb. xii. 25—28.] So, that this *note* alſo is eminently *characteriſtical* of this epiſtle.

§ 9. Peter ſeems to aſcribe to Paul an *eminency of wiſdom*, in the epiſtolary writing he refers to, [II. Pet. iii. 15.] ' according to the wiſdom given unto him.' As Paul, in all his other epiſtles, exerciſed great *wiſdom*; ſo alſo in that which he wrote to the *Hebrews*. It is not Paul's ſpiritual wiſdom *in general*, in the knowledge of the will of God and myſteries of the goſpel, which Peter here refers to; but that *ſpecial* holy prudence which he

exerciſed

exercised in composing this epistle, and maintaining the truth, about which he dealt with the *Hebrews*. And what an eminent *character* this also is of the epistle, we shall endeavour, God assisting, to evince in our exposition of it. His special *understanding* in all the mysteries of the Old Testament, unfolding things hidden, from the foundation of the world; his *application* of them to the mystery of 'God manifest in the flesh;' his various beautiful intermixtures of *reasonings* and *exhortations*; his adapting himself to their capacity, prejudices, and affections, urging them constantly with their own principles and concessions; these, I say, among many other things, manifest the *singular wisdom* which Peter signifies to have been used. It may also be observed, that—whereas Peter affirms, that among the things about which Paul wrote, there were (τινα δυσνοηΊα) *some things hard to be understood*—Paul, in a special manner, confesseth, that some of the things which he was to treat of in that epistle, were (δυσερμηνυΊα) *hard to be declared*, uttered, or unfolded; and, therefore, certainly *hard to be understood*, [Heb. v. 11.] which, in our progress, we shall manifest to be spoken, not without great and urgent *cause*, in many instances, especially that directed to by himself concerning Melchisedeck. So, that this also gives another *characteristical note* of the epistle testified to by Peter.

I have insisted the longer upon this testimony, because, in my judgement, it is sufficient of itself to determine the controversy; nothing of any importance, that I can meet with, being excepted to it. But because we want not other confirmations of our assertion, and those also, *every one* of them singly, overbalancing the conjectures that are advanced against it, we shall subjoin them also in their order.

§ 10. 2. The *comparing* of this epistle with the *others* of the same apostle, gives farther evidence to our assertion. I suppose it will be confessed, that they only are competent judges of the argument, who are well exercised in his writings. To *their* judgement, therefore, alone we appeal. Now the *similitude* between this and other epistles

tles of St. Paul is threefold—in *words*, phrases, and manner of expression ;—in the *matter* or doctrines delivered ;—and particularly in the *spirit, genius*, and *manner of writing*, peculiar to this *apostle*. Many things are required to enable any one to judge aright of this matter; he must, as BERNARD says, "drink of Paul's spirit, who would understand his writings." Without this *spirit*, they are somewhat obscure, intricate, sapless, and unsavoury; when, to them in whom it is, they are all sweet, gracious: in some measure *open*, plain, and powerful. A great and constant *exercise* to an acquaintance with his frame of spirit in writing, is also necessary. Unless a man have contracted, as it were, a familiarity, by a constant converse with him, no critical skill in words or phrases, will render him a competent judge. This enabled CÆSAR to determine aright concerning the writings of CICERO. And he that is so acquainted with this apostle, will be able to discern his *spirit*, as AUSTIN says his mother, MONICA did divine revelations, *(nescio quo sapore)*, *by an inexpressible spiritual savour.*—Moreover, an *experience* of the power and efficacy of his writings is required. He, whose heart is cast into the *mold of the doctrine* delivered by him, will receive quick impressions from his spirit exerting itself in any of his writings. He that is thus prepared to judge, will find, that *heavenliness* and perspicuity in unfolding the deepest evangelical mysteries—that peculiar *exaltation* of Jesus Christ, in his person, office, and work—that spiritual *persuasiveness*—that transcendent *manner* of arguing and reasoning—that wise *insinuation* and pathetical pressing of well-grounded exhortations—that *love*, tenderness, and affection to the souls of men—that *zeal* for God, and *authority* in teaching,—which enliven and adorn all his other epistles, shine in this in an eminent manner, from the beginning to the end. And this consideration, whatever may be the apprehension of others, concerning it, is what gives me satisfaction above all that are pleaded in this cause.

§ 11. 3. The *testimony* of the *first churches*, of whose testimony any records are yet remaining, may also be
pleaded

pleaded in this cause. Above thirty of the *Greek* fathers, and fifty of the *Latin*, have been reckoned up by the learned reporting this primitive tradition. I shall not trouble the reader with a catalogue of their names, nor the repetition of their words; because the whole of what in general we assert, is acknowledged by the *eastern church* where this epistle was first made *public*; and surely they could discover the truth in this matter of fact, better than the *western* church, or any in the following ages.

§ 12. 4. The *Epistle itself* discovers the author several ways.

(1.) The *general argument* and scope of it declares it to be Paul's. Hereof there are two parts:—The *exaltation* of the person, office, and grace of our Lord Jesus Christ, with the excellency of the gospel, and its worship; and—a discovery of the *nature*, *use*, and *expiration* of Mosaical institutions; their present unprofitableness, and the ceasing of their obligation to obedience. The *first* part, we may grant, was equally the design of all the apostles, though we find it, in a peculiar way, insisted on in the writings of Paul. The latter was his special work and business; partly *ex instituto*; and partly from the occasional opposition of the Jews. The apostles of the circumcision, suitable to the nature of their work, accommodated themselves to be the prejudicate opinion of the *Jews*; and the *rest* of the apostles had little occasion to deal with them or others on this subject. Paul, in an eminent manner, bore the burden of that day; having well settled *all other churches*, who were troubled in this controversy, by some of the Jews, he at last treats with themselves directly, giving an account of what he had elsewhere *preached* and taught to this purpose, and the grounds on which he proceeded; and this not without great success, as the burying of the Judaical controversy not long after fully manifests.

(2.) The *method* of his procedure is the same with that of his other epistles, which also was peculiar to him. He first lays down the *doctrinal* mysteries of the gospel, vindicating them from oppositions and exceptions; and then descends to *exhortations* to obedience deduced from them, with an enumeration of such moral duties as those to whom he wrote, stood in need to be minded of.

(3.) His way of *argument* in this and his other epistles is the same; which is *sublime* and *myſtical*, accommodated rather to the *spiritual reaſons* of believers, than the artificial rules of philoſophers. That he ſhould more abound with *teſtimonies* and quotations out of the Old Teſtament in this, than his other epiſtles, is nothing more than the *matter* whereof he treats, and the perſons to whom he wrote, neceſſarily required.

(4.) *Many things* in this epiſtle evidently manifeſt, that he who wrote it, was not only *mighty* in the ſcripture, but alſo exceedingly well *verſed* and ſkilful in the *cuſtoms*, practices, opinions, *traditions*, expoſitions, and applications of ſcripture then received in the Jewiſh church, as we ſhall fully manifeſt in our progreſs. Now, who could this be but Paul? For, as he was brought up under one of the beſt and moſt famous of their maſters in thoſe days, and profited in the knowledge of their religion *above his equals*; ſo, for want of this kind of learning, the Jews eſteemed the chief of the other apoſtles, Peter and John, to be (ιδιωται) 'ignorant and unlearned,' [Acts iv. 13.]

(5.) Sundry particulars towards the *cloſe* of the epiſtle openly proclaim Paul to have been the writer of it. As the mention that he makes of his *bonds*, and the compaſſion that the *Hebrews* ſhewed him in his *ſufferings*, and whilſt he was a priſoner, [chap. x. 34.] and the mention of his dear and conſtant companion, Timothy, [chap. xiii. 23.] who was at Rome with Paul, in his bonds, [Phil. i. 13, 14.] Now, ſurely it is ſcarcely credible, that any other in Italy, *where Paul then was*, and newly releaſed out of priſon, ſhould write to the churches of the *Hebrews*, and therein make mention of his *own bonds*, and the bonds of Timothy, a man unknown to them, but by the means of Paul, and not once intimated any thing about his condition. Beſide, the *conſtant ſign* and token of Paul's epiſtles, which himſelf had publicly ſignified to be ſo, [II. Theſ. iii. 17, 18.] is ſubjoined to this; ' *Grace be with you all.*' That this originally was written with *his own*

own hand, there is no ground to queſtion, but rather appears to be ſo *becauſe it was written*; for he affirms, that it was his *cuſtom* to ſubjoin that ſalutation with his own hand.

Now, this was an evidence to *them* to whom the *original* of the epiſtle firſt came; but not to thoſe who had only tranſcribed *copies* of it. The *ſalutation* itſelf was their token, being peculiar to Paul. And all theſe circumſtances will yet receive ſome farther force from the conſideration of the *time* wherein this epiſtle was written.

Exercit. 3.

OF THE TIME WHEN, AND LANGUAGE IN WHICH, THE EPISTLE TO THE HEBREWS WAS WRITTEN.

§ 1. (I.) *Of the time when the epiſtle was written. It was after Paul's releaſe out of Priſon; before the death of James; before the ſecond of Peter.* § 2. *The time of Paul's being ſent to Rome.* § 3. *The affairs of the Jews at that time; and the martyrdom of James.* § 4. *The ſtate of the Hebrew churches; which were zealouſly addicted to Moſaical inſtitutions.* § 5. *The troubles of the Jews; and the Chriſtians warned to leave Jeruſalem.* § 6. *Cauſes of their unwillingneſs to leave it.* § 7. *The occaſion and ſucceſs of the epiſtle.* § 8. (II.) *Of the language wherein it was written. Not written in Hebrew.* § 9. *Not tranſlated by Clemens.* § 10. *But has ſtrong marks of a Greek original.*

§ 1. (I.) THE time when the epiſtles were written, often threw conſiderable light on many paſſages; for inſtance, we learn, that the ſhipwreck at Mileta [Acts xxvii.] is not what St. Paul refers to, [II. Cor. xi.] when he ſays he was a 'night and a day in the deep;' becaufe that epiftle was written fome years *before* his failing towards Rome. The time of Paul's imprifonment at Rome was *expired* before the writing of this epiftle; for he was not only abfent from Rome, in fome other part of Italy, when he wrote it, [chap. xiii. 24.] but alfo fo far at liberty, as to entertain a refolution of going into the Eaft, when Timothy fhould come to him, [chap. xiii. 23.] The date of it muft be alfo *prior* to the martyrdom of James at Jerufalem; fince he affirms, that the Hebrew church had not yet refifted unto blood, [chap. xii. 4.] It is alfo certain, that it was not only *written*, but *well known* to the believing Jews, before the writing of the *fecond* epiftle of Peter, which was not long before the apoftle's death, which happened, as is generally agreed, in the thirteenth year of Nero.

§ 2. From thefe obfervations it appears, that our beft guide is Paul's being fent prifoner to Rome; which was in the firft year of Festus, after he had been detained two years in prifon, at Cæfarea, by Felix, [Acts xxiv. 27. xxv. 26, 27.] and this moft probably correfponds with the *fourth* or *fifth* year of Nero, which was the *fifty-ninth* year from the nativity. Two years after, the *feventh* of Nero, and *fixty-firft* of our Lord, he obtained his liberty, which was about thirteen years after the determination of the controverfy about *Mofaical inftitutions*, [Acts xv.] Now, prefently after his liberty, whilft he abode in fome part of Italy, expecting the coming of Timothy, before he had entered upon the journey he had promifed to the Philippians, [chap. ii. 24.] he wrote this epiftle.—The *time* being thus fixed, it may be proper to confider,

§ 3. What was the general ftate and condition of the Hebrews in thofe days?—That the church had a great fhare of fuffering, in the outrage and mifery of thofe days, about the death of Festus, who died in the province, and the beginning of the government of Albinus, who fucceeded him, none can queftion, [vid. Joseph. Wars of the Jews, B. ii.] This is what the apoftle mentions, [chap. x. 31—34.] '*Ye endured*, &c.' And this was the lot of all honest and sober-minded men in those days, it being not a *special persecution*, but a *general calamity* that the apostle speaks of. For a *direct* attack upon the church was first made by ANANUS, who was a rash young fellow, by sect a Saducee, and yet advanced to the priesthood. During the interval between the death of FESTUS, and the settling of ALBINUS, this cruel Saducee, placed in power by AGRIPPA, summons James before himself and his associates, where he is condemned, and immediately stoned.

§ 4. The churches at this time in Jerusalem and Judea were very numerous. The oppressors, robbers, and seditious of all sorts, being wholly intent upon the pursuit of their own ends, filling the nation with tumults and disorders, the disciples of Christ, who knew that the time of their preaching the gospel to their countrymen was but short, and even now expiring, followed their work with diligence and success, being not greatly regarded in the dust of that confusion which was raised by the nation, while rushing into its fatal ruin.

All these churches were, together with the profession of the gospel, zealously addicted to the observance of the law of Moses. The *synod* indeed at Jerusalem had determined, that the *yoke of the law* should not be put on the necks of the *Gentile* converts, [Acts xv.] but eight or nine years after that, when Paul came up to Jerusalem again, [chap xxi. 20—22.] James informs him, that the many thousands of the Jews who believed, did all zealously observe the law of Moses; and, moreover, judged that all those who were Jews by birth, ought to do so also; and on that account were like enough to assemble in a disorderly multitude, to inquire into the practice of Paul himself, who had been ill-reported of amongst them. On this account they kept their assemblies distinct from those of the *Gentiles*, all over the world.* All those Hebrews, then, to whom Paul wrote this epistle, continued in the use and practice of *Mosaical* worship, as celebrated in the

* HIERON. in Gal. i.

temple

temple, and in their *synagogues*, with all other legal inſtitutions whatever. Whether they did this out of an unacquaintedneſs with their liberty in Chriſt, or out of a pertinacious adherence to their own prejudicate opinions, I ſhall not determine.

§ 5. From this time forward, the body of the Jewiſh people ſaw not a day of peace and quietneſs; tumults, ſeditions, outrages, robberies, murders, increaſed all over the nation. And theſe things, by various degrees, made way for that fatal war; which, beginning about *ſix* or *ſeven* years after the death of James, ended in the utter deſolation of the people, city, temple, and worſhip, foretold ſo long before by Daniel the prophet. This was that day of the Lord, the ſudden approach of which the apoſtle declares to them, [Heb. x. 36, 37.] ' For ye have need ' of patience; that after ye have done the will of God, ye ' may receive the promiſe; for *yet a little while*, and he ' that ſhall come will come, and will not tarry;' (μικρον οσον οσον) ' *a very little while*,' leſs than you think of. The manner of it he declares, [Heb. xii. 26—28.] And by this means, he effectually diverted them from a pertinacious adherence to thoſe things, whoſe diſſolution, from God himſelf, was ſo nigh at hand; which argument was alſo afterwards preſſed by Peter, [II. Pet. iii.]

Our bleſſed Saviour had long before warned his diſciples of all theſe things; particularly of the deſolation that was to come upon the Jews, with the tumults, diſtreſſes, perſecutions, and wars, which ſhould precede it; directing them to the exerciſe of patience in diſcharging their duty, until the approach of the final calamity; and of which he adviſed them to free themſelves by *flight*, or a timely departure out of Jeruſalem and Judea, [Matt. xxiv. 15—21.] This, and no other, was the *oracle* mentioned by EUSEBIUS, whereby the Chriſtians were warned to depart out of Jeruſalem. It was given, as he ſays, (τοις δοκιμοις) to *approved men* amongſt them. For, although the prophecy itſelf was written by the evangeliſts, yet the ſpecial meaning of it was not known and divulged amongſt all. The leaders of them kept it *ſecret* for a ſeaſon, leſt an

exaſpe-

exasperation of the people being occasioned thereby, they should have been obstructed in the work which they had to do before its accomplishment; and this was the case relative to other things, [II. Thes. ii. 5, 6.] But now, when the present work of the church among the Jews was to come to its close, the elect being gathered out of them, and the final desolation of the city and people appearing to be at hand, by a concurrence of all the signs foretold by our Saviour, those entrusted with the sense of that *oracle*, warned their brethren to provide for that flight, whereto they were directed. That this flight and departure probably with the loss of all their possessions, was grievous to them, may be easily conceived.

§ 6. But what seems most especially to have perplexed them, was their relinquishment of that worship of God, whereto they had been so zealously addicted. That this would prove grievous to them, our Saviour had before intimated, [Matt. xxiv. 20.] Hence were they so slow in their obedience to that heavenly *oracle*, although excited with the remembrance of what befell *Lot's wife* in the like tergiversation. Nay, as it is likely, from this epistle, many of them, who had made profession of the gospel, rather than they would now utterly forego their old worship, deserted the faith, and, cleaving to their unbelieving countrymen, perished in their apostacy; whom our apostle, in a special manner, forewarns of their inevitable and sore destruction, by that fire of God's indignation which was shortly to devour the *adversaries*, to whom they associated themselves, [Heb. x. 25—31.]

§ 7. Paul, who had an inexpressible zeal, and overflowing affection for his countrymen, being now in Italy —considering the present condition of their affairs, how pertinaciously they adhered to the Mosaical institutions, how near the approach of their utter abolition was, how backward they would be while they possessed that frame of spirit, to save themselves by *flying* from the midst of that perishing generation; what danger they were in to forego the profession of the gospel, when it would not be retained without a relinquishment of their former Divine

service

service and ceremonies—writes this epistle to them, wherein he strikes at the very root of all their dangers and distresses. For, whereas all the danger of their abode in Jerusalem and Judea, and so of falling in the destruction of the city and people; all the fears the apostle had of their apostacy into *Judaism*; all their own disconsolations in reference to their flight and departure,—arose from their adherence to, and zeal for the law of Moses; by declaring to them the nature, use, end, and expiration of his ordinances and institutions, he utterly removes the ground and occasion of all the evils mentioned.

This was the season wherein the epistle was written; and these are some of the principal occasions (though it had other reasons also, as we shall see afterwards) of its being written. And I no way doubt, (though the particular events of those days are buried in oblivion) but that through the grace of him, who moved and directed the apostle to write, it was made signally effectual towards the professing *Hebrews*, both to free them from that yoke of bondage, wherein they had been detained; and to prepare them with cheerfulness to the observance of *evangelical* worship, leaving their countrymen to perish in their sin and unbelief.

§ 8. (II.) Some, from a supposed dissimilitude of style in this, compared with Paul's other epistles, and because it was written to the *Hebrews*, have thought, that it was originally written in *Hebrew*.—But if so,

1. Whence comes it to pass, that no *copy* of it, in that language, was ever seen or heard of, by the most diligent collectors of all fragments of antiquity in the primitive times? Had ever any such thing been extant, whence came it in particular, that ORIGEN, that prodigy of industry and learning, should be able to attain no knowledge or report of it? Again,

2. If it were incumbent on Paul in writing to the Hebrews, to write in their *own* language, why did he not also write in *Latin* to the Romans? But,

3. It is very improperly supposed, that the Hebrew tongue was then the common language of the Jews; for

it was known only to the learned amongſt them, and a corrupt *Syriac* was the common dialect of the people even at Jeruſalem.

4. It is, moreover, as unduly averred, that the *Hebrew* was the mother tongue of Paul himſelf, or that he was ignorant of the *Greek*, ſeeing he was born at Tarſus, in Cilicia, where the latter muſt have been the language he was brought up in.

5. The epiſtle was written for the uſe of all the Hebrews in their ſeveral diſperſions, eſpecially that in the Eaſt, as Peter witneſſeth, they being all alike concerned in the matter of it, though not ſo immediately as thoſe in Judea and Jeruſalem. Now, to thoſe the *Greek* language, from the days of the Macedonian empire, had been in *vulgar* uſe, and continued to be ſo. Nay,

6. The Greek tongue was ſo well known, and ſo much uſed in Judea itſelf, that it was called *the vulgar* amongſt them; ſo that the pretence of ſome of the *Rabbins*, concerning a *prohibition* againſt learning the Greek tongue, is built on ſuppoſitions evidently falſe; and may be eaſily convicted of ſelf-contradiction.

§ 9. Again, the epiſtle is ſaid to be *tranſlated* by CLEMENS; but where, or when, we are not informed. Was this in *Italy before* it was ſent to the Hebrews? To what end then was it written in *Hebrew*, when it was not to be uſed, but in Greek? Was it ſent in *Hebrew before* the ſuppoſed *tranſlation?* then in what language was it communicated to others, by them who *firſt* received it? CLEMENS was never in the *Eaſt*, to tranſlate it. And if all the firſt copies of it were diſperſed in Hebrew, how came they to be ſo utterly loſt, as that no report or tradition of any one copy did ever remain? Beſides, if it were tranſlated by CLEMENS, in the *Weſt*, and that tranſlation alone preſerved, how came it to paſs, that it was ſo well known, and generally received in the *Eaſt*, *before* the Weſtern churches admitted it; this tradition, therefore, is alſo every way groundleſs and improbable.

§ 13. Moreover, the ſtyle is freer from *Hebraiſms* than could be expected in a *tranſlation*; and it abounds with Greek

Greek elegances, that have no countenance given them by any thing in the Hebrew tongue, [see chap. v. 8.] The word (ברית) *Berith* being constantly rendered by διαθηκη, and the words concerning Melchisedeck, [chap. vii. 11.] strongly militate against its Hebrew original.— When John reports the words of Mary, (ραββονι) *Rabboni*, and adds of his own (ο λεγεται διδασκαλε) *that is to say, master*, [John. xx. 16.] doth any man doubt but that he wrote in Greek, and therefore so rendered her Syriac expression? And is not the same thing evident concerning our apostle, from the interpretation he gives of the Hebrew words? And it is in vain to reply, that these words were *added* by the translator, seeing the very *argument of the author* is founded in the interpretation of those words which he gives us.

It appears, then, that the assertion, " that this epistle was written in Hebrew," is altogether groundless; the evidence for its Greek original being such as few other books of the New Testament can afford concerning themselves, should the same question be made about them.

Exercit. IV.

CONCERNING THE ONENESS OF THE CHURCH.

§ 1. *Mistake of the Jews about the nature of the promises.* § 2. *The promise of the Messiah under the notion of a covenant, the foundation of the church.* § 3. *The church confined to the person and posterity of Abraham, who was called and separated for a double end.* § 4. *Who properly the seed of Abraham.* § 5. *Mistakes of the Jews about the covenant.* § 6. *Abraham the father of the faithful, and heir of the world, on what account.* § 7. *The church still the same.* § 8. *Conclusion.*

§ 1. THE Jews, at the time when this epistle was written, (and their posterity, in all succeeding generations, follow their example and tradition) were not a little confirmed in their obstinacy and unbelief, by a misapprehension of the true sense of the Old Testament *promises*. For, finding many glorious promises made to the *church* in the days of the Messiah, especially concerning the great access of the *Gentiles* to it, they looked upon themselves the posterity of Abraham, according to the flesh, as the first, proper, and indeed only subjects of them; to whom, in their accomplishment, others were to be *proselyted* and joined, the substance and foundation of the church remaining still with them. But the *event* answered not their expectation. Instead of inheriting all the promises merely upon their *carnal* interest and privilege, they found that themselves must come in on a *new account*, to be sharers in common with others, or be rejected, whilst those others were admitted to the inheritance. This filled them with wrath and envy, which greatly strengthened their unbelief. They could not bear with patience an intimation of letting out the ' vineyard ' to other husbandmen.' With this principle and prejudice of theirs, the apostle dealt directly in his epistle to the Romans. [See chap. x. xi.]

On the same grounds he proceedeth with them in this epistle; and because his answer to their objection from the *promises* lies at the foundation of many of his reasonings with them, the nature of it must be here previously explained.

§ 2. Now, though the *promise* of the Messiah given to Adam, an *absolute promise* proceeding from mere grace, was the support and encouragement of mankind to seek the Lord; yet, as it was the foundation of the church, it included the nature of a *covenant*, virtually requiring a re-stipulation to obedience. For the promise was given to this end, that men might have a new foundation of obedience, the first covenant being disannulled. Hence, in the after explications of the promise, this condition of *obedience* is expressly added. So upon its renewal to Abraham, God required, that he should ' walk before ' him, and be upright.' This promise, then, as it hath

the

the nature of a *covenant*, including the *grace* that God would shew to sinners in the Messiah, and the *obedience* that he required from them, was, *from* the first giving of it, the foundation of the church and its worship. And to this church, thus founded on the covenant, were all the following promises and privileges exhibited. On this account, the church, *before* the days of Abraham, though scattered up and down in the world, and subject to many changes in its worship, by the addition of new revelations, was still but *one and the same*; because founded on the same covenant, and interested thereby in all its benefits.

§. 3. In process of time, God was pleased to confine this church, as to the ordinary visible dispensation of his grace, to the person and posterity of Abraham. Upon this restriction of the church covenant and promise, it was, that the Jews of old managed a plea in their own justification against the doctrine of the Lord Jesus Christ, and his apostles. 'We are the children of Abra-'ham,' was their continual cry; on that account, they presumed the promises all belonged to them alone. Which persuasion hath cast them, as we shall see, upon a woeful and fatal mistake.—Two privileges did God grant to Abraham upon his *separation* to a special interest in the preceding promise and covenant.

First, that according to the *flesh*, he should be the father of the Messiah, the promised seed; who was the very life of the covenant; the fountain and cause of all the blessings contained in it. That this privilege was *temporary*, having a limited season, the nature of the thing demonstrates; for, upon his natural exhibition in the flesh, it was necessarily to cease. In pursuit of this were his posterity separated from the rest of the world, and preserved a peculiar people, that through them, according to the flesh, the promised seed might be brought forth in the fulness of time. [Rom. ix. 5.]

Secondly, together with this he had also another *privilege*, namely, that his faith, whereby he was personally interested in the *covenant*, should be the *pattern* of the faith of the church in all generations. On *this* account he became the '*father* of all believers;' for 'they that are 'of *faith*, the same are the children of Abraham,' [Gal. iii. 7. Rom. iv. 11.] and also, '*heir* of the world;' [ver. 13.] in that all who should believe throughout the world, being thereby implanted into the covenant made with him, should become his *spiritual* children.

§ 4. Answerable to this two-fold end of the separation of Abraham, there was a *double seed* allotted to him. A seed according to the *flesh*, separated to the bringing forth of the Messiah; and a seed according to the *promise*, such as by the righteousness of faith should be interested in the promise—all the elect of God. Not that these two seeds were always *subjectively* diverse; [Rom. ix. 10, 11.] for sometimes the *same seed* was the seed of Abraham, both according to the flesh and according to the promise; though sometimes those according to the flesh were not of the promise; and so on the contrary. Thus Isaac and Jacob were the seed of Abraham, both according to the flesh and the promise; and multitudes afterwards of the carnal seed of Abraham, separated to bring forth the Messiah, were not of the seed according to the promise, because they did not personally believe. And many afterwards, who were not of the carnal seed of Abraham, were yet designed to be made his spiritual seed, by faith, that in them he might become *heir of the world*, and all nations of the earth be blessed in him.

§ 5. And herein lay the great mistake of the Jews of old, wherein they are followed by their posterity unto this day. They thought no more was needful to interest them in the covenant of Abraham, but that they were his seed, 'according to the flesh.' And they constantly pleaded the latter privilege, as the ground and reason of the former; not reflecting, that they can have no other privilege on *that* account, than Abraham himself had in the flesh; which was, that he should be set apart as the special channel through whose loins God would derive the promised seed into the world; when the very nature

ture of the thing shews, the separation and privilege were to *cease*. For to what purpose should it be continued, when the end for which it was designed was fully effected? Seeing, therefore, that this *carnal privilege* was come to an end, with all its attendant ordinances, by the actual coming of the Messiah, to which they were subservient; if they did not by faith in the promised seed attain an interest in the privileges of the *spiritual blessing*, it is evident that they would on no account be considered as actual sharers in the covenant of God.

§ 6. We have seen, then, that Abraham was the *father* of all that believe, and *heir* of the world, on the account of his *faith*, and not of his separation according to the *flesh*. And in the covenant made with him lies the foundation of the church in all ages: wheresoever this covenant is, there all the *promises and privileges* of the church are. Hence it was, that at the coming of the Messiah there was not *one church* taken away, and *another* set up in the room of it; but the *church* continued the *same* in those that were the children of Abraham according to *faith*. The Christian church is not ANOTHER CHURCH, but the very same that was before the coming of Christ, having the same faith, and interested in the same covenant. It is true, that the former carnal privileges of Abraham and his posterity expiring, on the grounds before mentioned, the *ordinances of worship* which were suited thereto, did necessarily cease also; and this cast the Jews into great perplexities, and proved the last trial that God made of them. For—whereas both the carnal and spiritual privileges of Abraham's covenant, which had been carried on together in a mixed way for many generations, came now to be separated, and trial must be made, [Mal. iii.] who of the Jews had interest in both, and who in the one only—those who had only the carnal privilege contended for a share on that single account in the other also, that is, in all the promises annexed to the covenant. But the foundation of their plea was taken away; and the

church

church to which the promises belong remained with them who were the heirs of Abraham's *faith* only.

§ 7. It remains, then, that the church, founded in the covenant, abode at the coming of Christ, and doth abide ever since, among those who are the children of Abraham by faith. The *old* church was not taken away, and a *new* one set up; but the same church was continued in those, *only* those, who by *faith* inherited the promises. Great external alterations were indeed then made; new ordinances of worship were appointed, suited to the new light and grace granted then to the church, while the old were abolished; and the Gentiles came in to the faith of Abraham, together with the *Jews*, to be fellow-heirs with them in his blessing. But none of these, nor all of them together, made any such alteration *in* the church, but that it was still ONE and the same. The *olive tree* was the same, though some branches were broken of, and others grafted in; the Jews fell off, and the Gentiles came in their room.

§ 8. And this determines the difference between the *Jews* and the *Christians* about the *promises* of the Old Testament; they are all made to the *church*. No individual person can claim interest in them but by virtue of his membership therewith: this church is, and always was, one and the same; with whomsoever it remains, the *promises* are theirs directly and properly; and among those promises this is one, that God will be a God unto them and their seed for ever.

EXERCIT. V.

OF THE JEWISH WRITINGS.

§ 1. *The present Jewish notion about the written word and oral tradition.* § 2. *Their general distribution of the Old Testament.* § 3. *Their smaller divisions.* § 4. *The Massora.* § 5. *Their pretended oral law.* § 6, 7. (I.) *What they intend by it.* § 8, 9. (II.) *The whole disproved.* § 10.

§ 10. *Agreement of the Jews and Papists about traditions.*

§ 1. THE apostle dealing with the Hebrews about the *revelation* of the will of God made to their fathers, assigns it in general unto their speaking to them (εν τοις προφηταις) *in the prophets*, [chap. i. 1.] This *speaking* to them the present Jews affirm to consist of two parts:

1. That which Moses and the following prophets were commanded to *write* for the public use of the church; and,

2. What was delivered only by *word of mouth* unto Moses, and which, being continued by oral tradition until after the last destruction of the temple, was afterwards committed to writing.—And because those who would read our Exposition, or the epistle itself, with profit, had need of some insight into the opinions of the Jews about these things, I shall, for the sake of them who want either skill, leisure, or means to search after them elsewhere, give a brief account of their faith concerning these two heads of revelation, and therein discover both the principle, nature, and means of their *apostacy* and infidelity.

§ 2. The scripture of the Old Testament they call (מקרא) *mikra*, the *reading*, and divide it into *three* parts— The *law*—the *prophets*—the *writings* by divine inspiration, usually called the *Hagiographa*, or *holy writings*. Thus R. BECHAI, (in *Cad Hackemach*) " The *law* (i. e. the whole writing) is divided into *three* parts; the *law*, the *prophets*, and the *holy writings*." And that all are generally comprized under ' the law,' thus they observe, (in *Midrash Tehillim*, Psalm lxxviii. 1.) " The Psalms are the law, and the prophets are the law," that is, the whole scripture.

This distribution, intimated by our Saviour, [Luke xxiv. 27.] evidently arises from the *nature* and *subject matter* of the books themselves, and it was the received division whilst the Jewish church continued. But the *Post-talmudical doctors* overlooking, or wilfully neglecting, the true reason of this distribution, have fancied others, taken

taken from the different *manners* and *degrees* of revelation by which they were given. Yea, in the *eleven* degrees of divine revelation affigned by MAIMONIDES, (*Mor. Nebu.* Par. II.) that by *infpiration* is caft into the *loweft* place. How groundlefs and fanciful is this diftinction! For, though God was pleafed to ufe *various ways* in reprefenting things to the minds of the prophets, it was in them all the *infpiration of the Holy Ghoft* alone that enabled them infallibly to declare the mind of God to the church. [II. Pet. i. 21.]

They make the *Revelation to Mofes* the moft excellent; and next in degree they place the *fpirit of prophecy*; and of the laft fort they reckon the *infpiration of the Holy Ghoft*.

The 'law,' or the books of Mofes, they call (מקרא) the *five*, or the *Pentateuch*, from the number of the books. Thefe they divide into *fections*, whereof they read *one* every fabbath day in their fynagogues; Genefis into *twelve*, Exodus into *eleven*, Leviticus into *ten*, Numbers into *ten*, and Deuteronomy into *ten*, which all make *fifty-three*; whereby, reading one each day, and two on one day, they read through the whole in the courfe of a year, beginning at the feaft of tabernacles. [See Acts xv. 21.]

The books given by the '*fpirit of prophecy*,' they make of two forts:

1. The *former prophets*, which are all the *hiftorical* books written before the captivity, Ruth only excepted, that is, Jofhua, Judges, Samuel, Kings.

2. The *prophetical books*, peculiarly fo called, Daniel only excepted, that is, Ifaiah, Jeremiah, Ezekiel, and the twelve minor prophets.

Thofe which, according to them, are written by the '*infpiration of the Holy Ghoft*,' are the *poetical* books, Pfalms, Job, Proverbs, Canticles, Lamentations, and Ecclefiaftes; to which they add Ruth, Daniel, and the hiftorical books written after the captivity, Chronicles, Ezra, and Nehemiah, which make up the *canon* of the Old Teftament.

Why

Why fundry of thefe books, particularly Ruth and Daniel, fhould be caft into the laft fort, they can give no tolerable account; and thofe written after the captivity are plainly of the fame nature with thofe which they call the former prophets: in fhort, they have not any reafon for this diftribution.

§ 3. The 'law' they divide into *leſſer ſections* of two forts, *open* and *cloſe*, which have their diftinct marks in their bibles; and many fuperftitious obfervances they have about the beginning and ending of them.* They divide it, moreover, into 153 (סדרים) *ſedarim, diſtinctions*; of which Genefis contains 42, Exodus 29, Leviticus 23, Numbers 32, Deuteronomy 27; which kind of diftinctions they alfo obferve throughout the fcriptures.†

Befides, they diftribute the prophets into what they call *Haphters*, that anfwer to the fections which are read every fabbath day in their fynagogues; which divifion they affirm to have been made in the days of ANTIOCHUS EPIPHANES, (whom they call הרשע *that wicked one*) when the reading of the law was prohibited.

§ 4. Having for a long feafon loft the promife of the Spirit, and therewith all faving fpiritual knowledge of the mind and will of God in the fcripture, the beft of their employment about it hath been in reference to the words and letters of it; wherein their diligence hath been of ufe in preferving the copies of it free from corruption: for—after the canon of the Old Teftament was completed in the days of *Ezra*, and *points* or *vowels* added to the letters, to preferve the knowledge of the tongue, and facilitate the reading and learning of it—it is incredible what induftry and curiofity they have ufed about the *letter* of fcripture. The collection of their pains to this purpofe is called the *Maſſora*, begun, it may be, from the days of Ezra, and continued until the time of com-

---

* Of the firft fort there are in Genefis 43, of the latter 48, &c. &c.

† Befides, they obferve, that ו in גחון Lev. xi. 42. is the *middle letter* of the law; דרש Lev. x. 16. the *middle word*, and Lev. xiii. 33. the *middle verſe*.

posing the *Talmud*, with some additional observations annexed to it since. The composers of this work they call (בעלי המסורה) the *men* or *masters of the Massora*, whose principal observations were gathered and published by R. Jacob Chaïim, and annexed to the *Venetian* bibles, whereas, before, the *Massora* was written in other books innumerable. In this their *critical doctrine* they give us the number of *verses*, *words*, and even *letters* in the bible, and how often each letter is severally used, &c. the sum of which is gathered by Buxtorf, in his excellent treatise on that subject. And herein is the knowlege of their masters bounded; but are more blind than moles in the spiritual sense of it. And thus they continue an example of the righteous judgement of God, in giving them up to the counsels of their own heart; and an evident instance how unable the *letter* of scripture is to furnish men with the saving knowledge of the will of God, while they enjoy not the *spirit* promised in the *covenant* made to the church, [Isa. lix. 21.]

§ 5. To that ignorance of the mind of God in the scripture, they have added another prejudice against the truth, in a strange figment of an *oral law*, which they make equal, yea, in many things superior, to the written law. The scripture becoming with them a *lifeless letter*, it was impossible that they should content themselves with what it reveals. For as the word, whilst improved according to the mind of God, is found full of sweetness and life, wisdom and knowledge; so, when it is enjoyed merely on an outward account, without a dispensation of suitable light and grace, it will yield men no satisfaction; which makes them turn aside to other means. This being eminently so in the Jews, and the *medium* they have fixed on to supply a supposed want in the scripture, proving to be the great engine of their obstinate infidelity; I shall

I. Declare what it is that they intend by the *oral law*; and then,

II. Briefly shew the absurdity and falseness of their pretensions about it.

§ 6.

§ 6. (I.) This *oral law* they affirm to be an unwritten *tradition* and *expofition* of the written law of Mofes, given to him on mount Sinai, and committed by him to Jofhua and the *Sanhedrim*, to be by them delivered by *oral tradition* to thofe who fhould fucceed them in the government of the church. It doth not appear, that in the days of Chrift or his apoftles, whilft the *temple* was yet ftanding, there was any ftated opinion amongft them about this *oral law*; nay, it is evident there was no fuch law then acknowledged; for the Sadduces, who utterly rejected all the main principles of it, were not only tolerated, but alfo in chief rule, one of them being high prieft. That they had multiplied many fuperftitious obfervances under the name of *traditions*, is moft clear;— but it doth not appear that they knew whom to affign their original to, and therefore called them indefinitely ' the *traditions of the elders*,' or, ' thofe that lived of old.' After the deftruction of their temple, when they had loft the life and fpirit of that worfhip which the fcripture revealed, betaking themfelves only to their traditional figments, they began to bethink themfelves how they might give countenance to their apoftacy from the perfection and doctrine of the written law. For this end they began to fancy that thefe *traditions* were no lefs from God than the *written law* itfelf. For, when Mofes was forty days and forty nights on the mount, they fay, that in the *day-time* he wrote the law from the mouth of God, and in the *night* God inftructed him in the unwritten expofition of it, which they have received by tradition from him. For when he came down from the mount, after he had read to them the *written law*, as they fay, he repeated to Aaron, Eleazer, and the *Sanhedrim*, all that fecret inftruction which he had received in the *night* from God, which it was not lawful for him to write; and he committed the whole efpecially to Jofhua. Jofhua did the fame to Eleazer; as he alfo did to his fon Phineas; after whom they give us a catalogue of feveral prophets that lived in the enfuing generations whom they employ in this fervice.

The last person, who, according to them, preserved the *oral law* absolutely pure, was that Simeon, whom they call ' *the just*,' mentioned by Jesus, the son of Syrach; [chap. i.] And it is very observable, that the latter *Jews* have left out Simeon, the son of Hillel, whom their ancient masters placed upon the roll of the preservers of this treasure, supposing he might be that Simeon who in his old age received our Saviour in his arms, when he was presented in the temple, [Luke ii. 25.] a crime sufficient, among them, to brand him with perpetual ignominy. How happy were it, if they *alone* were concerned in " turning men's glory into shame !"

§ 7. After the destruction of the temple and city, when the *evil husbandmen* were slain, and the vineyard of the Lord let out to others, the kingdom given to another nation, and therewith the covenant sanctified use of the scripture; the remaining Jews having wholly lost the mind of God therein, betook themselves vigorously to their *traditions*. A while after (about two hundred years after the destruction of Jerusalem) Rabbi Judah surnamed, The Prince and the Holy, took upon him to gather their scattered traditions, and cast them into some form and order, in writing, that they might be to the Jews a rule of life and worship for ever.*

This collection of his they call *Mishna*, or *Mishnaioth*, being, as is pretended, a *repetition of the law* in an exposition of it; whereas indeed it is a *farrago* of all sorts of traditions, true and false; with a monstrous mixture of lies and fables, useless, foolish, and wicked. The things contained in it are by themselves referred to five heads:

1. The *oral law* received by Moses on mount *Sinai*, preserved by the means before declared.

2. Oral *constitution* of Moses himself after he came down from the mount.

3. *Constitutions and orders* drawn, by various ways of arguing, out of the *written law*.

* Maimon. in *Jad Chazacha*. The author of *Sedar Olam*, Tzemach, David, &c.

4. The

4. The *answers* and *decrees* of the Sanhedrim, and other wise men in former ages.

5. *Immemorial customs*, whose original being unknown, are supposed to be divine.

The whole is divided into *six parts*, noted with the initial letter of the word which signifies the chief things treated of in it.* To this *Mishna* of R. JUDAH they annex the *Tasiphot*, or additions of R. CHAIAH, his scholar, expounding many passages in his master's works; and to them, moreover, is subjoined a more full explanation of the *Mishna*, which they call *Baracelot*, being a collection of some *Anti-talmudical* masters.

About three hundred years after the destruction of the temple, R. JOHANNAN, composed the *Jerusalem Talmud*, consisting of expositions, comments, and disputes upon the whole *Mishna*, excepting the last part about *purifications*. An hundred years after that, or thereabouts, R. ASE composed the *Babylonian Talmud*, or *Gemara*; thirty-two years, they say, he spent in this work; yet leaving it unfinished; seventy-one years after, it was completed by his disciples. And the whole work of *both these Talmuds* may be referred to five heads:

1. They expound the text of the *Mishna*.
2. They decide questions of right and fact.
3. They report the disputations, traditions, and constitutions of the doctors that lived between them and the writing of the Mishna.

---

* As follows:

1. (1) *Zeraim*, *seeds*, divided into *eleven Massichtot*, or treatises, containing in all *seventy-five* chapters.

2. (מ) *Moad*, *appointed feasts*, divided into *twelve* treatises, containing *eighty-eight* chapters.

3. (נ) *Nashim*, of *Women*, distributed into *seven* treatises and *seventy-one* chapters.

4. (נ) *Nezikim*, of *Losses*, divided into *eight* treatises and *seventy-four* chapters.

5. (ק) *Kodoshim*, of *Sanctifications*, containing *eleven* books and *ninety* chapters.

6. (ט) *Teharoth*, of *Purifications*, in *twelve* books and *a hundred and twenty-six* chapters.

4. They

4. They give allegorical monstrous expositions of the scripture, which they call *Midrashoth*; and

5. They report stories of the like nature.

This, at length, is their *oral law* grown into; and, in the learning of these things consists the whole religion of the Jews; there being not the most absurd saying of any of their doctors in those huge heaps of folly and vanity, that they do not equal, nay, that they are not ready to prefer, to the written word; that perfect, and only guide of their church, whilst God was pleased with it. In the dust of this confusion, they dwell, " *loving this darkness* more than light, because their deeds are evil." Having, for many generations, entertained a prejudicate imagination, that those traditional figments, amongst which their crafty masters have inserted many filthy and blasphemous fables against our Lord Christ and his gospel, are of *divine authority!* and having utterly lost the *spiritual sense* of the written word, they are by it sealed up in blindness and obdurateness; and shall be so until the *veil* be taken away, when the appointed time of their deliverance shall come.

§ 8. (II.) A brief discovery of the falseness of this fancy of their *oral law*, which is the foundation of all that huge building of lies and vanities that their *Talmuds* are composed of, shall put an end to this discourse.

1. The very story of the giving of the law on mount Sinai sufficiently discovers the folly of this imagination. The Jews are ready, on all occasions, not only to prefer their pretended *oral law* to that which is written; but also openly profess, that without it, the other is of no use to them. I desire, then, to know,—whence it is, that all the *circumstances* of giving and teaching the *less necessary* (as the written law is deemed) are so exactly recorded; but not *one word* is spoken of this *oral law*, either of God's revealing it to Moses, or of Moses teaching it to Joshua, or any others? Strange! that so much should be recorded of every circumstance of the less principal, *lifeless law*, and not *one* word of either substance or circumstance of the other. How know they, that any such law was given
to

to Mofes, as they pretend? What *teſtimony*, or record of it, was there made at the time of its giving, or for two thoufand years afterwards?

2. Did their forefathers, at any time before the captivity, *tranfgreſs* the oral law, or did they not? If they fay they did not, but *kept* it, we may then fee, that the moſt ſtrict obſervance of it could not preſerve them from all manner of wickedneſs. What a defpicable *fence* muſt it have been to the written law! If they ſhall fay that it was not kept, but *broken* by them; 'I defire to know whence it comes to paſs, that, whereas God, by his prophets, doth reprove them for all their other fins, and in particular, for their contempt of his *written law*, the ſtatutes, ordinances, and inſtitutions of it, he no where once mentions their fuppoſed greater guilt of defpifing the *oral law*; but there is as univerſal a filence concerning its *tranfgreſſion*, as there is of its inſtitution? Can we have any greater evidence of its being fictitious, than this; that whereas it is pretended it is their main *rule* of obedience, God *never reproved* them for the tranfgreſſion of it; though, whilſt he owned them as his church and people, he fuffered none of their fins to paſs unreproved, eſpecially not any of equal importance with this upon their principle?

3. Mofes was commanded to write the *whole law* that he received from God, which he accordingly did; [Exod. xxiv. 3, 4. xxxiv. 28. Deut. xxxi. 9—24.] but where was the *oral law*, which they fay was not to be written, when Mofes was commanded to write the *whole law* that he had received of God? This new law was not then coined, being, indeed, nothing but the product of their apoſtacy from the law which was written.

4. The fole ground and foundation of this *oral law* lies in the pretended imperfection of the *written law*. This is what they plead for the neceſſity of it; the written law extends not to all neceſſary caſes that occur in religion, many things are redundant, many wanting, of which they gather numerous inſtances; fo that they will grant, that if the *written law* had been perfect, there had been no need of this traditional one. But whom, in this matter,

ſhall

shall we believe, a few ignorant Jews, or God himself, bearing witness, that his '*law is perfect*,' and requiring no more in his worship, but what is in this prescribed? [See Psal. xix. 8. Prov. xxx. 5, 6. Deut. iv. 1, 2.] and this perfection of the written law, though it be perfectly destructive of their traditions, not only the KARÆI, among themselves, earnestly contend for, but also sundry of their GEMARISTS acknowledge, especially when they forget to oppose the gospel.

5. God every where sends his people to the *written law* of Moses for the rule of their obedience. If there is such an *oral law*, it is one that God would not have any one to observe; nor did ever reprove any one for its transgression.

§ 9. And yet this figment is the bottom of the present *Judaical religion* and obstinacy. When the apostle wrote this epistle, their obstinacy had not yet arrived at this rock of offence; since their falling on it, they have increased their blindness, misery, and ruin. *Then* they were contented to try their cause, by what God spake to their fathers *in the prophets*, which kept open a door of hope, and gave some advantages for their conversion; but that door is now shut up until God shall *take away this veil* from their faces, that they may see to the *end* of the things that were to be abolished.

By this means principally have they, for many generations, both shut *out* the truth, and *secured* themselves from conviction. For, whatever is taught in the *scripture*, concerning the person, office, and work of the *Messiah*—seeing they have *that* which they esteem a revelation of at least *equal* authority; teaching them a doctrine quite of another nature, and more suited to their carnal principles and expectations—they readily discard, and will rather rest in any evasions, than yield to its testimony. And whilst they have a firm persuasion, received by the tradition of many generations, that the written word is *imperfect*, but an *half* revelation of the mind of God—which yet is in itself unintelligible, and not to be understood, but according to their oral law now recorded in their *Talmuds*

Talmuds, what can the moſt plain and cogent teſtimonies avail to their conviction?

§ 10. And this hath been the fatal means of the *grand apoſtacy* of both churches, *Jewiſh* and *Chriſtian*; for the *Roman church* hath at length arrived at almoſt the ſame iſſue, by the ſame degrees. I ſhall, therefore, ως εν παρωδω) manifeſt their *agreement* in this principle of their traditions, which have been the ruin of them both.

1. The Jews expreſsly contend, that their *oral law*, their *maſs of traditions*, was from God himſelf; partly delivered to Moſes on mount Sinai, and partly added, by him, from Divine revelations, which he afterwards received.—And this is the perſuaſion of the Romaniſts, about their *cabal of traditions*; they plead them all to be of a Divine original, partly from Chriſt, and partly from his apoſtles, by living tradition. Let one convention of their doctors determine, that *images* are to be adored; another, that *tranſubſtantiation* is to be believed; and a third, add a *new creed*; let one doctor advance the opinion of *purgatory*, another of *juſtification by works*; all is one, theſe things are not then firſt *invented*, but only declared out of that unſearchable *treaſure of traditions*, which they have in their cuſtody.

2. This *oral law* being thus given, the *preſervation* of it, ſeeing Moſes is dead long ago, muſt be inquired after. Now the Jews aſſign a three-fold depoſitory of it; firſt, the *whole congregation*; ſecondly, the *Sanhedrim*; and thirdly, the *high prieſt*. To this end they affirm, that what Moſes then received was *three times* repeated, upon the deſcent of Moſes from mount Sinai; and that his after additions had the ſame promulgation. Firſt, It was repeated by himſelf to *Aaron*; ſecondly, by them both to the *elders*; and, thirdly, by the elders, to the whole *congregation*.—In the ſame manner do the Romaniſts lay up the *ſtock* of their traditions. In general they make the *church* the repoſitory of them. To the Sanhedrim have *councils* conveniently ſucceeded in the ſame office. But the *high prieſt*, the *pope*, is the principal conſervator of this *ſacred treaſury* of traditions; and upon their ſucceſſion

doth the *certainty* of them depend. And whilſt there is a *Pope at Rome*, the knowledge of the *new oral law* will not fail; as the *old* one did not, whilſt the Jews had an high prieſt, though in the purſuit of it they *crucified the Meſ-ſiah*, and continue to reject him to this day.

3. The Jews, in favour of their traditions, affirm, that the written word without them is *imperfect*, and not to be underſtood, but as it is interpreted by them.—And the firſt queſtion of the Romaniſts generally is, "How do you know the ſcriptures to be the word of God?" And then they fail not to aſſert, firſt, that the ſcripture is imperfect; and, ſecondly, that what is delivered therein can no way be rightly and truely underſtood, but by the help of thoſe *traditions* which they have in their cuſtody. But although theſe are *advantageous inventions*, yet their advocates cannot be allowed the credit of their being the firſt authors, ſeeing they are expreſsly *borrowed* from the Jews.

4. When theſe two laws, the laws of God and their own, come in competition, many of the Jews prefer that of their own *invention* before the other, both as to certainty and uſe; hence they make it the foundation of their church, and the only ſafe *means* to preſerve the truth. It ſeems they have at leaſt ſhewed themſelves more benign towards mankind, than they would allow God to be, inaſmuch as they have committed this ſecret law to writing. And to this purpoſe is their confeſſion, (in מזבח הזהב *The golden altar)* "It is impoſſible for us to ſtand, *(or abide)* upon the foundation of our holy law, which is the written law; unleſs it be by the *oral law*, which is the expoſition thereof." Wherein they not only declare their judgements concerning their *traditions*, but alſo expreſs the reaſon of their obſtinate adherence to them; which is, that without it they cannot maintain themſelves in their *preſent Judaiſm*. And ſo, indeed, is the caſe; innumerable teſtimonies of ſcripture riſing up directly againſt their infidelity, they were not able to keep their ſtation, but by an horrible corrupting of them through their traditions. On this account it is a common thing with them, in the advice they give to their diſciples, to

prefer

prefer the study of the *Talmud* before the study of the *scripture*, and the *sayings* of their wife men before the *sayings* of the prophets; and plainly express an utter disregard of the written word, any farther than as they suppose the sense of it explained in their *oral law*.—Neither are they here forsaken by their associates; for the principal design of all the books which have been lately published by the Romanists, (and they have not been a few) hath been to prove the certainty and sufficiency of their *traditions* in matters of faith and worship, above that of the written word.

5. There are some few remaining, among the *Eastern Jews*, who reject all this story concerning the oral law, and professedly adhere to the written word only. These the masters of their present religion brand as *hereticks*; calling them (קראים) *scripturists* or *biblists*, while at the same time the greatest part of their *Talmud*, the sacred treasury of their *oral law*, is taken up with differences and disputes of their masters *among themselves*, with a multitude of various and contradictory conceptions about their traditional reveries.—Thus deal the Romanists also with their adversaries; this they charge them with: they are *hereticks*, they are *biblists*; and, by adhering to scripture alone, have no certainty among themselves, but run into diversities of opinions, as having deserted the unerring rule of their *cabala*; when the world is filled with the noise of their *own conflicts*, notwithstanding their pretended relief. And as the *Jewish* traditions have been committed to writing, so the *Romish* are recorded in the *rescripts* of popes, decrees of councils, and *constitutions* of the canon law, and the like *sacred* means. But here the Jews deal far more ingeniously than they; for the former tell us plainly, that now their *whole* oral law is written, and that they have no reserve of their *authentic* traditions undeclared. But here the Romanists fail us; for although they have given us 'heaps upon heaps' of traditions, by the means before-mentioned, yet they plead, that they have still an *inexhaustible* treasure of them laid up in their church stores,

and the breast of their holy father, to be drawn forth at all times, as occasion may require. What a convenient reserve! what an enviable privilege!

PART II.
Concerning the Messiah.

EXERCIT. I.

MESSIAH, THE DELIVER FROM EVIL, PROMISED OF OLD.

§ 1. *The subject stated.* § 2. *The original moral state of things.* § 3. *Of sin and punishment entering into the world.* § 4. *The first effect of Adam's sin was punishment.* § 5. *The second effect, the moral corruption of nature.* § 6. *Man's manifold misery on the entrance of sin into the world, recapitulated.* § 7. *Men made the subjects of mercy, and not angels.* § 8. *Evidences that there is a way provided for man's recovery.* § 9. *Men's deliverance not attainable by themselves.* § 10. *Not by angels.* § 11. *Not by the law of Moses,* 12. *Either moral or ceremonial; but by a new covenant of grace.* § 13. *The first promise of grace,* § 14. *And the threatening annexed to it.* § 15 *The promise renewed to Abraham.* § 16. *Other scripture testimonies, in reference to a deliverer.* § 17. *This deliverer, the* MESSIAH. § 18—22. *Additional testimonies, chiefly from the Targums.* § 23. *Conclusion.*

§ 1. WE now proceed to the *basis* that the apostle stands upon, in the management of his whole design.

For

For in all *parænetical* difcourfes, as this epiftle for the moft part is, there are always fome principles taken for granted, which give life and efficacy to the exhortations. And thefe are:

Firft, That there was a Meffiah, or Saviour of mankind from fin and punifhment, promifed upon the firft entrance of fin into the world; in whom all acceptable worfhip of God was founded, and in whom all the religion of the fons of men was to center. [Exercit. 1—3.]

Secondly, That this Meffiah, long before promifed, was actually exhibited in the world, and had finifhed the work committed to him, when the apoftle wrote this epiftle! [Exercit. 4—6.]

Thirdly, That Jefus of Nazareth was the Meffiah, and that what he had done and fuffered, was the work and duty promifed of old concerning him. [Exercit. 7, 8.]

There is not a line in the epiftle to the Hebrews, that doth not *virtually* begin and end in thefe principles; not a doctrine, not an exhortation, that is not built upon this triple foundation. They are alfo the great truths of the *Chriftian Religion.* The confirmation and vindication of the *firft* of thefe principles is what our prefent difcourfe intends.

§ 2. The very firft apprehenfions of the nature of God, and the condition of the univerfe, declare that man was formed free from *fin,* which is his voluntary fubduction of himfelf from under the government of his Maker; and free from *trouble,* which is the effect of his difpleafure on that fubduction or deviation, (in which two the whole nature of evil confifteth) fo that it muft have fome other original.

Furthermore, in this firft effect of immenfe power, God glorified himfelf, not only by the wifdom and goodnefs wherewith it was accompanied; but alfo by that *righteoufnefs* whereby, as the fupreme *rector and governor* of all, he allotted to his rational creatures the law of their obedience, annexing a reward thereto, confifting in a mixture of juftice and bounty. For, that obedience fhould be rewarded is of juftice; but that *fuch* a reward as the
eternal

eternal enjoyment of God should be proposed to the *temporary* obedience of a creature, was of mere grace and bounty. And that mankind should have continued in the state and condition wherein they were created, supposing an accomplishment of the obedience prescribed to them, is manifest from the very notions we have of the nature of God; for we no sooner conceive that *he is*, but withal we assent, that ' he is the *rewarder* of them that diligently ' seek him,' [Heb. xi. 6.] it being inseparable from his nature, as the sovereign ruler of the works of his hands. And thus was the *continuance* of this blessed state of the creation provided for, and laid in a tendency to farther glory; being absolutely exclusive of any distance between God and man, besides that which is natural, necessary, and infinite from their *beings*. There was no sin on the one side, nor disgust on the other. This secured the order of the *universe*. For, what should cause any confusion there, whilst the *law of its creation* was observed, and which could not be transgressed by brute and inanimate creatures.

§ 3. That this state of things hath been altered from time immemorial; that there is a corrupting spring of sin and disorder in the nature of man; that the whole world lieth in ignorance, darkness, evil, and confusion; that there is an alienation and displeasure between God and mankind—God revealing his wrath and judgements from heaven, whence, at first nothing might be expected but fruits of goodness, and pledges of love; and man, naturally dreading the presence of God, and trembling at the effects of it, which at first was his life, joy, and refreshment—*reason*, itself, with prudent observation, will discover. The whole creation groans out this complaint, as the apostle witnesseth, [Rom. viii. 20, 21] and God makes it manifest in his judgements every day, [Rom. i. 18.]

That things were not made at first in that state and condition wherein they are now; that they came not thus immediately from the hands of infinite wisdom and goodness, is easily discernible. God made not man to be at a *perpetual quarrel* with him, nor to fill the world with tokens

of

of his *displeasure*, because of sin. This men saw of old, by the light of nature; but what it should be that opened the floodgates to all that evil and sin, which they saw and observed in the world, they could not tell. But what they could not attain to—and for the want of which they wandered in all their apprehensions about God and themselves, without certainty or consistency—we, by divine revelation, are clearly acquainted with. The sum of it is briefly proposed by the apostle, [Rom. v. 12.] ' By ' one man sin entered into the world, and death by sin.' Sin and death are comprehensive of all that is *evil* in any kind. All that is *morally* so, is sin; all that is penally so, is death. Whatever there is of disorder in the nature of things below; whatever is irregular, horrid, unequal, or destructive in the universe; whatever is penal to man in this life, or to eternity; whatever the wrath of the holy righteous God, " revealing itself from heaven," hath brought, or ever shall bring, on the works of his hands—are to be referred to this head.

Now, the work which we assign to the Messiah is, the *deliverance* of mankind from this state and condition.

§ 4. The first consequent and effect of the sin of Adam was, the *punishment* wherewith it was attended, [Gen. ii. 17.] " *Dying thou shalt die.*" Neither can it be reasonably pretended to be singly death to his own person, which is intended in that expression. The *event* sufficiently evinceth the contrary. Whatever is evil to himself and his whole posterity, with the residue of the creation, so far as he or they might be any way concerned therein, hath grown out of this commination; which is sufficiently manifested in the first execution of it, [Gen. iii. 16—19.] The *malediction* was but the execution of the *commination*. It was not consistent with the justice of God to *increase* the penalty (beyond what was threatened) after the sin was committed. The threatening, therefore, was the *rule* and measure of the *curse*. But this is here extended by God himself, not only to all the miseries of man, (Adam and his whole posterity) in this life—in labour, disappointment, sweat and sorrow, with *death* under the curse—but to the whole earth also, and consequently, to those superior regions and orbs of heaven, by whose influence the earth is, as it were, governed and disposed to the use of man, [Hos. ii. 21, 22.]

It may be yet farther inquired, what was to be the *duration* of this punishment? Now, there is not the least intimation of a term wherein it should expire, or that it should not be commensurate to the existence of the sinner. God (as the righteous judge) lays the *curse* on man, and there he leaves him—leaves him for ever! A miserable life he was to spend, and then to *die* under this curse of God, without hopes of emerging into a better condition.

Supposing, then, *Adam* to die penally under the curse of God (as without extraordinary relief he inevitably must have done) the righteousness and truth of God being engaged for the execution of the threatening against him,—I desire to know, what should have been the state and condition of his soul? Doth either *revelation* or *reason* intimate, that he should not have continued for ever under the same penalty and curse, in a state of death, or separation from God? And if he should have done so, then was *death eternal* in the commination. This, which is termed by our apostle, (η οργη ερχομενη, I. Thes. i. 10.) 'the wrath 'to come,' is what the Messiah delivers from.—And what was inflicted on those who *first* sinned, all their posterity are liable to. Are they not all subject to death, as was *Adam?* Are the miseries of man in his labour, or the sorrows of women in child-bearing, taken away? Is the earth itself freed from the effects of the curse? Do they not die who never sinned after the similitude of Adam's transgression? The Jews themselves acknowledge that all death is *penal;*[*] that Adam was a common *head* to all mankind;[†] and some of the most sober of them, that his

---

[*] R. Ame in *Talm. Tract. Sabbat.* citat. in *Sepher Ikharim.* Lib. IV. cap. xiii. Maimon. *More Nebuch.* Par. III. cap. xvii.

[†] Manass. Ben Israel, *De Fragilitate,* et *De Termino Vitæ.* Aben Ezra in Gen. iii. 22.

sin was imputed to all his posterity.* The latter masters, I acknowledge, are in this whole matter lubricous and uncertain, especially ever since they began to understand the plea of Christians, for the necessity of satisfaction to be made by the sufferings of the Messiah from the doctrine of the fall. Hence ABARBINEL, in his commentary on Isa. liii. expressly argues against those sufferings of the Messiah, from the non-necessity of them, with reference to the sin of Adam. Some of them also contend, that it was not so sorely revenged, as we plead it to have been. "Ask an Heretic (a *Christian*) saith LIPMAN (in his *Nizzachon*) how it can enter into their hearts to think that God should use such great severity against the sin of Adam, that he should hold him bound for so small a matter, namely, for the eating of an apple, that he should destroy him in this world and that to come, and not him only, but all his posterity?"—But the blind pharisee disputes not so much against *us*, as against *God himself*. Who was it that denounced death in case he transgressed? Who was it that pronounced *him miserable*, and the *world accursed* on the same account? Are we to blame if the Jews are not pleased with the ways of God? Besides, although to eat an apple be in itself but a small thing, yet to *disobey* the command of the great God, is not such a small matter as the Jew supposeth.

§ 5. The second consequent of the first sin of man is the *moral corruption* of nature, the spring of all that evil of actual sin that is in the world. And herein we have a full consent from the Jews, delivered after their manner, both in the Targums, Talmuds, and private writings of their principal masters. For, an *evil concupiscence* in the heart of man, from his very conception, they generally acknow-

* R. MENAHEM. *Rakanatensis* in Sect. *Bereshith*, &c. The following sentence is remarkable: "When he (Adam) sinned, the whole world sinned, whose sin we bear and suffer, which is not so in the sin of his posterity." JOSEPH ALBO in *Seher I:harim*, Lib. I. cap. xi. *Targum*, in Ruth iv. Vid. LUD. CAPELL. in Annot. John iii.

VOL. I.   R   ledge.

ledge. The name they give it, is (יצר הרע *figmentum malum*) the *evil figment* of the heart, properly enough, from Gen. vi. 5. " And God faw that the wickednefs of man was great in the earth ; and that the *whole figment of the thoughts*, or computation of his heart, was only evil, every day." Hence have they taken the above-mentioned term, which, perhaps, is a more proper name than that ufed by Chriftian divines, *(originale peccatum) original fin*. And it is a ludicrous ignorance in fome of the *late Rabbins*, who profefs to deny original fin, and yet in the mean time grant this *evil figment* in all mankind, which was not in Adam in his innocency. The *Targumifts* term it in the *Chaldee* tongue (יצרא בישא) to the fame purpofe. On Pfal. xci. 12. " That thy foot ftumble not at the *evil figment* which is like a ftone ;" that is, that it feduce thee not, that it caufe thee not to offend, to ftumble and fall in fin. [See James i. 14.] And Pfal. cxix. 70. they call it abfolutely *the figment*, or *evil foam* of the heart. ' The fig-
' ment of their heart is made thick, as with fatnefs ;' an expreffion not unufual in the fcriptures, to fet out impenitency and fecurity in finning, [Ifa. vi. 10.] Moreover, they do not unfitly defcribe it by another property, [as Ecclef. ix. 14.] ' The evil figment, or concupifcence, ' which is like to a great king ;' namely, becaufe of its *power*; on which account, in the New Teftament, it is faid (βασιλευειν) *to reign as a king*, becaufe of the fubjection of it, (εν ταις επιθυμιαις) *in the lufts*, or concupifcence *of the heart*, [Rom. vi. 12.] and (κυριευειν) *to have dominion*, [v. 14.] which is to the fame purpofe with that of the *Targumift*. And thus we have ample teftimony to this *moral corruption* of nature in the *Targums*, the moft ancient records now extant of the Judaical apprehenfions about thefe things.

The *Talmudifts* have expreffed the fame thoughts about this inbred and indwelling fin ; and, to fet forth their conceptions about it, they have given it feveral *names* not unfuitable to thofe defcriptions of it which are given us by the Holy Ghoft in the New Teftament ; as (רע *malum*) *evil*;

EXER. I. THE DELIVERER FROM EVIL. 111

evil; a name, as they fay, given by himfelf,* [Gen. viii. 21.] and anfwerably it is termed in the New Teftament, (η αμαρτια) *that fin*, that *evil thing* that dwelleth in us, [Rom. vii.] They obferve that Mofes calleth it (ערלה) *præputium*) *uncircumcifion*, [Deut. x. 16.] and therefore (in *Tract. Sand.* chap. xi.] to the queftion. When an infant may be made partaker of the world to come? R. NACHMAN, the fon of ISAAC, anfwereth, " Prefently after he is *circumcifed*;" circumcifion being admitted of old, as the fign of the taking away by grace of the natural *evil figment* of the heart: and accordingly it is called by our apoftle (ακροβυςια) *uncircumcifion*, [Col. ii. 13.] Again; they obferve that David calls it (שמא) *an unclean thing*, [Pf. li. 10.] by the rule of contrarieties; ' Create ' in me a *clean* heart, O God;' whence it appears that the heart of itfelf is *unclean*. And the apoftle gives it us under the fame name and notion, [I. Thef. iv. 7. I. Cor. vii. 14.] They alfo call it (שונא) *an enemy* or *hater*; and to the fame purpofe it is called in the New Teftament (εχθρα) *enmity* or *hatred*, [Rom. viii. 7.] Ifaiah calls it (מבשל) *the offence*, or the ftumbling block, [Ifa. lvii. 17. See alfo Rom. v. 18. Jam. i. 14, 15.] The caufe of our ftumbling and falling. Ezekiel calls it (אבן) *a ftone*, [chap. xxxvi. 26.] Nor doth any allufion better fet out the nature of it from its effects; (καρδια σκληρη και αμετανοητος) ' an hard and impenitent heart,' [Rom. ii. 5.] †

But the (יצר הטוב) " *the new man*, or *good concupifcence*, comes not on our nature until the age of thirteen years;" fo the *Midrafh*, feeling in the dark after that fupply of grace, which is fo clearly revealed in the gofpel. So MANASSEH BEN ISRAEL; " This vitiofity and contagion proceeding from the fin of our firft parents, hath invaded both faculties of our rational fouls, the underftanding and the will.‡ And for the continuance of this, or

---

* R. MOSES HADDARSHAN, a R. JOSE, in *Berefhith Rabba*.
† Vid. *Neve Shalom*, Lib. X. Cap. ix. *Midrafh Coheleth* in Eccleſ. iv. 13.
‡ Præf. *De Fragilit.* Vid. *Tractat. Sandrim*, fo. 91. KIMKI, in Pfal. li.

its abode in us, they express it, (in *Bereshith Rabba*) " So long as the righteous live they wage war with their concupiscence." And they variously set forth the *growth* of it, where it is not corrected by grace. At first, they say, it is like a *spider's thread*, but at last like a *cart-rope*; [from Isa. lix. 5. and v. 18.] And again, in the beginning it is like a *stranger*, then as a *guest*, but lastly as the *myster* of the house. [See Jam. i. 14, 15.]*

§ 6. More testimonies of this nature, from the writings that are of authority amongst them, might be produced, but that these are sufficient for our purpose. What we aim at, is, to evidence their conviction of that manifold misery which came upon mankind on the entrance of sin into the world. And in proof of two things have we produced their suffrage and consent.

1. The change of the primitive condition of man, by his defection from the law of creation. This made him obnoxious in his whole person, and all his concernments, to the displeasure and curse of God, to all the evil which in this world he feels, or fears in another; to death temporal and eternal: and hence did all the disorder which is in the universe arise, which must be acknowledged by all men who will not brutishly deny what their own consciences dictate to them, and which the condition of the whole lower world proclaims, or irrationally ascribe such things to God as are utterly inconsistent with his wisdom, goodness, righteousness, and holiness. And,

2. We have manifested their acknowledgement, that a principle of sin, or moral evil, hath invaded the nature of man; or that from the sin of our first parents there is an evil concupiscence in the heart of every man, continually and incessantly inclining the soul to all moral evil whatever.

From both these it unavoidably follows, on the first notions of the righteousness, holiness, veracity, and faithfulness of God, that mankind in this estate and condition can justly expect nothing but a confluence of evil in this world, and at the close of their pilgrimage to perish with a ruin commensurate to their existence. For God in wisdom

* *Bereshith Rabba*, Sect. xxii.

dom and righteousness, as the sovereign Lord of his creatures, having given them a law, good and equal, and having appointed the penalty of death and his everlasting displeasure to the transgression thereof; and withal having sufficiently promulgated both the law and the penalty; the transgression prohibited actually ensuing, himself being judge, it remains—either, that all this constitution of a law, and threatening of a penalty, was vain and ludicrous, as Satan in the serpent pretended—or, that mankind is rendered absolutely miserable and cursed, and that for ever. Now which of these is to be concluded, divine revelation, reason, and the event of things, will readily determine.

That God, without the least impeachment of his righteousness or goodness, might have left all mankind *remediless* in this condition, is manifest, both from what hath been discoursed concerning the means whereby they were brought into it, and his dealing with *angels* on the like occasion. The *condition* wherein man was created, was *morally* good and upright; the state wherein he was placed outwardly, happy and blessed; the *law* given him just and equal; the *reward* proposed to him glorious and sure; and his *defection* from this condition *voluntary*. The execution of a righteous sentence upon the *voluntary* transgression of a *just* law hath no unrighteousness in it. And this was the sum of what God did in this matter, as to the misery that came on mankind; and who should judge him, if he left man for ever to ' eat of the fruit of his ' own ways, and to be filled with his own devices?'

Hence Adam, when his ' *eyes were opened*' to see the nature of *evil*, in that actual sense which he had in his conscience of the guilt he had contracted, had not the least expectation of relief and mercy. And the *folly* of the course he took in *hiding* himself, argues sufficiently both his present amazement, and that he knew of nothing better to betake himself to; therefore doth he give that account of the *result* of his thoughts, and what alone he now looked for; ' I heard thy voice, and was afraid.' Nor would any *revelation* that God then had made of himself,

self, either by the *works* of his power and wisdom, or by any inbred impression on the souls of men *concreated* with them, give encouragement to them who had sinned against him to expect relief. Besides, he *had* dealt thus with *angels*. Upon their first sin he spared them not, but at once, without hope of recovery, cast them under the ' chains ' of darkness, to be kept to the final judgement of the ' great day.' Now God dealt not unsuitably to any of the excellencies of his nature, when he left the *apostatizing angels* to perish without remedy. Had he dealt so also with *apostatizing mankind*, who were drawn into a conspiracy against him by the head of the defection, had not his ways been holy and righteous?

§ 7. Yet doth not this great instance of God's dealing with angels absolutely conclude his leaving of mankind in remediless misery. He might *justly* have done so; but thence it doth not follow that he *necessarily* must. And although the chief, and indeed only, reason of his extending grace and mercy to men, and not to angels, was his own sovereign will and pleasure, concerning which who can say unto him, ' What doest thou?' Yet there was such a difference between these two original transgressors, as may manifest a *condecency* or suitableness to his righteousness and goodness in his various proceedings with them: for there are sundry things that put an aggravation on the rebellion of angels above that of men; and some that render their ruin less destructive to the glory of the universe, than that of mankind would have been. For,

1. The angels were created in a state and *condition* far superior to, and much more excellent than that of men. The place of their first habitation which they left, [Jude vi.] was the *highest heavens*, the most glorious receptacle of created beings; in opposition to which they are said to be cast to the *lowest hell*, [II. Pet. ii. 4.] whereas man was placed on the *earth*, which, although then beautiful and excellently suited to his condition, was yet every way inferior to the glory and lustre of the other.

2. Their several *employments* also did greatly differ; the work of angels was immediately to attend the *throne of God*,

God, to minister before him, to give him glory, and to execute the commands of his providence in the government of the works of his hands, [Psalm lxviii. 17. Dan. vii. 10. Ezek. i. 5—7. Heb. i. 14. Rev. v. 11.] the highest pitch of honour that a mere creature can be exalted to. Man, during his natural life, was to be employed in ' tilling and dressing the ground,' [Gen. ii. 15.] a labour that would have been easy, useful, and suitable to his condition; but yet in honour, advantage, and satisfaction, unspeakably beneath the duty of the others.

3. Their *enjoyments* also greatly differed. For the angels enjoyed the immediate glorious presence of God without any external created resemblances of it, when man was kept at a greater distance, and not admitted with such immediate communion with God, or enjoyment of his glorious presence. Now all these, and the like considerations, although on the one side they do not in the least *extenuate* the sin of man in his apostacy, yet they *greatly aggravate* the wickedness, ingratitude, and pride of the fallen angels.

4. Moreover they differed in their *intellectual perfections*, whereby they were enabled to discover the excellencies, and to know the mind of God. For although man had all the light, knowledge, and wisdom *concreated* with him, and so *natural* to him, which were any way needful to enable him to perform aright the obedience required of him, in the observance whereof he should have been brought to the enjoyment of God; yet it came far short of that *excellency* of understanding, that piercing wisdom, which those *spiritual beings* were endowed with, to fit them for that near contemplation of the glory of God whereunto they were admitted, and that ready apprehension of his mind which they were to observe.

5. There was likewise a difference in the *manner* of their defection. Our first parents were *seduced* or deceived, [I. Tim. ii. 14. II. Cor. xi. 3.] and therefore calls Satan their murderer, [John viii. 44.] they were circumvented by his craft and policy; but the angels had nothing

thing without them to excite them, or lay fnares for them.

6. Although the condition of mankind, being to be propagated by natural generation from one common ftock, made it neceffary that our firft parents fhould have a greater truft repofed in them—by reafon of their *reprefenting* their whole pofterity in that covenant wherein they ftood before God—than any of the angels could have, feeing the latter ftood every one for himfelf, yet they were but *two perfons* that actually finned at firft, and thofe one after another, one feduced by another; whereas the angels in multitudes inconceivable, by a joint confpiracy at the fame inftant, combined together againft the authority and law of their creation, and, as it fhould feem, appointed one among themfelves for the head of their apoftacy. Now although, as was faid, none of thofe things can in the leaft *extenuate* the fin of man, which was the product of inconceivable infidelity and ingratitude, yet they contain fuch aggravations of the fins of angels, as may evidence a condecency to divine wifdom and goodnefs in paffing them by in their fin and mifery, and yet giving relief to mankind.

7. We may add to what hath been faid, the concernment of the glory of God in the *univerfe*. For if man had been left for ever without relief, the whole human race, or kind of creatures partakers of human nature, had been utterly loft; nothing of that kind could ever come to the enjoyment of God, nor could he ever have been glorified by them in a way of thankfulnefs and praife, which yet was the end why he made that fort of creatures; for the *whole race* of them, as to the event, would have been mere objects of wrath and difpleafure; but in the fall of angels they were only a certain number of *individuals* that finned, the *whole kind* was not loft as to the end of their creation; angelical nature was preferved as to its orderly dependence on God, in thofe millions that kept their obedience and primitive condition, which is continued to them with a fuperaddition of glory and honour. God, then, having made unto himfelf

self *two families* for his praise, amongst whom he would dwell, that above of angels, and this below of mankind, had sinning man been utterly cast off, one family had been lost for ever, though so great a remnant of the other was preserved; wherefore, it seemed good to his infinite wisdom, both to *preserve* that portion of his superior family which sinned not, and to *recover* a portion of that below, and to make them up into one family, in one new head, his son Jesus Christ, in whom he hath now actually gathered into one, all things that are in heaven and earth, to his praise and glory, [Ephes. i. 10.]

§ 8. There is, then, no *necessary reason* inducing us to believe, that God hath left all mankind to perish under the curse, without any remedy; yea, there are, on the contrary, many evidences, that there is a way provided for their recovery; for,

1. The glorious properties of the nature of God, which he designs to manifest and exalt, in all his external works, do in a sense *require* that there should be *salvation* for *sinners*. God had, in the creation of all things, glorified his greatness, power, wisdom, and goodness. His sovereignty, righteousness, and holiness he had in like manner revealed in that holy law, which he had prescribed to angels and men, for the rule of their obedience, and in the assignation of their reward. Upon the sin of angels and men, he had made known his severity and vindictive justice, in the curse and punishment inflicted on them. But there were yet remaining undiscovered, in the abyss of his eternal essence, *grace,* and *pardoning mercy,* which in none of his works had as yet exerted themselves, or manifested their glory. The creatures know nothing in God, but as manifested in its effects. His *essence,* in itself, dwells in light inaccessible. Had never any stood in need of grace or mercy, or had never been made partakers of them, it could not have been made known, that there was that kind of *goodness* in his nature, which yet it is his principal design to glorify himself in. And there is nothing in himself, which the Lord more requireth our con-

formity to himself in, than in this condescension, goodness, grace, and readiness to forgive; which manifests how dear the glory of them is to him.

2. To what end shall we conceive the providence and *patience* of God to be exercised towards the race of mankind for so long a season? We see what is the general event of the continuance of mankind in the world; God saw it, and complained of it long ago, [Gen. vi. 5, 6.] Shall we now think, that God hath no other design in his patience towards the children of men for so many generations, but merely to suffer them all without exception, to sin against him, dishonour him, provoke him, that so he may at length everlastingly destroy them? That this, indeed, is the *event* with many, or even with the most, through their own perverse wickedness, blindness, and love of sinful pleasures, cannot be denied. But to suppose that God hath no other design, but merely by his patience to bear with them a while in their folly, and then to avenge himself upon them, is unsuitable to his wisdom and goodness. It cannot be, then, but that he would long since have *cut off* the whole race (to prevent its propagation) if there were *no way* for them to be delivered out of this perishing condition.

3. That there is a way of deliverance for mankind, the *event* hath manifested in two remarkable and undeniable instances:

(1.) In that *sundry persons* who were, as others, ' by ' nature children of wrath,' and under the curse, have obtained an undoubted and infallible interest in the love and favour of God, and this *testimony*, ' that they pleased ' him.' Some persons, in all generations, have enjoyed the friendship, love, and favour of God; which they would never have done, unless there had been some way for their deliverance out of the state of sin and misery, before described. For, therein every man, upon a just account, will find themselves in the state of Adam, who, when ' he heard the voice of God, was *afraid*.'

(2.)

THE DELIVERER FROM EVIL.

(2.) God hath been pleased to require from men, a *revenue of glory*, by way of worship, prescribed them after the entrance of sin. This he hath not done to the angels that sinned; nor could it have been done consistently with righteousness to men, without supposing a *possibility* of deliverance from under his wrath. For in every prescription of duty, God proposeth himself as a *rewarder*, which he is only to them that please him; and to please God, without the *deliverance* inquired after, is impossible. *Deliverance*, then, from this condition, may on just grounds be expected. Our next inquiry is, *how* it might be effected.

§ 9. The great relief must be brought about—either by *men* themselves, or by some *other* for them. About what they can do themselves, we may be quickly satisfied. The nature of the *evils* under which they suffer, and the *event* of things in the world, sufficiently discover the disability of men to be their own *deliverers*. Besides, who should contrive the *way* of it for them? one single person, more, or all? How easily the impossibility of it might be demonstrated on any of these suppositions, is too manifest to be insisted on.

There are but two ways conceivable (setting aside the consideration of what shall be afterwards fixed on) whereby mankind, or any individual amongst them, may obtain deliverance from this evil:

1. That God, without any farther consideration, should remit it, and exempt the *creation* from under it. But although this way seems *possible* to some, it is, indeed, utterly otherwise. Did not the sentence against this evil proceed from his *righteousness*, and the essential rectitude of his nature? Did he not engage his *truth* and faithfulness, that it should be inflicted? And doth not his *holiness* and justice require that it should be so? What should become of his glory; what should he do unto his great name, if now, without any cause or reason, he should, contrary to all those engagements of his holy perfections, wholly remit and take it off? nay, this would plainly
justify

justify the serpent in his calumny, that, whatever he pretended, yet indeed, that no execution could ever ensue. How also can it be supposed, that any of his *future comminations* should have a just weight upon men, if that first great and fundamental one should be evacuated? or what *authority* would be left unto his *law*, when he himself should dissolve the sanction of it? Besides, if God should do thus—which reason, revelation, and the event of things manifest, that he neither would, nor *could* (for he cannot deny himself)—it would have been His work, and not an acquisition of men themselves. But this way of *deliverance* is, at best, but *imaginary*. Therefore,

2. There is no other way for man, if he will not perish eternally under the punishment due to his apostacy and rebellion, but to find out some way of *commutation*, or making a *recompence* for the evil of sin, to the law and righteousness of God. But herein his utter insufficiency quickly manifests itself; for whatever he is, or hath, or can claim any interest in, lies no less under the *curse*, than he doth himself; and that which is under the *curse* can *contribute* nothing to its removal. That which is, in its whole being obnoxious to the greatest punishment, can have nothing wherewith to make *commutation* for it; for that must first be accepted for itself, which can either make *atonement*, or be received for any other in exchange. And this is the condition of every *individual* of mankind, and will be so to eternity, unless relief arise from another quarter. It is farther evident, that all the endeavours of men must needs be unspeakably disproportionate to the end aimed at, from the concernment of the other parts of the creation, in the *curse* against sin. What can they do to restore the universe to its first glory and beauty? How can they reduce the creation to its *original harmony?* Wherewith shall they *recompense* the great God, for the defacing of so great a portion of that impress of his glory and goodness that he enstamped upon it? In a word, they, who from their *first date*, to their *utmost period*, are always under the *punishment*, can do nothing for the *total*
removal

removal of it. The experience also of five thousand years hath sufficiently evinced how *insufficient* man is to be a saviour to himself. All the various and uncertain notions of Adam's posterity in religion, from the extreme of atheism, to that of sacrificing themselves and one another, have been designed in vain towards this end. Nor can any of them, to this day, find out a better, or a more likely way for them to thrive in, than those wherewith their progenitors deluded themselves. And in the issue of all we see, as to what man hath been able *of himself* to do towards his own *deliverance*, that both he, myself, and the whole world, are continued in the same state wherein they were upon the first entrance of sin, *cumulated*, as it were, with another world of confusion, disorder, mischief, and misery. The corrupt spring of *moral evil* that is in man's nature, is *universal* and endless: it mixeth itself with all, and every thing that man doth, or can do, as a *moral* agent, and that always, and for ever, [Gen. vi. 5.] It is, then, impossible that it should have an end, unless it either destroy, or spend itself; but *ever sinning*, which man cannot but be, is not the way to *disentangle* himself from sin.

§ 10. If, then, any deliverance be ever obtained for mankind, it must be by *some other*, *not involved* in the same misery as themselves. This must be either God himself, or good angels; other *rational agents*, there are none that we know of. If we look to the *latter*, we must suppose them to undertake this work, either by the appointment of God, or of their own accord, without his previous command or direction. The latter cannot be supposed. As remote as men are from all thoughts of recovering *fallen angels*, so far were they from contriving the recovery of *man*.

But it may be said, that God himself might *design* them to work this deliverance. But this makes *God*, and not them, to be the Saviour, and them only the *instrument* of this work. But yet he has neither done so in fact, nor were they *meet* to be so employed. Whatever is *purely penal*.

penal in the misery of man, is an effect of the righteous judgement of God. This, therefore, could be no otherwise diverted from him, but by the *undergoing* of it by some other in his stead. And two things are indispensably required, to qualify any for that purpose: *First*, that they were not themselves *obnoxious* to it, either *personally*, or upon the *common account*; should they be so, they ought to look to their *own* concernment in the first place. *Secondly*, that they were such, as that their benefit of *undergoing* the penalty might, according to the rule of justice, redound to them, in whose stead they underwent it; otherwise they would suffer in vain. Now, although the angels might answer the former of these, in their *personal immunity* from obnoxiousness to the curse; yet the latter they were totally unsuited for. They had no *relation* to mankind, except that they were the *workmanship* of the same Creator. But this is not sufficient to warrant any substitution of that kind. Had angels been to be delivered, their redemption must have been wrought in the *angelical nature*, as the apostle declares, [Heb. ii. 16.] But what justice is it that *man* should sin, and *angels* suffer? or, from whence should it arise, that, from *their* suffering, it would be righteous that he should go free? by what notions of God could we have been instructed in the wisdom and righteousness of such a proceeding? To which add, that this God *hath not done*; and we may safely conclude, that it *became Him* not so to do.

§ 11. But what need all this inquiry? The Jews, with whom we have to do in this matter, plead constantly, that God hath appointed for men, at least to themselves, a way of *deliverance* out of this condition; and this is, according to them, by observing the law of Moses. This they trusted in of old, [Rom. ix. 32.] this they continue to make their refuge at this day.* And whereas they can-

---

* Answers to certain *questions* proposed to the Jews, published by BRENIUS, [Quest. v.]—This gentleman, (and it would be well if he had no *modern imitators*) in his reply, hath betrayed the most

cannot deny, but that they sometimes sin against the moral precepts of this law, and so stand in need of help against the *Helper*, they fix in this case upon a double relief. The one is their own *personal repentance*; and the othe rthe *sacrifices* that are appointed in the law. But whereas they now are, and have been for many generations, deprived of the privilege, as they esteem it, of offering sacrifices according to the law, they hope that their *own repentance* with their death, which they pray may be *expiatory*, will be sufficient to obtain for them *forgiveness of sin*. Only they say this might better, and more easily, be effected, if they might enjoy the benefit of sacrifices. But where do they find that their *sacrifices* were ever designed for this end, to enable them the *more easily* to obtain the remission of sins, by another means which they use? For it was said directly, that the sacrifice on the day of expiation did expiate their sin, and make atonement for it, that they might not die; and not that it helped them in procuring pardon another way. But this is now taken from them, and what shall they do? Why, rather than they will come to him, who was *represented* in that sacrifice, and on whose account alone it had all its efficacy, they will find out some new way of doing that, which their sacrifices were appointed to effect; and this they must do, or openly acknowledge that they all *perish* eternally.

If the remedy be only the observance of the *law of Moses*, as the Jews pretend, I desire to know what became of them; what was their estate and condition, who lived and died *before* the giving of that law? Not only the patriarchs before the flood, some of whom had this testimony, 'that 'they pleased God,' and one of whom was taken *alive* to heaven, but Abraham also himself, who received the promises, must, on this supposition, be excluded from a participation of deliverance, and perish eternally.—But the

most important doctrines of the Christian religion.—When will men have done attempting, what is no less ungrateful than impious, to rob the MESSIAH of his crown and scepter, and then " recommend him to the Jews?"

con-

contrary appears from this very confideration, and is undeniably proved by our apoftle, in the inftance of Abraham, [Gal. iii. 17.] that he 'received the *promife*,' and was taken into *covenant* with God, four hundred and thirty years before the giving of the law. And that covenant conveyed to him the love and favour of God, with deliverance from fin and the curfe, as themfelves will not deny. There was, therefore, a remedy in this cafe provided, *long before* the giving of the law on mount Sinai; and, therefore, the law was *not given for that purpofe*. If they fhall fay, they had a way of deliverance, but God provided *another* afterwards; as this would be fpoken without warrant, or authority from fcripture, fo I defire to know both *what* that way was, and *why* it was rejected. Of God's appointment it feems it was, and effectual it was to them that embraced it; but why it fhould be laid afide, who can declare?

§ 12. Again, there are two parts of the law; the *moral precepts* of it, and he inftituted *worfhip* appointed in it. Unto this latter part do the facrifices of it belong. But neither of thefe are fufficient to the end propofed; nor jointly can they attain it; for,

1. The *moral precepts* of it are the fame with thofe that were written in the heart of man, by nature, or the law of his creation, which he tranfgreffed in his firft rebellion. And he muft be delivered from that guilt, before any new obedience can be accepted of him. His old debt muft be fatisfied for, before he can treat for a new reward, which infeparably follows all acceptable obedience. But this the precepts of the law take no notice of, nor direct to any way for its removal. Hence our apoftle concludes, that *it could not give life*, but was weak and infufficient in itfelf to any fuch purpofe.

Befides, it could not abfolutely preferve men in its own obfervance; for it required that obedience, which never any *finner* did, or could, in all things, perform; as the fcriptures of the Old Teftament abundantly manifeft. For they tell us, that 'there is no man that finneth not,'

[*I. Kings*,

EXER. I.   THE DELIVERER FROM EVIL.

[*I. Kings* viii. 46. II. Chron. vi. 36.] That, 'if the 'Lord fhould mark iniquity, no man could ftand,' [Pfal. cxxx. 3.] And that, 'if he enter into judgement (ac- 'cording to the law) no man living can be juftified in 'his fight,' [Pfal. cxliii. 2.] To this purpofe fee the excellent difcourfe, and invincible reafonings of our apoftles, [Rom. iii. and iv.] This the holy men of old confeffed; this the fcriptures bear teftimony to, and this experience confirms, feeing every tranfgreffion of that law was put under a curfe, [Deut. xxvii. 26.] If, then, there is no man that *finneth not*, and every fin is put under a *curfe*, the *preceptive* part of the law can be no means of delivery. Neither is there any teftimony given concerning any one under the Old Teftament, that he was any other way juftified before God, but by *faith and pardon of fins*, which are not of the works of the law. This the Jews themfelves confefs concerning Abraham; " Thou findeft, that Abraham, our father, inherited not this world and the world to come, any otherwife than *by faith*; as it is faid *he believed God*."*

2. It remains, then, that the *facrifices of the law* muft yield the relief, or we are ftill at a lofs in this matter. And thefe the Jews would willingly place their chief confidence in, as they did of old. Since, indeed, they have been driven from their obfervance, they have betaken themfelves to other helps, that they might not appear to be utterly hopelefs. And, therefore, being driven from all other hopes,† they truft, at length, to their *own death!* (for in *life* they have no hope) making this one of their conftant prayers, " Let my death be the expiation of all fins." But this is the *curfe*, and, therefore, is no means to avoid it. Omitting, therefore, thefe horrid follies of men under *defpair*, an effect of that 'wrath, 'which is come upon them to the uttermoft,' the thing itfelf may be conceived.

* Vid. etiam *Berefhith Rabba*, Sect. xxiv.
† Vid. BUXTORF. *Synagog. Judaic.* Cap. xx.

VOL. I.   T   That

That the sacrifices of the law, in themselves, should be a means of delivering men from the guilt of sin, and of reconciling them to God, is contrary to the *light of nature*—their own *proper use*—and *express* testimonies of the Old Testament. For, can any man think it reasonable, that the blood of bulls and goats should, of itself, make an *expiation* of the sin of men; *reconcile* them to God, the Judge of all; and impart to them an everlasting righteousness? Our apostle sufficiently declares the manifest impossibility of it, [Heb. x. 4.] They must have very mean and low thoughts of God; his holiness, justice, and truth; of the demerit of sin, of heaven and hell, who think them all to depend on the blood of a *calf or a goat*. The sacrifice of them, indeed, might, by God's appointment, represent *that* to the minds of men, which is effectual to the whole end of appeasing God's justice, and of obtaining his favour; but that they should themselves effect it, is impossible.—Their primitive and *proper use* doth also manifest the same. For they were to be frequently repeated, and, in all the repetitions of them, there was still new mention made of sin. They could not, therefore, by themselves, take it away; for, if they could, they would not have been *reiterated*. It is apparent, therefore, that their use was to *represent*, and bring to remembrance, that which did perfectly take away sin. Besides, the scripture expressly *rejects* all the sacrifices of the law, when they are trusted in for any such end and purpose, which demonstrates, that they were never appointed to that end. To which we may add, that during the observance of the whole law of Moses, whilst it was in force by the appointment of God himself, he still directed those who sought for acceptance with him, to a *new covenant* of grace, the benefits of which they were then, by faith, made partakers of, and which was afterwards more fully to be declared. [See Jerem. xxxi. 31—34. Heb. viii. 12, 13.] And this plainly overturns their whole foundation. For, to what purpose should God call them from resting on the Sinai covenant, to look for mercy and

grace

grace by *another*, if that had been able to give them the defired help?

§ 13. The firft intimation that God gave of *redeeming grace* is contained in the *promife* fubjoined to the curfe denounced againft our firft parents, and their pofterity in them, [Gen. iii. 15.] 'The feed of the woman fhall 'bruife the ferpent's head, and the ferpent fhall bruife his 'heel.' If there be not a promife of *deliverance* expreffed in thefe words, whence is it, that the execution of the fentence of death againft fin is fufpended? Unlefs we will allow an *intervention*, fatisfactory to the righteoufnefs and truth of God, to be expreffed in thefe words, there would have been a truth in the fuggeftion of the ferpent, that notwithftanding what God had faid, they were not to die.—The whole evil of fin, and its curfe, that mankind then did, or were to fuffer, proceeded from the *friendfhip* contracted between the *woman* and the *ferpent*, and her fixing faith in him. God here declares, that he will break that *league*, and put *enmity* between them. But being now, both of them, in the fame finful and accurfed condition, this could not be without a change of condition in one of them. Satan is not divided againft himfelf; nor is at enmity with them that are left wholly in this eftate. A change of condition, therefore, on the part of the *woman and her feed*, is plainly promifed; that is, by a *deliverance* from the ftate of fin and mifery wherein they were. Without this the *enmity mentioned* could not have enfued.

In purfuit of this enmity, the feed of the woman was to 'bruife the head of the ferpent.' The *head* is the feat of his power and craft. Without the deftruction of the evil and pernicious effects, which by his counfel he had brought about, his *head* cannot be *bruifed*.

Again, there is an intimation of the *manner* how this work is to be brought about. God takes it upon himfelf; 'I will put *enmity*;' it is an iffue of his fovereign wifdom and grace. But he will do it in and by the *nature* of man, the 'feed of the woman.' And this is the MESSIAH; or, "God joining with the nature of man," to deliver mankind from fin and eternal misery. By this relief God declared himself to be—"a God of pardon, gracious, and tenderly merciful." If this be not acknowledged, it must be confessed, that all the world—at least to the flood, if not to the days of Abraham, in which time we have testimonies concerning some, that they walked with God, and pleased him—were left without any certain ground of faith, or hope of acceptance with him. For, without some knowledge of this mercy, and the provision of a way for its exercise, they could have no such persuasion. This, then, we have obtained—that God presently upon the entrance of sin into the world, and the breach of its public peace thereby, promised a reparation of that evil in the whole extent of it, to be wrought by the seed of the woman; that is, the MESSIAH. Many testimonies of the like import might be collected out of Jewish writings, which may be deemed unnecessary;* and as to the Divine writings of the New Testament, however explicit, [as II. Cor. xi. 3. II. Tim. ii. 14. Rom. v. 11—15. Heb. ii. 14, 15. I. John iii. 8. Rev. xii. 9. and chap. xx. 1—3.] we forbear to press them upon the Jews.

* That Satan accompanied the serpent in tempting Eve, and was principally intended in the curse, the Jews themselves acknowledge: *Targum* BEN. UZZIEL. MAIMON. *More Nebuch.* P. II. Cap. xx. *Bereshith Rabba*, Sect. x. *Midrash Vaiikra*, Cap. xiii. 2.—ABEN EZRA, Comment. in loc. cites the opinion of their Doctors, particularly R. SAADIAS HAGGAON, and R. SAMUEL BEN HOPHNI; though he disputes their opinions on the weak pretence—" That Satan goeth not on his belly, nor eateth dust;" which pretence he is obliged to hold on the absurd hypothesis,—That the serpent was deprived of *voice and understanding*, making him before a *rational subsistence*, though expressly reckoned among the *beasts* of the field.—What will not a desperate cause drive men to? Rather than ascribe the fall of man to diabolical intrigue, and abide by its genuine consequences, they will not scruple to admit---That a *rational creature* is metamorphosed into a *brute* for tempting man!

The two *Targums* agree, that the words contain a remedy for the effect of Satan's temptation, to be wrought by the MESSIAH. Vid. R. BECHAI the elder, Comment. in loc. R. JUDAH, and the author of *Caphtor Vaparach*, &c.

§ 14.

§ 14. Besides, it is most evident from the thing itself; for, who can imagine, that this great alteration, which ensued on the works of God—which caused him to pronounce them accursed, and to inflict so great and sore a punishment on Adam, and all his posterity—should arise from the actings of a brute creature? where is the glory of this dispensation? How can we attribute it to the wisdom and greatness of God? What is there in it suitable to his righteousness and holiness? What rule of justice will admit, that the accessary should be punished with greater sufferings than the principal? Neither doth this punishment, as to its principal part, the 'bruising of the head,' befall *all* serpents—yea, comparatively but a *few* of them, perhaps, not one of a million—whereas *all* mankind were liable to the penalty denounced against them. Were no more men intended herein than are " *bitten on the heel by serpents,*" the matter were otherwise; but *death* is passed upon *all*, inasmuch as all have sinned.—This, therefore, is openly and plainly the deliverance inquired after; MESSIAH shall defeat the counsel, and destroy the work of Satan.

Moreover, there is a declaration made, how this *victory* shall be obtained, and this deliverance wrought; *viz.* by the ' feed of the woman,' which is twice repeated in the words, once expressly, (and *her feed*) and it is included in the pronoun (הוא) *it*. And as by feed in the *former* place the *posterity* of the woman—some to be born of her race, partakers of human nature—may be intended, as the subject of the enmity mentioned; so, in the *latter* some *single person*, some *one* of her posterity or feed, that should obtain the victory, is expressly denoted. For, as all her feed in common do never go about this work, the greatest part of them continuing in a willing subjection to Satan; so, if all of them should combine to *attempt* it, they would never be able to accomplish it, as we have proved at large. Some *one*, therefore, to come of *Her*, with whom God would be present in an especial manner, is here expressly promised; and this is the MESSIAH.

God

God having, in infinite wisdom and grace, provided this way of relief, and given this intimation of it, *that revelation* became the foundation and centre of all the religion in the world. For, as those who received it by faith, and adhered to it, continued in the worship of the *true God*, expressing their faith in the *sacrifices*, that he had appointed typically to represent and exemplify, before their eyes, the work itself, which, by the promised seed, was to be accomplished; so also, all that *false worship*, which the generality of mankind *apostatized* into, was laid in a general persuasion, that there was a way for the *recovery* of the favour of God; but what that was they knew not, and therefore wandered in woeful uncertainties.

§ 15. But we have farther expositions of this first promise, and farther confirmations of this grace, in the scripture itself. For, in process of time, it was renewed to Abraham, and the accomplishment of it confined to his family. For his gratuitous call from superstition and idolatry, with the separation of him and his posterity from all the families of the earth, was *subservient* only to the fulfilling of the promise before treated of. The first mention of it we have Gen. xii. 1—3. ' Now, the Lord
' had said to Abraham, get thee out of thy country, and
' from thy kindred, and from thy father's house, to a
' land that I will shew thee. And I will make of thee a
' great nation, and I will bless thee, and make thy name
' great, and thou shalt be a blessing. And I will bless
' them that bless thee, and curse them that curse thee;
' and in thee shall all the families of the earth be blessed.'
And this is again expressed, Gen. xviii. 18. ' All the
' nations of the earth shall be blessed in him.' And chap. xxii. 18. ' And in thee shall all the nations of the earth be
' blessed'. And when he doubted of the accomplishment of this promise, because he was *childless*, and said, ' behold to me thou hast given no seed,' as knowing that therein lay the promise, [chap. xv. 3.] God tells him, that he who should come ' forth of his own bowels
' should be his heir,' [ver. 4.] which was afterwards restrained to Isaac, [chap. xvii. 21.] Thus he is called and separated from his own family and kindred, and from all other

other nations, and a *peculiar portion* of the earth affigned him and his for their habitation. Now, the fpecial end of this Divine difpenfation was, to be a means of accomplifhing the former promife, or the bringing forth of him who was to be the *deliverer* of mankind from the *curfe*; for,

1. It is faid, that Abraham hereupon fhould be (ברכה) *a bleffing*; not only bleffed thyfelf, but alfo the means of conveying bleffings, the *great bleffing*, unto others. And how was this done in Abraham? it can be nothing, but that he was *feparated* to be the peculiar channel, by which the promifed *bleffing feed* fhould be brought forth into the the world.

2. It is faid, that all the ' families of the earth (ונברכו) ' *fhall be bleffed* in him,' [Gen. xii. 3.] that is, not in his perfon, but in his *feed*, [chap. xxii. 18.] the promifed feed that fhould come of him. And [chap. xxii. 18. התברכו] in *Hithpael*, ' *blefs themfelves*.' And this is fpoken of *all nations*, all families, the pofterity of Adam in general, and not any one nation exclufively. They are all curfed in Adam, as hath been declared, and God here promifeth, that they fhall be bleffed in the feed of Abraham, and by him, ' the feed of the woman.' And this bleffing muft involve in it all the good things of which, by the curfe, they were deprived. In this promife was the *ore* laid up, which, after many generations, was brought forth and ftamped with the image of God.

3. The curfe to *Satan* is here again renewed; ' I will ' blefs them that blefs thee, and I will curfe HIM that ' curfe thee.' The bleffing is to *many*; but the curfe refpecteth *one* principally; that is, Satan, as the fcripture generally expreffeth the oppofite *apoftate* power under that name. Neither is there any juft caufe of the variation of the number, unlefs we look on the words as a purfuit of the firft promife, which was accompanied with an efpecial malediction on Satan, and who acts his enmity in all obloquy and curfing againft the bleffed feed, and thofe that are bleffed therein.

§ 16.

§ 16. After the giving of this promise, the whole Old Testament beareth witness, that a person was to be born of the posterity of Abraham, in whom the nations of the earth should be saved; that is, delivered from sin and curse, and made eternally happy. It is said, (לו יקהש עמים) ' *to* ' *him* shall be *the gathering of the people*;' the people of the world, distinct from Judah, shall gather themselves to him; that is, for safety and deliverance, or to be made partakers of the *promised blessing*. Hence Balaam, among the Gentiles, prophesied of him, [Numb. xxiv. 17—19.] And Job, among the children of the East, that were not of the posterity of Isaac, professed his faith in him, [Job. xix. 25.] ' I know that my Redeemer liveth, or ('ח) *is* ' *living*; and afterwards he shall stand on the earth,' or rise on the dust. He believed that there was (גאל) *a Redeemer* promised, one that should free him from sin and misery. Though he was among the Gentiles, yet he believed the promise, and expected his own personal redemption, by the blessed seed. And thus, although God confineth the posterity of Abraham after the flesh, to the land of Canaan, yet, because in the promised seed he was to be " *heir of the world*," he gives to the Messiah, ' the heathen to be his in- ' heritance, and the uttermost parts of the earth for his ' possession,' [Psal. ii. 8.] And upon the accomplishment of the work assigned him, he promiseth, that ' all the ' ends of the world shall remember, and turn to the Lord; ' and all the kindreds of the nations shall worship before ' him,' [Psal. xxii. 27.] a plain declaration of the Gentiles coming in for an interest in the redemption wrought by him. [See Psal. xlv. 16.] For these *rebellious ones* was he to receive gifts, that the ' Lord God might dwell ' among them,' [Psal. lxviii. 18.] so, that by him 'Egypt and ' Ethiopia were to stretch forth their hands to God,' [ver. 31.] yea, ' all kings were to bow down to him, and all nations ' to serve him,' [Psal. lxxii. 11—17.] In the *last days*, the days of the Messiah, *many* people, yea, all nations, are to be brought to the house of the Lord, and to worship him acceptably, [Isa. ii. 2—4.] and expressly, [chap. xi. 10.] The *root of Jesse*, which the Jews grant to be

the

the Meffiah, is to ftand for an enfign to the people, and to it fhall the *Gentiles* feek; even for that falvation and deliverance which he had wrought; and they are preferred therein, before Ifrael and Judah, [ver. 12.] *Egypt and Affyria*; that is, the other nations of the world are to be brought into the fame covenant of the Meffiah with *Ifrael*, [Ifa. xix. 25.] For *all flefh* was to fee the glory of the Lord, and not the Jews only; and the *Ifles*, or the utmoft parts of the earth, were to *wait for the law* of the promifed Meffiah, [chap. xlii. 4.] And the whole of what we affert is fummed up, chap. xlix. 6. where God fpeaks to the promifed feed, and fays, " It is a light thing, that thou fhouldft be my fervant, to raife up the tribes of Jacob, and to reftore the preferved of Ifrael; I will alfo give thee for a light to the Gentiles, that thou mayeft be my falvation to the end of the earth;" where he is as fully promifed to the *Gentiles*, to be their falvation, as ever he was to Abraham, or his pofterity. [See Ifa. li. 5. and liii. 12.] And on this account doth God call to men in general, to come into his covenant; promifing to them an intereft in the *mercies of David*, becaufe he hath given this feed as a witnefs to them, as a *leader and commander*, or a captain of their falvation, [Ifa. lv. 1—4.]

§ 17. Thus do both the law and the prophets bear witnefs to the *promifed Deliverer*, and the *deliverance* to be wrought by him. And this is he, whom *Jews* and *Chriftians* call (משיח) MESSIAH, *the Anointed*. Thofe who were of old confecrated to God in the great offices of *kings, priefts*, and *prophets*, were by his appointment to be anointed; at leaft fome of them on *fpecial occafions* were fo. Thence were they called (משיחים) *anointed ones*. And becaufe this anointing with oil was not appointed for *its own fake*, but for fomewhat *fignified* thereby, thofe who received the thing fignified, although not actually and literally anointed with oil, are all called " anointed ones;" alfo, [Pfal. cv. 15.] Now, this promifed feed, this faviour or deliverer, being appointed of God, to perform his work in the difcharge of a *triple office*, of king, prieft, and prophet to his people, and being furnifhed with those gifts and endowments which were signified by the anointing oil is, by an *antonomasia*, called "the Messiah." Or (מלך המשיח) "Messiah the king." [Dan. ix. 25. משיח נגיד] "Messiah the prince," ruler, or leader; and [ver. 26.] *Messiah* absolutely.

This name is but twice, or thrice at most, used in the Old Testament, directly and immediately to denote the *promised seed*; namely, Dan. ix. 25, 26. whereto, Psal. ii. 2. may be added. But this name, on the reasons before given, prevailing in the *Judaical church*, it is frequently made use of in the *Targums*, and some other of their chief writings where he is treated of; although he be not expressly named in the original. ELIAS, (in his *Methurgamim*) reckons up *fifty* of those places, whereunto *one and twenty* more are added by BUXTORFIUS. A few here follows:

§ 18. On Gen. iii. 15. *Targ.* JONATH. "The seed of the woman shall bruise the head of the serpent, and they shall obtain healing, or a plaister for the heel, in the days of MESSIAH the king."—On Gen. xxxv. 21. "Which is the place (*i. e.* Edar, which was near Bethlehem) from whence the king MESSIAH shall be revealed 'in the end of the days.' This tradition is taken from Mich. iv. 8.—On Gen. xlix. 1. "The time (*i. e.* the precise time) wherein the king MESSIAH was to come, was hid from him, and therefore he said, Come, and I will declare unto you, what shall befall you in the end of the days;" because the *precise time* of his coming was hidden even from the best of the prophets, unto whom the glory of the *Divine Majesty* was in other things revealed.—Gen. xlix. 10. '*Until Shiloh come*.' All the three *Targums* agree in the application of these memorable words to the MESSIAH, which is an illustrious prophecy concerning him, and which the Jews, with none of their cavilling exceptions can evade.

On Exod. xii. 42. *Hierusal. Targ.* "Moses shall come forth from the midst of the wilderness, and the king MESSIAH from the midst of Rome." That of the MESSIAH coming

coming out of Rome is *Talmudical*. And we may here, once for all, observe, that although they believe that their Messiah is to be a *mere man*, born after the manner of all other men, yet they never speak of his *birth* as a thing they looked for; they only speak of his *coming*, or most commonly of his being *revealed*; and their great expectation and inquiry is, when he shall be *discovered* and revealed. And this proceedeth out of a secret self-conviction, that he *was born* long since, even at the time promised and appointed; only that he is *hidden* from them, as, indeed, he is, though not in the sense by them imagined. But what connection has the *night of the passover* with the coming of the Messiah? They cannot imagine, that he shall come to them whilst they are celebrating that ordinance, which is *not lawful* for them, unless they were at Jerusalem, whither they believe they shall never return until he come and go before them. It is, then, from some tradition amongst them, that their deliverance out of Egypt was a *type* of the deliverance by the MESSIAH, whose sacrifice and suffering were represented in the *pascal lamb*, which gave occasion to this gloss.—Chap. xl. 9. *Targ.* JONATH. " The king MESSIAH, who shall deliver Israel in the end of the days."—Numb. xxiii. 21. xxiv. 7, 17, 20, 24. All the *Targums* agree, that the MESSIAH is intended in these prophecies of Balaam. On those words, ' There shall come a star out of Jacob, and ' a sceptre out of Israel,' they jointly say, " A king shall arise out of Jacob, and the MESSIAH shall be anointed." And an illustrious prophecy it is, no doubt, concerning *his* coming and dominion, who is the " root and the offspring of David, the bright and morning star."—Likewise, Deut. xviii. 15—19. This place is an eminent prophecy concerning the MESSIAH, and his prophetical office; and from it, the Jews themselves (in *Midrash Coheleth*, Cap. 1.) say, " The latter *Redeemer* is to be like the former."

§ 19. Moreover, I. Sam. ii. 20. *Targ.* " He shall exalt the kingdom of this MESSIAH."—II. Sam. xxiii. 3. *Targ.* " He said he would appoint to me a king, which is the

Messiah, who shall arise and rule in the fear of the Lord."
—Ruth iii. 15. *Targ.* " It was said in the prophecy, that six righteous persons should come of Ruth, David, and Daniel, with his *companions*, and the king Messiah."

§ 20. Again, Psal. ii. 2. *Targ.* " Against his Messiah." The *Talmudists*, in several places, acknowledge this psalm to be a prophecy of the Messiah, and apply sundry passages thereof to him. And those words, ' Thou art my son, this day have I begotten thee,' are not amiss expounded by them, (in *Tract.* Succah. Cap. v.) " I will this day reveal to men, that thou art my son;" for so are they applied by our apostle, when dealing with the Jews, [Acts xiii. 33. Heb. i. 5.] to his " resurrection from the dead," whereby he was declared the Son of God with power, [Rom. i. 4.] All the principal expositors amongst them, as Rashi, Kimchi, Aben Ezra, Bartenora, or R. Obodia, acknowledge, that their ancient doctors and masters expounded this psalm concerning the Messiah.—Psal. xxi. 1. *Targ.* " The king Messiah shall rejoice;" and ver. 7. *Targ.* " Messiah the king."— Psal. xlv. 2. *Targ.* " Thy beauty, O king Messiah, is more excellent than that of the sons of men."—Psal. lxviii. and lxix. 32. [in *Shemoth Rabba*, Sect. xxxv.] " All nations shall bring gifts to the king Messiah." The same exposition is given in *Midrath, Esther*, Cap. i. ver. 1. and R. Obodia Haggaon on the place.— Psal. lxxii. 1. *Targ.* " Give the sentence of thy judgement to the king Messiah." And Rashi says of ver. 16. " Our *masters* interpret this of the cates, or dainties in the days of the Messiah, and expound the whole psalm concerning Messiah the king." It is evident, that in this psalm much light was communicated to the church of old, concerning the office, work, grace, compassion, and rule of the Messiah, with the calling and glorious access of the Gentiles to him.*—Psal. lxxx. 15. " The vineyard which thy right hand hath planted; and the

---

* Vid. *Midrash*, on the title of Psal. lxx. and Aben Ezra, *ibid.*

branch

branch thou haſt made ſtrong for thyſelf;" ſo our tranſlation; but all old tranſlations, as the *Seventy*, *vulgar Latin*, and *Syriac*, interpret the Hebrew term (בן) not in analogy to the preceding allegory of the *vine*, but from ver. 17. and render it, (ἐπι υιον ἀνθρωπȣ, *super* FILIUM *hominis*), *and upon the* SON *of man*, whom thou madeſt ſtrong for thyſelf. *Targ.* " And for the king MESSIAH, whom thou haſt ſtrengthened, or fortified, for thyſelf." And in ver. 17. he is expreſſly called (בן־אדם) " *the ſon of man*, whom thou madeſt ſtrong for thyſelf." The *Targum* here alſo acknowledgeth the true MESSIAH, for whoſe ſake the church is bleſſed, and by whom it is delivered; though ABEN EZRA ſuppoſes the words may reſpect *Meſſiah Ben Ephraim*, an *idol* of their own.

§ 21. We are now entering on the *prophets*, who " teſtified before-hand the ſufferings of Chriſt, and the glory that was to follow," (I. Pet. i. 11.) I deſign only to report ſome of the moſt eminent places, concerning which, we have the common ſuffrage of the Jews in their general application to the Meſſiah. Among theſe, that of ISAIAH ii. 2—4. occurs in the firſt place: " And it ſhall come to paſs in the laſt days, that the mountain of the Lord's houſe ſhall be eſtabliſhed in the top of the mountains, and ſhall be exalted above the hills, and all nations ſhall flow unto it; and many people ſhall go and ſay, Come ye, and let us go up unto the mountain of the Lord, to the houſe of the God of Jacob; and he will teach us of his ways, and we will walk in his paths; for out of Zion ſhall come forth a law, and the word of the Lord from Jeruſalem. And he ſhall judge among the nations, and ſhall rebuke many people, and they ſhall beat their ſwords into plough-ſhares." KIMCHI gives it for a rule, that the expreſſion, " *in the latter days*," always denotes the times of the MESSIAH, which I ſuppoſe is not liable to any exception. And as he giveth a tolerable expoſition of the "eſtabliſhing of the *mountain of the Lord* on the top of the mountains," aſſigning it to the glory of the worſhip of God, above all the falſe and idolatrous worſhip of the Gentiles, which they obſerved on the mountains and high

high places; fo, concerning thofe words, ver. 4. 'He
'fhall judge among the nations,' he faith, "This judge,
or he that judgeth, is the King Messiah." The like
faith Aben Ezra alfo on the fame place, and Jarchi on
the fame words in the prophecy of Micah. And as this is
true, fo, whereas Jehovah alone is mentioned in the foregoing verfes, to whom and no other this expreffion can
relate, how is it poffible for them to deny that the Messiah is the Lord, the *God of Jacob* alfo? For undeniably
it is *he* concerning whom it is faid, ' that he fhall judge
' among the nations;' and by their confeffion that it is
the Messiah who is the *Shophet*, the judge, here intended, they are plainly convinced out of their own mouths,
and their infidelity condemned by themfelves.

We have, then, evidently in thefe words *three articles*;
firft, that the Meffiah fhould be God and man; the God
of Jacob, who fhould in a bodily prefence judge the people,
and fend forth the law among the nations;—*fecondly*, that
the Gentiles fhould be called to faith in him, and the
obedience of his law;—*thirdly*, that the worfhip of the
Lord in the days of the Meffiah fhould be far more glorious than at any time whilft the firft temple was ftanding.
—Again, Ifa. iv. 2. *Targ.* " At that time fhall the Messiah of the Lord be for joy and honour." And this
prophecy is alfo by the moft learned of the Rabbins applied to the Messiah. Kimchi interprets (צמח) the
branch, by that of Jer. xxiii. 5. ' I will raife up to David
' a righteous *branch*, a *king* fhall reign and profper.'—
Ifa. ix. 6. *Targ.* " God the mighty one, abiding for ever,
Messiah, whofe peace fhall be multiplied unto us in his
days."—Chap. xi. 1. *Targ.* " And a king fhall come
forth from the fons of Jeffe, and Messiah fhall be
anointed from the fons of his fons;" i. e. his pofterity.—
Ver. 6. *Targ.* " In the days of the Messiah of Ifrael
peace fhall be multiplied in the earth—and the wolf fhall
dwell with the lamb." That this chapter contains a prophecy of the Meffiah and his kingdom, and that immediately and directly, all the Jews confefs; hence is that

part

part of their usual song in the evening of the sabbath.*
Chap. xvi. 1. *Targ.* " They shall bring their tribute unto
the MESSIAH of Israel." So also ver. 5. " Then shall
the throne of the MESSIAH of Israel be prepared in goodness."—Chap. xxviii. 5. *Targ.* " The MESSIAH of the
Lord of Hosts."—Chap. xliii. 1. *Targ.* " Behold my
servant the MESSIAH." And KIMCHI on this place,
" Behold my servant," adds, " That is, the King MES-
SIAH." And ABARBINEL confutes both R. SAADIAS and
ABEN EZRA with sharpness who were otherwise minded.
—Chap. xliii. 10. *Targ.* " My servant MESSIAH, in
whom I rest."—Chap. lii. 13. *Targ.* " Behold, my servant the MESSIAH shall prosper."

§ 22. Once more; Jer. xxiii. 5. *Targ.* " And I will
raise up to David, MESSIAH the righteous." This is he
who in the next verse is called " Jehovah our righteousness." The Jews generally agree that it is the Messiah
who is here intended. For the preservation of the name
of this righteous branch (יהוה צדקנו) ' Jehovah our righteousness,' we may bless God for the *original*; for the
old translations are either mistaken, corrupt, or perverted.†
—Chap. xxx. 21. *Targ.* " Their king shall be anointed
from amongst them; and their MESSIAH shall be revealed unto them."—Chap. xxiii. 13—15. *Targ.* " And the
people shall be yet gathered by the MESSIAH;" and a

* התנערי מעפר קומי
לבשי בגדי תפארתך עמי
על יד בן ישי ביתהלחמי
קרבה אל נפשי גאלה

Which, with a little variation, may be thus rendered:
    Shake thyself from dust, arise,
    People cloath'd in glorious guise,
    For from Bethl'hem Jesse's son
    Brings my soul redemption won.

† The Jews endeavour to evade the testimony, by producing
instances of the application of this name to other things; as the
altar built by Moses, the *arch*, and the *city* of Jerusalem. But
it is one thing to have the name of God *called* on a place or thing
to bring the occasion of it to remembrance, but another to say,
that this is *the name* of such a person, ' Jehovah our righteous-
' ness.'

prophecy

prophecy of him it is no doubt, as the 15th verse makes it evident, where all the Jews acknowledge him to be intended by the *branch* of righteousness, which shall spring up to David.—Hof. iii. 5. *Targ.* " And shall obey the MESSIAH, the son of David, their king."—Chap. xiv. 8. *Targ.* " They shall sit under the shadow of the MESSIAH."—Micah iv. 8. *Targ.* " And thou MESSIAH of Israel, who art hid because of the sins of the congregation of Zion, to thee the kingdom shall come." This *gloss*, I confess, draws upon the lees of *Talmudical rabbinism*; for they fancy that their MESSIAH was long since born, even at the *appointed time*, but is kept hid, they know not where, because of the sins of Israel.—Chap. v. 2. *Targ.* " Out of thee shall the MESSIAH come forth before me to exercise rule over Israel."—Zech. iii. 8. *Targ.* " Behold I bring forth my servant the MESSIAH, who shall be revealed."

§ 23. I have not insisted on these places, as if they were *all* the testimonies to the same purpose that might be taken out of the prophets, seeing they are a very small portion of the *predictions* concerning the person, grace, and kingdom of the Messiah, and not all those which are eminent in that kind; but because that they are such as wherein we have either the consent of all the Jews with us in their application, or we have the suffrage of the more ancient and authentic masters to reprove the perverseness of the *modern rabbins*.

And this is he whom we inquire after. One who was was promised from the foundation of the world to relieve mankind from under the state of sin and misery whereunto they were cast by their apostacy from God. This is he who from the first promise of him, or intimation of relief by him, was the hope, desire, comfort, and expectation of all that aimed at reconciliation and peace with God. Upon whom all their religion, faith, and worship, was founded, and in whom it centered. He, for whose sake, or for the bringing of whom into the world, Abraham and the Hebrews his posterity were separated to be a peculiar people distinct from all the nations of the earth;

in the faith of whom, the whole church from the days of Adam, that of the Jews especially, celebrated its myftical worship, endured persecution and martyrdom, waiting and praying continually for his appearance. He whom all the prophets preached and promised; describing before-hand his sufferings, with the glory that was to ensue. He of whose coming a catholic tradition was spread over the world, which the old serpent, with all his subtilty, was never able to obliterate.

Exercit. II.

APPEARANCES OF THE SON OF GOD UNDER THE OLD TESTAMENT.

§ 1. *Ends of the promises and prophecies concerning the Messiah. Other ways of revealing him.* § 2. *What meant in the Targums by* THE WORD OF GOD. § 3—8. *Various appearances of the Son of God to the patriarchs.* § 9. *Apprehensions of the Jewish masters on this subject.*

§ 1. WE have seen how plentifully God instructed the church of old by his prophets, in the knowledge of the person, office, and work of the Messiah; which he did, partly, that nothing might be wanting to the faith and consolation of believers; and partly that his righteous judgements in the rejection and ruin of those who obstinately refused him, might be justified and rendered glorious. Nor were these *promises* and *predictions* alone the means whereby God would manifest him to their faith. For,

There are two things concerning the Messiah, which are the pillars and foundation of the church;—his *divine nature*; and—his work of mediation in the *atonement* for sin which he was to make by the sacrifice of himself. For the declaration of these, to them who according to the promise looked for his coming, there were two special means graciously designed of God. The *one*, which referred to his atonement, was his instituted *worship*, and the various *sacrifices* which he appointed to be observed in the church, as types and representations of that one perfect oblation which he was to offer in the fulness of time. The *other way*, which concerns his divine person, was by these visions and appearances of the Son of God as the head of the church, granted to the fathers. In our inquiry after the *prognostics* of the *Messiah's* advent, we shall manifest, that a revelation was made of a *distinct person* in the Deity, who in a peculiar manner managed all the concernments of the church after the entrance of sin.

§ 2. There is frequent mention in the *Targumists* of (מימרא דיי) ' the *word of the Lord*;' and it first occurs in them on the first appearance of a *divine person*, after the sin and fall of man, Gen. iii. 8. The text is; ' And ' they heard *the voice* (קול *the word*) of the Lord God, (מתהלך) *walking* in the garden.' The participle ' *walking*,' may be as well referred to the ' *voice*,' as to *the Lord God;* (*vocem domini Dei ambulantem.*) And although the word (קול) which we render ' *voice*,' most commonly signifies (λογον προφορικον, *verbum prolatum*,) *the outward voice*, and *sound* thereof, yet, when applied to God, it frequently denotes his (λογον ενδιαθετον) *internal word*, his *almighty power*, whereby he effects whatever he pleaseth. This expression therefore may also denote (τον λογον τε Θεε, και' εξοχην) ' the *word of God*,' i. e. *God himself*, his *essential* word, the *person* of the Son; for our first parents heard this ' *Word walking* in the garden,' before they heard the outward sound of any voice or words whatever, [Gen. iii. 9.] The *Chaldee paraphrast* observing that some special presence of God is expressed in the words, renders them, " And they heard the voice of the *Word* of the Lord God *walking* in the garden." So all the *Targums*; and that of Jerusalem begins the next verse accordingly: " And (מימרא) *the word* of the Lord God called

called to Adam." And the expreſſion they afterwards make uſe of in places innumerable, and in ſuch a way as plainly to denote a *diſtinct perſon* in the Deity.*

The Jews diſcern that '*walking*' in this place relates immediately to *the voice*, and not to the Lord God, and therefore endeavour to evade the force of it, but to no tolerable purpoſe.

It is therefore *moſt probable* that in the great alteration which was now coming upon the whole creation of God, mankind being to be caſt out of covenant, the ſerpent and the earth being to be curſed, and a way of recovery for the elect of God to be revealed, that he, ' by whom all ' things were made,' and by whom all to be brought again to God were to be renewed, did, in an eſpecial and glorious manner, appear to our firſt parents, as he in whom this whole diſpenſation centered, and to whom it was committed. And as after the promiſe given he appeared (εν μορφη ανθρωπινη) *in an human ſhape*, to inſtruct the church in the myſtery of his future incarnation, and under the name of *angel*, to ſhadow out his office as *ſent* unto it, and employed in it by the Father; ſo here, *before* the promiſe, he diſcovered his diſtinct glorious perſon, as the eternal voice or word of the Father.

§ 3. Again, Gen. xviii. 1—3. the reaſon why *Abraham* ſat ' in the door of the tent,' given in the text, is,

---

* Vid. PHILON. *De Confuſione Linguarum.* That place Hoſ. i. 7. among others, is expreſs to this purpoſe, where the words of the prophet are thus rendered by the *Targumiſt*; " I will ſave (or redeem) them (במימרא) *by the word* of the Lord their God." And it is not unworthy conſideration, that as the wiſeſt and moſt contemplative of the *philoſophers* of old had many notions about (ο λογος αιδιος) *the eternal word*, which was with them, (δυναμις της ολης κτισεως ποιητικη) *the creative power of the univerſe*; to which purpoſe many ſayings might be obſerved out of PLATO, *Chalcidius*, PROCLUS, PLOTINUS, and others, whoſe expreſſions are imitated by our own writers, JUSTIN MARTYR, CLEMENS, ATHANAGORAS, TATIANUS, and many more. And indeed the ſame may be obſerved of the *Mahometans* themſelves; for this is the name they give to Jeſus in their *Alcoran* (כלמה אללה) *the Word of God*. *So prevalent* hath this notion of the SON OF GOD been in the world.

because it was about *the heat of the day*, or *as the day grew hot*; in opposition to, the time of God's appearance to *Adam*, which was in the *cool air of the day*. For as, when God comes to curse, nothing shall refresh the creature, however suitable for the purpose in its own nature; it shall wither in the *cool of the day*; so, when he comes to bless, nothing shall hinder the influence of it upon his creatures, however any thing in itself may, like the *heat of the day*, be troublesome or perplexing.

He lift up his eyes and looked, and, 'lo, three men 'stood by him.' It seems to be a *sudden* appearance that was made to him; he looked up and saw them; and this satisfied him that it was an *heavenly* apparition.

The business of God with Abraham at this time was to renew unto him the promise of the blessed seed, and to confine it to his posterity by Sarah; even now when he was utterly hopeless of it, and began to desire that Ishmael might be the heir. To this signal work of mercy was adjoined the intimation of an eminent effect of *vindictive justice*, wherein God would set forth an example of it to all ensuing generations, in the destruction of Sodom and Gomorrha. And both these were the proper works of him, on whom the *care of the church* was in an especial manner incumbent, all whose blessedness depended on that promise; and to whom the *rule of the world*, the present and future judgement of it, is committed; that is, the person of the Son. And hence in the *overthrow* of these cities, HE who is to be their future judge, is said to set forth an *ensample* of his future dealings with ungodly men. [II. Pet. ii. 6.]

A *distinction* of persons in the Deity, although not a precise *number* of them, is hence demonstrable. For it is evident that HE of the three who appeared unto Abraham, and to whom he made his supplication for the sparing of Sodom, was JEHOVAH, the judge of all the world, [Gen. xix. 22—25.] And yet all the *three* were set upon the work, that *one* being the prince and head of the embassy; as he who is Jehovah, is said to be sent by Jehovah, [Zech. ii. 8, 9.] In the story itself it is manifest that they were

all

all employed in the same work; *one* as *Lord* and prince, the other two as his ministering servants.—And this is further cleared in that expression of Moses, [Gen. xix. 24.] ' The Lord rained upon Sodom and Gomorrha brimstone ' and fire from the Lord, out of heaven.' There is, therefore, in this place, an appearance of God in an human shape; and of *one distinct person* in the Godhead; who now represented himself to Abraham in the form in which he would dwell amongst men, when *of his seed* he would be made flesh. This was one signal means whereby Abraham ' *saw his day and rejoiced*,' which himself ascribes to his *pre-existence*, and not the promise of his *coming*. [John viii. 56—58.] A solemn *prelude* it was to his taking flesh, a *revelation* of his divine nature and person, and a *pledge* of his coming in human nature, to converse with men.

§ 4. Gen. xxxii. 24, 26, 30. ' And Jacob was left ' alone,' &c. This story is twice noticed in the scripture afterwards; once by Jacob himself, [Gen. xlviii. 15, 16.] and once by the prophet Hosea, [chap. xii. 3, 4.] In the first place he is called a *man*; ' there *appeared a man*;' in the second, Jacob calls him an *angel*, ' *the angel that re-* ' *deemed me*;' and in the third, he is expressly said to be God, ' *the Lord of hosts*.'

Jacob was now passing with his whole family into the land of Canaan, to take seisure of it by virtue of the promise, on the behalf of his posterity. At the very entrance of it, he is met by his greatest adversary, with whom he had a severe contest about the promise and inheritance itself. This was his brother Esau, who, coming against him with a power, which he was in no way able to withstand, he feared, would utterly destroy both his person and posterity, [ver. 11.] In the promise about which their contest was, the blessed seed, with the whole church state and worship of the Old Testament, was included; so that it was the greatest controversy, and had the greatest weight depending on it, of any that ever was amongst the sons of men. Wherefore to settle Jacob's right, to preserve him with his title and interest, *he* who was principally concerned in the whole matter, appeared to him.

This

This *man* in appearance, this *angel* in office, was in name and nature ' *God* over all, blessed for ever.' For, in the first place, Jacob prays solemnly unto him for his blessing, [Gen. xxxii. 26.] and refuses to let him go, or to cease making his earnest supplications until he had blessed him. Accordingly he *blesseth* him, and giveth him a *double token* of it—the touch of his thigh, and the change of his name—giving him a name to denote his prevalency with God; that is, with himself. From hence Jacob concludes that he had *seen God*; and calls the name of the place, the *face of God*. In the second place, [Gen. xlviii. 16.]—besides that he *invocates* the angel for his *presence* with, and *blessing* on the children of Joseph; which cannot regard any but God himself, without gross idolatry—it is evident that the angel who redeemed him, [ver. 16.] is the same with *the God who fed him*; that is, the God of his fathers.

And this is yet more evident in the prophet; for with regard to this story of his power over the angels, he says, ' he had power with GOD;' and proves it because he had ' power over the ANGEL, and prevailed.' And he shews whereby he thus prevailed; it was by ' weeping ' and making supplications unto him,' which he neither did, nor lawfully might do, to a created angel. Again, this angel was he whom he found, or ' who found him ' in Bethel,' [Gen. xxviii. 20—22. and xxxv. 1.] which was no other than HE to whom *Jacob made his vow*, and with whom he entered into solemn covenant, that he should be ' *his God*.' And therefore the prophet adds expressly in the last place, [Hos. xii. 5.] that it was the *Lord God of hosts* whom he intended.

From what has been spoken, it is evident, that he who appeared to Jacob, with whom he earnestly wrestled, by tears and supplications, was *God*; and because he was sent as the *angel* of God, it must be some distinct person in the *Deity*, condescending to that office; and appearing in the form of a *man*, he represented his future assumption of human nature. And by all this, did God instruct the church in the mystery of the ' person of the MESSIAH,' and who

who it was that they were to look for in the bleffing of the promifed feed.

§ 5. Exod. iii. 2—6. 'And Mofes came to the moun-
' tain, &c.' He who is here revealed, affirms of himfelf, that he is 'the God of Abraham,' [ver. 16.] and alfo defcribes himfelf by the glorious name—I am that I am, [ver. 14.] in whofe name and authority, Mofes dealt with Pharaoh in the deliverance of the people, and whom they were to ferve on that mountain, upon their coming out of Egypt. He, whofe (רצין) *merciful good-will* Mofes prays for, [Deut. xxxiii. 16.] And yet he is exprefsly called an *angel*, [ver. 2.] namely, the angel of the covenant, the great angel of the prefence of God, in whom was the name and nature of God; and he thus appeared—that the church might know and confider *who* it was that was to work out their fpiritual and eternal falvation, of which that deliverance was a type and pledge.

§ 6. Exod. xix. 18—20. ' And mount Sinai was al-
' together on a fmoak, &c.' As to him that prefided and ruled the whole action, fome Chriftians think it was a *created* angel, reprefenting God, and fpeaking in his name. But if this be fo, we have no certainty of any thing that is affirmed in the fcripture, that it may be referred directly and immediately to God; but we may, when we pleafe, fubftitute a *delegated angel* in his room. For in no place, not in that concerning the creation of the world, is God himfelf more exprefsly fpoken of. Befides, the pfalmift [Pfal. lxviii. 17.] affirms, that when thofe chariots of God were on mount Sinai, Jehovah himfelf was in the midft of them. And this prefence of God the Hebrews varioufly call (יאקר, שכינה, הכבוד) whereby they now underftand a *majeftical* and *fanctifying* prefence. In reality it intends him who is the ' brightnefs of his Father's glory, and the ' exprefs image of his perfon;' who was delegated to this work, as the great angel of the covenant, giving the law in the ftrength of the Lord, in the majefty of the name of the Lord his God.

§ 7. Exod. xxiii. 20—22. ' Behold I fend an angel,' &c. The angel here promifed, is he who went in the midft of the people in the wildernefs, whofe glory appeared among them. It is faid to the people concerning him (השמר לפניו) "*beware of him,*" or rather, *take heed to thyfelf before him,* before his face, in his prefence. The verb (שמר) in *Niphal,* is *fibi cavit; cave tibi.* And this is the caution that is ufually given to the people, requiring that reverence and awe which is due to the holinefs of the prefence of God. It is added, (ושמע בקולו) "*and obey his voice.*" This is the great precept which is folemnly given, and fo often reiterated in the law, with reference to God himfelf. Again, (אל תמר בו) "*provoke him not,*" or rebel not againft him. This is the ufual word whereby God expreffeth the tranfgreffion of his covenant; a rebellion that can be committed only againft *God alone.*—Of thefe precepts a *two-fold reafon* is given, whereof the *firft* is taken from the fovereign authority of the angel; 'for he 'will not *pardon* your tranfgreffions;' that is, as Jofhua 'afterwards tells the fame people, 'he is an *holy* God, he 'is a *jealous* God, he will not forgive your tranfgreffions, 'nor your fins,' [Jofh. xxiv. 19.] namely, fins of rebellion, that break and difannul his covenant. And who can *forgive fins* but God? To fuppofe here a created angel, is to open a door to idolatry; for he, in whofe power it is abfolutely to pardon fin and punifh it, muft certainly be *worfhipped* with religious adoration. Another reafon is taken from his *name,* 'for my name is in him.' A more *excellent name* than any of the angels enjoy, [Heb. i. 4.] He is God, JEHOVAH, that is his name, and his nature anfwereth thereto. Hence [ver. 22.] it is added, 'if, indeed, thou obey his voice, and do all that I fpeak." His voice is the voice of God, in his fpeaking God fpeaketh. Moreover, [Exod. xxxiii. 14, 15.] God fays, concerning this angel (פני) *my prefence, my face* fhall go with thee; which prefence Mofes calls his *glory,* [ver. 18.] his *effential* glory, which was manifefted to him, [chap. xxxiv. 6.] though but obfcurely, in comparifon of what it was to them, who, in his human nature (wherein dwelt the 'fulnefs of the Godhead bodily,' [Col. ii. 9.] beheld his glory, 'the glory as of the only begotten of

'the

'the father,' [John i. 14.] For this face of God is he, whom if any one seeth, 'he seeth the Father,' [John xiv. 9.] becaufe he is 'the brightnefs of his glory, and 'the exprefs image of his perfon,' [Heb. i. 3.] he who accompanied the people in the wildernefs, [I. Cor. x. 4.] and whofe *merciful good pleafure* towards them Mofes prayed for [Deut. xxxiii. 16.] that is, the 'Father of 'lights, from whom defcendeth every good and perfect 'gift,' [Jam. i. 17.] Thefe things evidently exprefs *God*, and none other; and yet he is faid to be an *angel* fent of God, in his name, and to his work; fo that he *can be* no other, but a certain perfon of the Deity, who accepted of this delegation, and was therein revealed to the church, as he who was to take upon him the feed of Abraham, and to be their eternal Redeemer.

§ 8. Josh. v. 13—15. 'And it came to pafs,' &c. The appearance here is of a *man*, a man of war, as God is called, [Exod. xv. 3.] armed with his fword drawn in his hand, as a token of the bufinefs he came about. At firft fight Joshua apprehends him to be a *man only*, which occafioned his inquiry, Art thou for us, or for our adverfaries? which difcovers his courage and undaunted magnanimity; for doubtlefs the appearance was *auguft* and glorious. But he anfwers to this whole queftion, (לא) *I am not*; that is, *not a man* either of your party, or of the enemy's, but quite another perfon, 'the prince of the 'hoft of the Lord.' And this was another illuftrious manifeftation of the Son of God to the church of old, accompanied with many inftructive circumftances. As

1. From the form wherein he appeared, namely, of a *man*, as a pledge of his future incarnation.

2. The *title* that he affumes to himfelf, 'the Captain of 'the Lord of hofts,' he to whom the guidance and conduct of them to reft, not only temporal, but eternal, was committed; whence the apoftle, in allufion to this place and title, calls him 'the Captain of our Salvation,' [Heb. ii. 10.] and

3. The *perfon* to whom he fpake, when he gave himfelf this title, was the 'captain of the people,' at that time,

time, teaching both him and them that there was another supreme captain of their *eternal* deliverance.

4. From the *time and place* of his appearance, which was upon the first entrance of the people to *Canaan*, and the first opposition they met with; so engaging his presence with the church in all things which oppose them in their way to eternal rest.

5. From the *adoration* and worship which Joshua gave him, which he accepted of, contrary to the duty and practice of created angels, [Rev. xix. 10. and xxii. 8, 9.]

6. From the *prescription of the ceremonies* expressing religious reverence, ' put off thy shoes,' with the reason annexed, ' for the place whereon thou standest (קדש הוא) *it is holiness*, made so by the presence of God; a precept similar to that given to Moses by the God of Abraham, Isaac, and Jacob, [Exod. iii. 5.]—By all these things was the church instructed in the person, nature, and office of the Son of God; even in the mystery of his eternal distinct subsistence in the Deity, his future incarnation and condescension to the office of being the head, and Saviour of his church.

These manifestations of the Son of God to the church of old, as the angel or messenger of the Father, subsisting in his own Divine person, are all of them revelations of the promised seed, the great and only Saviour and Deliverer of the church in his eternal pre-existence, and pledges of his future incarnation, for the accomplishment of the whole work committed to him. And many other instances of the like nature may be added out of the former and latter prophets, which, because in most important circumstances they are coincident with these, need not here particularly be insisted on.

§ 9. One signal instance of the Jewish masters' apprehensions, concerning the Divine appearances, as an evidence of the truth insisted on, shall be here related in the words of Moses Nechmanides Gerundensis, on Exod. xxiii. His words run thus: " This angel, if we speak exactly, is the angel the *Redeemer*, concerning whom it is written, *my name is in him*, [Exod. xxiii. 21.] that angel,

angel, I say, who said to Jacob, I am the God of Bethel, [Gen. xxxi. 13.] He, of whom it is said, And *God* called to Moses out of the bush, [Exod. iii. 4.] And he is called an *angel*, because he governeth the world. For it is written, [Deut. vi. 21.] *The Lord our God* brought us out of Egypt; and elsewhere, [Numb. xx. 16.] He sent his *angel*, and brought us out of Egypt. Moreover, it is written, [Isa. lxiii. 9.] And the *angel* of his face *(presence)* saved them, namely, that angel who is the face of God; of whom it is said, [Exod. xxxiii. 14.] My face shall go before thee, and I will cause thee to rest. Lastly, it is that angel of whom the prophet speaks, [Mal. iii. 1.] And the *Lord*, whom ye seek, shall suddenly ' come ' to his temple; the *angel* of the covenant, whom ye de- ' light in.' His following words are to the same purpose: Mark diligently what is the meaning of these words, ' *My* ' *face* shall go before thee.' For Moses and the Israelites always desired the *chief angel*; but who that was, they could not truely understand; for, neither could they learn of any others, nor obtain it by prophecy. But the *face of God* signifieth *God himself*; as all interpreters acknowledge. But no man can have the least knowledge hereof, except he be skilled in the mysteries of the law." He adds, moreover, " My face shall go before thee; that is, the angel of the covenant, whom ye desire; in whom my face shall be seen; of whom it is said, in an acceptable time have I heard thee; my name is in him; I will cause thee to rest; or cause that he shall be gentle and kind to thee; nor shall lead thee with rigour, but quietly and mercifully."—This R. Moses bar Nachman wrote about the year 1220, in Spain, and died at Jerusalem 1260, and is one of the chief masters of the Jews. There are many things occurring in his writings, beyond the common rate of their present apprehensions; and in the places above cited, he plainly everts one of the principal foundations of their present infidelity. For he not only grants, but contends and proves, that the angel spoken of was *God*, and being sent of God, as his angel, he must be a *distinct person* in the Deity, as we have proved. The reason,

reason, indeed, he fixeth on, why he is called an *angel*—because he governeth the world—though true in itself, is not so proper. For he is so called, because of his eternal designation, and actual delegation by the Father, to the work of saving the church, in all conditions, from first to last. And as he acknowledgeth, that his being called the *face of God*, proves him to be *God*, so it doth no less evidently evince his personal distinction from *him* whose *face* he is; that is, ' the brightness of his glory and the ' express image of his person.' And what he adds of the mercy and benignity which, by the appointment of God, he exerciseth towards his people, is remarkably suitable to the tenderness and mercy which the great Captain of our salvation exerciseth, by God's appointment, towards all those whom he leads and conducts to glory.

Exercit. 3.

THE FAITH OF THE JEWS CONCERNING THE MESSIAH.

§ 1. *The state and expectations of the Jews at the birth of Christ.* § 2. *The faith of their forefathers lost among them.* § 3. *The reason why the true Messiah was rejected by them.* § 4. *Their state after this.* § 5. *The things concerning the Messiah mysterious; yet seeming inconsistencies reconciled in the gospel.* § 6. *The notion of the Jews about two Messiahs. Messiah Ben Joseph.* § 7. *Messiah Ben David. The faith and expectations of the Jews concerning him.* § 8. *Their perplexity about the time of their coming.* § 9. *A description of him and his kingdom, out of Maimonides.* § 10. *Ground and reason of their present unbelief.* 1. *Ignorance of their miserable state by nature.* § 11. 2. *Ignorance of acceptable righteousness, and of the judgement of God concerning sin.* § 12. 3. *Of the nature and*

and end of the law. § 13. 4. *Carnal affections.* § 14. 5. *Their envy against the Gentiles, which is increased by their oppressions.* § 15. *Conclusion.*

§ 1. WE have proved the promise of a *person* to be born, and anointed to the work of relieving mankind from sin and misery, and to bring them back to God. And what *kind* of person he was to be, we have also shewed. It now remains, that we consider the faith of the Jews concerning him. That the minds of men were intently fixed on the coming of the MESSIAH, the last of the prophets clearly testifies, [Mal. iii. 1.] 'The Lord, 'whom ye seek; the angel of the covenant, whom you are 'desiring, shall come suddenly.' As the time of his coming drew nigh, this *expectation* was increased and heightened; so that they continually looked out after him, as if he were to enter among them every moment. No sooner did any one make an appearance of something extraordinary, but instantly they were ready to say, Is not this the MESSIAH? This gave advantage to various impostors, as *Theudas*, and *Judas* of Galilee, to deceive many to their ruin. Yea, the Jews had divulged such report of their *expectations*, with the predictions and prophecies they were built upon, that the whole world took notice of it. This was the state of the Jewish church, not long before the destruction of the second temple. And so fixed they were in their opinion, that he was to come about that season, that during the last desolating siege of the city, they looked *every day* when he would come and save them.

§ 2. But, together with this earnest expectation and desire, they had utterly *lost the sight and faith of their forefathers* about the nature, work, and office of the promised MESSIAH. For, being grown carnal, and minding only things earthly and present, they utterly overlooked the *spiritual genealogy* of the 'seed of the woman,' from the first promise; and wresting all predictions to their ambitious, covetous, corrupt inclinations and interests,

terests, they fancied him to themselves, as one that was to deliver them from *outward troubles*, and to satisfy them with the glory and desirable things of this world, without respect to *sin*, or the *curse*, or deliverance from them. And hence the Sadduces, who denied the immortality of the soul, and consequently all rewards and punishments in another world; yet *no less desired* the coming of the Messiah, than the Pharisees and their disciples. And the truth is, they had brought their principles to a better consistency than the others had done. For if the promised Messiah was only to procure them the good things of *this world*, and whilst they lived in it, it was in vain to look for another world to come, and the blessings thereof. To look for *eternal life*, and yet to confine the promise of the seed to the things of this life only, there was neither solid ground, nor colourable reason. So that the Pharisees laid down the principle, and the Sadduces naturally drew their conclusion from it. Some, in the mean time, among them, God's favoured secret ones, as Simeon, Anna, Joseph, Zecharia, and Elizabeth; but especially the blessed Virgin, with many more, retained, no doubt, the *ancient faith* of their forefathers. But the *body* of the people, with their *leaders*, being either *flagitiously* wicked, or *superstitiously* proud, fancied a Messiah suited to their own lusts and desires. And this *prejudicate opinion* of a terrene, outward, glorious kingdom, was that which—working in them a neglect of those spiritual and *eternal* purposes for which he was promised—hardened them to an utter rejection of the true Messiah when he came to them.

§ 3. That this was the ground on which they rejected the promised Messiah, is evident from the story of the gospel. But after they had done this, and murdered the Prince of Life, to justify themselves in their wickedness and unbelief, they still with all earnestness looked after *such* a Messiah as they had framed in their own imagination: and herein they grew more earnest and furious than ever; for they had not only their own false pre-conceived opinion strengthened by their carnal interests and desire of earthly things to actuate them, but also their

repu-

reputation and pretence to the love and favour of God, to heighten them in their prefumptions. For this is the force of pride and carnal wifdom, to purfue thofe mifcarriages with violence wherein they had been wickedly engaged, and to lay hold on any pretence that may feem to juftify them in what they have done; and on this account they expofed themfelves as a prey to every feducer, who made the leaft appearance of being fuch a Meffiah as they thought fit to receive. This at laft drove them to a fecond fhipwreck in the bufinefs of BARCHOCHEBA, who, pretending himfelf to be their Meffiah fent to deliver them from the *Roman* yoke, and to fet up a kingdom amongft them,* drew them all the world over into that fedition, outrage, and war, which ended in an almoft univerfal extirpation of them from the face of the earth.

§ 4. From this time forward the remaining Jews, with their pofterity, utterly rejected the faith of their father Abraham, and the reft of their progenitors, who thereby obtained a *good report*, ' that they pleafed God.' A Meffiah promifed to *Adam*, the common father of us all, one that fhould be a *fpiritual* Redeemer from fin and mifery, a *Goel*, or redeemer from death and wrath, a peace-maker between God and man; one that fhould work out *everlafting falvation*, the great bleffing in which all the nations of the earth were to have an intereft, a *fpiritual* and eternal prophet, prieft, and king, God and man in one perfon; they neither looked for any more, nor defired. A *temporal* king and deliverer, promifed to *themfelves alone*, to give them eafe, dominion, wealth, and power, they would now have, or none at all. They would not think it thankworthy towards God himfelf to fend them a Meffiah to deliver them from fin.

§ 5. Our apoftle tells us, [I. Tim. iii. 16.] ' That
' without controverfy, great is the *myftery of godlinefs*, God
' was manifefted in the flefh, juftified in the fpirit, feen
' of angels, preached to the Gentiles, believed on in the
' world, received up into glory.' All things which con-

* Vid. Talm. Tract. Saned. Dift. Cheleck.

cern the Messiah, his perfon, office, and work, are exceedingly *myſterious*, as containing the principal effect of the wifdom and goodnefs of God, and the facred depths of the counfel of his will. Hence the things fpoken of in the Old Teſtament are to carnal reafon full of feeming inconfiftencies; as for inftance, it is promifed of him, that he ſhould be the *feed of the woman*, [Gen. iii. 15.] *of the feed of Abraham*, [Gen. xxii. 18.] and of the *poſterity of David*; and yet that his name fhould be, the mighty God, the everlasting Father, the Prince of peace, [Ifa. ix. 6.] and of him it is faid, ' Thy throne, O God, is for ever and ever,' [Pfal. xlv. 6.] and that he is the ' Lord our righteoufnefs,' [Jer. xxiii. 6.] and that he is the ' Lord of hofts,' [Zech. ii. 8.] Moreover it is declared, that he fhall ' fit upon his ' throne for ever,' and ' reign, whilft his enemies are ' made his footftool,' [Ifa. ix. 7. Pfalm ii. 7, 8. xlv. 6, 7.] and yet, that he fhall be *cut off*, [Dan. ix. 26.] that he fhall be ' pierced in his hands and feet,' [Pfalm xxii. 16.] ' *ſlain* by the fword of God,' [Zech. xiii. 7.] and that ' in his *death* he fhall have his *grave* made among the ' wicked,' [Ifa. liii. 9.] Alfo, that he ' fhall come with ' great glory, and on the *clouds of heaven*, [Dan. vii. 13, 14.] and that he ' fhall come *lowly*, riding on an afs, ' and a colt the foal of an afs,' [Zech. ix. 9.] That the ' *foul* of the Lord was *well pleaſed* with him, and always ' delighted in him,' [Ifa. xliii. 1.] and yet that it ' plea' fed him to *bruiſe* him, and put him to grief, [Ifa. liii. 10.] ' to forfake him,' [Pfal. xxii. 1.] That he was to be a ' king and prieft upon his throne,' [Zech. vi. 13.] and yet thefe things were literally confiftent, the kingdom being annexed to the family of David, and the priefthood to the pofterity of Aaron, by divine conftitution; that he ſhould be honoured and worſhipped of all nations, [Pfalm xlv. 11, 12. lxxii. 10, 11, 15.] and yet that he fhould be rejected and defpifed as one altogether undefirable, [Ifa. liii. 3.] That he ' fhould ftand and ' feed, or rule in the name and majefty of God,' [Mic. v. 4.] and yet complains, ' I am a worm, and no man,

' a re-

'a reproach of men; and defpifed of the people,' [Pfalm xxii. 6.] All which, with fundry others of the like nature concerning his office and work, are *clearly reconciled* in the *New Teftament*, and their concurrence in the perfon of our Lord Jefus Chrift openly and fully declared.

At the time of his coming, the Jews were generally as ignorant of thefe things as Nicodemus was of *regeneration*; they knew not how they could be. And therefore whenever our Saviour intimated to them his divine nature, they were filled with rage and madnefs, [John viii. 58, 59.] They would ftone him, becaufe, being a man, he declared himfelf to be God, [John x. 30, 31, 33.] and yet, when he proved it to them that the MESSIAH was to be fo, (inafmuch as, being David's fon, David in the fpirit called him Lord) they were confounded, not being able to anfwer him a word. [Matt. xxii. 42—46.] When he told them that the Son of Man, the MESSIAH, muft be *lifted up*, that is, in his death on the crofs, they objected to him out of the law, that 'Chrift abideth for ever,' [John xii. 34.] and they knew not how to *reconcile* thefe things. Hence fome of his own difciples thought he could not be the Meffiah, when they faw that he died, [Luke xxiv. 20, 21.] and the beft of them feem to have expected an outward temporal kingdom. But of all thefe difficulties and feeming inconfiftencies, there is a bleffed *reconciliation* revealed in the gofpel, and an application made of them to the perfon of the Lord Jefus, the office he bore, and the work that he accomplifhed.

§ 6. Whereas the fcripture hath declared to us fuch a Meffiah, as fhould have the natures of *God* and *man* in one perfon, which perfon fhould in the nature of man fuffer and die, and reign for fpiritual ends and purpofes; they have rejected the *divine nature* of this perfon, and fplit that which remaineth into *two perfons*—to the one they affigned one part of his work, as to *fuffer* and *die*; to the other, another part, to *conquer* and *reign* according to their carnal apprehenfions of thefe things—they have, I fay, feigned *two Meffiahs*, between whom they have diftributed the *whole work* of him who is promifed, according to their grofs conception of it. And one of thefe is to come, they fay, before the other, to prepare his way for him. This firft they call Meffiah BEN JOSEPH, becaufe he is to be of the *tribe of Ephraim*; the other Meffiah, BEN DAVID. And they dream, that one ARMILLUS fhall conquer many nations, fight againft Jerufalem, flay Meffiah BEN JOSEPH, and afterwards be confumed with fire from heaven, through the power of BEN DAVID. And this fhall be the end of Meffiah BEN JOSEPH, or EPHRAIM.—Thus do they at their pleafure difpofe of this creature of their own; for having framed him themfelves, he is their own to do with him what they pleafe, alive or dead.

We need not ftay long in the removal of this *Mormo* out of our way; fhould they invent twenty other Meffiahs, as they have done this, and which, on the fame grounds, and with as good authority, they may, the cafe would ftill be the fame. Who gave them power to fubftitute themfelves in the place of God, to give *new promifes*, to appoint *new Saviours*, and to invent new ways of deliverance? The fcripture is utterly filent of any fuch perfon, nor have they any *Antetalmudical* tradition concerning him. And what their mafters have invented in the *Talmuds*, is of no more authority than what they coin every day themfelves; the truth is, this whole ftory of ARMILLUS and BEN JOSEPH is a *Talmudical romance*; the one the *giant*, and the other the *knight*. But thefe fictions *feria ducunt*. Poor creatures are hardened by them, to their eternal deftruction. But is the world bound to believe what every one, whom they are pleafed to call *Rabbi*, can imagine, though never fo contrary to the principles of that religion, which themfelves pretend to own and profefs? So, indeed, fome of them feem to fay; for they fcruple not to affert, that if their mafters teach the "*right hand to be the left*;" yea, "*heaven to be hell*," yet their authority is not to be queftioned. But God, I hope, of his great goodnefs, will not fuffer poor mankind to be always fo deluded. All the promifes of God, all the prophecies from the foundation of the world, concern only *one Messiah*, of the seed of Abraham, of the tribe of Judah, and of the family of David. All the faith of the church of old, as we have proved, respected that *one* only. And who will lay any weight upon what is spoken, or promised, concerning him, if the Jews have power to invent *another* at their pleasure?

Again, their masters have not only dealt dishonestly and blasphemously, but *foolishly* also in this matter, in that they have not suited their *own creature* to the ends for which they had made him. The end, as was shewed before, why they advanced this imagination, was, to give continuance to what is spoken in scripture, or retained by themselves in tradition, concerning the *sufferings* of the Messiah. And it is somewhat strange to me, that having raised up this BEN JOSEPH, they did not use him *worse* than they have done; but by a foolish pity have spoiled their own whole design. They have a tradition among themselves, that the Messiah must " bear a *third part* of the afflictions, or persecutions, that ever were, or shall be in the world." And what proportion doth a man's being *slain in battle*, where his army is victorious (which is all the hardship this BEN JOSEPH is to meet with) bear to the afflictions which befell the church in every age? And it is mere lost labour, to compare the death of this warrior with what is delivered in scripture, concerning the Messiah. Every one, not judicially blinded, must needs see, that there is no affinity between them.

The *fifty-third* chapter of Isaiah is acknowledged by the *Targum*, and sundry of the principal masters of their faith, to be a prophecy concerning HIM. Now, the person there spoken of, is one whom the JEWS are to *reject* and *despise*, whom God is to afflict and bruise, by causing the " sins of the whole church to meet upon him." One, who by his sufferings, is to fulfil the pleasure of the Lord, making his soul an offering for sin, justifying the elect, and conquering Satan by his death. On the contrary, their fictitious Messiah is to be *honoured of all the Jews*, to raise arms to fight a battle, and therein, after the manner of other men, to be slain. So that a story was never worse told, nor to less purpose. No other use can be made of it, that I know of, but only to consider in it the blindness of poor obstinate sinners given up to hardness of heart, and a spirit of folly, for the rejection of him, whom God *sealed, anointed,* and *sent* to be the Saviour of the world. Leaving him, therefore, in the embraces of this cloud, we may,

§ 7. Consider the other expected MESSIAH, whom they call BEN DAVID, in whom principally they place their confidence. First, therefore, they contend, that he shall be a *mere man*; and there is nothing that they strive to avoid more than the testimonies of scripture, which shew that the promised Messiah was to be God and man in one person. They contend also, that he shall be born after the *manner of all other men.* About the *place* of his birth they are not fully agreed; for although they all acknowledge the prophecy of Micah, about *Bethlehem,* to relate to him, [Mic. v. 2.] yet knowing that *town* now to have been desolate for many generations, and waste without inhabitants (which would seem to prove that he *is come already)* they contend, that it is said he shall be born at *Bethlehem*; because he is to spring of David, who was born there; for of the tribe of Judah, and family of David, he must proceed; although they have neither distinction of tribes, nor succession of families, left in the world amongst them! To relieve themselves from that difficulty, they feign that he shall restore to them all their genealogies.

§ 8. About the *time* of his coming they are woefully perplexed. But many tokens they have of it, when it doth come; for they heap up, out of some allegorical passages in the scripture, such stupendous prodigies, as never were, nor shall be in the world. One of the principal of them is ' the sounding of the great trumpet, which all ' Israel shall hear, and the world tremble at,' [from Isa. xxvii. 13.] To this they add the " finding of the *ark* and *sacred fire."* His *office,* when he comes, is to be a *king,* to which he shall be anointed by *them,* when they are gathered together. And the work he is to do, is—*in war,* to fight with ARMILLUS, *Gog*, and *Magog*, to conquer the Edomites and Ishmaelites; that is, the Romish Christians, and Turks or Saracens; and in so doing, to erect a glorious kingdom at Jerusalem.—In peace he is to rule righteously, not only over Israel, but also all the nations of the world; who, if they have any difference amongst them, shall refer all to his determination and umpirage.— *In religion*, he shall build the *third temple*, mentioned by Ezekiel; restore the sacrifices, and cause the law of Moses to be most strictly observed. But that which is the head of all, he shall free the Jews from their captivity, restore them to their own land, make princes and lords of them all, giving them the wealth of all nations, either conquered by him, or brought voluntarily to him; feast them on *Behemoth*, *Zis*, and the wine of paradise; so that they shall see want and poverty no more.

This is the substance of their persuasion, concerning his coming, person, office, and work. *When* he shall come, whether he shall live *always*, or die at an hundred years old; whether he shall have *children*, and if he have, whether they shall succeed him in his throne; whether the Jews that are dead, shall rise at his coming, and their *galgal*, or *rolling* in the earth, from all parts of the world, into the land of Canaan, shall then happen or no; whether the *general resurrection* shall not succeed then immediately upon his reign, or at least within *forty* years after; or how long it will be to the end of the world, they are not at all agreed. But this is the substance of their persuasion and expectation; that he shall be a *mere man*— that the deliverance which he shall effect, shall be *mighty wars*, wherein the Jews shall be always victorious—and that, in the dominion and rule which they shall have over all nations, the *third temple* shall be built, the law of Moses be observed by him and them, and the *Noachical* precepts be imposed on all others. As for any *spiritual salvation* from sin and the curse of the law, of justification and righteousness by him, or the procurement of *grace and glory*, they utterly reject all thoughts about them.

§ 9.

§ 9. With these opinions, many of them have mixed prodigious *fancies*, rendering their estate under the Messiah in this world not much inferior to that which MAHOMET hath promised to his followers in another. And some of them, on the other hand, endeavour to pare off what superfluities they can spare, and to render their folly as plausible as they are able. Wherefore, that it may appear what is the *utmost height* of their conceptions in this matter, and what the most contemplative persons amongst them fix upon, I subjoin a description of him and his *kingdom*, in the words of MAIMONIDES, one of the wisest and soberest persons that hath been amongst them, since their last fatal dispersion. Observing the fond and frivolous imaginations of their *Talmudical* masters, about the Messiah, he gives many rules and instructions about the right understanding of their sayings, to free them from open impieties and contradictions; to which he subjoins, as he supposeth, the true notion of the MESSIAH and his kingdom, in the ensuing words: " As the days of the Messiah, they are the time when the kingdom shall be restored to Israel, and they shall return to *Palestine*. And this king shall be potent, the metropolis of whose kingdom shall be *Sion*; and his name shall be famous to the uttermost parts of the earth. He shall be greater than Solomon, and with him shall the nations make peace, and yield him obedience, because of his justice, and the miracles that he shall perform. If any one shall rise against him, God shall give him up into his hand to be destroyed. All the scripture declares his happiness, and the happiness we shall have by him. Howbeit, nothing in the nature of things shall be changed, only Israel shall have the kingdom; for so our wise men say expressly, There is no difference between these days and the days of the Messiah; but only the subduing the nations under us." So, indeed, says R. SAMUEL, and some others of them.—But he goes on, " In those days victuals shall be had at an easy rate, as if the earth brought forth cates and clothes." And afterwards; " The Messiah shall die, and his son, and his son's son, shall reign after him; but his kingdom shall endure long, and men shall live long in those days; so that some think his kingdom shall continue a thousand years. But the days of the Messiah are not so much to be desired, that we may have store of corn and wealth, ride on horses, and drink wine with music; but for the society and conversation of good men, the knowledge and righteousness of the king, and that then, without wearisomness, trouble, or constraint, the whole law of Moses shall be observed."*

This is the sum of the creed of the *most sober* part of the Jews, concerning the Messiah, whom they look and long for; for the same author tells us, that there were *very few* so minded; generally they look after nothing but dominion, wealth, and pleasure. But all of them own him a *temporal king*, a mighty warrior, subduing the nations to the Jews; a furious *Camillus*, or an ALEXANDER, or a CÆSAR; of redemption from sin, death, and hell; of pardon of sin, justification, and righteousness; of *eternal salvation* by him, they know nothing, they believe nothing. MAIMONIDES thinks, indeed, that his kingdom shall long continue; not like MANASSE of late, who supposeth, that it might not abide above *forty years*, and those immediately preceding the day of judgement.— When he *comes*, let them make their best of him; we have already received the ' *Captain of our Salvation*.'

§ 10. But what seduced them into these *low, carnal,* and earthly imaginations?

1. *Ignorance of their miserable condition by nature*, both as to sin and wrath, justly claims the first place. The Messiah, as we proved at large, was first promised to relieve mankind from that state, whereinto they were cast by the apostacy of Adam, the common root and parent of them all. Such as are men's apprehensions of that condition; such also will be their thoughts concerning the Messiah, who was promised to be a deliverer from it. They who know themselves to be cast out of the favour of God, by sin, made *obnoxious* to his eternal displeasure, and disabled

---

* Maimon, in Tract. Saned. Cap. x.

to do any thing that shall pleafe him (as being caft into a
ftate of *univerfal enmity* againft him) muft needs look on
the Meffiah, promifed through the grace, goodnefs, and
wifdom of God, to be one that muft, by fuitable ways
and means, free them from fin and wrath; procure for
them the favour of God; enable them to ferve him again
acceptably, and fo bring them at length to their *chief end*,
the everlafting enjoyment of himfelf. Upon the matter,
the Jews know no mifery, but what confifts in *poverty*,
captivity, and want of rule and dominion. And what
fhould a *fpiritual Redeemer* do to thefe men? What
beauty and comelinefs can he have, for which he fhould
be defired?

§ 11. 2. *Ignorance of the righteoufnefs of God*, both as
to what he requireth, that a man may be juftified before
him, and of his *judgement* concerning the defert of fin,
hath the fame effect upon them, [Rom. x. 3, 4.] The great
end for which the Meffiah was promifed, as we have in
part declared, and fhall afterwards be farther evinced, was
to make ' atonement for fin,' and bring in an ' ever-
' lafting righteoufnefs,' [Dan. ix. 24.] A righteoufnefs was to be brought in, that might anfwer the juftice
of God, and abide its trial. There is not any thing that
more openly difcovers the miferable blindnefs of the prefent Jews, than the confideration of what they infift upon
as their righteoufnefs before God. The faith and obedience of their *forefathers*, the privilege of *circumcifion*, fome
outward obfervances of *Mofaical* precepts, with anxious fcru-
pulous abftinences, felf maceration, prayers by *tale and number*, and the like bodily exercifes, are the fum of what
they plead for themfelves. Now, if thefe things, which
are abfolutely in their own power, will make up a
righteoufnefs acceptable to God, cover all the fins whereof
they know themfelves to be guilty, to what end fhould
they look for a *Redeemer*, ' to bring in everlafting *righteouf-*
' *nefs*,' or make *atonement* for fin? Why fhould they look
out for a relief in this cafe, feeing they have enough at
home to ferve their turns? Let them that are ' weary
' and heavy leaden' feek after fuch a Deliverer; they have

no need of him, or his salvation. According, therefore, as this building of *self-righteousness* went on and prospered amongst them, faith in the Messiah, as to the *true ends* for which he was promised, decayed every day more and more, until at length it was utterly lost. For, as our apostle tells them, ' if righteousness were by the law, the ' promise of the Messiah was to no purpose ;' and if the *law* made things *perfect*, the bringing in of another priesthood and sacrifice was altogether needless.

As to their judgement of God, concerning the desert of sin ;—their *afflictions* and persecutions, the *death* of their children, and their own death, especially if it be of a *painful distemper*, they suppose will make a sufficient propitiation for all their sins. Such mean thoughts have they of the majesty, holiness, and terror of the Lord ! Of late also, lest there should be a failure on any account, they have found out an invention to give their sins to the *Devil*, by the *sacrifice of a cock*, the manner of which is described at large by BUXTORF.* Let the Messiah provide well for them in this world, and they will look well enough to themselves, as to that which is to come.

§ 12. 3. And hence ariseth also their *ignorance of the whole nature, use, and end of the Mosaical law*, which also contributes much to the producing of the same effect upon them. They look upon the law and their observance of it, as the only means of obtaining righteousness, and making atonement with God ; so they did of old, [Rom. ix. 32—34.] In the observance of its *precepts*, they place all their righteousness before God, and by the *sacrifices* of it, they look for the atonement of all their sins. But, if righteousness may be obtained, and atonement made without him, to what end serves the *promise* concerning him ? The truth is, having thus taken from him the whole office and work to which he was designed of God, and that he might not be thought altogether useless, they have cut out for him the work and employment before-mentioned. For looking on righteous-

---

* Vid. BUXTORF. *Synagog. Judaic.* Cap. xx.

VOL. I.   A a   ness

ness and atonement, with the consequent of them, eternal salvation, as the proper effects of the law, they thought meet to leave to their Messiah the work of procuring to them liberty, wealth, and dominion, which they found by experience the law was not able to do. But, indeed, had their eyes been opened in the knowledge of God and themselves, they would have found the law no less insufficient to procure, by itself, an *heavenly*, than an *earthly* kingdom for them.

But here, by the way, some may possibly inquire, how the Jews, if they look for atonement and the remission of sins, by the *sacrifices* of the law, can expect to have their present sins pardoned, without which they cannot be eternally saved, seeing they are *confessedly destitute* of all legal sacrifices whatever? Have they found out some other way, or do they utterly give over seeking after salvation? This very *question* being put to one of them, he answers, " That they now obtain the pardon of their sins by *repentance and amendment of life*, according to the promises made in the prophets to that purpose ;" and concludes, " Although there are now no sacrifices, which were a means *(tanto facilius)* the *more easily* to obtain the forgiveness of sins, yet it may be obtained by *repentance*, and a departure from evil ways." This is their hope, which, like that of the hypocrite, is as the giving up of the ghost. For,

(1.) Though repentance and amendment of life are required in them who seek after the forgiveness of their sins, and many promises are made to them; yet, is this all that God required, that sin might be forgiven? They are sufficient, indeed, in their *own place*, but are they so *absolutely also?* Did not God, moreover, require and appoint, that they should make use of *sacrifices*, to make atonement for sin, without which it should not be done away? [See Lev. xvi.] And

(2.) What is the meaning of that plea, that by sacrifices, indeed, remission of sins might be " *more easily*" obtained, but an avowal that it may be obtained without them? Doth this, " *more easily*" respect God, or man?

If

If they say it respects *God*, I desire to know, if he can pardon sin without sacrifices, why he cannot do it *as easily* as with them ? or what is he *eased* of by sacrifices ? If it respects *themselves*, as indeed it doth, then it may be inquired, what it is that they shall be *eased* of, in their obtaining the pardon of sins by the use of sacrifices, when again restored to them? Surely the present *inconvenience* of which they hope to be *eased*, can be nothing but *that* which they now are forced to make use of, for that end and purpose—*repentance and amendment of life.* If, then, they had their *sacrifices*, the former might be spared, or at least much might be abated of what, at present, is necessary. This, then, it seems, was the end why God instituted sacrifices—that these Jews might obtain pardon of sins *without* either *repentance* or *amendment !* And this is that which they love as their souls ; namely, that they may live in their sins, and be acquitted of all danger, by sacrifices and outward services. But

(3.) *Atonement* for sin is expressly necessary, or else all the institutions of *sacrifices*, for that end, were vain and ludicrous ; and, therefore, notwithstanding their pretence of repentance (which was *always* required) no Jew can, upon his own principles, now in the total cessation of all sacrifices, obtain either pardon of sin here, or salvation hereafter. But to proceed ;

§ 13. 4. Their corrupt *carnal affections* have, moreover, greatly contributed to their obstinacy in their unbelief. Hence they have coined their self-pleasing imaginations concerning the Messiah, and the work that he hath to do. Wealth, ease, liberty, dominion, or a share in power and rule, are the things that please their *carnal minds.* But whilst they are obstinately fixed in the expectation of such things, to tell them of a *spiritual and heavenly kingdom*, wherein the poorest and most persecuted person on the earth may have as good an interest, and enjoy as much benefit by it, as the greatest monarch in the world, and you do but cast away your words into the wind.

Since the propagation of the gospel, and the success of it in the world, *envy*, another corrupt lust, against the Gentile believers hath exceedingly perverted their minds in their notions about the Messiah. They cannot endure that the *Gentiles* should be equal sharers with themselves in the promise of the Messiah. They would have him to themselves alone, or not at all; and this keeps up their desires and expectations of such a one as they have fancied for their own ends and purposes. Again,

§ 14. 5. Their envy against the *Gentiles* is greatly increased and excited by the *oppressions* and *sufferings* from them, which they undergo. I speak not now of their present and past sufferings from nominal *Christians*—which in many places have been *unrighteous* and *inhuman*, and so undoubtedly a great occasion of hardening them in their obstinacy—but of their long-continued oppressions, under the power of the *Gentiles in general*. Having been greatly harrassed and wasted by them in most ages, and having a *Deliverer* promised to them, they are strongly inclined to fancy such a deliverance, as, being peculiarly theirs, should enable them to *avenge* themselves on their old enemies and oppressors. And how hard it is for them to lay aside these thoughts, unless they are freed by Divine grace, from the carnal affections now mentioned, is not difficult to guess.

§ 15. This is the faith and expectation of the *present Jews* all over the world, concerning the MESSIAH, in whom they place their confidence. A *mere man* he is to be; a *king* over the Jews at Jerusalem, who shall conquer many nations, and give peace, prosperity, and plenty to all the Israelites in their land. But what great matter is there in all this? Have not other men done as much, or more for their citizens and people? Can they fancy that their Messiah should be more victorious than ALEXANDER? They dare not hope it. At a disputation before the *Pope* and *Cardinals* at *Rome*, which they have recorded in *Shebat Jehudah*, they openly professed that they never expected so great glory by *their* Messiah, as that which they saw them attended with. But do these things answer

answer the *promises* made concerning him, from the foundation of the world? Is *this* the meaning of the promise given to *Adam*? Was this the end of the call and separation of *Abraham*? or the intention of the promise made to him, that in ' his seed all the nations of the ' earth should be *blessed*?' Is this only the import of it, that towards the end of the world many of them shall be *conquered*? Was this the intent of the *oath* made to David, and of the *sure mercies* confirmed to him and his thereby? Do all the promises in the prophets set out in words so glorious and magnificent, end in a *warrior*, inferior it may be to many of those whose destruction they prophesied of? Or, is not this rather a way to expose the whole Old Testament to scorn and reproach? Was this the expectation of the *fathers* of old? Is *this* that which they desired, prayed for, longed for, esteeming all the glory of their present enjoyments as nothing in comparison of it? What is there in *this Messiah*, that he should be the hope and desire of all nations? Did God set him forth as the great effect of his love, grace, goodness, and faithfulness towards them, and then bring forth a *military king*? Was the church in travail for so many generations, to bring forth this *fighter*? Had they no eye of old to *spiritual* and *eternal* things in the promise of the Messiah?

What is become all this while, of the *work* every where in the scripture assigned to the true Messiah? Who shall ' break the serpent's head?' Who shall take away the curse that entered as the inseparable attendant on sin? Who shall be a *blessing* to all nations? To whom shall the Gentiles be gathered for salvation? Who shall be a priest after the order of *Melchisedeck*? Who shall have a *body prepared* him to offer instead of the sacrifices of the law? Who shall have his hands and feet *pierced* in his sufferings, and his vesture parted by lot? Who shall make his soul an offering for sin? Who shall be *bruised*, grieved, and afflicted by God himself, because he shall bear the iniquities of his people? Who shall make *atonement* for transgressors, and bring in an everlasting righteousness?
Who

Who shall for ever make *intercession* for transgressors? Who shall sit at the right hand of God in his rule over the whole world? But these men, indeed, take a ready way to destroy all religion, and to turn the *whole bible* to an idle story of earthly things, without either life, spirit, or heavenly mystery in it.

EXERCIT. 4.

THE PROMISED MESSIAH IS LONG SINCE COME.

§ 1. *Introduction. The time of the Messiah's coming, first determined by the prophecy of Jacob, concerning Shilo.* § 2 —4. *The words of it briefly explained.* § 5—8. *The argument deduced from it.* § 9. *Haggai's prophecy concerning the glory of the second house.* § 10. *What house intended.* § 11—13. *What the glory of it.* § 14, 15. *The argument from it, concerning the Messiah, confirmed. A parallel testimony from Malachi.*

§ 1. THE SECOND great *principle*, supposed by the apostle in all his epistle to the Hebrews, and which he lays as the foundation of all his arguments, is, that the MESSIAH, whom we have proved to have been promised from the foundation of the world, was *actually come*, and had finished the work appointed for him, when he wrote that epistle.

Now, this determination of time inquired after, was first made by Jacob, [Gen. xlix. 8—9.] But here we may remark, respecting the line of succession, that as, after the promise given to Abraham, the Messiah might have sprung from any family whatever of his posterity, by Isaac, until the limitation was made by Jacob to the person of *Judah*; and *after* that limitation, might have done so from any family of his tribe or posterity, until the confinement of that privilege to the person of *David*; so no restriction

striction being afterwards added, his production by any person of his posterity, whether in an alliance nearer to, or farther from the *reigning line*, was all that was included in the promise.

The great *masters* among the Jews are exceedingly perplexed with the testimony above quoted, and have, therefore, invented endless ways for the enervating of it, openly and loudly *contradicting* one another almost about every word in the text. It were, therefore, not only endless to consider all their several expositions, but also *useless*, being so fully confuted by each other.*

2. The subject here spoken of is *Judah*; that is, the *tribe* of Judah. Now, this tribe may be considered either *absolutely* in itself, as it was in a separated state in the wilderness, without the *mixture* of any, not of his posterity; or with respect to that accession, which was afterwards made to it occasionally from the other tribes. As, first, from the lot of *Simeon* falling within its lot in the first inheritance of the land, [Josh. xix. 1.] whence that tribe, though still keeping its distinct genealogy, was reckoned to Judah, and became one people with them. Secondly, by the cleaving of the tribe of *Benjamin*, whose lot lay next to it, to the reigning house of David, in the fatal division of the people, [I. Kings xii. 20, 21, 27.] upon which both these tribes were after called by the name of *Judah*, [ver. 20.] and the people of both called (יהודים) *Jews*. Thirdly, by the falling off of the tribe of *Levi* to it, with multitudes of other good men, out of all the tribes of Israel, upon the idolatry and persecution of Jeroboam, [II. Chron. xi. 13—17.] by which means that one tribe quickly became more numerous and potent than all the rest. Lastly, by the mixture and addition of those great numbers which, out of *all* the tribes of Israel, joined themselves to them upon their return from Babylon, and the restitution of the worship of God amongst them in its proper place. Now, it is *Judah, with all these accessions*, that is intended in this prophecy, and yet so, as

* Vid. A. R. Meir, Aben Ezra, Targ. Onkel, &c.

that in the production of the Messiah, the genuine offspring of Judah was still to have the pre-eminence.

§ 3. That which is foretold concerning this *Judah*, is, that it should have (שבט) a *scepter*, and (מחקק) a *lawgiver*, or a *writer of laws*, for others to observe. What time this should come to pass is not limited; only thus far, that after it once possessed this privilege, it was not to cease till the Shiloh came. Political government in that tribe, the foundation itself of executing this promise, was not laid until about six hundred and twenty years after this time; when the kingdom was given to David. Nor is the *kind of government* expressed; only that they should be a people having the principle of government among themselves. Whilst they continued such, the *scepter* and *scribe* departed not from them, whatever might be the variety in the outward form. Accidental alterations in the modes of governing make no essential change in the state of the people, or nature of the government. Thus the first constitution of rule in that tribe was absolutely *monarchical*; this being imprudently managed by Rehoboam, he lost the ten tribes, who would never afterwards submit to the royal family of Judah. Its *retrieval*, after the Babylonish captivity, was *ducal*, or by an honorary president, with a mixture of *aristocracy* and *democracy*. Upon the ceasing of these rulers, extraordinarily called, the aristocracy in *Sanhedrim* prevailed; whereunto succeeded a *mixt monarchy* in the *Hasmoneans*; and their interest being ruined by intestine divisions, Herod, by craft and force, intruded himself.

Neither did this usurpation make any essential change in the polity of the nation; for although the rule was not always in the hands of Jews, and *Herod* was a foreigner, and notwithstanding the turbulent government of the Herodians, with the interposition of the Roman arms, the nation, and, what constitutes a people, its *laws and polity*, were still continued. In this state things continued amongst them, until the destruction of the commonwealth by Vespasian, and of the city and temple by Titus; only as a presage of the departure of scepter and scribe,

scribe, the power of judgement, as to the lives of men, was some years before taken from the Sanhedrim, [John xviii. 31.]

By the fixation of *rule*, in general, in Judah, we are freed from any concern in the disputes of learned men, about the precise time of the departure foretold.* And, indeed, if any thing more be intended in this prediction, than that the tribe of Judah should continue in a natural *political* state, with government in itself, it will be utterly impossible to determine exactly upon the accomplishment of this prophecy.

§ 4. During the continuance of this *scepter* and *law-writer*, it is promised that the SHILO should come. The word (שילה) *Shilo*, which comes from (שלה) *shala*, to *prosper*, or *save*, is used only in this place, and signifies a *prosperer*, *deliverer*, or *saviour*; that is, the MESSIAH. The Jews lay a double exception to the interpretation we give of the original particles (עד־כי) which we render *until*; first, that the former (עד) signifies *for ever*; so that the meaning is, that the scepter and law-writer shall not depart from Judah *for ever*, *because* the ' Shilo shall come ;' the latter particle (כי) being often casual. But although the former may *sometimes* signify as much as ' *for ever*,' (while mostly it signifies *adhuc, yet,* or *as yet)* it neither doth, nor can when it is joined, as here, with the other particle (כי) which limits the duration intimated by the *subject* and sense of the ensuing words they have a respect to. They except again, that (עד) is burdened with the accent *jethib*, which distinguisheth the sense, and puts a stop upon it. But of this they can give no instance when it hath *athnac* immediately preceding it, as in this place it hath. Besides, *scepter* and *law-giver* are long since *actually departed* from Judah, and in their judgement the *Shilo* not yet come ; which perfectly destroys the verity of the prediction.

* As BARONIUS, SCALIGER, CASAUBON, BULLINGER, MONTACUE, PERERIUS, A. LAPIDE, CAPELLUS, SCULTETUS, RIVETUS, SPANHEMIUS, &c.

§ 5. Having taken this brief view of the words, we may now draw our argument from them: " The Messiah, according to this prediction, must come whilst the rule and government of Judah were *continued*, or *before they were utterly taken away*; but they are long since taken away, even since the destruction of the nation, city, and temple, by Titus; and, therefore, the Messiah is long since come."—To manifest the uncontroulable evidence of this testimony, and our argument from it, there is no more necessary, but that we demonstrate;

First, that by *scepter* and *law-writer*, *rule* and *government* are intended.

Secondly, that the promised *Shilo* is the Messiah.

Thirdly, that all *rule* and national polity was utterly long since taken away from Judah, even in the destruction of the city and temple. The last being a matter of fact, must be evinced from history, and the state of things in the world, from those days, whereon there will be no rising against this testimony, by any thing but that pertinacious obstinacy, to which the Jews are judicially given up.

§ 6. The *first* thing proposed, that by *scepter* and *lawgiver*, rule and government are intended, is evident not only from the *words* themselves, which are plain and expressive, but from the context also. The dying patriarch Jacob, [Gen. xlix. 3—8.] foretelling, among other things, the erection of a rule and government amongst his posterity, it might have been expected, that of course it should have been fixed in *Reuben*, his first-born, according to the line of its descent from the foundation of the world; but he deprives him of it, [ver. 4.] Though he was in the course of nature, " the excellency of his dignity, and the excellency of his strength," [ver. 3.] yet he faith, ' thou shalt not excell;' shalt not preserve that excellency in thy posterity, nor have the pre-eminence of rule. In like manner he passeth by the next in order, *Simeon* and *Levi*, taking from them all expectation of that privilege. But coming to Judah, there he fixeth the seat of rule, [ver. 8.] ' Judah, thou art he whom
' thy

'thy brethren shall praise,' alluding to his name; thou shalt be exalted to that rule amongst them, from the right of which the others fell by their transgression. And this *rule*, saith he, shall consist, as all prosperous dominions do, in two things:—First, In the regular obedience of those who *de jure* are subject to it, 'thy father's children 'shall bow down before thee;' thou shalt have the authority over the rest of my posterity. Secondly, In the conquest of the enemies and adversaries of the dominion itself; 'thine hand shall be in the neck of thine enemies; 'as a lion's whelp thou art gone up from thy prey;' to which the words insisted on are subjoined; '*The scepter shall not depart*; that is, the scepter of *rule* amongst thy brethren, and prevalency against thine enemies; however, it may be weakened or interrupted, shall not utterly depart, or be removed, until the *Shilo* come. Thus the context (the principal guide of a true interpretation) stands clear and perspicuous.

The *Targumists** have, with one consent, given us the same account of the sense and import of these words; nor was it ever denied, by any of the Jews, until they found themselves necessitated to it by their corrupt interest; and those who do object, only cavil at words and syllables; and even this will do them no service.

The Hebrew word (שבט) which we render *scepter*, is originally and properly a *rod*, or staff; all other significations of it are *metaphorical*. Among them the principal is that of *scepter*, an ensign of rule and government. Nor is it absolutely used in any other sense; but in that very frequently, [Psal. xlv. 6.] 'A *scepter* (שבט) of upright-' ness is the scepter of thy kingdom.'—[Numb. xxiv. 17.] 'A *scepter* shall arise out of Israel;' that is, a prince or a ruler; *Targum*, " Christ shall arise out of Israel." And this sense of the words is made more evident by its conjunction with the word (מחקק) *law-giver*; he that pre-

---

* Thus ONKELOS: " The *ruler* (he that hath dominion) shall not be taken from the house of Judah." And thus JONATHAN: " Kings and rulers shall not cease from the house of Judah." With which the *Jerusalem Targum* agrees.

scribes, and writes law with authority, [See Psal. cxiii. 8. Isa. xxxiii. 22.] These two words, then, *in conjunction*, absolutely denote *rule* and *dominion*.*

§ 7. Our *second* inquiry is, concerning the *subject* of the promise under consideration, which is " *the Shilo*," whereby we say the *promised seed* is intended. Most learned men look upon it as derived from the verb (שלה) to be *quiet, safe, happy, prosperous* ;† whence also is [שליה Psal. cxxii.] *peace, safety, prosperity*, and *abundance*. But the weight of our argument lies not in the precise etymology and signification of the word ; what we insist on, is, that it is the MESSIAH who is intended in that expression. For,

1. This is manifest from the context and words themselves. The promise of the MESSIAH was the *foundation* of that nation and people ; the reason of the call of Abraham, and of the erection of a kingdom and a state in his posterity. This promise concerning him, and covenant founded in him, was always the chief matter of the *patriarchal benedictions*, when they blessed their children and posterity. Now, unless we grant *him* to be intended in this expression, there is no mention of him at all in this *prophetical eulogy* of Jacob. Besides, his posterity being now to be distributed into twelve distinct tribes, and each of them having his peculiar blessing appropriated to him—wherein it is certain and confessed by all the Jews,

---

* The cavils of a few moderns, as MANASSEH, BEN ISRAEL, &c. deserve not a refutation, being contrary to all sound principles of criticism, and the authority of their own ancient Rabbins, and to historical facts.

† To this *etymology* of the word agree GALATINUS, FAGIUS, MELANCTHON, PAGNINUS, DRUSIUS, SCHINDLER, BUXTORFIUS, AMAMA; and generally all the most learned in the Hebrew tongue. He that would be farther satisfied about the import of the word may consult REYMANDUS, PORCHETUS, and GALATINUS, in their discourses against the Jews on the subject ; KIMCHI, PAGNINUS, MERCER, SCHINDLER, PHILIP ab AQUINO, and BUXTORF, in their Lexicons; MUNSTER, FAGIUS, DRUSIUS, and GROTIUS, in their Annotations on the text; HELVICUS, RIVETUS, EPISCOPIUS, BOETIUS, and HOORNBECKIUS, in their Dissertations on it.

that

that this privilege of bringing forth the MESSIAH was henceforth reſtricted to Judah—it muſt be done in this place, or there is no footſtep of it in the ſcripture. And it is very ſtrange, that Jacob, reckoning up the *privileges* and advantages of Judah above his brethren, ſhould omit the chief of them, from whence all the reſt did flow. And the very tenour of the words manifeſts this intention; fixing on that which was the fountain and end of all bleſſing in the *promiſed ſeed*, he paſſeth over his *elder* children, and determines on Judah, with the continuance of rule to the coming of it.

2. That which in the text is affirmed, concerning this *Shiloh*, makes it yet more evident who it was that is intended; " And to him (ולו יקהת עמים) *the gathering of the people*;" (Sept. προσδοκια εθνων, *Vulg. expectatio gentium*) ' *the expectation of the nations.*'—ONKELOS; "And him ſhall the people obey," or to him they ſhall *hearken*. BEN-UZZIEL; "Becauſe of him the people ſhall faint;" that is, ceaſe their oppoſition, and ſubmit to him. *Targ. Jeruſal.* "And to him ſhall all the kingdoms of the earth be ſubject." All to the ſame purpoſe. The noun (יקהת) in conſtruction (from יקהה) is from the verb (יקה) *to hear*, attend, obey. It is but once more uſed in the ſcripture, [Prov. xxx. 17.] where it is rendered *doctrine*, or teaching given out with authority, and, therefore, to be *obeyed*. So that primarily it may ſeem to denote *obedience to doctrines*. That which in all theſe interpretations is aimed at, and in which they all agree, is, that the *Gentiles*, (people, heathen) ſhould be called and gathered unto the *Shilo*; ſhould *hear his doctrine*, and be made ſubject to him. Now, as this was eminently contained in the great fundamental promiſe, concerning the Meſſiah, made to Abraham, namely, that ' in him *all the nations* ' of the earth ſhould be bleſſed;' ſo, there is not any deſcription of him, in the following prophets, more eminent than this; that unto him ' the gathering of the peo- ' ple ſhould be,' which, in many places, is made the characteriſtic note of his perſon and kingdom. Now, he to whom the Gentiles ſhall ſeek, whoſe doctrine they ſhall

learn

learn, whose law they shall obey, to whom they shall be subject, in whom they shall be blessed, and to whom they shall be gathered, for all these ends and purposes, is the true and only MESSIAH, and this is the *Shilo* here mentioned.

§ 8. It remaineth, *thirdly*, that we should also evidence, that all rule and polity is long since taken away from Judah, and that for many generations there hath been no such thing as a *tribe* of Judah, in any national or political condition or constitution in the world. And had we not here to do with men obstinate to the last degree, there would need very few words in this matter. But they must have *that* proved to them, which all the world sees and knows, and takes care to make good, and which themselves, as occasion serves, confess and bewail. Is it not known to all the world, that for these *sixteen hundred years* last past, they have been scattered over the face of the earth, leading a *precarious* life, under the powers of princes, and of commonwealths, as their several lots in their *dispersion* have fallen. *(Sine Deo, sine homine rege)* cast out of God's especial care, they wander up and down without *law*, government, or authority. And, therefore, if there be any truth in this prophecy, if there be a certainty in any thing in this world, it is certain that *scepter* and *law-giver* are long since departed from Judah.

§ 9. We shall now proceed to other sacred testimonies in proof of our position. The first we shall fix upon is, that of *Haggai* ii. 3—9. to which we shall add Mal. iii. 1. The occasion of the former words must be sought from the story of those times in *Ezra*, and the whole discourse of the prophet in that place. The people returning from their captivity with Zerubabel, in the days of Cyrus, had laid the foundation of the temple; but having begun their work, great opposition was made against it, and great discouragements they met with. The kings of *Persia*, who first encouraged them to this work, and countenanced them in it, [Ezra i. 7—9.] being possessed with false reports and slanders, began to withdraw their assistance, as should seem in the days

days of Cyrus himself, [Ezra iv. 5.] and at length *expressly forbade* their proceedings, causing the whole work to cease by force, [ver. 23.] Besides this outward opposition, they were, moreover, greatly discouraged by their own poverty, and disability for the carrying on their designed work in any measure, so as to answer the beauty and glory of their former house, built by Solomon. Hence the elders of the people, who had seen the former house in its glory, wept with a loud voice when they saw the foundations of this laid, [Ezra iii. 12, 13.] as foreseeing how much the splendor and beauty of their worship would be eclipsed and impaired; for, as the measures of the fabric itself, assigned to it by Cyrus, [Ezra vi. 3.] did no way answer Solomon's structure; so they had no ability or means to make provision for the ornaments of it, wherein its magnificence principally consisted. Being, therefore, thus hindered and discouraged, the work ceased wholly, from the end of Cyrus's reign, to the second year of Darius Hystaspes. For there is no reason to suppose, that this intermission of the work continued to the reign of Darius Nothus. However, it is evident, that the old discouragement was still pressing upon them. The former house was glorious and magnificent, famous and renowned in the world, and full of comfort to them, from the visible pledges it contained of the Divine presence. To remove this discouragement, or to support them under it, the Lord, by his prophet, makes them a promise; ' The glory of this latter house shall be great ' above that of the former,' [Hag. ii. 9.]

To clear our argument intended from these words, we must consider—what was this *latter house?* and—wherein the glory of it did consist?

§ 10. We are to inquire, first, *what house* it is whereof the prophet speaks; now, this is most evident in the context, (הבית הזה) " *this house*"—saith he, pointing to it, as it were with his finger; that which your eyes look upon, and which you so much despise in comparison of the former—*this house* shall be filled with glory. It is true, this temple was three hundred years after rebuilt by Herod.

rod, in the eighteenth year of his reign; which yet hindered not but that it was still the *same temple*. For the structure was never destroyed, nor the materials of it at once taken down; it, therefore, still continued one and the same house, though much enlarged and beautified. And, therefore, the Jews, in the days of our Saviour, overlooked, as it were, the re-edification of the temple by Herod, and affirm, that *that house*, which was then standing, ' was forty-six years in building,' [John ii. 20.] as they supposed it to have been upon the *first return* from captivity; for the whole work and building of Herod was finished within the space of eight years.*

§ 11. The *glory* promised to this house is, in the next place, to be considered. This is expressed both absolutely and comparatively; *absolutely*, [Hag. ii. 7.] ' I ' will fill this house with *glory*;' *comparatively*, with reference to the temple of Solomon, which some of them had seen, [ver. 9.] ' The glory of this latter house shall ' be *greater* than that of the former.'—To understand aright this promise, we must reflect a little upon the glory of the first house, which the glory of this second was to excel.

1. It was very glorious, from its principal architect, which was God himself. He contrived the whole fabric, and disposed of all the parts of it. For when David delivered to Solomon the pattern of the house, and the whole worship of it, he tells him, ' All these things the Lord ' made me understand in writing, by his hand upon me, ' even all the work of this pattern,' [I. Chron. xxviii. 19.] God gave him the whole in *writing*; that is, divinely and immediately inspired him, by his holy Spirit, to set down the frame of the house, and all the concernments of it, according to his own appointment and disposal. This rendered the house *glorious*, as answering the wisdom of him by whom it was contrived. And herein it had the

* *Targ.* JONATH. ABEN EZRA, KIMCHI, and others, interpret the words, as belonging to *that house*, which was built by Zerubabel and Joshua; nor do any of the ancient Jews diffent.

advan-

advantage above all the fabrics that ever were on earth; and in particular above the second temple, whose builders had no such idea of their work given them by inspiration.

2. It was *glorious* in the greatness, state, and magnificence of the fabric itself. Such a building it was, as was never paralleled in the world, which sundry considerations will make evident to us; as,

(1.) The grand and magnificent *design* of Solomon, the wisest and richest king that ever was, in the building of it. When he undertook the work, and sent to Hyram, king of *Tyre*, for his assistance, he tells him, ' that the ' house he was to build was to be great, because their ' God was great above all Gods,' [II. Chron. ii. 5.] Nay, saith he, ' the house which I am about to build, shall be ' *wonderful and great*.' No doubt, he designed the structure to be magnificent to the utmost that his wisdom and wealth would extend to. And what shall he do that comes after the king? What shall any of the sons of men think to contrive and erect, so that it may *surpass in glory*, that in which Solomon laid out his utmost? There can, doubtless, be no greater fondness, than to imagine, that it could, in any measure, be equalled by what was done afterwards by Zerubabel, or Herod.

(2.) The vast and unspeakable sums of *treasure* which were expended in the building and adorning of it. I know there is some difference among learned men, about reducing the Hebrew signatures of money to our present account. But let the estimate be as low, as by any can reasonably be imagined (and setting aside what Solomon expended of his *own)* the provision left by David towards the work—an *hundred thousand* talents of gold, and a *thousand thousand* talents of silver; besides brass and iron without weight, with timber and stone, [I. Chron. xxii. 14.]—on the ordinary computation and balance of coins, amounted to no less than—the gold, to 450,000,000l. and the silver to 3,750,000,000l. besides what was dedicated by his *princes*, and out of his peculiar treasure. He that would be satisfied, what immense sums Solomon added of his own to this, may consult VILLAPANDUS on this subject. And what might be the product of this expence, wisely managed, is not easy to be conceived. It seems to me, that the *whole revenue of Herod* was scarce able to find bread for Solomon's workmen; so unlikely is it, that his fabric should be equal to that other. It was surely a *glorious* house, that all this charge was expended about.

(3.) It appears farther from the number of *workmen* employed in the structure. We need not augment the number by conjectures, seeing there is evident mention in scripture ' *an hundred and four-score, and three thousand six* ' *hundred ;*' besides the *Tyrians* that were hired, who, by their wages, seem also to be a great number, [II.Chron. ii. 10.] There was an ' *hundred and fifty-three thousand and* ' *six hundred*' strangers of the posterity of the Canaanites, [II. Chron. ii. 17, 18.] and *thirty thousand* Israelites, [I. Kings v. 13.] Neither was all this multitude engaged in the work only for a few days or months, but for full *seven* years, [I. Kings vi. 38.] And herein, as JOSEPHUS observes, the speed of the work was almost as admirable as its magnificence. And what a glorious structure might be raised by such numbers of men, in such a space of time, when nothing was wanting to them, which, by the immense treasure before-mentioned, could be procured, may easily be conceived. It doth not appear, that the *whole number of the people*, rich and poor, who were gathered together under Zerubabel, after the return from the captivity, did equal the numbers of Solomon's *builders* ; nor can it be imagined, that Herod employed so many in the whole work, as Solomon had to *overlook* his labourers :

3. The glory of the *worship* of this temple consummated its beauty. Now, this was principally founded on the glorious entrance of the DIVINE PRESENCE into it, upon its consecration by the prayer of Solomon. Hereof God gave a double pledge.

(1.) The *falling of the fire* from heaven to consume the first offerings, and leave a *fire* to be kept alive perpetually

petually upon the altar, a type of the effectual operation of the Holy Spirit, making all our sacrifices acceptable to God, [II. Chron. vii. 1.] And this the Jews expressly confess to have been wanting in the *second* temple.

(2.) The *glory of the Lord*, as a cloud filling the whole house, and resting upon it, [II. Chron. vii. 2, 3.] This foundation being laid, and attended with the sacrifice of *many thousands* of cattle, the whole worship was gloriously carried on, according to the institution revealed to David, by the spirit of God. And the better to enable them to a right performance hereof, some chief ministers, as Heman, Ethan, and Jeduthan, were themselves inspired with the spirit of prophecy. So that plainly here we had the utmost glory, that a ' *wordly sanctuary and carnal ordinances*' could extend to.

§ 12. Having taken this brief view of the glory of Solomon's temple, we may now inquire, What was the *glory* promised to this *second* house, concerning which the prophet affirms expressly, that it shall *excell* the first. Though this house was built *higher* by Herod, yet it was erected precisely on the old foundation. But not to enter at present into a consideration of the *measures* of the *former* structure; let the latter temple be thought as wide and as long as the former, and some cubits higher, does this give it a greater glory than the other? a glory *so much greater*, as to be thus eminently promised to be brought in with the shaking of heaven, earth, sea, and dry-land? Can any thing more fondly be imagined? It had not the *hundredth part* of the glory of Solomon's house; for, besides all the glorious *golden vessels* and ornaments of it, besides all the treasures disposed in it, besides sundry of the most magnificent parts of the building itself, there were *five things* wanting in the last, wherein the *principal* glory of the first house consisted.—*The ark propitiatory and cherubims*,—*The Divine Majesty, or presence*,—The *holy spirit of prophecy*,—*Urim and thummim*,—*Fire from heaven*, to kindle the everlasting fire on the altar. They that acknowledge all these things to have been wanting in the second temple, as the Jews generally do, and the *Talmud* expressly, [in יומא Cap. v.] cannot well compare the glory of it with that of the other, seeing they were the most eminent pledges of the presence of God.

§ 13. What then is the *true glory* promised to this house, wherein it was to have the pre-eminence above the former? Now, this is expressly said, to be—the coming into it of the desire of all nations. ' The desire of all ' nations shall come ; and I will fill this house with glory ' —and the glory of this latter house shall be greater than ' that of the former, saith the Lord of hosts,' [Hag. ii. 7 —9.] This is directly affirmed to be the glory promised, and nothing else is in the least intimated wherein it should consist. And there are *three* circumstances of this glory expressed in the text:—The *way* whereby it should be brought in ; ' I will shake the heavens, and the ' earth, and the sea, and the dry land ; and will shake all ' nations ;'—The *season* wherein this was to be brought about ; ' Yet once, it is a little while ;' and—The *event* of it ; ' And in this place will I give peace, saith the Lord ' of hosts.'

The Jews by these words—' the desire of all nations'— generally understand the *desirable things* of the nations, their silver and gold, which above all things are to them most desirable. But,

1. This is directly contrary to the *context*; for it is the plain design of the Holy Ghost to take off the thoughts of the people from that kind of glory, which consisted in a coacervation of ornaments of silver and gold, which, being all of them always in his power, he could, at that time, have furnished them with ; but that he would have them look for *another glory*.

2. It is perfectly *false* as to the event ; for when was there such an outward shaking of all nations under the second temple, as that thereon they brought their silver and gold unto it, and that in such abundance, as to render it more rich and glorious than the house of Solomon? So to wrest the words is plainly to aver, that the promise was *never fulfilled*; for nothing can be more ridiculous than to make a comparison between the riches and

trea-

treasures of Solomon's temple, and those which at that time were laid up in the second.

3. Open force is offered to the *words themselves*, for they are not, ' All nations shall bring their (החמות) *desi-* ' *rable things*,' but ' The (המדת) *desire* of all nations shall ' come.' So woeful is the consideration of men rebelling against *light*, that they care not into what perplexities they run themselves, so as they may avoid it.

§ 14. We say, then, that these words contain a prophecy of the Messiah, and of the *real glory* that should accrue to the second temple, by his coming to it whilst it was yet standing. This is the import of the words (ובאו חמדת כל הגוים) *Vulg. Et veniet desideratus cunctis gentibus*) *and the desire of all nations shall come.* The original word (החמדה from חמד) is properly (*desiderium*) *desire*, but is no where used in the scriptures, except for a thing or person *desired*, or desirable, loved, valued, or valuable; and it being said here *emphatically*, that this desire shall *come*, nothing but a desired or desirable *person* can be intended thereby; and this was no other but the MESSIAH, the bringing of whom into the world was the end of building that temple, and of the whole worship performed therein; and by his *coming into it*, the complement of its true glory was obtained.

The promise of him of old to Abraham was, that in him ' all nations of the earth should be blessed;' he is therefore rightly called their *desire*—or he that, *de jure*, ought to be *desirable* above all things to them—the *desire of all nations*; for he in whom all their blessedness and deliverance were laid up, may be properly called their ' desire,' because containing all things truly desirable, and because, like desire fulfilled, it was perfectly satisfactory to them when enjoyed.

The only difficulty in the interpretation of the words lies in their unusual construction: the verb (באו *venient*) *shall come*, is of the plural number, and (חמדת) *the desire*, whereto we refer it, of the singular; (*desiderium omnium gentium venient.*) But it is not unusual in the Hebrew tongue, where two substantives are joined in construction,

tion, that the verb agrees in number and perfon, not with that which it directly and immediately refpects, but with that by which it is *regulated*; [fo II. Sam. x. 9. fo Job xv. 20. and I. Sam. ii. 4. fo likewife Hof. vi. 5, &c. &c.] This conftruction, then, though *anomalous*, is in that language fo frequent, as not to create any difficulty in the words, and yet poffibly may not be without a farther fenfe, intimating the *coming of the nations* to Chrift upon his coming into the temple.

' I will fhake the heavens and the earth, the fea and ' dry land, and I will fhake all nations.' All agree that thefe words are to be interpreted *figuratively*; yet it cannot be denied, that a great concuffion and fhaking of the world, and all the nations of it, is intended, otherwife nothing is fignified by them. And this muft be with reference to that *houfe*, and the worfhip thereof, in a tendency to its glory. Now I defire to know, what work among the nations in the whole world it is, that was wrought with refpect to the temple, which is here intended? The nations came, indeed, under *Antiochus*, and almoft ruined it; under *Craffus*, and robbed it; under *Pompey*, and profaned it; under *Titus*, and deftroyed it. But what tended all this to its *glory*? But refer thefe words to the coming of the MESSIAH, and all things in them contained were *clearly fulfilled*.

Take the words either literally or metaphorically and they fuit the event: take them *literally*; and at his birth a *new ftar* appeared in the heavens; *angels* celebrated his nativity, *wife men* came from the Eaft to inquire after him, *Herod* and all Jerufalem were fhaken at the tidings of him, and upon his undertaking the work, he wrought *miracles* in heaven, earth, fea, and dry land; upon the whole creation of God.—Take them *metaphorically*, as they are rather to be underftood, for the mighty change which God would work in his worfhip, and the ftirring up of the nations of the world to receive him and his doctrine, and the event is yet more evident. All nations under heaven were quickly fhaken and moved by his coming. Some were ftirred up to inquire after him, fome to oppofe pose him, until the world, as to the greatest and most noble parts of it, was made subject to him. Evident it is, that since the creation of all things, never was there such an alteration and concussion in the world as that wherewith the MESSIAH and his doctrine was brought into it, and which is therefore so expressed by the prophet.

§ 15. Concerning the work which God will thus do '*once more*'; it is said to be 'a *little while*, that is, a little while ere it be accomplished. It is not the nature of the work, but the *season* or time wherein it should be wrought, that is denoted in these words; but this season is not called a *little while* absolutely, but with respect to the former duration of the people, or church of the Jews, either from the calling of Abraham, or the giving of the law to Moses. And this space of *four hundred years* is comparatively but ' a *little* while, so termed, to stir up believers to a continual expectation of it, it being now nearer to them than to their forefathers, who beheld the time of its performance a very *great way off*. And this also serves for the conviction of the Jews; for whereas their forefathers of old did confess, and themselves at present cannot with any modesty deny, that the Messiah is here intended, whom they suppose not yet to be come, how can this space of time from the days of Haggai in any *sense* be called a *little while*, seeing it far exceeded all the space of time that went before, from the call of Abraham, which is the first epocha of their privilege and claim.

The last circumstance that favours our interpretation of this place, is taken from the *event*; 'And in this place ' I will give peace, saith the Lord of hosts.' We say, then, that by *peace*, here, must be understood—either outward *temporal* peace, or *spiritual* peace between God and man, and between Jews and Gentiles in their joint communion in the same divine worship: if they say the *former*, I desire to know when this promise was accomplished under the second temple? In short, to say that

this

this was the peace intended, is to say directly, that God promised what he never did or will perform.

We have sufficiently proved, that the principal work of the Messiah was to make peace between *God and man,* by taking away *sin,* the cause of distance and enmity. this then is the peace here promised: this God gave at Jerusalem while the second temple was standing. For ‘ he is our peace who hath made both one, and hath ‘ broken down the middle wall of partition between us, ‘ having abolished in his flesh the enmity, even the ‘ law of commandments contained in ordinances for to ‘ make in himself of twain, one new man, so making ‘ peace. And that he might reconcile both to God in ‘ one body by the cross, having slain the enmity thereby, ‘ and came and preached peace to them that were afar ‘ off, and to them that were nigh.,’ [Ephes. ii. 14—17.] Thus did God give peace at Jerusalem, both to the Jews and Gentiles, by him that was ‘ the desire of all nations.’

I shall add yet farther strength to it *from a parallel testimony*; ‘ Behold, I send my Messenger, and he shall ‘ prepare the way before me, and the Lord whom ye seek ‘ *shall suddenly come to his temple,* even the Messenger of ‘ the covenant, whom ye delight in; behold, he shall ‘ come, saith the Lord of hosts,’ [Mal. iii. 1.] Now that he should come whilst the temple *stood,* is here confirmed by a double prophetical testimony, the temple being utterly and irreparably destroyed now above 1600 years ago, it must be acknowledged that the MESSIAH is long since come, unless we will say, that the word of God is vain, and his promise of none effect.

EXERCIT.

EXERCIT. 5.

DANIEL'S PROPHECY EXPLAINED AND VINDICATED.

§ 1. *The subject proposed.* § 2. *Preliminary remarks, and statement of the subject.* § 3. (I.) *That the prophecy refers to the coming of the Messiah, as appears* § 4. 1. *From the context.* § 5. 2. *From the names and titles given the person spoken of.* § 6. 3. *From the work to be done in his day.* § 7. *To restrain transgression.* § 8. *To pardon sins.* § 9. *To make reconciliation for iniquity.* § 10. *To bring in everlasting righteousness.* § 11. *To seal vision and prophecy.* § 12. *Messiah shall be cut off.* § 13. *He shall confirm the covenant.* § 14. *And cause the sacrifice to cease,* § 15. 4. *From the confession of the ancient, and perplexities of the modern Jewish masters.* § 16. (II.) *Chronological computation of the times determined in Daniel's weeks. Some difficulty attending the subject, how accounted for.* § 17. *Within what limits the computation must be sought. It must be included between the first year of Cyrus, and the destruction of the temple.* § 18. *The number of years contained in that space of time.* § 19. *The end of the limited time, being clear in the prophecy, should regulate and fix the beginning. Not the destruction of the temple, but the cutting off of the Messiah, the precise end of Daniel's weeks.* § 20. *Hence it follows, that the first decree of Cyrus is not the precise* BEGINNING *of the weeks.* § 21. *Nor the decree of Darius, either Hystaspes or Nothus.* § 22. *But it was the decree of* ARTAXERXES LONGIMANUS, *given unto Ezra, that was intended by the angel; which appears not only from its exactly answering to the time, but also from the circumstances of that decree.*

§ 1. THERE remains yet one place more giving clear and evident testimony to the truth under demonstration, to be considered and vindicated. And this is the illustrious prediction and calculation of time granted to Daniel, by the angel Gabriel, [Dan. ix. 24—27.] 'Seventy weeks are determined upon thy people, and upon thy holy city, to finish the transgression, and to make an end of sins, and to make reconciliation for iniquity, an to bring in everlasting righteousness, and to seal up the vision and prophecy, and to anoint the Most Holy. Know, therefore, and understand, that from the going forth of the commandment, to restore and build Jerusalem, unto Messiah, the Prince, shall be seven weeks, and three-score and two weeks, the street shall be built again, and the wall in troublous times. And after three-score and two weeks shall Messiah be cut off, but not for himself; and the people of the prince that shall come, shall destroy the city and the sanctuary; and the end thereof shall be with a flood, and to the end of the war, desolations are determined. And he shall confirm the covenant with many for one week; and in the midst of the week, he shall cause the sacrifice and the oblation to cease, and for the overspreading of abominations he shall make it desolate, even until the consummation, and that determined, shall be poured upon the desolate.'

§ 2. In treating of this illustrious prophecy, we shall

I. Prove that it refers to the coming of the Messiah, and the time wherein he should so come.

II. Ascertain the chronological computation of the time designed, in an exact account of the space limited from the beginning to the end.

§ 3. (I.) It is evident, in general, that here is given out, by the Holy Ghost himself, a computation of the time wherein the Messiah was to come, and to perform his allotted work; which warrants the kind of argument we now insist upon. No small part this was of the church's reasure of old, and a blessed guide it would have been to the faith and obedience of those, who were most immediately concerned therein, had it been diligently attended to. But having sinfully neglected it in its due season,

they have ever since wickedly opposed it. To Daniel, this information was granted as a *great favour*, and a seasonable relief, upon his deep humiliation and fervent supplications, as himself records; ' Whilst, saith he, I
' was speaking and praying, (with fasting and sackcloth,
' and ashes, ver. 3.) and confessing my sins, and the sins
' of my people Israel, and presenting my supplications be-
' fore the Lord my God, for the holy mountain of my
' God; yea, whilst I was speaking in prayer, the man
' Gabriel, whom I had seen in the vision of the beginning,
' being caused to fly swiftly, touched me about the time
' of the evening oblation; and he informed me, and
' talked with me, and said, O Daniel, I am now come
' forth to give thee skill and understanding. At the be-
' ginning of thy supplications, the commandment came
' forth, and I am come to shew thee, for thou art great-
' ly beloved; therefore, understand the matter, and consi-
' der the vision, *seventy weeks*,' &c. [20—23.] This was the answer God gave him, upon his great and fervent prayer for the church, for his relief and support; whence it is manifest, that the great blessing of the church was involved in it. And the computation of time mentioned was granted as a light to guide the Jews, that they might not be shipwrecked at the appointed time. But when that time drew nigh, they wholly disregarded it, being generally grown dead and carnal, and filled with prejudices against the proper work of the Messiah. And since the misery that is come upon them, for not discerning this time and judgement, most of them cry out against all computations of time about the Messiah's coming,* although they are plainly called and directed thereto by God himself. Neither can they conceal the vexation which from hence they receive, by finding the design of the prophecy so directly against them. Hence this place of Daniel, with respect to the *time* of the Messiah, and Isa¦ liii. for his *office* and work, are generally esteemed the

* *Talm.* Tract. *Sanedr. Shebet. Jehuda.* MAIMON. in *Jad. Chazekah,* Tract. *De Regib.* Cap. xii.

racks and tortures of the *Rabbins.*—For the computation itfelf, the Jews univerfally acknowledge, that the *fevens* here denote *fevens of years*; fo that the whole duration of the 70 *fevens,* comprifeth 490 *years.**

§ 4. But that it is the *true Meffiah* is here intended, appears from

1. The *context* and fcope of the place.

(1.) This whole revelation was granted to Daniel, for his relief in the profpect that he had of the enfuing calamities of the church: and was recorded by him, for its encouragement and fupport in thofe diftreffes, as were alfo the prophecies of Haggai and Malachi, before infifted on. Now, the *only general promife* which God, for the confolation of the church of old, renewed unto them in all ages, was this concerning the *Meffiah*, wherein all their bleffednefs was contained.

(2.) Unlefs the Meffiah, and his bleffed work be here intended, there is not one word of *comfort* or relief to the church in this whole prophecy. The *context*, therefore, evidently befpeaks the *true Meffiah* to be here intended.

§ 5. 2. The names and *titles* given to the perfon fpoken of, declare who he is that is defigned. He is called (משיח) THE MESSIAH, *the anointed,* (κατ' ἐξοχην) *by way of eminence,* and abfolutely. The addition of [משיח נגיד ver. 25.] MESSIAH THE PRINCE, makes it yet more evident. For as this word is often ufed to denote a *fupreme ruler,* one that 'goeth in and out before the people,' in rule and government, [as II. Sam. vii. 8. I. Kings i. 35. xiv. 7, &c.] fo it is peculiarly affigned to the MESSIAH, [Ifa. lv. 4.] 'Behold, I have given him a witnefs to the people, ' a *leader,* (or *prince)* and commander to the people.' And to afcribe this name of ' *Meffiah the Prince*' abfolutely to any but the *promifed feed,* is contrary to the whole tenor of the Old Teftament.

Moreover, he is called, (ver. 24. קדש קדושים) *the moft holy, (fanctitas fanctitatum)* in the abftract, the *holinefs of holineffes.* The moft holy place in the tabernacle

* R. SAADIAS HAGAON, JARCHI, KIMKI, &c.

and

and temple was so called, but *that* cannot be here intended. The time is *limited* (למשח) ' *to anoint* (or make ' *a Messiah* of) the most holy ;' but by the Jews' confession, the holy place in the *second* temple was never *anointed*. It must, therefore, be the *person* typified by the holy place, in whom the fulness of the Godhead was to dwell, that is here said to be *anointed*.*

§ 6. 3. The *work* here assigned to be done in the days of the Messiah, declares who it is that is intended ; as—finishing transgression—the making an end of sin—making a reconciliation for iniquity—the bringing in of everlasting righteousness—the sealing up of the vision and prophecy—his being cut off, and not for himself—confirming the covenant with many—causing the sacrifice and oblation to cease, [Dan. ix. 24—27.] All these, especially as coincident, demonstrate the person of the Messiah. He that shall call to mind what hath been evinced concerning the nature of the *first promise* ; the faith of the ancient Judaical church ; the person, office, and work of the Messiah ; will, upon the first consideration of these things, conclude that *this is he*. For we have in these things, the substance of all the temple institutions, the center of all promises, and a brief delineation of the whole work of the promised seed. Wherefore, although it be not an exposition of the place that we have undertaken, but merely a demonstration of the concernment of the Messiah therein ; yet, because the consideration of the particular expressions above-mentioned will corroborate the present argument, I shall briefly explain them.

§ 7. The first thing is (לכלא הפשע *ad cohibendum prævaricationem*) ' *to restrain, coerce, make an end of transgression*.' The verb (כלא) is to *shut*, to *shut up* ; to *forbid*, to *refrain*, to *restrain*. For the *latter* sense, we might refer to Psalm cxix. 101. (כלאתי) ' *I have refrained*, (or kept) my feet from every evil way*.' [Psal. xi.

---
* The words of NACHMANIDES (*in loc.*) are remarkable: "This Holy of Holies is the *Messiah*, who is sanctified from the sons of David."

[12.]

12.] 'Thou, Lord (הכלא לא) *wilt not withhold*, or re-
'strain, thy mercy from me.' For the *former*, to Jer.
iii. 3. Hag. i. 10. I. Sam. xxv. 33, &c.—Hence (כלא
carcer) a prison, wherein men are put under restraint.—
From the similitude of letters, and sound in pronuncia-
tion, some suppose it to have an affinity, in signification,
with the word (כלה) to *consummate*, to *end*, to *finish*.
But there is no sufficient proof of this coincidence. For,
although the latter sometimes may signify to *restrain* or
shut up, [as Psal. lxxiv. 11.] yet, the former no where
signifies to *consummate*, or to *finish*.

The first thing, therefore, promised with the Messiah,
and which he was to do at his coming, was, to *restrain
transgression*, to *shut it up* from overflowing the world so
universally as it had done. *Transgression*, from the day of
its first entrance into the world, had passed over the whole
lower creation, like a flood; but God would now, by the
Messiah, coercively set bounds to it. By his Spirit, by
his grace, by his doctrine, and the efficacious power of his
gospel, he set bounds to the rage of wickedness, rooted
out the old idolatry of the world, and turned *millions* of
the sons of Adam unto righteousness. But the Jews, who
deny his coming, can give no instance of any other *restraint* laid upon the prevalency of transgression, within
the time limited by the angel; and so directly deny the
truth of the prophecy, because they will not apply it to
HIM, to whom alone it belongs.

§ 8. The *second* thing is (חטאות לחתם) *to seal up sins*.
The expression is *metaphorical*. To *seal*, is either to *keep
safe*, or to *hide* and cover; the former can have no
place here, being perfectly inconsistent with what is spoken
immediately before, and what follows directly after, in
the text; and the most proper sense of the word is, to
cover or *conceal*, and thence to *seal*, because thereby a
thing is *hidden*. Now, to *hide* sin or transgression, in
the Old Testament, is to *pardon* it, or *forgive* it. As
then the former expression respecteth the restraining of
the *power* and progress of sin, by the grace of the gospel,
[as Tit. ii. 11, 12.] so this expression respects the pardon

don and removal of its *guilt*, by the mercy proclaimed and tendered in the gospel. Hence is God said to ' cast our ' sins behind his back ; to *cover them*, and to cast them into ' the bottom of the sea.' That this was no way to be done, but by the Messiah, we have before evinced. Neither can the Jews assign *any other way* of the accomplishment of this part of the prediction, within the time limited. For, setting aside this only consideration of the pardoning of sin, procured by the mediation of the Messiah ; and there was never any age wherein God did more severely bring forth sin to judgement, as themselves at large experience.

§ 9. *Thirdly*, this season is designed (לכפר עון) ' *to make reconciliation for iniquity*;' to make atonement. [See Heb. ii. 17.]

When the word is applied to God, as the agent, it is to *hide*, to cover, to pardon sin, to be gracious to sinners ; and when so applied to men, in the use of any of his institutions, it is to *propitiate*, appease, atone, make atonement. This latter was the work for which he was promised to our first parents. That he *was to do it*, we are taught in the Old Testament ; and *how* he did it, we learn in the gospel. To expect this work from any other, or to be wrought by any other ways or means, is fully to renounce the first promise, and the faith of the holy fathers from the foundation of the world.

§ 10. What is mentioned in the *fourth* place answers the former (להביא צדק עלמים) ' *to bring in everlasting righ-* ' *teousness*.' There was a *legal* righteousness amongst the people before, consisting partly in their blameless observance of the institutions, and partly in their ritual atonements for sin, made annually and occasionally. But that neither of these could constitute their righteousness *everlasting*, needs not a formal proof. Wherefore, an *evangelical righteousness*, which is absolute, perfect, and enduring for ever, is promised to be brought in by the Messiah ; the righteousness which he wrought in his life and death, doing and suffering the whole will of God, and which procureth, as well as terminates in—not a *temporal*

deli-

deliverance, but—the 'everlasting salvation' mentioned in Isa. xlv. 17. To declare the nature, and the way of bringing in this righteousness, is the great design of the gospel, [Rom. i. 16, 17.] And I desire to know of the Jews, how it was brought in within the time limited? According to *their* principles, the time here determined was so far from bringing in everlasting righteousness, that by their own confession, it brought in nothing but a deluge of *wickedness*, by the abounding sins of their own nation, and the oppression of the Gentiles. This, therefore, is the proper work of the Messiah, foretold by the prophets, and expected by all the fathers; and he alone, whoever he be, that brings in this EVERLASTING RIGHTEOUSNESS, is the *promised seed*, the true and only Messiah.

§ 11. The *fifth* particular here foretold, is (לחתם חזון ונביא) 'to *seal vision and prophet*;' prophet for *prophecy*. The expression being metaphorical, is capable of a *tripple* interpretation, and every one of them proper to the Messiah, his work, and the times wherein he came; but applicable to no other.

1. To *seal*, is to consummate, to establish, and confirm, [Isa. viii. 16. John iii. 33. Rom. iv. 11.] In this sense, *vision* and *prophecy* were *sealed* in the Messiah; each one of them had a respect to the coming of the just one, the promised seed. God had spoken of him by the mouths of his holy prophets, from the foundation of the world. In the bringing of him forth, he sealed the truth of their predictions, by their actual accomplishment. The law and the prophets were until John, and then they were to be fulfilled. This was the season wherein all vision and prophecy centered; and this the person, who was the principal subject and end of them; he, therefore, and his coming, is here foretold.

2. To *seal*, is to finish, conclude, and put an end to any thing, [Isa. xxix. 11.] Thus also were *vision* and *prophecy* then *sealed* among the Jews. They were shut up and finished. The privilege and use of them were no more to be continued in their church. And this also

fell

fell out accordingly; for by their own confeſſion, from that day to this, they have not enjoyed either *viſion* or *prophet*.

3. By *ſealing* the confirmation of the doctrine concerning the Meſſiah, his perſon, and office, by *viſion* and *prophecy*, may be intended. The viſions and prophecies that went before, by reaſon of their darkneſs and obſcurity, left the people, in ſundry particulars, at great uncertainty; but now all things were cleared and confirmed. The *ſpirit of prophecy* accompanying the MESSIAH, and by him given to his diſciples, as foretold by Joel, [chap. ii. 28, 29.] was, in his Revelations, expreſs and clear, confirming all things belonging to his perſon and doctrine. Neither had theſe words any other accompliſhment than what we contend for.

§ 12. *Sixthly*, it is affirmed, that (יכרת משיח) "*Meſſiah ſhall be cut off*." Not *(occidetur)* ſhall be *ſlain* (as the Vulg. Latin renders the word) but *(excidetur)* ſhall be *cut off*; that is, *penally*, as one puniſhed for ſin. For the word (כרת) when it includes death, conſtantly denotes a *pœnal execiſion*, or cutting off *for ſin*. [See Gen. xvii. 14. Exod. xii. 15. Numb. xv. 30, &c.] This the Jews themſelves acknowledge to be the meaning of the word.* It is then foretold, that the Meſſiah ſhall be *cut off pœnally* for ſin, which he truly was, when he was made a *curſe* for ſin, all our iniquities meeting upon him.

And this alſo is intimated in the enſuing particles (ואין לו) '*and not to* (or *for) him*' For an objection is prevented, that might ariſe about the *pœnal* exciſion of the Meſſiah; for how could it be, ſeeing he was very juſt and righteous? To this it is anſwered, by way of conceſſion, that it was not on his *own* account, not *for himſelf*, but *for us*; as it is at large declared, [Iſa. liii.] Or, '*not to him*,' may be a farther declaration of his ſtate and condition; that, notwithſtanding theſe carnal apprehenſions, which the Jews would have of his outward ſplendor and riches, he ſhould have nothing in this world, not

---

* Vid. R. SAADIAS GAON, in *Hæmunoth*, Cap. viii.

'where to lay his head,' nor any to stand up for him. And this is that part of the *prophecy*, for the sake of which, the Jews so pertinaciously contend, that the true Messiah is not intended in it; for, say they, he shall not be *pœnally cut off*. But who told them so? Shall we believe the angel, or them? Will they not suffer God to send his Messiah in his *own way*, but they must interfere and tell him, that it *must not* be so? To cast away all prophecies, because they suit not men's carnal hearts, what is it else, but to reject all authority of God and his word? That is what hath proved their ruin; they will not receive a Messiah that shall suffer, and be *cut off for sin*, though God foretold them expressly, that it must be so.

§ 13. It is added, *seventhly*, concerning the person whose coming is foretold, that (הגביר גרית לרבים) ' he ' *shall confirm* (or strengthen) *the covenant with* (or to) ' *many*.' The *covenant* spoken of, absolutely, can be none but that everlasting *covenant* which God made with his elect, in the promised seed; and the great promise of which was the foundation of the covenant with Abraham. And hence, God says, that he will 'give him for ' a covenant to the people,' [Isa. xlii. 6. and xlix. 8.] And the salvation which they looked for, through him God promiseth, ' through the blood of the covenant,' [Zech. ix. 11.] This covenant was *strengthened to many* in the ' *week*' wherein he suffered, even all that believed in him, and was ratified in his blood, [Heb. ix. 15.] And after he had declared it in his own *ministry*, he caused it to be proclaimed by his gospel. At the time here determined, the *special covenant* with Israel and Judah was broken, [Zech. ix. 10.] and they were thereon cut off from being a church or people. Nor was there, at that season, as all know, any other *ratification* of *the covenant*, but only what was made in the death of the Messiah.

§ 14. Then also, *eighthly*, did he ' cause to cease ' the sacrifice and gift,' or offering. First, he caused it to *cease*, as to force and efficacy, or any *use in the worship of God*, by his own accomplishment of all that was prefigured and intended by it. Hereby it became as a

dead

dead thing, unprofitable, and made ready to difappear, [Heb. viii. 13.] And then, fhortly after, he caufed it utterly to be taken away, by a perpetual *defolation* brought upon the place where alone facrifices and offerings were acceptable to God, according to the law of Mofes.—And this various work of his is our third evidence, that this prophecy belongs to the Meffiah. Moreover,

§ 15. 4. Befides the confeffion of the *ancient Jews* confenting to the truth contended for, we have, for our confirmation therein, the woeful perplexities of their *latter mafters*, in their attempts to invade the force of this teftimony. For fome ages they have abhorred nothing more, than that the true Meffiah fhould be thought to be here intended. For if that be once granted, they know that it brings an inftant *ruin* upon the pretences of their infidelity; and that not merely upon the account of his *coming*, againft which they have invented a forry relief, but principally on account of his being *pœnally cut off*, which can by no means be reconciled to their prefumptions and expectations. But if He be not here intended, it is incumbent on them to declare *who* is. For the utmoft extent of the time limited in the prediction, being long fince expired, the prophecy hath certainly had accomplifhment in fome one or other; or otherwife the whole angelical meffage never was, nor ever will be, of any ufe to the church of God.

But here *our mafters* are by no means agreed amongft themfelves; nor do they know what to anfwer to this inquiry. And if they guefs at any one, it is not becaufe they think it poffible he fhould be defigned, but becaufe they think it impoffible for them to keep life in their caufe, without making fome reply when the fword of truth lies at the heart of it. Some of them, therefore, affirm the Meffiah fpoken of to be *Cyrus*, whom God calls his *anointed*, [Ifa. xlv. 1.] But what the *cutting off*, or *death* of Cyrus, fhould make in this prediction, they know not. And if, becaufe Cyrus is once called the *anointed* of the Lord, he muft be fuppofed to be intended in that place, where no one word or circumftance is applicable

plicable to him; they may as well say, that it is *Saul*, the King of Israel, who is spoken of, seeing he is also called the ' *anointed* of the Lord,' [I. Sam. xxiv. 6.] But that which casts this fancy beneath all consideration, is, the *time* allotted to the *cutting off* of the Messiah.

ABARBINEL, and after him MANASSE BEN ISRAEL, with some others of them, fix on the *younger Agrippa*, the last King of the Jews, who, as they say, with his son *Monabasius*, was *cut off*, or slain at Rome, by *Vespasian*. Neither is there in this conceit any colour of probability. For neither was *that Agrippa* properly ever king of the Jews, having only Galilee under his jurisdiction; nor was he ever *anointed* to be their king, nor designed of God to *any work*, on the account of which he might be called his *anointed*; nor was he of the posterity of Israel, nor did he any thing deserving an illustrious mention in this prophecy. Besides, in the last fatal war, he was still of the Roman party, nor was he *cut off*, or slain by *Vespasian*; but after the war he lived at Rome in honour; and in the third year of Trajan died in peace.* So that there is nothing of truth, no colour of probability in this desperate figment.

Their last evasion is, that by ' Messiah the Prince,' the office of *magistracy* and *priesthood*, and in them, all *anointed* to authority are intended. These, they say, were to be ' *cut off*' in the destruction of the city. But this evasion, also, is of the same nature with the former; yea, more vain than they, if any thing may be allowed to be so. The angel twice mentioneth the Messiah in his message; first, his *coming* and *anointing*, [ver. 25.] and then his *cutting off*, [ver. 26.] If the same person or thing be not intended in both places, the whole discourse is equivocal, no circumstance being added to distinguish between *them*, who are called by the same name in the same place. And to suppose that the Holy Ghost, by one and the same name, within a few words, continuing his speech of the same matter without any note of distinction, should

* As JUSTEES, the *Tiberian*, assures us in his History, whose words are reported by PHOTIUS, in his *Bibliotheca*.

signify things so diverse from one another, is to leave no place for understanding any thing that is spoken by him. The Messiah, therefore, who was to *come*, and to be *anointed* and *cut off*, is one and the same individual person. Now, it is expressly said, that there shall be seven weeks and sixty-two weeks; that is, *four hundred and eighty-three years* from the going forth of the decree to Messiah the prince. I desire, therefore, to know, whether that space of time was passed before they had any *magistrates* or *priests*, to be afterwards cut off? This pretence, therefore, may pass with the former. And this perplexity of the modern *Jews*, in their attempts to apply this prophecy to any other thing or person besides the TRUE MESSIAH, confirms our exposition and application of it. There is no other that they can imagine, to whom any one thing here mentioned may seem to belong; much less can they think of any, in whom they should *all center* and agree. It is then the promised Messiah, the hope and expectation of the fathers, whose *coming* and *cutting off* is here foretold.

§ 16. (II.) More fully to demonstrate our assertion, and to rescue this illustrious prophetic testimony from the withered grasp of prejudice, let us now advert to the *computation of Daniel's weeks*. That there is some difficulty in finding out the *exact* computation of time here limited, all chronologers and expositors confess. Nor is it necessary to suppose, that Daniel himself exactly understood the beginning and the end of the weeks mentioned. The hiding of the *precise* time intended was greatly subservient to the providence of God, in the work he had to do by the Messiah, and what that people were to do to him. The *general notation* of it sufficed for the direction of the godly, and the conviction of unbelievers, as it doth to this day. And it may be, we shall not find any computation that will answer in all particulars and *fractions* to a day, month, or even year. And that, either because of the great darkness and confusion of some of the times falling under the account, or else, because perhaps it was not the mind of God, that ever the time should be so

pre-

precisely concluded, or that any thing which he revealed for the strengthening of the church's faith, should depend upon *chronological* niceties. It shall suffice us, then, to propose and confirm such an account of these weeks, which, while it infallibly compriseth the substance of the prophecy, contains nothing in it contrary to the scriptures, and is not liable to any just and rational exception.

§ 17. In the first place, we may wholly lay aside the consideration of those who would date the weeks from any time whatever before the *first year* of the reign, and *first decree* of Cyrus. And of the like nature is the account of SOLOMON JARCHI, among the Jews, who dates the time limited from the destruction of the temple by the Chaldeans. But both these accounts are expressly contrary to the words of the angel, who fixes the beginning of the time designed to the *going forth of a decree* for *building Jerusalem*. To these we may add all that would extend these weeks beyond the destruction of the city and temple by Titus, as some of the Jews would do, with a view that the prophecy should comprise their second fatal destruction by Adrian, which is no way concerned in it.

The *seventy weeks* mentioned we must then seek for, *between* the first year of Cyrus, when the *first decree* was made for rebuilding the temple, and the *final destruction* of it by the Romans. This space we are confined to by the *text*; the seventy weeks are ' from the going forth of ' the word to cause to return, and to build Jerusalem,' [ver. 25.]

Now, the kingdom of Cyrus had a double *first year*; the one absolutely of his reign over *Persia*, the other of his rule over the *Babylonish* monarchy, which he had conquered after the death of *Darius Medus*. Now, it is the first year of the *second* date of the kingdom of Cyrus, which may have any relation to the time here limited; for whilst he was king of *Persia only*, he could have nothing to do with the *Jews*, nor make any decree for the building of the temple, both the people and place being then under the dominion of another. Besides, it being
said

said, [Ezra i. 1.] that he made his decree in the *first year* of his reign, himself plainly declares, that he had obtained the *Eastern monarchy* by the conquest of *Babylon.* ' The Lord God of Heaven hath given me the whole king- ' doms of the earth,' [ver. 2.] which words can in no sense, be applied to the kingdom of *Persia*, supposing the monarchy of *Babylon* still to continue.

The whole space of time then here limited is *seventy weeks*, [ver. 24.] The beginning of these seventy weeks is the going forth of the *decree*, or word to *restore* or build Jerusalem, [ver. 25.] The first decree or command that *could* have any relation to this matter, was that made by Cyrus, in the first year of his empire. We must then, in the first place, find out the direct space of time between the first year of Cyrus, and the destruction of the temple; and then inquire, whether the whole, or what part of it, is denoted by these seventy weeks.

§ 18. It is generally agreed by all historians and chronologers, that Cyrus began his reign over *Persia* in the first year of the fifty-fifth *olympiad*; probably the same year that *Nabonidus*, or *Darius Medus* began his reign over Babylon. And this was the year in which Daniel set himself solemnly to seek the Lord for the delivery of the people out of captivity, *he* who was so long before prophesied of to be their deliverer, being now come to a kingdom, [Dan. ix. 1.] In the twenty-seventh year of his reign, or the first of the sixty-second *olympiad*, having conquered the Babylonian empire, he began the first year of his *monarchial* reign, from whence Daniel reckons his third, which was his *last*, [Dan. x. 1.] And herein he proclaimed to the Jews, to return to Jerusalem, and to build the temple, [Ezra i. 1.] The city and temple were destroyed by Titus in the third year of the two hundred and eleventh *olympiad*. Now, from the *first* year of the sixty-second olympiad, to the *third* of the two hundred and eleventh olympiad, inclusive, are 599 years; and within that space of time we are to inquire after the 490 years here foretold.

Of this space of time, the *Persian* empire, from the twenty-seventh of Cyrus, or first of the whole monarchy, and the first of the sixty-second olympiad, continued two hundred and two years, as is generally acknowledged by all ancient historians, ending on the second year, inclusive of the one hundred and twelfth olympiad, which was the last of Darius Codemanus.*

After his death, *Alexander*, beginning his reign in the third year of the hundred and twelfth olympiad, reigned six years. From him there is a double account, by the two most famous branches of the Grecian empire. The first is by the Syrian, or *ara* of the *Seleucidæ*, which takes its date from the tenth year after the death of Alexander, when, after some bloody contests, Seleucus settled his kingdom in Syria.†

* For after this

1. Cyrus reigned	3 years.
2. Cambyses and Smerdes Magus	8
3. Darius Hisdaspes	34
4. Xerxes and Artabanus	21
5. Artaxerxes Longimanus	41
6. Darius Nothus	19
7. Artaxerxes Mnemon	43
8. Ochus	23
9. Arses	3
10. Darius Codomanus	7
In all	202

† According to the Syrian account,

1. Alexander reigned	6 years.
2. From Alexander to Seleucus	10
3. Seleucus	30
4. Antiochus Soter	21
5. Antiochus Theos	15
6. Seleucus Callinicus	20
7. Seleucus Ceraunus	2
8. Antiochus Magnus	37
9. Seleucus Philopater	12
10. Antiochus Epiphanes	12
11. Eupator	2
12. Demetrius Soter	10
13. Alexander Vales	2
In all	179

So

So that the time of the Grecian empire in Syria, from the death of Darius Codomanus, to the liberty of the Jews, and erection of the supreme government amongst them, was one *hundred and seventy-nine years*, which being added to the two hundred and two years of the *Persian* empire, makes up three *hundred and eighty-one* years. To the same issue comes also the account by the other branch of the Grecian empire in *Egypt*.*

The rule of the *Hasmoneans*, with the reign of Herod the Great, who obtained the kingdom by means of their division, continued until the birth of Christ, one *hundred and forty-eight* years. For Jonathan began his rule in the second year of the hundred and fifty-seventh olympiad; as may be seen by adding the Sellucian æra to the hundred and fourteenth olympiad, wherein Alexander died; and our Lord Christ was born in the second year of the hundred and ninety-fourth olympiad, in the last year, or last year but one, of Herod the Great. This sum, therefore, of a hundred and forty-eight years, being added to the forementioned, from the beginning of the empire of Cyrus, which is three hundred and eighty-one years, makes up, in all, five hundred and twenty-nine years.

From the birth of our Lord Christ, in the second year of the hundred and ninety-fourth *olympiad*, to the destruction of the city and temple, in the third year of the two hundred and eleventh olympiad, are seventy years; which makes up the whole sum before-mentioned, of

---

* According to the Egyptian account,

1. Alexander	- - -	6 years.
2. Ptolemeus Lagi	- -	39
3. Philadelphus	-	38
4. Evergetes	- -	24
5. Philopater	-	19
6. Epiphanes	- -	23
7. Philometer	-	30
In all	- -	179

five

five hundred and ninety-nine years, from the first of the empire of Cyrus, to the destruction of Jerusalem.†

PETAVIUS and MOUNTACUE reckon from the first of *Cyrus*, to the eighteenth of *Tiberius*, wherein our Lord Christ suffered, five hundred and ninety-four years, which differs very little from the account we have insisted on; and this being every way consistent with itself, and the stated æras of the nations, and abridging the time to the *shortest space* that will endure the trial, we shall abide by it. Now, the number of nine hundred and ninety-nine years exceeds the time limited in the prophecy, by the space of a *hundred and nine* years. Hence it evidently appears, that the seventy weeks of Gabriel, (490 years) are not commensurate to the *whole space* of time between the first decree of Cyrus, in the first year of his general empire, and the final desolation of the city and temple by Titus. One hundred and nine years must be taken from it, either at the beginning, or at the end; or partly at the one, and partly at the other.

§ 19. We shall first consider the *end* of them, which being clear in the prophecy, will regulate, fix, and state the *beginning*. Two things in general are insisted upon in this prophecy: first, the *coming* of the *Messiah* the prince, his anointing unto the work which he had to do, and his cutting off, as we before declared; and secondly, the *ceasing* of the *daily sacrifice*, with the destruction of the city and temple, by war, and a flood of desolation. Now, these things happened not at the *same time*; for the city and sanctuary were destroyed thirty-seven years after the cutting off, or death of the Messiah. We are to inquire,

† From Cyrus to Darius Codomanus - 202 years
From Darius Codomanus, to Alexander Vales; or, in the Egyptian line, to Philometer - } 179
From Philometer, to the birth of Christ; or, during the Hasmonean rule, with Herod the Great } 148
From the birth of Christ, to the destruction of Jerusalem - - - } 70

From the first of Cyrus, to the destruction of the city - - } Total 599

there-

therefore, *which* of these it was, that the time mentioned determined for. Now it is the coming, anointing, and cutting off of the Messiah, that is the thing chiefly intended in this prophecy. This we have proved undeniably before; manifesting that the vision was granted to Daniel, and given out by him, for the *consolation* of himself and the church, as was the way of the Holy Ghost in all his dealings with the fathers of old. To this the desolation and destruction of the city and temple was only a consequent of what was principally foretold. And it is doubtless unreasonable to expect the duration of the time beyond the *principal* subject matter treated of, and on the account whereof alone, the computation is granted, to that which is only *occasionally* mentioned. Besides, the computation itself is pointed directly by the angel to the Messiah, and his cutting off. ' Seventy weeks are determined upon ' thy people, know, therefore, that from the going forth ' of the commandment, to Messiah the prince shall be,' &c. ' And after sixty-two weeks shall the Messiah be cut ' off.' But there is no reference of the time limited to the desolation of the city and sanctuary.

Moreover, it is expressly said, that the time limited extends itself only to the death of the Messiah, or a very few years farther; for he was to *come* after seven weeks and sixty-two weeks, which are the whole time limited within one week, or seven years. Now, his coming, here intended, is not the time of his *incarnation*, but that of his *unction* at his baptism, which fell out at the end of sixty-nine weeks. After these sixty-nine weeks, or *seven* and *sixty-two* weeks, he is to be ' cut off;' that is, in the middle, or towards the end of the last week, when he had confirmed the covenant by preaching three years and a half of that seven years which remained. And if we shall say, that his unction was to be *after* the sixty-nine weeks, we must grant it to be in the first or second year of the last week; whereto add the three years and a half of his preaching, and the remaining *fraction* of one or two years can no way disturb the account, there being nothing more frequent than such an omission, for the sake of an intire and round number. Here, then, muft we fix the *end* of the four hundred and ninety years, *viz.* in the *death* of the Meffiah; and fo wholly lay afide the account of thofe who would extend the time determined to the defolation of the city and temple.

§ 20. We muft, therefore, in the firft place, abate from the whole account of five hundred and ninety-nine years before ftated, the fum of *thirty-feven* years, which enfued after the death of our Saviour, until the deftruction of Jerufalem; and the remnant is *five hundred and fixty-two* years; which exceeds the number of feventy weeks by *feventy-two* years. It appears, then, that the beginning of the weeks cannot be the *decree of Cyrus*; for to name four hundred and ninety, for five hundred and fixty-two, would feem rather to be a rude conjecture, than an exact prophecy; nor is there any neceffity for fuch a fuppofition. Befides, the word ufed by the angel (חתך) plainly proves, that a *precife duration* of time is intended; for it fignifies to *cut out*, or *cut off*; that is, to fet apart, *limit*, or *determine*. It is, therefore, a precife portion of time *cut out*, *limited*, and *apportioned*, for the accomplifhment of the work foretold, fubject only to the inconfiderable fraction before noticed.*

§ 21. Others there are, who, refolving to date thefe weeks from the firft of Cyrus, and to make four hundred and ninety years the exact meafure of the time from thence to the death of the Meffiah, and not being able to difprove the computation from Alexander to that time, fall alfo

---

* The Jewifh mode of attempting to folve the difficulty, by dating the weeks from the deftruction of the temple, by the Chaldeans, and ending them in the defolation of the fecond houfe, is beneath farther notice; as excluding in their computation thofe tranfactions which are equally notorious to mankind, as that there ever was fuch a thing as the Perfian empire. And to fuppofe that there were no more kings of *Perfia* than are mentioned in the books of Ezra and Nehemiah, is no lefs futile than it would be to fay, that there were never above three or four kings of the *Affyrian* empire, becaufe there are no more mentioned in fcripture. But if a full chronological account was not *intended* in thofe books, this (ανισἱοργησια) *non-infertion in hiftory*, is beneath all confideration.

upon the Perfian empire, and cut it fhort above fifty years of the general account, to fit it to the place they have provided for it. To this end they reject the account of the Chaldeans, Grecians, and Romans, concerning the time of its continuance, as fabulous, and give us a new *arbitrary* account of the reign of thofe kings whom they will allow. But independent of the extraordinary liberty required to warrant fuch a procedure, it is deftitute of all probability. The word *decree*, or commandment, mentioned to Daniel is, that for the *building* of Jerufalem; that is, the *reftoring* of it into a condition of rule and government, and not merely the fetting up of houfes. Confequent to this, their 'building of the walls' alfo, for the defence of the people is mentioned. Of this it is faid, that it fhould fall out in a *troublefome time*, or a time of ftreights, as accordingly it fell out in the days of Nehemiah. In the whole, there is not the leaft mention of *building the temple*, which, had it been intended, could not, I fuppofe, have been omitted. But in the *decree of Cyrus*, the principal thing mentioned and aimed at is, the re-edification of the *temple*, the *city*, and the *walls* thereof, being not fpoken of, [Ezra i. paffim.] It feems, then, evident, that the decree mentioned by Daniel, for the building of the city and walls, and *that* given out by Cyrus, for the building of the temple, were divers. Befides, this decree of Cyrus, although foretold long before, and made famous, becaufe it was the *entrance* into the people's return and fettlement, took effect for fo fhort a fpace of time, being obftructed within lefs than three years, and utterly fruftrated within four or five, that it is not likely to be the date of this prophecy, which feems to take place from fome *good fettlement* of the people. That alone which is pleaded with any colour for this decree of Cyrus, is the prediction recorded, Ifa. xliv. 28. It is prophefied of him, that he fhould fay to 'Je-'rufalem, thou fhalt be built; and to the temple, thy 'foundations fhall be laid.' But it is neither here foretold, that Cyrus fhould make any *decree* for the building of Jerufalem, or that it fhould be done in *his days*, as

indeed

indeed it was not until an *hundred years* after, as it is evident from the story in Nehemiah. The whole intention of this prophecy is, that he should cause the people to be set at liberty from their captivity, and give them leave to return to Jerusalem, which he accordingly did, and thereupon, both the building of the city and temple ensued, though not without the intervention of other decrees. The account, therefore, before laid down, being established, it is certain enough, that the decree mentioned by Gabriel, from the going forth whereof the seventy weeks are to be dated, was *not that* of the first of Cyrus, for the return of the captivity and building of the temple. We must, therefore, inquire for some *other decree*, from whence to date the weeks.

§ 22. The second decree of the kings of Persia, in reference to the Jews, was that of Darius, made in his second year, when the work of the building of the temple was carried on through the prophecy of Haggai and Zechariah, mentioned in Ezra vi. granted by Darius, upon appeal made to him from the neighbouring governors; and it was a mere revival of the decree of Cyrus, the roll whereof was found in Achmetha, in the province of the Medes, [ver. 2. See Hag. i. 12. ii. 10. Zech. i. 1.]

Upon the roll of the kings of Persia, we find *three* called by the name of Darius, as the Jews term him. (1.) *Darius Hysdaspes*, who succeeded Cambyses, by the election of the princes of Persia, upon the killing of Smerdes Magus, the usurper. (2.) *Darius Nothus*, who succeeded Artaxerxes Longimanus. (3.) *Darius Codomanus*, in whom the Persian empire had its period, by Alexander the Great. That the last of these can be no way concerned in the decree, is notorious; the two others are disputed. Most learned men grant, that *Darius Hysdaspes* was the author of this decree; and indeed that it was so, at least, that it can be ascribed to no other Darius, we shall soon undeniably prove. And it is not unlikely that he was inclined to this favour and moderation towards the Jews, by his general design to relieve men from under the oppressions preffions that were upon them during the reign of Cambyfes, and to renew the acts of Cyrus, their firft emperor, who was renounced amongft them, to ingratiate himfelf with mankind, and confirm himfelf in that kingdom, whereto he came not by fucceffion. And it is not improbable, that this was he who was the hufband of *Efther*. Now, Cyrus reigned after his firft decree *three* years; Cambyfes with Smerdes *eight*; and Darius, before he iffued out this decree, two years; in all thirteen years. Now, deduct this from five hundred and sixty-two, and there yet remains five hundred and forty-nine years, which exceeds the number of years inquired after by *fifty-nine* years. So that neither can this be the *commandment* intended; not to mention, that this command was a mere renovation, or a new acknowledgement of the decree of Cyrus, about the rebuilding of the temple; and fo, doubtlefs, was not defigned as the *fignal epocha* of the time here determined.

The great SCALIGER, who would date the weeks from this decree of Darius, knowing that the time would not fuit with the reign of *Darius Hyfdafpes*, contends, that *Nothus*, who fucceeded *Longimanus*, was the author of it; and extends the whole time to the deftruction of the city and temple; that fpace of time, according to his computation, being elapfed from the fecond year of Darius. But the truth is, as may be feen from our former account, that from the *fecond* year of *Darius Nothus*, to the deftruction of the city, was but four hundred and eighty years. Befides, we have before proved from the text, that the time determined was to expire in the death of the MESSIAH. Neither is it confiftent with the prophecy of *Jeremiah*, that the temple fhould be wafte fo long a fpace; that is, about one hundred and feventy years. Again, *Haggai* plainly declares, that when the work of the temple was carrying on, in the fecond year of Darius, many were yet alive, who had feen the firft temple, [Hag. ii. 3.] As multitudes were upon the laying of its foundation, in the days of Cyrus, [Ezra ii. 12.] But this was impoffible, had it been in the days of Nothus, a hundred and

and fixty or feventy years after it was deftroyed.—It appears, then, that *Darius Nothus* was not the author of the decree mentioned; as alfo that the times of the weeks cannot be dated from the *fecond year* of Darius Hyftafpes, who was the author of it.

§ 23. After this, there is mention made of two other commands, or decrees, relating to the temple and people, both granted by the *fame Artaxerxes*, one in the *feventh* year of his reign, to Ezra, [chap. vii. 7.] the other in the *twentieth* year of his reign, to Nehemiah, [chap. ii. 1.] And from one of thefe muft the account inquired after be dated. Now, fuppofing that one of thefe decrees muft be intended, it is evident, that *Longimanus*, and not *Memor*, was the author of them; for from the feventh year of Memor, which was the fecond of the ninety-fifth olympiad, to the eighteenth year of Tiberius Cæfar, wherein our Saviour fuffered, being the third of the two hundred and fecond olympiad, are only four hundred and twenty-eight years, *fixty-two* fhort of the whole. Now, thefe fixty-two years added to the beginning of the account, from the feventh of Memor, fall in exactly on the *feventh* of *Longimanus*; from the feventh of Longimanus, then, to the feventh of Memor, are fixty-two years, and from the feventh of Memor, to the eighteenth of Tiberius, are four hundred and twenty-eight; in the whole four hundred and ninety, the number inquired after.*

And there wants not reafon to induce me to fix on this decree, rather than any other, being, indeed, the moft famous, and moft ufeful to the people of all the reft. By what means it was obtained, is not recorded. Evident it is, however, that Ezra had great favour with the king,

---

* From the feventh of Longimanus, to the feventh of Memor - - -	62 years.
From the feventh of Memor, to the eighteenth of Tiberius - - -	428
From the going forth of the decree, in the feventh year of Artaxerxes Longimanus, to the death of Chrift - - -	490

and that he had convinced him of the greatness and power of that God, whom he served, [Ezra viii. 22.] Besides it was not a mere *proclamation of liberty*, like that of Cyrus, which was renewed by Darius; but a *decree*, a *law* made by the *king* and his seven *counsellors*, [Ezra vii. 14.] the highest and most irrefragable legislative power amongst the Medes and Persians. Moreover, together with the decree Ezra had a formal *commission*; he is said not only to have *leave* to go, but to be '*sent*' by the *king and his counsel*. Besides, the former decrees barely respected the *temple*; and it seems, that in the execution of them the people had done little more than building the *bare fabric*; all things, as to the true order of the worship of God, remaining in great confusion, and the civil state utterly neglected. But now, in this commission, Ezra is not only directly to set the whole worship of God in order, at the charge of the king, [Ezra vii. 16—23.] but also that he should appoint a *civil government* and magistracy, with supreme power, to be exercised as occasion required, [ver. 25, 26.] This alone, and no other, was the *building of the city*, mentioned by Gabriel; for it is not walls and houses, but policy, rule, and government, that makes a city.

And it is very considerable what a conviction of the *necessity* of this work was then put upon the spirits of the governors of the Persian empire; for the king himself calls Ezra ' The scribe of the law of the God of Heaven,' and declares that he was persuaded, that if this work was not done, ' there would be wrath from heaven upon him- ' self, his kingdom, and his son,' [ver. 23.] The seven counsellors also join in that law, [ver. 28.] So that no command that concerned that people, before or after, was accompanied with that solemnity, or gave such glory to God as this did. Besides, the whole work of *reforming* the church, the restitution of divine *worship*, and the recognition of the sacred *oracles*, by Ezra, make it manifest, that *this decree*, and no other, was intended by the angel Gabriel.

EXERCIT. 6.

THE EVASIONS OF THE MODERN JEWS ANSWERED.

§ 1. *That the Messiah's coming is delayed, and their dispersion continued, because of the sins of their forefathers, answered.* § 2. *Because of their own sins, answered.* § 3. *That the deliverance from Babylon was nothing but a trial, whereby God would make an experiment, answered.* § 4. *That the Messiah was born the same day that the second temple was destroyed, considered.* § 5. *That the promise of the Messiah's coming at the season we plead for, was not absolute, but conditional, answered.* 1. *This militates against the promise to the Gentiles.* § 6. 2. *Against Divine fore-knowledge.* § 7. 3. *Against its own pretensions.* § 8. 4. *Against the nature of the promised covenant.* § 9. 5. *Against the Messiah's ever coming.*

§ 1. BUT the Jews endeavour to evade the force of all this evidence, by various pleas; and particularly by pleading, that it is *for their sins* the coming of the Messiah is prolonged, whereby they are left in their present long dispersion. We readily grant, in a sense, it is on on account of *their sins*, that they have *no Messiah*. But we must inquire, what they intend thereby? I ask, therefore, whether it be for the sins of their *forefathers*, who lived before the last final dispersion, or for *their* sins, who have since lived in their several generations, that they are thus utterly forsaken? If they shall say, it is for the sins of their *forefathers*; then I desire to know, whether they think God to be *changed* from what he was of old; or, whether he be not still every way the same, as to all the promises of the covenant? Supposing they will say, that he is still the same, I desire to know, whether he did not, in former times, in the days of their judges and kings, especially in the Babylonish captivity, punish them for their sins, with that contemperation of justice

justice and mercy, which was agreeable to the tenor of the covenant? This, I suppose, they will not deny, the scripture speaking fully to it, and the righteousness of God requiring it. I desire, then, to know, what were the *sins of their forefathers*, before the destruction of the second temple, and their final dispersion, which, according to the rules of the covenant, so much exceeded the sins of them who lived before the desolation of the first temple, and the captivity that ensued? For we know that the sins of these former were punished only with a dispersion, which continued to more than seventy years; after which they returned again to their own land; whereas their present captivity and dispersion have now continued above *twenty times* seventy years. Now, of all the sins, which on the general account of the law of God, the sons of men can make themselves guilty of, *idolatry* is doubtless the greatest; the chusing of *other Gods* is a complete renunciation of the true God, and therefore is this sin forbidden at the very front of the law, as intimating, that if the command of owning the true God, and him alone, be not adhered to, it is to no purpose to apply ourselves to those that follow. Now, it is known to all, that this sin of IDOLATRY abounded amongst them under the *first* temple, and that also for a long continuance, attended with *violence, adulteries, persecution,* and oppression; but that those under the *second* temple had contracted the guilt of *this sin,* the present Jews do not pretend; and we know that they hated all appearance of it. Nor are they able to assign any other sins whatever, wherein they went higher in their provocations, than their progenitors under the first temple. What then is the cause of the *different events* and success between them? It cannot be, but that either they have contracted the guilt of some sin, wherewith God was more displeased, than with the *idolatry* of their forefathers, or that the *covenant* made with them is expired, or that there hath been a coincidence of both these; and that, indeed, is the fact. The Messiah came, in whom the carnal covenant was to expire, and they *rejected* and slew him; which has deserved their rejection from it, and their present disinheritance.

§ 2. Sometimes they will plead, that it is for their *own sins*, and the sins of the generations that *succeeded* the destruction of the second temple, that they are kept thus long in captivity. But we know, that they use this plea only as a covering for their obstinate blindness and infidelity. Take them from this dispute, and they are continually boasting of their *righteousness* and holiness; for they do not only assure us, that they are better than all the world besides, but also much better than their forefathers; and that on the day *of expiation*, that is, once a-year, they are as holy as the angels in heaven! Then I would fain know—whereas it is a principle of their faith, that all Jews, excepting *apostates*, are so holy and righteous, that they shall all be saved, shall all have a portion in the blessed world to come—whence is it, that none of them are so righteous as to be restored to the land of Canaan? Is it not strange, that the righteousness which serves the turn to bring them all to heaven, will not serve to bring any one of them to Jerusalem? this latter being more openly and frequently promised to them, than the former.

Again, *repentance* from their sins is a thing wholly in their own power, or it is not; if they shall say, it is in their own power, as generally they do, I desire to know, why they defer it? The glorious imaginations they have of the *levelling of mountains*, the *dividing* of rivers, the *singing* of woods, and *dancing* of trees, and of *coaches* and chariots of kings to carry them; as also the riding upon the shoulders of their rich neighbours into *Jerusalem*, the conquest of the world, the eating of *Behemoth*, and drinking the wine of *Paradise*; the riches, wives, and long life they shall have in the days of the Messiah—all these brave things make them, as they pretend, patiently to endure all their long exile and calamity. And will not all these fine things prevail with them for a little repentance, which they may perform when they please; and so obtain them all in a trice? If they are so evidently blind, about what

what they look upon as their only great concernment in this world, have they not great cause to be jealous, left they are also equally blind in other things, and particularly in that wherein we charge them with blindness? This, it seems, is the state of things; unless they repent, the Messiah will not come; unless he come, they cannot be delivered out of their calamity, nor enjoy the promises. To repent is a thing in their own power, and yet they had rather endure all miseries, and forego all the promises of God, than take in hand, and go through with it. And what shall we say to such a perverse generation of men, who openly proclaim, that they will live in their sins, though they have never more to do with God to eternity!

§ 3. Some have asserted, "That the deliverance from Babylon was nothing but a trial, whereby God would make an experiment, whether, together with the restitution of their kingdom and temple, those enormous sins of adultery, murder, and idolatry, which they had committed, could be cut off, and expiated; but instead of a discharge of their former arrears, which they were obliged to, they heaped up new debts by their sins."—But this is plainly a worthless fiction; as no man can produce one word from the scripture, where it treats of these things, in the least giving countenance thereto; or can shew, how this procedure is suitable to the justice of God; either to the general notion that we have of it, or as to any other instance recorded of it in the scripture. On the contrary, the prophets that treated concerning that dispensation of God, in places innumerable, plainly contradict this imagination.

God punisheth not the sins of their fathers upon their children, unless the children continue in the sins of their fathers. This he declareth at large, Ezek. xviii. Now, what were the sins of this people under the first temple, before their captivity? They reckon *adultery, murder,* and *idolatry.* It is, no doubt, but many of them were adulterers, and that sin among others was charged upon them by the prophets; but it is evident, that their *princi-*

cipal ruining fins were their *idolatry* and perfecution of the prophets. Now, were the Jews, that is, the *body of the people*, guilty of thefe fins under the *fecond* houfe ? It is known, that from all grofs *idolatry* they preferved themfelves, which had been in an efpecial manner, their ruin before ; and as for *killing* the prophets, they acknowledge that after Malachi they *had* none, but thofe whom they will not own to be prophets.

Suppofe that all thofe under the fecond houfe continued in the fins of their forefathers, which yet is falfe, and denied by themfelves, as occafion requires ; yet what have the Jews done for *fixteen hundred years*, fince the deftruction of that houfe ? They plead themfelves to be holy, and (applying the prophecy, Ifa. liii. to themfelves) proclaim themfelves to be innocent and righteous ; at leaft they would not have us to think, that the generality of them are adulterers, murderers, and idolaters ; whence is it, then, that the punifhment of their fathers' fins lies upon them fo long ? What rule of juftice is obferved herein ? What inftance of the like difpenfation can they produce? For our parts, we affirm, that they *continue* to this day in the *fame fin*, for which their forefathers, under the fecond houfe, were rejected and deftroyed ; and we know the righteoufnefs of God in their prefent captivity.

They fay, they abhor the fins of their forefathers, repent of them, and obtain remiffion of their fins, through their obferving the law of Mofes ; wherein, then, is the faithfulnefs of God in his promifes to them ! Why are they not delivered out of captivity ? Why not reftored to their land, according to exprefs teftimonies of the covenant made with them to that purpofe ? There is no colour of truth nor reafon, therefore, in this *evafion*, which they invented, to preferve themfelves in their obftinate blindnefs and unbelief.

§ 4. Being preffed with the teftimonies before infifted on, out of Haggai, concerning the glory of the fecond temple, and the coming of the defire of all nations into it, they have a tradition, that the Meffiah was born the fame day, that the fecond temple was deftroyed. " RABBI JODEN, in
the

the name of RABBI IBBO, faid, *The Meffiah was born in the day that the houfe of the fanctuary was deftroyed,*" &c.* Again, they have a tradition out of the fchool of one ELIAS, a famous mafter among them, of the *Jannarei*, or *Ante-Talmudical* doctors, which they have recorded in the *Talmud*, about the continuance of the world, which is as follows: " It is a tradition of ELIAS, that the world fhall continue fix thoufand years; *two thoufand void* (which the glofs of R. SOLOMON JARCHI reckons from the creation, to the call of Abraham) *two thoufand of the law* (to the deftruction of the fecond temple) and *two thoufand* for the days of the *Meffiah.*" It is incredible how the latter *Rabbins* are perplexed with this tradition of their *Mafters*, which is recorded in the *Talmud* as facred.† But what is become of him all this while? O " he was carried away by the four winds of heaven, and kept in the great fea four hundred years!" Is not this, you will fay, very ridiculous? True; but he who is offended with the citation of fuch things out of their *Talmudical doctors*, is defired only to exercife patience, until he fhall be able himfelf to report from them, things more ferious and of greater importance. And yet, from *them* muft we learn the perfuafions of the ancient Jews, or be ignorant of them. This evafion, therefore, needs nothing better than itfelf to confute it.

§ 5. They fometimes grant, that the time fixed on was determined for the coming of the Meffiah; but add withal, that the promife of his coming at that feafon was not *abfolute*, but *conditional*; namely, on fuppofition, that the Jews were righteous, holy, and worthy to receive him. And nothing is more common with them, than this condition: ' if they *deferve* it,' ' if they *repent*,' the Meffiah will come, ' the time is already paft, but becaufe of our ' fins he is not come.' ' If Ifrael could repent but one ' day he would come.' There was a time limited and

---

* Tract. *Bezaroth*, Diftinct *Hajakorr*. In *Berefhith Rabba*, on Gen. xxx. they have a long ftory to the fame purpofe.
† Tract. *Saned.* Diftinct. Chelec.

deter-

determined, they grant, for the coming of the Messiah; this time is signified in general in the scripture to be before the destruction of the second temple, and the utter departure of scribe and law-giver from Judah; but all this designation of time, they add, was but *conditional*, and the accomplishment of it had a respect to their righteousness, repentance, good works, and merits; but which failing, their Messiah is not yet come.——To this issue is their infidelity at length arrived. But there are reasons innumerable, which expose the *vanity* of this pretence. Some of them I shall briefly insist upon:

1. We have before proved, that not the Jews only, but the Gentiles also, even the whole world, was concerned in the coming of the Messiah. The prophets every where declare, that the Gentiles, the nations of the world, were equally concerned with the Jews in the promise of the Messiah's coming, if not principally intended, because of their greatness and number. The time of exhibiting this remedy to them he promised also, and limited, stirring them up to an expectation of its accomplishment, as that whereon all their happiness depended; and shall we now suppose, that all this love, grace, and mercy of God towards mankind, and his faithfulness in his promises, were all suspended on the goodness, righteousness, merits, and repentance of the Jews? Shall we suppose, that God, who so often testifies concerning them, that they were a people, wicked, obstinate, stubborn, and rebellious, should make them keepers of the everlasting happiness of the whole world? Shall we suppose, that he hath committed the fountain of his grace and love, which he intended and promised should overflow the whole earth, and make all the barren wildernesses of it fruitful, to be stopped by them at their pleasure? As if he should say in his promises, " I am resolved, out of my infinite goodness and compassion towards you, O ye poor miserable sons of Adam, to send you a Saviour and a Deliverer, who, at such a time, shall come and declare to you, the way of life eternal, shall open the door of heaven, and save you from the wrath that you have deserved; but I will

will do it on *this condition*, that the Jews, an obstinate and rebellious people, be good and holy, righteous and penitent, for unless they be so, the Saviour shall not come, nor is it possible it should, until they be so." Is this worthy of the Most High?

§ 6. 2. When God limited the time of the Messiah's coming, he either foresaw what would be the state and condition of the Jews, or he did not. If they say he *did not*; then, besides that, they deny him to be God, by denying those essential attributes of his nature, which the very heathen acknowledge in their deities; they also utterly overthrow all the predictions of the Old Testament; for there is not any of them, but depends upon a supposition of the presence of God; and this is nothing but to countenance their unbelief with perfect atheism. If they say he *did* foresee, that their conditions and manners would be according to the event, so as to know that it was impossible the Messiah would come at the time determined; I ask, to what end and purpose doth he so often, and at so great a distance of time, predict and promise that he should come, and so that not one word of his predictions should be fulfilled? Why, I say, did he *fix on a time* and season, foretell it often, limit it by signs infallible, give out an exact computation of the years, from the time of his predictions, and call all men to an expectation of his coming accordingly; when, it seems, by his foresight, he knew that, by reason of all the Jews wanting merit and repentance, no such thing could possibly take place? This were not to promise and foretell in infinite veracity, but purposely to deceive. The *condition*, then, pretended, cannot be put upon the promise of the coming of the Messiah, without a direct denial of some, and, by just consequence, of all the essential properties of Jehovah. There is not in the whole scripture the least intimation of such a condition, as that which they pretend the promise insisted on to be clogged with. It is no where said, no where intimated, that if the Jews repented, and merited well, the MESSIAH should come at the time mentioned; no where threatened, that if they did not so, his coming should be put off to an uncertain day. He was to come *to turn* men from ungodliness, and not because they *were turned* before his coming.

§ 7. 3. The suggestion overthrows the rise of the promise, and the whole nature of the thing promised. The spring of the *promise* was mere love, and sovereign grace; there was not any thing in man, Jew or Gentile, that should move the Lord to provide a remedy for them who had destroyed themselves. Now, to suspend the promise of this love and grace, on the righteousness and repentance of them to whom it was made, is perfectly to destroy it, and to place the merit of it in man; whereas it arose purely from the grace of God. Again, it utterly destroys the nature of the *thing promised*, which is a salvation from sin and misery. To suppose that this shall not be granted, unless men, as a condition of it, *deliver themselves* from their sins, is to assert a plain contradiction, and wholly to destroy the promise. He was not promised to men, because they *were* penitent and just, but to *make* them so. And to make the righteousness of Jews and Gentiles, the *condition* of his coming, is to take his work out of his hand, and to render both him and his righteousness useless. The Jews, on several accounts, are *self-condemned*, in the use of this pretence. Their great sins, they say, are the cause, why the coming of the Messiah is retarded. But what those sins are, they cannot declare. We readily grant them to be wicked enough; but withal, we know their great wickedness to consist, in that which they will not acknowledge; not in being unfit for his coming, but in *refusing* him when he came. They instance sometimes in their *hatred* one to another, their mutual *animosities*, and frequent *adulteries*, and want of observing the *sabbath*, according to the rules of their present superstitious scrupulosity. But take them from the rack of our arguments, and you hear no more of their confessions, no more of their sins and wickedness, but they are immediately all righteous and holy, all beloved of God, and better than their forefathers; yea, as before hinted, on the day of expiation they are as *holy*, if we believe

lieve them, as the *angels* in heaven. There is not one fin amongst them! Is it not strange, then, that the Messiah did not, at one time or other, come to them on that day?

§ S. 4. The vain plea is directly contrary to the nature of the covenant, which God promised to make at the coming of the Messiah, or that which he came to ratify and establish, and the reason which God gives for the making of that covenant, [Jer. xxxi. 31—33.] The foundation of the new covenant lies in this, that the people had 'disanulled and broken the former made with 'them.' Now, surely they do not disannul that covenant, if they are righteous according to the tenor of it; and unless they are righteous, they say, the Messiah will not come; that is, the new covenant shall not be made, unless by them it be first made needless! Again, the nature of the covenant lies in this, that God in it *makes* men righteous and holy, [Ezek. xi. 19.] So that righteousness and holiness cannot be the *condition* of making it,—unless it be of making it useless. This, then, is the contest between God and the Jews; he takes it upon himself to *give* men righteousness, by the covenant of the Messiah, and they take it upon themselves to *be* righteous, that he may make that covenant with them.

§ 9. 5. If the coming of the Messiah depend on the righteousness and repentance of the Jews, it is not only possible, but *very probable*, that he may *never come*. Seeing that they have not repented all this while, what *assurance* have we, nay what *hope* may we entertain, concerning the remnant of future trial? Greater calls to repentance from God, greater motives from themselves and others, they are not like to meet with. And what grounds have we to expect, that they who have withstood all these calls, without any good fruit, by their own confessions, will ever be any better? Upon this supposition, then, it would be very probable, that the Messiah should never come.

Exercit. 7.

JESUS OF NAZARETH THE ONLY TRUE AND PROMISED MESSIAH.

§ 1. *Introduction and subject stated.* § 2. (I.) *That Jesus came within the time limited.* § 3. (II.) *That no other came within that season, that could claim the character.* § 4—6. (III.) *That the scriptural characteristic notes of of the Messiah belong to Jesus Christ, and center in his person.* 1. *He came from the true flock.* § 7. 2. *The place of his birth.* § 8—13. 3. *Born of a Virgin.* § 14, 15. 4. *What he taught.* § 16—19. 5. *What he suffered.* § 20—25. 6. *His miracles.* § 26. 7. *The success of his doctrine and religion.*

§ 1. IF, then, the Messiah, came not within the time limited, all expectation from the scripture of the Old Testament must come to nought; nor can the Jews, on that supposition, in any measure defend the truth of it against an infidel. And, indeed, the ridiculous fable of his being born at the time appointed, but *kept hid to this day,* they know not where, is not to be pleaded, when they deal with men not bereaved of their senses, or judicially blind. We ask them, then, if Jesus of Nazareth be not the MESSIAH, where is he? or who is he, that came in answer to the prophecies insisted on? Three things then remain to be proved:

I. That our Lord Jesus Christ came, lived, and died within the time limited for the coming of the MESSIAH.

II. That no other came within that season, that either pretended, with any colour of probability, to that dignity, or was ever owned to be such by the Jews themselves.

III. That all the scriptural characteristical notes of the Messiah center in the person of our Lord Jesus.

§ 2. (I.) That Jesus came and lived in the *time* limited, some short space before the departure of the scepter and scribe from Judah, the ceasing of the daily sacrifices, and final desolation of the second temple, we have all the evidence that a matter of fact so long passed is capable of. The histories of the church are express, that he was born during the empire of Augustus Cæsar, in the latter end of the reign of Herod over Judea, when Cyrenius was governor of Syria; that he lived to the time when Pontius Pilate was governor of Judea, under Tiberius, about thirty-six or thirty-seven years before the destruction of the nation, city, and temple, by Titus. Neither did the most malicious and fierce impugners of his religion, such as CELSUS, PORPHYRY, and JULIAN, ever once attempt to attack the truth of the story, as to his real existence, and the *time* of it. So that herein we have as concurrent a suffrage as the whole world in any case is able to afford. The best historians of the nations, who lived near those times, give their testimony to what is recorded in our gospel. CORN. TACITUS expressly assigns the time of his death to the reign of *Tiberius*, and the government of *Pilate*. The same also is confirmed by FLAV. JOSEPHUS.*

§ 3. (II.) We secondly affirmed, that no other person came, within the time limited, that could pretend to be the Messiah. This the Jews themselves confess; nor can they think otherwise, without condemning themselves; for if any such person came, seeing they received him not, nor do own him to this day, their guilt would be the same that we charge upon them, for the refusing of our Lord Jesus. It remaineth, that either Jesus is the true Messiah, as coming from God, in the season limited for that purpose, or that the whole promise concerning the Messiah is a mere figment, the whole Old Testament a fable, and both the old and present religion of the Jews a delusion. At that season the Messiah must come, or there is an end of all religion. If any came, then, whom they

* *Antiq.* Lib. xviii. Cap. 4.

had

had rather embrace for their Messiah, than our Lord Jesus, let them own him, that we may know who he was, and what he hath done for them. If none such there was, as they will not pretend there was, their obstinacy and blindness, in refusing the only promised Messiah, is such, as no reasonable man can give an account of, who doth not call to mind the righteous judgement of God, in giving them up to blindness and obstinacy, as a just punishment for their rejection and murdering of his only Son.

§ 4. (III.) We come next to consider those *characteristic notes* that are given in scripture concerning the Messiah; and to shew, that they all agree to Jesus of Nazareth, and center in his person. The principal of them we shall now state, and vindicate against the exceptions of the Jews; particularly,

The stock whereof he came—the *place* of his birth—and *manner* of it—what he *taught*—what he *did*—and what he *suffered*. And as these are the principal of those signs and notes, that God gave out to discover the Messiah in his appointed time, being very sufficient for that purpose; so, upon the matter, they comprize all the signs and tokens whereby any person may be pre-signified.

1. For, the *family*, or lineage whereof he was to come. After the promise had for a long time run in general, that he should be of the seed of the woman, it was restricted to the *seed of Abraham*, [Gen. xv. 17.] and that alone, until God added that peculiar limitation to it, ' in *Isaac* shall ' thy seed be called,' [Gen. xxi. 12.] After this, in the family of Isaac, *Jacob* peculiarly inherited the promise; and his posterity being branched into twelve tribes, the nativity of the Messiah was confined to the tribe of *Judah*, [Gen. xlix. 10.] Out of that tribe God afterwards raised the kingly family of *David*, to be a type of the kingdom of the Messiah; and hereupon he restrained the promise to that family, though not to any particular branch of it. After this, no other restriction was ever afterwards added. It was not, then, at any time, made necessary by promise, that the Messiah should proceed from the *royal* branch

branch of the house of David, but only that he should be born of some of his posterity; by what family soever, poor or rich, in power or subjection, he derived his genealogy from him. And by the signal providence of God, no one since the destruction of the city and temple, can demonstrate that original. And yet, for what end should this token of him be given forth to know him by, when all genealogies of the people being utterly lost, it is impossible it should be of any use in the discovery of him?

The *genealogy* of Christ was written, and published to the world, by persons of unquestionable integrity, who had as much advantage to know the truth of the matter, about which they wrote, as any men ever had, or can have, in a matter of that nature. And their adversaries would undoubtedly have excepted against what they advanced, had they not been overpowered with the conviction of its truth. Had they had the least suspicion on the contrary, why did they not, in some of their consultations and rage against him and his doctrine, once object this to himself, or his followers, that he was not of the family of David, and so could not be the person he pretended himself to be. Besides, the persons who wrote his genealogy, sealed their testimony not only with their *lives*, but with their *eternal condition*; and higher assurance of truth can no man give.

§ 5. Suppose what some object be granted, that the genealogy recorded by *Matthew* be properly the genealogy of *Joseph*; what madness is it to imagine, that while avowedly proposing in the title of his genealogy, to manifest Jesus Christ to have been of the family of David, the Evangelist doth not prove and confirm what he had so designed, according to the *laws of genealogies*. No more is required for the accomplishment of the promise, but that the Lord Jesus should be *so* of the family of David, as it was required by the laws of families and genealogies, that any person might belong to it. Now, this might be by the legal marriage of his mother, to him who was of that family; for after that contract of marriage, whatever tribe or family she was of before, she was legally accounted

counted to be of that family into which, by her efpoufals, fhe was engrafted. And of that family, and no other, was he to be reckoned, who was born of her after thofe efpoufals. Now, that the reckoning of families and relations among the Jews, by God's own appointment, did not always follow natural generations, but fometimes *legal inftitutions*, is manifeft by the law of a man dying without iffue; for when the next kinfman took the wife of the deceafed, to raife up feed to him, he that was born of the woman, was, by law, not reckoned to be his fon by whom he was begotten, but was to be the fon, and fo of the family of him that was deceafed, to bear his name, and inherit his eftate, [Numb. xxxvi. 6.] And this legal cognation, Luke feems to intimate, [Luke i. 27.] where he fays, ' that the mother of Jefus was ' efpoufed to a man, whofe name was Jofeph, of the fa- ' mily of David ;' there being no apparent reafon to mention *his family*, but that the genealogy of his wife's fon was to relate thereto. And if this was the law of genealogies, as it evidently was, Matthew, recording the genealogy of *Jofeph*, to whom the bleffed Virgin was efpoufed, doth properly record that of *her fon*, according to the mind of him who gave both law and promife; and upon this *known rule of genealogies*, and legal relations, may Matthew proceed in his recital of the pedigree of Jofeph.

§ 6. Luke directly, and of fet purpofe, gives us the genealogy of the Bleffed Virgin Mary, the *mother* of our Lord; for the line of his progenitors, which he derives from Nathan, is not at all the fame with that of Jofeph from Solomon, infifted on by Matthew. It is true, there are a Zerubbabel and Salathiel in both genealogies, but this proves not both the lines to be the fame; for the lines of Solomon and Nathan might by marriage meet in thefe perfons, and fo leave it indifferent, which line was followed up to David; and the lines of Jofeph and Mary might be feparated again in the pofterity of Zerubbabel, Matthew following *one* of them, and Luke the *other*. This, I fay, is poffible, but the truth

truth is (as is evident from the course of generations insisted on) that the Zerubbabel and Salathiel, mentioned in Matthew, were not the same persons with those of the same name in Luke, those being of the house of Solomon, these of the house of Nathan. So that from David it is not the line of Joseph, but of the blessed Virgin, that is recited by Luke. And the words wherewith Luke prefaceth his genealogy, do no way impeach this assertion, (ως ενομιζετο υιος Ιωσηφ τυ Ηλὶ) ' as was supposed the son ' of Joseph the son of Eli ;' for, whereas these words (ως ενομιζετο) ' as was supposed,' are usually read in a parenthesis, the parenthesis may better be extended thus— ' being (as was supposed the son of Joseph) the son of ' Heli.'—Or Joseph may be said to be the son of *Eli*, because his daughter was espoused to him, otherwise the true natural father of Joseph was Jacob, as Matthew declares, Heli being the father of the blessed Virgin. So that both *legally* and *naturally* our Lord Jesus Christ was a descendant of the house of David, according to the promise. And as this was unquestionable among the Jews in the days of his conversation in the flesh ; so the present Jews have nothing of moment to oppose to these unquestionable records. This is the first characteristical note given of the Messiah, whereby he might be known. And it is signally corroborated by the providence of God, in that all genealogies among the Jews are now so confounded, and have been so for so many generations, that it is utterly impossible any one should rise amongst them, and manifest himself to be of this or that particular family. The burning of their genealogies by Herod, the extirpation of the family of David by Vespasian, and their long dispersion, have put an utter end to all probability about the genealogies amongst them.

§ 7. 2. Another characteristic note, pointing out the Messiah in prophecy, was the place where he should be born ; which, added to the time and the family, evidently designed his person. This place of his nativity is foretold in Mich. v. 2. ' And thou, Bethlehem Ephratah, ' is it (or, it is) little for thee to be amongst the thou-

'fands of Judah; out of thee fhall come forth
' unto me, he that fhall be a ruler in Ifrael, whofe
' goings forth are from of old, from the days of eternity.'
That of old this prophecy was underftood by the church of
the Jews, to denote the place of the Meffiah's birth, we
have an illuftrious teftimony in the records of the Chriftian church, [Matt. ii. 5, 6.] Upon the demand of
Herod, where the Meffiah fhould be born, the chief
priefts and fcribes affirm, with one confent, that he was
to be born at Bethlehem, confirming their judgement by
this place of the prophet. And afterwards, when they
fuppofed that he had been *born* in Galilee, becaufe he
lived there, they made this an argument againft him, becaufe he was not born, according to the fcripture, in
Bethlehem, the town where David was, [John vii. 41,
42.]*

When we confider the occafion of Jofeph and Mary
coming to Bethlehem, their being obliged to it by public
authority; and when we confider, that the decree for the
enrolment was of great charge and trouble to the
whole empire, and that no public ufe was ever made of
that enrolment; nor is it certain, that it was accomplifhed in many other parts of the empire; may we not
reafonably infer, that the infinitely wife Governor of all
the world puts this into the emperor's mind, and incites
him thus to fet mankind into a motion, that two perfons
of low condition might be brought out of Galilee into
Bethlehem, that Jefus, according to this prophecy, might
be born there. Had they gone of their own accord, it
might have given advantage to the Jews, to fay that the
mother of Jefus went to Bethlehem only with a view to be

---

* It is remarkable that the *Chaldee paraphrafe* renders the
words, ' Out of thee fhall come forth to me the ruler,' thus:
"Out of thee fhall come forth to me the MESSIAH, who fhall have
the dominion." R. SOLOMON expounds the place thus : " Little to
be in the thoufands of Judah; that is, thou deferveft to be fo,
becaufe of the profanation of Ruth, the Moabitefs, who was in
thee; out of thee fhall come forth to me the MESSIAH, the fon
of David."

deli-

delivered, that she might better report her son to be the MESSIAH. But by this admirable providence, all such objections are removed; their minds are determined by an authority not to be resisted; a journey they must make, at a time very unseasonable for the holy Virgin, being so near the time of her delivery, and be publicly enrolled of the *family of David*, upon the command of him who never knew ought of that business, and which none but himself could be instrumental to accomplish. Not long after this, that town of Bethlehem was *utterly destroyed*; nor hath it been for a *thousand and six hundred* years, either *great* or *small* among the thousands of Judah.

§ 8. 3. The *manner* of the Messiah's birth, that he should be *born of a Virgin*, is a third characteristical note given of him. The first promise sufficiently *intimated* that he was not to be brought into the world according to the ordinary course of mankind, but was to be (διακρίτικως) in a distinguishing manner the *seed of the woman*, to the exclusion of man. To make this design yet the *more evident*, God gives it forth directly in a word of promise, [Isa. vii. 10—16.] ' Moreover the Lord spake to Ahaz,
' saying, ask thee a sign of the Lord thy God, ask it
' either in the depth, or in the height above; but Ahaz
' said, I will not ask, neither will I tempt the Lord.
' And he said, Hear ye now, O house of David, is it a
' small thing for you to weary men, but ye will weary
' my God also? Therefore, the Lord himself will give
' you a sign: behold, a Virgin shall conceive and bear a
' Son, and call his name EMANUEL; butter and honey
' shall he eat, that he may know to refuse the evil, and
' chuse the good; for, before the child shall know to re-
' fuse the evil, and chuse the good, the land that thou
' abhorrest, shall be forsaken of both her kings.' This is the prophetic promise, the accomplishment whereof in our Lord Jesus we have recorded, Matt. i. 22, 23. ' All
' this was done, that it might be fulfilled, which was spo-
' ken by the prophet: Behold, a *Virgin* shall be with
' child, and shall bring forth a Son, and they shall call
' his name Immanuel.' Now, this being a thing utterly

above the courfe of nature, it is an infallible evidence, and *demonftrative note* of the true Meffiah. He, and *he alone*, was to be born of a Virgin; and Jefus of Nazareth alone was actually fo; therefore, Jefus alone is the Meffiah.

§ 9. The Jews being greatly preffed with this *prophecy*, and its *accomplifhment*, try all means to efcape, by breaking through one of them. And we might expect that they would principally attempt the ftory of the evangelift; but circumftances on that fide being fo cogent againft them, they are very faint in that endeavour. For, if it was fo indeed, that Jefus was not born of a *Virgin*, as it is recorded, and his difciples profeffed, why did they not charge them with an untruth? But though they infift not much upon the denial of the truth of the record; yet, to relieve themfelves, they contend, that the words of the prophet are not *applicable* to the birth of our Lord Jefus, which the evangelift reports them prophetically to exprefs.

We have formerly evinced, that the foundation and end of the Judaical church and ftate, and of the prefervation of the Davidical family, was folely the bringing forth of the promifed Meffiah. And this the *event* hath fully demonftrated in their utter rejection after the accomplifhment of that end. And on account of the *temporal* concernment of that people in the coming of the Meffiah, the promife of him was oftentimes *mixed*, and interwoven with the mention of other things, that were of *prefent ufe* and advantage to them; fo that it was not eafy fometimes to diftinguifh the things that are properly fpoken with reference to *him*, from thofe other things which refpected what was prefent; feeing both of them are together fpoken of to the fame general end and purpofe. Upon thefe principles we may eafily difcover the true fenfe and import of this prophetical prediction.

§ 10. Upon the infidelity of Ahaz, and the generality of the houfe of David with him, refufing a fign of deliverance tendered to them, God tells them by his prophets, that they had not only wearied his meffengers by their unbelief and hypocrify, but that they were ready to

weary

weary himself also, [ver. 13.] with their manifold provocations, during that *typical state* and condition wherein he kept them. However, for the *present*, he had promised them deliverance; and although they refused to *ask a sign* of him, according to his *command*, yet he would preserve them from their present fears, and utter ruin, and in his due time accomplish his great and wonderful intendment, miraculously by causing a *Virgin to conceive* and bring forth that Son, on whose account they should be preserved from utter destruction, as a church and state, until his coming. But how may it appear that it was the MESSIAH who should be thus born of a Virgin? This the prophet assures them, by telling them what he shall *be*, and accordingly *be called*: ' He shall be called IMMA-' NUEL,' or *God with us*, both in respect of his *person* and *office*; for he shall *be* God and man, and he shall *reconcile* God and man, taking away the enmity and distance caused by sin; a description of the Messiah, whereby he might be sufficiently known. And the prophet farther assures them, that this IMMANUEL shall be born truly a man, and *dwell amongst* them, being brought up with the *common food* of the country, until he came, as other men, to the years of discretion: ' *Butter and honey* shall ' he eat, until he know to chuse the good, and refuse the ' evil.' And this was enough for the consolation of believers, as also for the security of the people from the desolation feared.

But yet, because all this prophetical declaration was occasioned by the war raised against *Judah* by the kings of Israel and Damascus, God is pleased to add to the promise of their deliverance, a threatening of judgement and destruction to their adversaries; and because he would limit a certain season for the execution of his *judgement* upon them (as he had declared the safety and *preservation of Judah* to depend on the birth of Immanuel of a virgin, in the appointed season) he declares that their enemies should be cut off before the time that *any child* not yet born could come to the years of discretion, to chuse the good, or refuse the evil, [ver. 16.] Now, that

that this is the true import and meaning of the prophecy, will evidently appear in our vindication of it from the exceptions of the Jews againſt its application by Matthew to the nativity of Jeſus Chriſt.

§ 11. Firſt, they except that it is not a *virgin* that is here intended by the original word, (עלמה) which they ſay ſignifies *any young woman*. The whole controverſy from this place depending on the determination of this point; I ſhall therefore fully clear the truth of what we aſſert; and the Jews themſelves will not deny, but that if the conception of a *virgin* be intended, it muſt refer to ſome other than any in thoſe days.

I. The word (עלמה) here uſed, is from the root (עלם) *to hide*, or (נעלם) in *niphal, hidden*, reſerved. Hence the name of *virgins*; partly, from their being unknown by man, and partly, from the univerſal cuſtom of the Eaſt, wherein thoſe virgins who were of any account, were kept reſerved from all public or common converſation. Hence, by the Grecians alſo, they are called, (καταχλειςι) *ſhut up*, or *recluſes*, and their firſt appearance in public they termed (ανακαλυπτηρια) 'the ſeaſon of bringing them out *from their retirements*.' The original ſignification of the word then denotes a *virgin* preciſely.

2. The *conſtant uſe* of the word directs us to the ſame ſignification. It is *ſeven* times uſed in the Old Teſtament, and in every one of them doth ſtill denote a *virgin*, or *virgins*, either in a proper, or metaphorical ſenſe. Only one place is controverted by the Jews, [Prov. xxx. 19.] 'And the way of a man with a *maid*. But it is uſed here peculiarly with the prefix, (בעלמה) whence it is recorded by the *Seventy* in the abſtract, (εν νεοτητι) 'the way of a man *in in his youth*;' which ſenſe Jerom follows. ('*viam viri in* adoleſentiâ;') and it may thus ſeem to be differenced from the ſame word in all other places. But in reality, the meaning of the wiſe man is evident; (דרך גבר בעלמה) 'the way that a man taketh to corrupt a *virgin*,' which is ſecret, full of ſnares and evils. And when by *ſubtle* wicked ways the
ſeducer

seducer prevaileth againſt her chaſtity, ſhe afterwards (as experience but too often teaches) becomes a common proſtitute. And this I take to be the genuine meaning of the place; though it is not altogether improbable, that the wiſe man proceedeth [ver. 20.] to *another inſtance* of things ſecret; ſince the particle (כי) often ſignifies as much as, *ſo alſo*.

3. It is plainly ſome *marvellous thing* that is here ſpoken of. It is called, (אות) a *ſignal prodigy*, and is given by God himſelf, as ſomething greater, and *more marvelous* than any thing that Ahaz could have aſked, either in *heaven above*, or in *earth beneath*, had he made his choice according to the tender made unto him. 'The 'Lord God himſelf ſhall give you a ſign.' The emphaſis uſed in giving the promiſe, denotes the greatneſs and marvellouſneſs of the thing promiſed. The Jews cannot aſſign either *virgin* or *ſon*, that is here intended; whence it appeareth, that none can poſſibly in this promiſe be intended, but he whoſe birth was a *miraculous ſign*, as being born of a *virgin*, and who being born, was *God with us*.

§ 12. The Jews object, in the ſecond place, that the birth of the child here promiſed was to be *a ſign* to Ahaz, and the houſe of David, of their deliverance from the two kings who then waged war againſt them. But we do not ſay, that this was given them as a *peculiar ſign* of their preſent deliverance; for Ahaz himſelf had before refuſed *ſuch* a ſign. God therefore aſſigns a reaſon in general, why he would not utterly caſt them off, although they wearied him, but would yet deliver them, as at other times, *viz.* becauſe of that great work which he had to accompliſh among them, which was to be ſignal, marvellous, and truly miraculous. And many inſtances we have of things promiſed for *ſigns*, which were not actually to *exiſt* until after the accompliſhment of the things whereof they were a ſign, [as Exod. iii. 12. I. Sam. x. 3, 4; Iſa. xxxvii. 30. I. Kings, xxii. 25.] Beſides, this *ſign* hath the truth and force of a *promiſe*, although it was not immediately to be put in execution. Their *aſſurance*, therefore, consisted in this; that on God's declaration, as surely as he would accomplish the great promise of bringing forth the Messiah, and that he should be born of a virgin, so certain should be their present deliverance, which they so desired.

§ 13. It is farther urged, that the deliverance promised was to be brought about *before the child* spoken of should *know to refuse the evil, and chuse the good*; or should come to years of discretion, [ver. 16.] and what was this to him, that was to be born some hundreds of years after? but it doth not appear, that (הנער) *the child* mentioned, [ver. 16.] is the same with the (בן) *son* promised, [ver. 14.] The prophet, by the command of God, when he went unto the king with his message, took with him *Shear-jashul*, his son, [ver. 3.] This certainly was for some special end in the message he had to deliver, the child being then but an infant, and of no use in the whole matter, unless to be made an instance of something that was to be done. It is, therefore, probable, that *he* was (הנער) *the young child* designed, [ver. 16.] before whose growing up to discretion, those kings of Damascus and Samaria were destroyed. Or the expression may denote the time of *any child* being born, and coming to maturity of understanding, and consequently the promised child. In as short a space of time, as this promised child, when he shall be born, shall come to know to refuse the evil, and chuse the good, shall this deliverance be wrought.

§ 14. (IV.) Another *descriptive note* of the Messiah, is, what he was to *teach*. This Moses describes, [Deut. xxviii. 18, 19.] 'I will raise them up a prophet from 'among their brethren, like unto thee,' &c. This is that signal testimony concerning the Messiah, which Philip urged to Nathaniel, [John i. 45.] which Peter not only applies to him, but declares that he was solely intended in it, [Acts iii. 22, 23.) and Stephen seals that application with his blood, [Acts vii. 37.] Nor do the Jews deny that the Messiah was to be *a prophet*, or that he was *promised in these words*. It is evident from this

passage,

passage, that, in the *ordinary* course of God's dealing with the Jewish church, there was no prophet like to Moses. Hence, MAIMONIDES with his followers conclude, that nothing can ever be altered in their law, because no prophet was ever to arise with authority equal to him, who was their law-giver. But the words of the text are plain : the *prophet* here foretold, was to ' be like ' to him,' that is, he was to be a *law-giver* to the house of God, as our apostle shews, [Heb. iii. 1—5.] The words of the author of *Sepher Ikkarim* [Lib. iii. cap. x.] are remarkable : " It cannot be, that there should not at some time arise a prophet like unto Moses, or greater than he ; but thus, these words, ' there arose none like him,' ought to be interpreted, not as if none should ever be like him, but that none should be like him, as to some particular quality, or accident ; or that in all the space of time, wherein the prophets followed him, until prophecy ceased, none should be like to Moses; but hereafter there shall be one like him, or rather greater than he." Such a prophet was the Messiah to be, a *law-giver*, so as to abolish the old, and to institute *new rites* of worship. This rising up of the prophet, like to Moses, declares that the whole will of God, as to his worship, and the church's obedience, was not yet revealed. Had it been so, there would have been no need of a prophet like to Moses, to lay new foundations, as he had done. But being invested with that *authority*, it is declared, that whosoever refuseth to obey him, should be exterminated, and cast out from the privileges of being reckoned among the people of God.

§ 15. We are, then, in the next place, to consider the accomplishment of this promise, in the person of *Jesus of Nazareth*. Now, that he was a prophet, and so esteemed by the Jews themselves (until, through the envy of the Scribes and Pharisees, and their own unwillingness to admit of the purity and holiness of his doctrine, they were stirred up to oppose and persecute him, as they had done all other prophets, who, in their several generations, foretold his coming) that he was, I say,

a prophet, is evident from the record of the evangelical
ſtory; [See Matt. xxi. 46. Mark vi. 15. Luke vii. 16.
xxiv. 19. John ix. 17. vi. 14. Acts iii. 22, 23.] and
their preſent obſtinate denial of this fact is a mere con-
trivance to juſtify themſelves in their rejection and murder of him. But this is not all; he was not only a prophet in general, but he was *that prophet* foretold by Moſes
and all the prophets, who was to put the laſt hand to
divine revelations, by a full declaration of the whole
counſel of God, the peculiar work of the MESSIAH.
For,

1. The nature of this prophet's doctrine confirms our
aſſertion. Whatever *characters* of divine truth that can
rationally be conceived, are eminently imprinted on the
doctrine of Jeſus Chriſt. Whatever tends to the glory
of God as the firſt cauſe and laſt end of all things; whatever is ſuitable to excite and improve that which is good
in man, in the notions of his mind, or inclinations of
his will; whatever diſcovers his wants and defects, that
he may not exalt himſelf in his own conceit above his
real condition, or is needful to point out to him his end
or his way, his happineſs, or the method of attaining
it; whatever may teach him to be uſeful in ſociety, in
all thoſe relations in which he may ſtand; whatever is
uſeful to deter him from evil, or even to ſuppreſs the
hidden ſeeds of it, without the leaſt indulgence; whatever in ſhort, may contribute to ſtir up and direct him in
the practice of what is true, honourable, juſt, pure,
lovely, and of good report, is clearly revealed by this
prophet, and in the moſt heavenly manner.

2. The removal of types, carnal ordinances, clouds
and ſhades, with which the Moſaical diſpenſation abounded, with a clear explanation of the nature, reaſon, and
uſe of all thoſe inſtitutions, was a work no leſs glorious
than the very firſt revelation of the promiſe itſelf; and
this was what was reſerved for the great prophet, the
MESSIAH. For that God would preſcribe ordinances
and inſtitutions for his church, whoſe full nature, uſe,
and end ſhould be everlaſtingly unknown to *them*, is un-
rea-

reasonable to imagine. But Christ unveiled the mind of God in all these institutions; and we may assert, that there is not the meanest Christian, who is instructed in the doctrine of the gospel, but can give a better account of the nature, use, and end of the *Mosaical institutions*, than all the *profound Rabbins* in the world either can or ever could do; he that is ' least in the kingdom of ' God,' being greater in this light and knowledge than John the Baptist himself, who yet was not behind any of the prophets that went before him.

3. The *event* confirms the character of *that* promised *prophet* to the Lord Jesus; for whoever should not receive the word of the prophet, God threatens to require it of him, that is, as they themselves confess, to exterminate them from among the number of his people, or to reject them from being so. Now this was done by the body of the *Jewish* nation; they received him not, they obeyed not his voice; and what was the end of this their disobedience? *They who*, for their despising, persecuting, and killing the former prophets *were only* chastened, afflicted, and again quickly recovered, out of the worst and greatest of their troubles, *are*, upon their rejection of him, and disobedience to his voice, *cut off*, destroyed, exterminated from the place of their solemn worship, and utterly rejected from being the people of God. Whatever may be conceived to be contained in the commination against those who should disobey the voice of that prophet promised, is all of it to the full, and its whole extent, come upon the Jews, upon their disobedience to the doctrine of Jesus of Nazareth; which, added to the foregoing considerations, undeniably prove him to be *that prophet*.

§ 16. 5. There is yet another character given of the Messiah in the Old Testament, in what he was *to suffer* in the world, in the discharge of his work and office. This being that wherein the main foundation of the whole was to consist, and that which God knew would be most contrary to the apprehensions and expectation of that carnal people, is, of all other *descriptive notes* of him, most clearly and fully asserted. The first evident testimony given hereto, is in Psal. xxii. 1—22. It would be easy to evince, by a critical examination of every part, that it is the Messiah, and he alone, who is ultimately and absolutely intended in this Psalm; and the whole was so exactly fulfilled in Jesus of Nazareth, that it appears to be spoken directly of him, and no other. The *manner* of his sufferings is scarcely more clearly expressed in the story of it by the evangelists, than it is here foretold by David in prophecy, and therefore many passages out of this Psalm are expressed by them in their records. He it was, who pressed with the sense of God's dereliction, cried out, ' My God! my God! why hast thou for-' saken me?' He it was that was accounted ' a worm, ' and no man,' and who was reviled and reproached accordingly; at him did men ' wag their heads,' and him did they reproach with *his trust in God*; his ' bones were ' drawn out of joint,' by the manner of his sufferings; his hands and feet were pierced, and upon his vesture they did cast lots; upon his sufferings were the truth and promises of God declared and preached to all the world.

§ 17. We have yet another signal testimony to the same purpose, [Isa. liii.] As the *outward manner* of the Messiah's sufferings, with *their* actings who were instrumental therein, is principally considered in Psal. xxii. so the *inward nature*, together with the important end and effects of them, are declared in *this* prophecy. Nor is there any prophecy that fills the present *Rabbins* with more perplexities, or drives them to more absurdities and contradictions. That it is the Messiah, and none other, we have not only the evidence of the text and context, and the nature of the subject matter treated of, with the utter impossibility of applying the thing spoken of to any other person, without the overthrow of the whole faith of the ancient church, but also all the advantage from the confession of the Jews that can be expected, or need to be desired, from adversaries.—For

1. The most *ancient* and best records of their judgement expressly affirm the person to be the *Messiah*.

This

This is the *Targum* on the place, which themselves esteem to be of unquestionable, if not of divine, authority. The spring and rise of the whole prophecy, as the series of the discourse manifests, is in chap. lii. 13. and there the words, 'Behold my servant shall prosper, or 'deal wisely,' are rendered by JONATHAN; "Behold my servant, THE MESSIAH shall prosper." And among others, [chap. liii. 5.] is so paraphrased by him, as that none of the Jews will pretend any other to be intended. In the *Talmud* itself, (*Sanhed.* Tractat. *Chelek.*) among other names they assign to the Messiah, (חולי) *cholia* is one; because it is said in this place, 'that truly he bore (חלינו) 'our infirmity.' We have their *ancient Rabbins* making the same acknowledgement. To this purpose they say, (in *Bereshith Rabba*, on Gen. xxiv. 17.) "This is *Messiah* the king, who shall be in the generation of the wicked, and shall reject them.—And he shall set his heart to seek mercy for Israel, to fast, and to humble himself for them, as it is written Isa. liii. *he was wounded for our transgressions.* And when Israel sinneth, he seeketh mercy for them, as it is said again, *and by his stripes we are healed.*" And, not to repeat more particular testimonies, we have their full confession in *Alsheck*, on the place: "Behold our *masters* of blessed memory *with one consent* determine according as they received by *tradition*, that it is concerning MESSIAH *the king* these words are spoken." And therefore ABARBINEL himself, who of all his companions hath taken most pains to corrupt and pervert this prophecy, confesseth, that all their ancient wise men consented with BEN-UZZIEL in his *Targum*. So that we have as full a suffrage to this character of the Messiah, from the Jews themselves, as can be desired or expected.

2. To apply this to the Jewish people as a body, is contrary, not only to their *Targum* and *Talmud*, and their chief writers, but also, to the express words of the text, plainly describing *one* individual person. Contrary to the *context*, distinguishing the people of the Jews from him that was to suffer for them, [ver. 3—6.] Contrary to every

every particular affertion and paffage in the whole prophecy, no one of them being applicable to the body of the people. Hence JOHANNES ISAAC confeffeth, that the confideration of this place was the means of his converfion. Again,

3. The whole *work* promifed from the foundation of the world, to be accomplifhed by the Meffiah, is here afcribed to the perfon treated of, and his fufferings. *Peace with God* is to be made by his chaftifement, and healing of our wounds by fin is from his ftripes. He *bears the iniquity* of the church, that they may find acceptance with God. In his hand the *pleafure of the Lord*, for the redemption of his people, was to profper; and he is to *juftify* them for whom he died. If thefe, and the like things here mentioned, may be performed by any other, the Meffiah may ftay away, there is no work for him to do in this world. But if thefe are the things which God hath promifed that he fhall perform; then he, and none other, is here intended.

§ 18. They yet urge farther thefe words, [ver. 10.] ' He fhall fee his feed, he fhall prolong his days.' This, fay they, is not agreeable to any, but thofe who have children of their bodies begotten, in whom their days are prolonged. I anfwer,

1. It were well if they would confider the words foregoing; of his making his foul an offering for fin; that is, dying for it; and then tell us, how he that doth fo, can fee his carnal feed afterwards, and in them prolong his days.

2. He that is here fpoken of is directly diftinguifhed from the *feed*; that is, the people of God; fo that *they* cannot be the fubject of the prophecy.

3. It is not faid, that he fhall prolong his days *in his feed*, but he himfelf fhall prolong his days after his death; that is, upon his refurrection he fhall live eternally, which is called length of days.

4. The feed here are the feed fpoken of, Pfal. xxii. 30. ' A feed that fhall ferve the Lord,' and be all accounted to him for a generation; that is, a fpiritual feed,

seed, as the Gentiles are called, the 'children of Sion
' brought forth upon her travailing.' [Isa. lxvi. 8.] Besides, how the Messiah shall obtain this seed, is expressed in the next verse; ' by his knowledge shall my righteous servant justify many;' they are such as are converted to God by his doctrine, and justified by faith in him. And that *disciples* should be called the *seed*, the *offspring*, the *children* of their masters and instructors, is so common among the Jews, and familiar to them, that no phrases are more in use. [See Isa. viii. 18.]

§ 19. We may yet add some other testimonies to the same purpose. *Daniel* tells us, chap. ix. 25. (יכת משיח)
' *Messiah shall be cut off*;' i. e. from the land of the living, ' and that not for himself.' 'And Zech. ix. 9. it is said, that he shall be (עני) '*poor*;' and in his best condition, ' riding on an ass,' which place is interpreted by SOLOMON, JARCHI, and others, of the *Messiah*. He was also to be *pierced*, [Zech. xii. 10.] being the *shepherd*, [chap. xiii. 7.] " The *king*, as the *Targum*, that was to be smitten with the sword of the Lord." Agreeable to these testimonies, the Jews themselves have a tradition about the *sufferings* of the Messiah, which sometimes breaks forth amongst them. In *Midrash Tehillim*, on Psal. ii. " R. HANA, in the name of R. IDI, says, That the Messiah must bear the *third part* of the affliction that shall ever be in the world." And R. MACHIR, in *Abkath Hochel*, affirms, that God inquired of the soul of the Messiah, at the beginning of the creation, whether he would endure sufferings and afflictions for the purging away of the sin of his people; to which he answered, " That he would bear them with joy." And these sufferings of the Messiah are such, as that, without the consideration of them, no rational account can be given of any of their services or sacrifices. Now, these testimonies, it is evident, concerning the meanness, poverty, persecutions, and sufferings in this world, ascribed to the Messiah, strongly confirm the truth of our faith, as believers on Jesus.

§ 20.

§ 20. Unto thefe characters given of the Meffiah, it would be eafy to fubjoin fundry invincible arguments, proving our Lord Jefus Chrift to be the *identical perfon* promifed; particularly, we might infift on the MIRACLES he wrought,* which we might plead, not only from our own *records*, but alfo from the *notoriety* of the facts,—miracles *exceeding* thofe wrought by Mofes, whether we confider their *number*, or their *nature*; whether we confider the refident *power* of working them, or the *continuance* of that power; and efpecially when we reflect on the *communication* and *extent* of that power; and we might

---

* The pretence of the Jews, to preferve themfelves from the force of that conviction, which a confideration of Chrift's miracles extorts, is fo perfectly *monftrous*, and fo full of *ridiculous figments*, that nothing but a defign to expofe their prefent naked defperate folly and childifh endeavours to cover themfelves from the light of their own conviction, can give countenance to the repetition of it. The ftory they tell us is briefly this: "There was a *ftone* in the *Sanctum Sanctorum*, under the ark, wherein was written "*Shem Hamphorafh*," (fo the *Cabalifts* call the name Jehovah) and he that could learn this name, might, by the virtue of it, do what *miracles* he pleafed. Wherefore, the wife men fearing what might enfue thereon, made two *brazen dogs*, and fet them on two pillars before the door of the fanctuary; and it was fo, that when any one went in and learned that name, thofe *dogs*, as he came out, *barked* fo horribly, that they frighted him, and made him *forget* the name that he had learned. But *Jefus of Nazareth* going in, wrote the name in parchment, and put it within the fkin of his leg, and clofed the fkin upon it; fo that though he loft the remembrance of it at his coming out, by the barking of the brazen dogs, yet he recovered the knowledge of it again out of the *parchment in his leg*; and by virtue whereof he wrought *miracles*, walked on the fea, cured the lame, raifed the dead, and opened the eyes of the blind." We fhall only remark, that if the miracles of Chrift had not been openly performed, and undeniably attefted, no creatures that ever had the *fhape of men*, or any thing more of modefty, than the *brazen dogs* they talk of, would have betaken themfelves to fuch monftrous foolifh figments, to countenance the rejection of him. He that fhould contend, that the fun did not fhine all the laft year, and fhould give this reafon of his affertion, becaufe a certain man of his acquaintance climbed up to heaven by a ladder, and put him in a box, and kept him clofe in his chamber all that while, would fpeak to the full, with as much probability and appearance of truth, as the *grand rabbins* do in this tale.

also infift on the fuccefs of his doctrine, which would shew us, were we to attend to all the circumftances, that it is utterly improbable on any other principle, but that which he and his difciples conftantly maintained, *viz.* That he was the promifed Meffiah. But thefe things having been by others largely, and particularly infifted on, we need only to mention them. And, indeed, the bare propofal of them is fufficient to caufe all the *Jewifh exceptions* to vanifh out of the minds of fober and reafonable men. We, therefore, conclude the third part of our *general Thefis* concerning the Meffiah—That Jefus of Nazareth, whom Paul preached was HE.

EXERCIT. 8.

THE JEWS' OBJECTIONS AGAINST THE CHRISTIAN RELIGION ANSWERED.

§ 1. *Introduction, and the fubject ftated.* § 2. (I.) *Certain unqueftionable principles, to guide us in the interpretation of the promifes, which the Jews urge againft the Chriftian religion.* § 3. (II.) *The promifes referred to certain general heads, are fhewn to be confiftent with the Chriftian religion, and eminently fulfilled by it. The promifes of univerfal peace.* § 4—6. *Concerning the deftruction of idolatry.* § 7. *Concerning themfelves.*

§ 1. WHAT remaineth for a clofe to thefe differtations, is, a brief confideration of thofe objections and arguments, wherewith the prefent Jews endeavour, and their forefathers, for many generations, have laboured to defend their unbelief. But here let us not forget that it is about the *coming of the Meffiah* fimply, that we are difputing; this we affert to belong since past; the Jews deny him to be yet come, living in the hope and expectation of him, which at present is in them, but as the 'giving up of the Ghost.' And the method whereby this dying deceiving *hope* is supported in them, is principally by this one general argument; " That the *promises* made and recorded to be accomplished at the coming of the Messiah, are *not fulfilled*; and, therefore, the Messiah is not yet come." This fills up their books of controversies, and is constantly made use of by their expositors, when occasion offers. The Messiah, say they, was promised of old. Together with him, and to be wrought by him, many other things were promised. These things they see not at all fulfilled; nay, not those which contain the only work and business that he was promised for; and, therefore, they will not believe that he is come. On the contrary, we say and demonstrate, that *all the promises*, concerning the *coming of the Messiah*, are *actually fulfilled*; and those which concern his grace and kingdom, are in part already accomplished. To evidence the truth of this answer, I shall,

I. Lay down certain unquestionable principles, that will guide us in the interpretation of the promises concerning the Messiah.

II. Shew, that the promises the Jews refer to in their objections, are perfectly consistent with the Christian religion.

§ 2. (I.) 1. Among those unquestionable principles is this; that the promises concerning the Messiah *principally* respect *spiritual things*, and that *eternal salvation* which he was to obtain for his church. This we have proved at large before; and this the very nature of the thing itself, and the words of the promises, abundantly manifest. There is not one promise concerning grace, pardon, the love of God, and eternal blessedness by the Messiah, which contain the whole of his direct and principal work, but they are all, 'yea, and amen in Christ Jesus,' are all exactly made good and accomplished. And this is testified unto by *millions of souls* now in the unchangeable fruition of God,

God, and all that seriously believe in him, who are yet alive.

2. Hence it follows, that all promises concerning *temporal* things, at, or by his coming, are but *accessary* and occasional; such as do not directly appertain to his principal work, and the main design of his coming. Those which concerned the sending of the Messiah, for the accomplishment of his principal work, were *absolute*, and depended not upon any thing in the sons of men. The whole of it was a mere effect of sovereign grace. He was, therefore, infallibly to come at his appointed season. But those that concern the dispensation of God's *providence in temporal things*, may all of them be *conditional*. And evident it is, that they have one *condition* annexed to the fulfilling of every one of them; and that is, that those who would partake of them, do submit themselves to the *law* and *rule* of the Messiah. ‘The nation and kingdom that will not ‘serve thee shall perish; yea, those nations shall be ‘utterly wasted,’ [Isa. lx. 12.] The *real kingdom* of Christ being to continue through *many generations*, even from his coming in the flesh to the end of the world, and in such a *variety* of states and conditions, as God saw conducing to his own glory, and the exercise of his people's faith and obedience, the accomplishment of these promises in *several ages* and seasons, according to the counsel of the Divine will, is exceedingly suited to the nature, glory, and exaltation of it. And this one observation may be easily improved to the frustrating of all the objections of Jews from the *pretended non-accomplishment* of these promises.

3. Whereas spiritual things have the principal place and consideration in the work and kingdom of the Messiah, they are oftentimes promised in words, whose first signification denotes things temporal. All men know the worth and usefulness of the precious things of the creation, gold, silver, precious stones; of the desirable things of natural life, health, strength, long life; of the good things of men in civil conversation, wealth, riches, liberty, rule, dominion, and the like. Men know somewhat of

the worth of thefe things, whofe excellency they are fo well acquainted with, and whofe enjoyment they fo much defire. And yet, can any man be fo ftupidly fottifh as to think, that in the days of the Meffiah hills fhall leap, and trees clap their hands, and wafte places fing, and fheep of Keder, and rams of Nebaioth, be made minifters, and Jews fuck milk from the breafts of kings, and little children play with cockatrices, literally and properly? And yet thofe things, with innumerable of the like kind, are promifed. Do they not openly proclaim to the meaneft comprehenfion, that the expreffions of them are *metaphorical*, and that fome other thing is to be fought for in them?

4. By the feed of Abraham, by Jacob and Ifrael, in many places of the prophets, not their *carnal* feed, at leaft not *all* their carnal feed, is intended; but the children of the faith of Abraham, who are the inheritors of the promife. And this we have proved before, in our differtation about the *Onenefs of the Church* of the Old and New Teftament.

5. By *all people*, *all nations*, the Gentiles, all the Gentiles, or the like; not *all abfolutely*, efpecially at any *one time*, or feafon, are to be underftood; but either the *moft eminent* and moft famous of them, or elfe thofe in whom the church, by reafon of their vicinity, is more efpecially concerned. God oftentimes chargeth the Jews of old, that they had worfhipped the Gods of *all the nations*; whereby not all nations abfolutely, but only thofe that were about them, with whom they had commerce and communication, were intended. And thofe which, in an efpecial manner, feem to be defigned in thofe prophetical expreffions, are that collection of nations, whereof the *Roman empire* was conftituted, which obtained the common appellation of the *whole world*, being, for the main of them, the pofterity of *Japhet*, who were to be perfuaded to dwell in the tents of *Shem*.

6. It muft be obferved, that whatever is to be effected by the fpirit, grace, or power of the Meffiah, during the continuance of his kingdom in the world, is mentioned

in the promises, as that which was to be accomplished, *at*, or *by his coming*. But here, as we before observed, lieth the mistake of the Jews; whatever is spoken about his work and kingdom, they expect to have fulfilled, as it were, *in a day*, which, neither the nature of the things themselves will bear, nor is it any way suited to the glory of God, or the *duration* of this kingdom in the world. Indeed, all the things that are foretold about the kingdom of the Messiah, are referred to his *coming*, because before that they were not wrought, and they are produced *by his spirit and grace*, and the foundation of them all was perfectly and unchangeably laid in what he did and effected upon his first coming.

7. It is granted, that there shall be a time, during the continuance of the Messiah's kingdom in this world, wherein the *generality* of the nation of the Jews all the world over shall be called and effectually brought to the knowledge of the Messiah, our Lord Jesus Christ, with which mercy they shall receive deliverance from their captivity, restoration into their own land, with a blessed, flourishing and happy condition therein. But by whom shall these things be wrought for them? By their Messiah, say they, at his coming. But shall he do all these things for them, whether they *believe* him or no; whether they obey him or reject him, love him or curse him? Is there no more required to this delivery, but that he should *come to them?* Is it not also required, that *they should come to him?* Here then lies the only difference between us. They are in expectation that the Messiah will come to them; we, that they will come to the Messiah.

8. Suppose that there should be any particular promise or promises relating to the times and kingdom of the Messiah, either accomplished, or not yet accomplished, the full, clear, and perfect sense and intendment of which we are not able to discover; shall we therefore reject that faith and persuasion which is built on so many clear, certain, undoubted testimonies of the scripture itself, and manifest in the event, as if it were with the beams

beams of the sun? For as such a proceeding could arise from nothing but a foolish conceited pride, that we are able to find out God to perfection, and to discover all the depths of wisdom that are in his word; so, being applied to other affairs, it would overthrow all assurance and certainty in the world. What then we understand of the mind of God, we faithfully adhere to; and what we cannot comprehend, we humbly leave the farther revelation of it to his divine Majesty.

§ 3. (II.) We shall shew the perfect consistency of the promises referred to by the Jews, with the Christian religion.

First, then, they insist upon that UNIVERSAL PEACE in the whole world, which they take to be promised in the days of the Messiah. To this purpose they urge, Isa. ii. 2—4. ' And it shall come to pass in the last ' days, that the mountain of the Lord's house shall be ' established in the top of the mountains,' &c. We agree with the Jews, that this is a prophecy of the Messiah, and of his kingdom in this world; but we differ from them in the exposition of the ' mountain of the ' house of the Lord;' they take it to be *mount Moriah*, we, the *worship of God* itself. And whereas both of us are necessitated to depart from the *letter*, and allow a *metaphor* in the words—for they will not contend that the hill Moriah shall be plucked up by the roots, and taken and set on the tops of other mountains they know not where, nor can they tell to what purpose—so, our interpretation of the words, which admits only of the most usual figurative expression, the *place* being taken for the *worship* performed in it, on the account whereof alone it was ever of any esteem, is far more easy and natural than any thing they can make of the remainder of the words, supposing mount Moriah to be literally understood. And in this sense we affirm the first part of the prophecy to be long since accomplished, really and to the full. For,

1. The temporal outward peace of the world, (if any such thing be here intended) is not the *principal part* or sub-

subject of the promise; but rather the spiritual worship of God, which is evidently and openly fulfilled. That which is *temporal*, as to the times and seasons of it, is left to the sovereign will and wisdom of God for its accomplishment. Neither is it necessary that it should be fulfilled amongst *all nations at once*, but only amongst them who at any time, or in any place, effectually receive the laws of God from the Messiah.

2. That the words are not to be understood *absolutely*, according to the strictness of the letter, is evident from that part of the prediction in Micah, ' Every one shall ' sit under his own vine, and under his fig-tree,' there being many, not only persons but great nations in the world, that have neither the one nor the other.

3. The Jews themselves do not expect *such peace* upon the coming of the Messiah. War, great and terrible, with Gog and Magog, they look for. But I say,

4. That Christ at his coming wrought *perfect peace* between God and man, slaying the enmity and difference which, by reason of sin, was between them. This alone absolutely and properly is *peace*. And where this is, no wars and tumults can hinder, but that the persons enjoying it shall be preserved in *perfect peace*.

5. He hath also wrought true *spiritual peace* and love between all that sincerely believe in him, all his elect; which, although it frees them not from outward troubles, persecutions, oppressions, and afflictions in the earth, and that from some also that may make profession of his name; yet, they having peace with God, and among themselves, they enjoy the promise to the full satisfaction of their souls. And this peace of the *elect with God, and among themselves*, is the real intent of this prediction; though expressed in terms of outward peace in the world.

6. The Lord Christ by his doctrine hath not only *proclaimed* and offered peace with God to all nations, but also given precepts of peace and *self-denial*, directing and guiding all the sons of men to live in peace among themselves; whereas the Jews of old had express command for

for *war*, and destroying the nations among whom they were to inhabit, which gives a great *foundation* to the promises of peace in the days of the Messiah.

7. Let it be supposed (though not granted) that it is general outward peace, prosperity, and tranquillity that is here promised; yet, even then, the *precise time* of its accomplishment is not here determined. If it be effected during the kingdom and reign of the Messiah in the world, as we are given to expect, the prophecy is verified. Take then this prophecy in what sense soever it may be literally expounded; there is nothing in it that gives the least countenance to the judicial pretence from the words.

§. 4. The *second* collection of promises which is insisted upon, is of those which intimate the destruction of IDOLATRY and false worship in the world, with the *abundance of the knowledge of the Lord* taking away all diversity in religion that shall be in the days of the Messiah. Such is that of Jer. xxxi. 34. ' They shall teach no ' more every man his neighbour,' &c. Zeph. iii. 9. 'I will ' turn to the people a pure language, that they may call ' on the name of the Lord, to serve him with one con-' sent.' [Zach. xiv. 9.] ' And the Lord shall be king ' over all the earth,' &c. But for the present we see, say they, the contrary prevailing in the world. *Idolatry* is still continued; *diversities* of religion abound; nor can the Jews and *Christians* agree in this very matter about the Messiah; all which make it evident, that he who is promised to put an end to this state of things, is not yet come. We answer,

1. That these things are not spoken *absolutely* but *comparatively*; namely, that in those days there shall be such a plentiful effusion of the spirit of wisdom and grace, as shall cause the true saving knowledge of God to be more easily obtained, and much more plentifully to abound, than it did in the time of the law; when the people, by an hard yoke, and insupportable burden of carnal ordinances, were but obscurely, and with difficulty, instructed in some part of the knowledge of God. And that

that the words are *thus* to be interpreted, the many promises that are given concerning the instruction of the church, in the days of the Messiah, and his own office of being the great prophet of the church, which the Jews acknowledge, do undeniably evince.

2. That the terms of *all people* and *nations* are necessarily to be understood as before explained, for *many* nations, those in an especial manner in whom the church of Christ is concerned; neither can any one place be produced, where an *absolute universality* is intended.

3. That the *season* of the accomplishment of these and the like predictions is not limited to the day or year of the *Messiah's coming*, as the Jews, amongst other impossible fictions, imagine; but extends itself to the *whole duration* of the kingdom of the Messiah, as hath been shewed before.

4. That God sometimes is said to *do* that, for the effecting of which he maketh provision of outward means, though as to some persons and times they may be frustrated of their effect, or genuine tendency, which the Jews not only acknowledge, but also contend for in other cases.

§ 5. These things being supposed, we may quickly see what was the *event*, as to those promises, upon the coming of the true and only Messiah; for,

1. It is known to all, and not denied by those with whom we have to do, that at the coming of Jesus of Nazareth, setting aside that knowledge and worship of God which was in Judea, a little corner of the earth, and that also, by their own confession, then horribly defiled and profaned, the whole world was utterly ignorant of the true God, and engaged in the worship of *idols* and devils from time immemorial.

2. Although the Jews had taken great pains, and compassed sea and land, to make *proselytes*, yet they were very few, and those very obscure persons, whom they could at any time, or in any place, prevail with to receive the knowledge, or give up themselves to the worship of the God

of Israel; but of converting people or *nations* to his obedience, they never entertained the least hopes.

3. It is manifest to all the world, that upon the *coming of Jesus*, and by virtue of his gospel, all the *old idolatry* of the world was destroyed; and that the whole fabric of superstition, which Satan had been so many ages engaged in erecting, was cast to the ground, and those *Gods of the earth*, which the nations worshipped, utterly famished. Hence it is come to pass at this day, that no people or nations under heaven continue to worship those dunghill gods, which the old empires of the world adored as their deities, and in whose service they waged war against the *God of Israel*, and his people. And had it not been for Jesus Christ and his gospel, the *true God* had been, most probably, no more owned in the Gentile world, at this day, than he was at his coming in the flesh; and yet these poor blinded creatures can *see no glory* in him, nor in his ministry.

4. The Lord Jesus Christ, by his spirit and word, did not only destroy *idolatry* and *false worship* in the world, but also brought the greatest and most potent nations of it to the *knowledge of God*; so that, in comparison of what was past, 'it covered the earth as *the waters cover the* '*seas*.'

5. The *way* whereby this knowledge and worship of the' true God was dispersed over the face of the earth, spreading itself like an inundation of saving waters over the world, was, by such a secret energy of the spirit of Christ, accompanying his word and the ministration of it, that it wholly differed from the operous, burdensome, and, for the most part, ineffectual way of teaching, which was used by the priests, Levites, and scribes of old; there being much more of the efficacy of grace, than of the pains of the teachers, seen in the effects produced, according to the words of promise, Jer. xxxi. 34.

6. In this diffusion of the knowledge of God there was *way made* for the union, and joint consent in worship, of those that should receive it. For the *partition wall* between Jews and Gentiles was removed, and an holy

holy and *plain* way of spiritual worship was prescribed to all that should embrace the law of the Messiah.

7. Notwithstanding all that hath been already accomplished; yet there is still room and time remaining for the *farther* accomplishment of these predictions; so that before the close of the kingdom of the Messiah, not one tittle of them shall fall to the ground. And thus also the *open event*, known to all the world, manifests the due and full accomplishment of these promises, making it unquestionable, that the Messiah is long since come, and hath fulfilled the long-designed work.

§ 6. Neither are the exceptions of the Jews of any force to invalidate *our application* of these promises. We have shewed already, that these and the like predictions are to have a gradual accomplishment, not all at once, in every place. It is sufficient, that there is an everlasting foundation laid for the destruction of all false worship, which having had a conspicuous and glorious effect in the most eminent nations of the world, sufficient to answer the intention of the prophecy, shall yet farther, in the appointed seasons, root out the remainder of all superstition and apostacy from God. For what concerns Christians themselves, it cannot be denied, but that many who are *so called* have corrupted themselves, and contracted the guilt of that horrible iniquity which they charge upon them. But this being the crime of some certain persons, and not of the professors of *Christianity* at large, ought not to be objected to them. And I desire to know, by what means the Jews suppose that themselves and the nations of the world shall be kept from idolatry and false worship in the days of the Messiah? If it be, because their Messiah shall give such a perfect law, and such full instructions concerning the mind and will of God, that all men may *clearly know their duty*; we say, that this is already done in the highest degree of perfection conceiveable. But what if, notwithstanding this, men will follow their own vain reasonings and imaginations, and fall from the rule of their obedience into *will-worship* and superstition, what *remedy* have they provided

against such back-sliding? If they say, they have none
but only an endeavour to press upon them their duty to
the words and institutions of God; we reply, that we
have the same, and do make use of it to the same important end. If they shall say, that *their Messiah* will *kill*
them, or slay them with the sword; we confess, that
ours is not of that mind; and we desire them to take
heed, lest, in the room of the holy, humble, merciful
king, promised to the church, they look for a *bloody ty-
rant*, that shall exercise force over the minds of men,
and execute his unhallowed revenge on those whom he
likes not. And with respect to the multitude of *sects*,
which every where spring up, we reply, that as all agree
in the worship of the God of Israel, by Jesus Christ the
Messiah, which contains the sum of their religion; so,
their profession itself is not to be measured by the doctrines and conceptions of some amongst them, but by the
scripture, which they all receive and acknowledge.

§ 7. *Thirdly*, they insist upon the promises which concern THEMSELVES, and these, of all others, they most
mind, and urge against their adversaries. Nothing, they
say, is more certain and evident in the scripture, than
that the people of Israel shall be brought into a blessed
and prosperous condition by the Messiah, at his coming,
and in particular, that by him they shall be brought home
into their *own land*. But now, say they, instead of this,
that whole people is scattered over the face of the earth,
under great misery and oppression for the most part, without the least interest in the country promised to them.
And from hence it is, that they most obstinately conclude,
that the Messiah is not yet come; for until *they are rich*,
wealthy, and powerful, they will not believe that *God is
faithful*.

In the consideration of these promises, we must carefully distinguish between those which had their *full*, at least
their *principal* accomplishment in the return of the people
from the *captivity of Babylon*, and those which have a
direct regard to the days of the Messiah. It is known,
that the prophets do very usually set out that merciful
deli-

deliverance in *metaphorical expreſſions*, in order to ſet off the greatneſs of the mercy itſelf. But the preſent Jews, who look for the accompliſhing of all the moſt ſtrained allegories in a *literal* ſenſe, do wreſt them all to the times of the Meſſiah, when they hope they ſhall receive them in full meaſure; for they reckon of all things according to their outward gain and profit, and not according to the manifeſtation of the glory and love of God therein.

But let them know, that whatever is foretold and pro‑ miſed, concerning *themſelves* in the days of the Meſſiah, they have no colour of reaſon to expect, until they *receive him*, own and ſubmit to him, which, to this day, they have not done. When Moſes went out to viſit them of old in their diſtreſs, and ſlew the Egyptian that ſmote one of them; yet, becauſe they refuſed him, and would not underſtand, that it was by him God would deliver them, and endeavoured to betray him to death, their *bondage was continued* forty years longer. Nevertheleſs, at length, by the ſame Moſes were they delivered. In like manner, although the Jews have refuſed and rejected him who was promiſed to be the Saviour, and ſo continue to this day in their captivity, ſpiritual and temporal; yet it is HE, by whom, in the time appointed, they ſhall be delivered from the one and the other. But this ſhall not be done until they own and receive him; and when God ſhall give them hearts to do it, they will quickly find the bleſſed ſucceſs thereof. But all this, we ſay, muſt come to paſs, when the veil ſhall be taken from before their eyes, and they ſhall look on him *whom they have pierced*, and joyfully receive him whom they have ſinfully rejected for ſo many generations. And when, by his ſpirit and grace, they ſhall be turned from ungodlineſs, and have their eyes opened to ſee the myſtery of the grace, wiſdom, and love of God, in the blood of his Son, then ſhall they obtain mercy from the God of their forefathers, and returning again into their own land, *Jeruſalem ſhall be inhabited again*.

PART

PART III.

Concerning the Priesthood of Christ.

EXERCIT. I.

OF THE ORIGIN OF CHRIST'S PRIESTHOOD.

§ 1. *The doctrine of Christ's priesthood is more sparingly taught in other parts of scripture, but professedly in the Epistle to the Hebrews.* § 2. *The importance of the subject, and the opposition made to it, justify a particular discussion.* § 3. *Signification of the word* PRIEST. § 4. *Melchisedeck the first priest. A sacrificer. Corruption of the Targum. Legal institution of a priesthood, in reference to the Messiah.* § 5. *The origin of Christ's priesthood. The state of innocency could have no priesthood properly so called.* § 6. *This farther proved.* § 7. *Nor could it have any proper sacrifice.* § 8. *If man had not sinned, the Son of God would not have taken our nature upon him.* § 9. *Of the nature of the Divine counsels. The end of God in his works in general; and in the creation of man in particular.* § 10—13. (I.) PERSONAL *transactions in the holy Trinity, concerning man, Gen.* i. 26. § 14—18. *The same truth farther revealed and confirmed, Prov.* viii. 22—31. § 19. *The same truth expressed, Psal.* ii. 7. § 20. (II.) FEDERAL *transactions between the Father and Son, about the work of redemption.* § 21. *Explanation of terms. Covenants how ratified of old.* § 22. *A complete and proper covenant, what it requires.* § 23. *Of covenants, with respect to personal services.* § 24. *The covenant between Father and Son express.* § 25. *Counsel.* § 26. *Will.*

Will. § 27. *The things disposed of in the power of the parties.* § 28. *Matter.* § 29. *End.* § 30. *Conditions and limitations.* § 31. *Conclusion.*

§ 1. AMONGST the many excellencies of this epistle to the *Hebrews,* which render it as useful to the church, as the sun in the firmament is to the world; the revelation that is made therein, concerning the nature, singular pre-eminence, and use of the priesthood of our Lord Jesus Christ, may well be esteemed to deserve the principal place. The subject, indeed, as to the *substance* of it, is delivered in some other passages of the New Testament; but yet more sparingly than, perhaps, any other truth of the like importance. The Holy Ghost reserved it for this, as its proper place; where, upon the consideration of the *Old Testament* institutions, and their removal out of the church, it might be duly represented, as that which gave an *end* to *them* in their accomplishment, and *life* to those ordinances of *evangelical* worship, which were to succeed in their room.

When our Lord Jesus says, that he came ' to give ' his life a *ransom* for many,' [Matt. xx. 28.] he had a respect to the *sacrifice* that he had to offer, as a priest. The same also is intimated, where he is called the *Lamb of God,* [John i. 29.] Our apostle also mentioneth his *sacrifice,* and his *offering* of himself unto God, [Ephes. v. 2.] On which account he calleth him a *propitiation,* [Rom. iii. 25.] and mentioneth also, his *intercession* with the benefits thereof, [Rom. viii. 34.] The clearest testimony to this purpose is, that of the apostle John, who puts together both the general acts of his *sacerdotal* office, and intimates wihal, their mutual relation, [I. John ii. 2.] for his intercession as our *advocate* with his Father, respects his oblation as he was a *propitiation* for our sins. So the same apostle tells us, that ' he washed us in his own ' blood,' [Rev. i. 5.] when he expiated our sins by the sacrifice of himself. But for the principal acquaintance we have with these and sundry other evangelical mysteries,

espe-

especially in reference to the nature and use of *Mosaical institutions*, which make so great a part of the scripture, we are entirely obliged to the revelation made in this *Epistle*.

§ 2. And this doctrine concerning the *Priesthood* of Christ, and the sacrifice that he offered, is, on many accounts, deep and mysterious. This our apostle plainly intimates in sundry passages of this epistle. With respect hereunto, he saith, the discourse he intended was (δυσερμήνευτος) *hard to be uttered*, or rather hard to be *understood when uttered*, [chap. v. 11.] As also another apostle, that there are in this *epistle* (δυσνόητά τινα, II. Pet. iii. 16.) *some things hard to be understood*. Hence it is required, that those who attend to this doctrine, should be past living on *milk only*, or be contented with the first rudiments and principles of religion ; and that they may be able to digest *strong meat*, by having " their senses exercised, to discern good and evil," [chap. v. 12—14.] And when he resolves to proceed in the explication of it, he declares that he is leading them *on to perfection*, [chap. vi. 1.] or the highest and most perfect doctrine in the mysteries of the Christian religion.

Moreover, the doctrine concerning the *priesthood*, and sacrifice of the Lord Christ, which contains the principal foundation of the faith and comfort of the church, hath *in all ages*, by the craft and malice of Satan, been either directly opposed, or variously corrupted. But there is a generation of men whom the craft of Satan (who envies the *strong consolation* of the church, which he knows proceeds in a great measure from this truth) hath stirred up in this and the foregoing age, who have made it a great part of their preposterous and pernicious endeavours to overthrow this *whole office* of the Redeemer, and the efficacy of the sacrifice of himself depending on that office. This they have attempted with much subtlety and diligence, introducing a *metaphorical*, or imaginary *priesthood* and *sacrifice* in their room ; and so, robbing the church of its principal treasure, they pretend to supply the want of it with their own fancies. And there are more reasons

Exer. I. PRIESTHOOD OF CHRIST. 261

sons than one, why I could not omit a strict examination of their *reasonings* and *objections* against this great part of the mystery of the gospel.

§ 3. Our Lord Jesus Christ is, in the Old Testament, called (כהן) *Cohen*, [Psal. cx. 4.] 'Thou art *Cohen* for 'ever.' Also it is said of him, [Zech. vi. 13.] 'He 'shall be *Cohen* upon his throne.' We render it in both places a *priest* (ιερευς, *sacerdos*.) In this epistle he is frequently said to be (ιερευς and αρχιερευς, *Pontifex, Pontifex Maximus) a priest* and *high priest*. The meaning of these words must be first inquired into.

The verb (כהן) is used only in *pihil, cihen*; and it signifies (ιερεργειν, *sacerdotio fungi*, or *munus sacerdotale exercere) to be a priest*, or *to exercise the office of the priesthood*. The *Septuagint* mostly render it by (ιεραζευω, *sacerdotio fungor) to exercise the priestly office*. Some would have the word to be ambiguous, and to signify *(officio fungi, aut ministrare in sacris aut politicis) to discharge an office*, or *to minister in things sacred or political*. But no instance can be produced of its use to this purpose. The word is, therefore, *sacred*; or is used properly only in a sacred sense.

The *Arabic* (כהן) *Cahan*, is, to *divine*, to prognosticate, to be a *soothsayer*, to *foretell*; and *Caahan* is a *diviner*, a *prophet*, an *astrologer*, a *figure-caster*. This use of it came up after the priests had generally taken themselves to such arts, as were partly curious, partly diabolical, by the instigation of the false gods to whom they ministered.

§ 4. He who was first called (כהן) a *priest* in the scripture, probably in the world, was *Melchisedeck*, [Gen. xiv. 18.] Sometimes, though rarely, it is applied to express a *priest* of false gods; as of *Dagon*, [I. Sam. v. 5.] and of *Egyptian* deities, [Gen. xli. 45.] 'Joseph married 'the daughter of Potipherah, *priest* of *On*;' that is, of *Heliopolis*, the chief seat of the Egyptian religious worship. It is confessed, that this name is sometimes used to signify *secondary princes*, or princes of a *second rank*; but the Jews, after the *Targum*, offer violence to Psal. cx. 4. where they would have Melchisedeck to be called *Cohen*,

Vol. I.   N n   *because*

because he was a *prince*; for it is expressly said of him, he was *a king*, of which rank none is, on account of his office, ever called *Cohen*. I say, therefore, that *Cohen* is properly (θύτης) a *sacrificer*; nor is it otherwise to be understood, unless the abuse of the word be obvious, and a *metaphorical* sense necessary. The *Targumists* make a great difference in rendering the word. Where it intends a priest of God *properly*, they retain it; where it is applied to a *prince*, or ruler, they render it by (רבא) *rabba*; and where applied to an *idolatrous* priest, by (כומרא) *comara*. But in this matter of Melchisedeck, [Gen. xiv. 18.] they are peculiar: 'And he was (משמש) *meshamesh, a minister* 'before the high God.' And by this word they express the ministry of the priests, [Exod. xix. 22.] 'The priests 'who draw nigh (לשמשא) *to minister* before the Lord;' whereby it is evident, that they understood him to be a *sacred officer*, or a *priest* unto God. But in Psal. cx. 4. where the same word occurs again to the same purpose, they render it by (רבא) *a prince*, or great ruler: 'Thou 'art a *great ruler*, like Melchisedeck;' which is a part of their open corruption of that psalm, with a design to apply it unto David; for the author of *that Targum* lived after they knew full well how the prophecy in that Psalm was in our books, and, by Christians, applied to the Messiah, and how the ceasing of their law and worship was, from thence, invincibly proved in this epistle. This made them maliciously to pervert the words in their *paraphrase*, although they durst not violate the sacred text itself. But the text is plain; 'Melchisedeck was *Cohen* to 'the high God;' a *priest*, one called to the office of solemn *sacrificing* to God; for he that offereth not sacrifice to God, is not a priest to him; for this is the principal duty of his office, and from which the whole receives its denomination. But, that *Melchisedeck* was by office a *sacrificer*, appears, from Abraham's delivering up unto him, [Gen. xiv. 20.] 'The tenth of all;' that is, as our apostle interprets the place (των ακροθινιων) *of the spoils* he had taken; among which, there is no question but there were many *clean beasts* meet for sacrifice. For in their

herds

herds and cattle confifted the principal parts of the riches of thofe days, and thefe were the principal fpoils of war, [See Numb. xxxi. 32, 33.] Abraham, therefore, delivered thefe fpoils to Melchifedeck, as the *prieft* of the high God, to offer in *facrifice for him*. And it may be, there was fomewhat more in it, than the mere pre-eminence of Melchifedeck—whereby he was the firft and *only prieft in office*, by virtue of fpecial Divine call—namely, that Abraham himfelf coming immediately from the flaughter of many kings, and their numerous armies, was not yet prepared for this facred fervice.

Sacrificing had been hitherto left at liberty; every one who was called to perform any part of folemn religious worfhip, was allowed to difcharge that duty alfo. But it pleafed God, in the reducing of his church into peculiar order, the more confpicuoufly to reprefent what he would afterwards really effect in Jefus Chrift, to erect among them a peculiar office of priefthood; whereby an *inclofure* of facrificing was made to the office of the priefts; that is, fo foon as there was fuch an office, by virtue of fpecial inftitution, it belonged *exclufively* to that office.

Whereas, therefore, it is prophefied, that the *Meffiah* fhould be a *prieft*, the principal meaning of it is, that he fhould be a *facrificer*; one that had a right, and was actually called to offer facrifice unto God. This is the general and real notion of a *prieft* amongft all men throughout the world.

§ 5. We have feen that Jefus Chrift is a prieft; he was prophefied of under the Old Teftament, and declared to be fo in the New. The ultimate *origin* of this office lies in the eternal counfels of God; but our prefent defign is, to trace thofe *difcoveries*, which God hath made of his eternal counfels in this matter, through the feveral degrees of Divine revelation.

Our firft condition under the law of creation was a condition of innocency and natural righteoufnefs; and, therefore, God had not ordained an eftablifhment in it of either prieft or facrifice.—They would have been of no ufe in that ftate; for there was nothing fuppofed, which might be prefigured or reprefented by them. Wherefore God did not pre-ordain the priefthood of Chrift, with any refpect to the obedience of man under the law of *creation*; nor fhould any fuch have been upon a fuppofition of its continuance.

There is an indiffoluble relation between priefthood and facrifice; they mutually affert or deny each other. Where the one is *proper*, the other is fo alfo; and where the one is *metaphorical*, fo is the other. Thus, under the Old Teftament, the priefts who were properly fo by office, had proper carnal facrifices to offer; and under the New Teftament, believers being made priefts unto God; that is, fpiritually and metaphorically, fuch alfo are their facrifices, fpiritual and metaphorical. Wherefore, arguments againft either of thefe conclude equally againft both. Where there are no priefts, there are no facrifices; and where there are no facrifices, there are no priefts. We may, therefore, conclude—that there was no priefthood to be in the ftate of innocency; whence it will follow, that there could be no facrifice. And—that there was to be no facrifice properly fo called; whence it will equally follow, that there was no priefthood therein.—That which enfues on both, is, that there was no counfel of God concerning either priefthood or facrifice in that ftate.

§ 6. ' For every *high prieft* taken from among men, is
' ordained for men in things pertaining to God, that he
' may offer both gifts and facrifices for fins,' faith our apoftle, [Heb. v. 1.] What is here affirmed of the *high prieft* is true, in like manner, concerning *every prieft*; only the high prieft is here mentioned by way of eminence; becaufe by him our Lord Chrift, as to his office, and the difcharge of it, was *principally* reprefented. Every prieft is, therefore, one ' taken from among men;' he is *(naturæ humanæ particeps) partaker of human nature* in common with other men; and antecedently to his affumption of his office, he is one of the *fame rank* with other men; he is *taken*, or feparated *from among* them,

and

and is vested with his office, by the authority and according to the will of God.

This office, therefore, is not a thing which is *common* to all, nor can it take place in any state or condition, wherein the whole performance of divine service is equally incumbent on all individually; for none can be taken from among others, to perform that which those others are every one obliged personally to attend to. But every priest, properly so called (καθισ]α]ται υπερ ανθρωπων) *is ordained*, or appointed, *to act for other men.* He is set over a work in the behalf of those other men, from among whom he is taken, that he may take care of, and perform (τα προς τον Θεον) *things pertaining to God*; or do the things that in behalf of men are to be done with God; that is, (בפר אלהים) *to pacify God*, to make *atonement* and reconciliation, by offering (δωρα και θυσιας) various sorts of *gifts* and *sacrifices*, according to God's appointment. This *office*, therefore, could have no place in the state of innocency; for it will not bear an accommodation of any part of this essential character of priesthood. I acknowledge, that in the state of uncorrupted nature, there would have been some (υπερ τε Θεε, τα προς τον ανθρωπον) *to deal with others for God*; for some would have been warranted and designed, in virtue of natural relations, to instruct others in the knowledge of God, and his will. They were to be (υπερ Θεε) *for God*, or in his stead to them, to instruct them in their duty suitable to the law of their creation. But every one thus instructed, was, in his own name and person, to attend to the things of God, or what was to be performed on the behalf of men; for in reference to God, there would have been no *common root* or principle for men to stand upon. Whilst we were all in the loins of *Adam*, we stood all in him, and we also fell all in him; but (εφ᾽ ω παν]ες ημαρ]ον, Rom. v. 12.) so soon as any one had been born into this world, and should have a personal subsistence of his own, he was to *stand by himself*, and to be no more, as to his covenant interest, concerned in the obedience of his progenitors. Every one was in his own person to discharge all duties of worship

ship towards God. Nor is it conceiveable, how any one could be taken out from the residue of men, to discharge the works of religion officially towards God for them, without its being to the prejudice of their right, and the hindrance of their duty. It follows, therefore, that the office of a priest, acting for men towards God, was impossible in that state.

§ 7. This is also the case, with reference to *sacrifices*; because of the relation between them and the priesthood. Hence is that saying (in *Bereshith Rabb.*) " *As is the altar for sacrifice, so are the priests belonging to it.*" By *sacrifice*, in this inquiry, we understand those that are *properly* so; for that which is *proper*, in every kind, is first. Nor is there any place for that which is *improper*, or metaphorical, unless *something proper*, from whence the denomination is taken, have preceded; for in allusion thereunto, doth the *metaphor* consist. Now, in the state of innocency nothing went before, with respect to which any thing might be so called; as now our spiritual worship is, with respect to them, under the Old Testament.

Concerning these sacrifices, we may consider their *nature*, and their *end*. A sacrifice is (זבח, θυσια, *victima*; *sacrificium mactatum*;) a *slain* or *killed offering*; yea, the first proper signification of the verb (זבח) is *(mactavit, jugulavit, decollavit, occidet)* to *kill*, to *slay by effusion of blood*, and the like. The substantive also (זבח, *mactatio, jugulatio, occisio,)* conveys the same meaning. It is, therefore, evident, that there neither is, nor can be, any sacrifice, properly so called, but what is made by the *killing* or *slaying* of the thing sacrificed. And the offering of inanimate things under the law, as of flour, or wine, or the fruits of the earth, were *improperly* so called, by virtue of their conjunction with such as were properly so. They might be (עולות) *offerings*, or *ascensions*; but (וזבחים) *sacrifices* they were not. And the nature of a sacrifice principally consists—not in the *actings* of the sacrificer, but—in the *bringing* of it to be slain, and in the *slaying itself*

itself; all that followed, belonging to the religious manner of testifying thereby faith and obedience.

This also discovers the proper and peculiar *end* of sacrifice, properly so called; especially such as might prefigure the sacrifice of Christ, to which our present discourse is confined. All such sacrifices must respect *sin*, and an atonement to be made for it. There never was, nor ever can be, *any other leading end* of the effusion of blood in the service of the living God. This the nature of the action, and the whole series of divine institutions in this matter, fully manifest. For to what end should a man take another creature, in his power and possession, which also he might use to his advantage; and, slaying it, offer it up unto God, if not to confess a *guilt* of his own, or somewhat for which he deserved to die; and to represent a *commutation* of the punishment due unto him, by the substitution of another in his room, according to the will of God?

§ 8. Some have maintained, that if man had not sinned, yet the Son of God should have taken our nature on him. In answer to which, we shall here only say, that the assertion is (αγραφον) *unwritten* (αντιγραφον) *contrary* to what is written, and (αλογον) *destitute* of any solid spiritual *reason*, for the confirmation of it; and, therefore, must needs be false. I say, that to ascribe to God a purpose of sending his Son to be incarnate, without respect to the redemption and salvation of sinners, is to enervate and contradict the whole design of revelation, and particular testimonies without number. ORIGEN observed this; " If sin had not been, there would have been no necessity, that the Son of God should be made a lamb; but he had remained what he was in the beginning, *(Deus verbum)* GOD THE WORD. But because sin entered into the world, and stood in need of a *propitiation*, which could not be but by a *sacrifice*, it was necessary that a sacrifice for sin should be provided."*

* *Homil.* xxiv. in Numer.

From what hath been spoken, it appears, that there was no decree, no counsel of God, concerning either *priest* or *sacrifice*, with respect to the law of creation, and the state of innocency. A supposition, therefore, of the entrance of *sin*, and what ensued thereon, the curse of the law, lie at the foundation of all real priesthood and sacrifice. Having made these previous remarks, it remains, that we proceed to declare the *special origin* of the priesthood of Christ in the counsel of God.

§ 9. From what hath been discoursed, it is manifest, that the counsel of God, concerning the priesthood and sacrifice of his Son to be incarnate for that purpose, had respect to *sin*, and the *deliverance* of the elect from it. That which now lies before us, is, to inquire more expressly into the *nature of the counsels of God* in this matter, and their progress in execution. And as, in this endeavour, we shall carefully avoid all *curiosity*, or vain attempts to be 'wise above what is written;' so, on the other hand, study with sober diligence to improve what is revealed, to the end that we should so increase in knowledge, as to be established in faith and obedience.

God, in the *creation of all things*, intended to manifest his nature in its being, existence, and essential properties; and the things themselves that were made, had, in their nature and order, such an impress of Divine wisdom, goodness, and power, as *made manifest* the original cause from whence they proceeded, [Rom. i. 19 —21. Psal. xix. 1, 2, &c.] Wherefore the visible works of God, man only excepted, were designed for no other end, but to declare in general, the nature, being, and existence of God. But in this nature (as we learn from his word of grace) there are three persons distinctly subsisting. And herein consists the most incomprehensible and sublime *perfection* of the Divine Being. This, therefore, was designed to be manifested and glorified in the creation of man: herein God would glorify himself, as subsisting in *three distinct persons*, and himself in each of these persons distinctly. And as this was not designed immediately in other parts of the visible creation, but in this

this, which was the complement and perfection of them; therefore, the first exprefs mention of a *plurality* of perfons in the Divine nature, is in the creation of man. And therein alfo are the *perfonal tranfactions* intimated, concerning his prefent and future condition.

§ 10. (I.) This, therefore, is what, in the firſt place, we ſhall evince—" That there were from all eternity, PERSONAL *tranfactions* in the Holy Trinity, concerning mankind, in their temporal and eternal condition, which firſt manifeſted themfelves in our creation."

The firſt relation of the counfels of God, concerning this matter, we have, Gen. i. 26. (ויאמר אלהים נעשה אדם בעלמנו כדמותנו וירדו) '*And God faid, let* us *make* MAN *in* ' OUR *image according to* OUR *likenefs; and let* THEM *have* ' *dominion.*' This was the counfel of God concerning the making of (אדם) *Adam*; that is, not that *individual* perfon who was firſt created, and fo called; but of the *fpecies* of creature which, in him, he now proceeds to create; for the word '*Adam*' is ufed in this, and the next chapter, in a three-fold fenfe:—*Firſt*, for the name of the *individual* man who was firſt created. He was called *Adam* from *Adama*, the *ground*, from whence he was taken, [chap. ii. 19—21. I. Cor. xv. 47.] *Secondly*, it is taken *indefinitely* for *the man* fpoken of, chap. ii. 7. And ' the Lord created (האדם) *man*;' not he; whofe name was Adam, for the *He Hajediah* is never prefixed to any proper name; but the *man* indefinitely of whom he fpeaks. *Thirdly*, it denotes the *fpecies* of mankind; as in this place; for the reddition is in the *plural* number: ' And let *them* have dominion;' the multitude of individuals being included in the expreffion of the *fpecies*; hence it is added, [ver. 27.] ' So God created *man* ' in his own image, in the image of God created he *him*, ' male and female created he *them*;' which is not fpoken with refpect to *Eve*, who was not then made, but to the *kind*, or race of men, including *both fexes.*

Concerning them, God faith, (נעשה) *let us make* in the *plural* number; and ſo are the following expreffions of

God in the fame work (בְּצַלְמֵנוּ) ' *in* OUR *image,* (כִּדְמוּתֵנוּ) ' *according to* OUR *likeness.*' This is the *first* time that God fo expreffeth himfelf; as to all other parts of the creation, we hear no more but (וַיֹּאמֶר אֱלֹהִים) ' *and God* ' *faid*;' in which word alfo I will not deny, but refpect may be had to the *plurality of perfons* in the Divine effence, as the Spirit is expreffly mentioned, chap. i. 2. But here that myfterious truth is clearly revealed.

§ 11. It is an eafy way, which fome have taken in the expofition of this place, to folve the feeming difficulty: God, they fay, fpeaks in it plurally *(more regio) in a kingly manner.* " It is the manner of the Hebrews, faith GROTIUS, to fpeak of God as of a king; and kings tranfact important matters with the *counfel* of the chief men about them, [I. Kings xii. 6. II. Chron. x. 9. I. Kings xxii. 20.]" But the queftion is not about the manner of fpeaking among the *Hebrews* (of which yet no inftance can be given to this purpofe) but of the words of God himfelf, concerning *himfelf*; and of the reafon of the *change* of the expreffion ufed conftantly before. God is king of all the world, and if he had fpoken *more regio,* would he not have done it, with refpect to the whole creation, equally, and not fignally with refpect to man? Befides, this *mos regius* is a cuftom of much later date; and that which then *was not,* was not *alluded to.* And the *reafon* added, why this form of fpeech is ufed—becaufe " kings do great things on the counfel of their principal attendants"—requires, in its application, that God fhould confult with fome *created princes,* about the creation of man, which is an *anti-fcriptural* figment.

The ancients unanimoufly agree, that a *plurality of perfons* in the Deity is here revealed and afferted; yea, the counfel of *Syrmium,* though dubious, though *Arianizing* in their confeffion of faith, denounced an *anathema* to any that fhall deny thefe words, ' *Let us make man,*' to be the words of the Father to the Son, (Sacrat. Lib. II. Cap. xxv.) CHRYSOSTOM lays the weight of his argument for it, from the *change* in the manner of expreffion before ufed, as he juftly and folidly might. AMBROSE obferves,

(Apparet

(Apparet *concilio trinitatis* creatum effe hominem) "it appears that man was created *by a counsel of the Trinity.*" Nor have any of thofe, who of late have efpoufed this evafion, anfwered the arguments of the *ancients* in favour of this Catholic fenfe, nor replied with any likelihood of reafon to their exceptions againft the contrary interpretation THEODORET (in Quef. xx. in *Gen.*) urgeth, that if God ufeth this manner of fpeech, concerning himfelf, merely to declare his mind *more regis*, he would have done it *always*, at leaft he would have done it often. However, it would unavoidably have been the form of fpeech ufed in that kingly act of *giving the law* at Sinai; for that, if any thing, required the *kingly ftyle* pretended. But the abfolute contrary is obferved. God, in that whole tranfaction with his peculiar people and fubjects, fpeaks of himfelf conftantly in the *fingular* number.

There are two forts of perfons, who, with all their ftrength and artifices, oppofe our expofition of this place; namely, the *Jews* and the *Socinians*, with whom we have to do perpetually, in whatever concerns the *perfon* and *office* of Chrift the Meffiah.

The *Jews* are at no fmall lofs, as to the intention of the Holy Ghoft, in this expreffion. PHILO (de *Opificio Mun.*) knows not on what to fix, but after a pretence of fome fatisfactory reafon, adds; "The true reafon hereof is known to God alone." The reafon which he efteems moft probable, is taken out of PLATO, in his *Timæus*; for whereas, he faith, that there was to be in the nature of man a principle of *evil*, it was neceffary that it fhould be from another author, and not from the moft high God. Such woeful miftakes may be paffed over in PLATO, who had no infallible rule to direct him in his difquifition after truth; but in him who had the advantage of the fcriptures of the Old Teftament, it cannot be excufed, feeing this figment rifeth up in oppofition to the whole defign of them.—Some feek an evafion in fuppofing the verb (נעשה) to be the *firft perfon fingular in Niphal*; and not the *firft perfon plural in Kal*; *(homo factus eft)* man, or *Adam, was made* in our image and likenefs; that is, of

Moses and other men. Of this expofition ABEN-EZRA says plainly, "It is an interpretation for a fool;" and well refutes it from thefe words of God himfelf, Gen. ix. 6. JOSEPH KIMKI would have it, that God fpeaks to *himfelf*, or the *earth*, or the four *elements*. Some of them affirm that God, in thefe words, confulted "with his family above;" that is, the *angels*. Others fay it is God and "his houfe of judgement." Other vain and foolifh conjectures of their's, in this matter, I fhall not repeat. Thefe inftances are fufficient; for hence it is evident into what uncertainty they caft themfelves, who are refolved upon an oppofition to the truth. They know not what to fix upon, nor wherewith to relieve themfelves. Although they all aim at the fame, yet, what one embraceth another condemns, and thofe that are wifeft reckon up all the conjectures they think of together, but fix on no one, as true, or as deferving to be preferred before others. For *error* is no where ftable or certain, but fluctuates like the fabled ifle of *Delos*, beyond the fkill of men or devils, to give it a fixation.

§ 12. GEORGIUS ENIEDINUS, whofe writings, indeed, gave the firft countenance to the *Antitrinitarian* caufe, urges feveral objections (in his *Explicationes locorum Veteris & Novi Teftamenti*) moftly borrowed from the JEWS, invented by them out of hatred to the Chriftian faith. But thefe gentlemen always think it fufficient to their caufe, to put in *cavilling exceptions* to the cleareft evidence of any *Divine teftimony*, without caring to give any fenfe of their own, by which they will abide as the true expofition of them.

He, therefore, firft pleads: "If there is any ftrength in this argument, it only proves that there are *many* Gods." Sophiftical and vain cavil! Is not the *unity* of the Divine nature always fuppofed in our difquifition concerning the perfons fubfifting therein? Nor do we plead for *three* diftinct perfons in the Trinity, from *this place*. What we contend for here is, that there is a *plurality of fubfiftencies* in the Divine nature; but that thefe are *Three*, neither more nor lefs, we prove from other places

places of scripture, without number. Without a supposition of this *plurality of persons*, we say, no tolerable account can be given of the reason of this assertion, by any who acknowledge the *unity* of the Divine nature. And we design no more, but that there is implied *mutual counsel*, which, without a distinction of persons, cannot be imagined. This whole pretence, therefore, founded on vain and false supposition, that the testimony is used to prove a *certain number* of persons in the Deity, is altogether vain and frivolous. It is granted, that *one speaks* these words, not more together; but he so speaks them, that he takes those to whom he speaks into the society of the same work with himself; nor is the Divine *Speaker* otherwise concerned in, ' let us make,' and ' in our ' likeness,' than those *to whom* he speaks. And, indeed, it is not the *speaking of these words* before many concerned, that Moses expresseth, but the *concurrence* of many to the same work, with the same interest and concernment in it. And whoever is concerned (whether speaking, or spoken to) in the first word, ' let *us* make,' is no less respected in the following words: ' in *our* image ' and likeness.' They must, therefore, be of *one* and the *same nature*, which was to be represented in the creature to be made in their image.

Again, he objects, " That writers often introduce a person deliberating and debating with himself." But the whole of this, and what he would insinuate by it, is merely *petitio principii*, accompanied with the neglect of the argument which he pretends to answer. For he only says, that " One may be introduced, as it were, deliberating and consulting with himself," whereof yet he gives no parallel instance, either from scripture, or other sober writer; but he takes no notice that the words directly introduce *more than one* consulting and deliberating among themselves, about creating man in their image.

Again, what he concludes from his arbitrary supposition—that hence " it doth not follow, that God took counsel with others besides himself,"—is nothing to the argument in hand; for do we ever plead hence, that
God

God confulted with *others befides himfelf?* But this the words evince, that he who then confulted with himfelf, is, *in fome refpect*, more than one. But to invent *exceptions* againft our interpretation of any teftimony of fcripture, and never care to give one of their own which they will adhere to and defend, is contemptibly perverfe.

He next appeals to Ifa. i. 'Hear, O heavens, and 'give ear, O earth!' But in fuch *rhetorical apoftrophes*, they are, in truth, *men* that are fpoken to, and that *fcheme* of fpeech is ufed merely to make an impreffion on them of the things that are fpoken. Apply this to the words of God, in the circumftances of the creation of man, and it will appear fhamefully ridiculous. The fcripture expreflly denies, that 'God took counfel with any 'befides himfelf in the whole work of the creation,' [Ifa. lx. 12—14.] Creation is a pure act of infinite monarchical fovereignty, wherein there was no ufe of any intermediate *inftrumental caufes*; nor can God be reprefented, as confulting with any creatures in that ftupendous work, without a difturbance of the true notion of it.

Again, man was made in the image and likenefs of him that fpeaks, and all that are, as it were, conferred with. 'Let us make man in OUR image;' but man was made in the image and likenefs of *God alone*, as it is expreffed in the next verfe. And the *image* here mentioned doth not denote that which is made to anfwer another thing, but that which *another* is to anfwer to. 'Let us make man in *our image*;' that is, conformable to *our nature*. Now, God, and any other beings, as angels, have not *one common nature*, that fhould be the example, and *prototype* in the creation of man; their nature and properties are infinitely diftant; and that likenefs which is between angels and men, doth no way prove, that man was made in the *image* of angels, although angels fhould be fuppofed to be made before them. For more is required to that end than mere *fimilitude*; as an egg is *like* another, but not the *image* of another. A defign of conforming one to another, with its dependance on that other, is required; and *fo* was man made in the image of *God alone*. This

This opponent makes no inquiry why, seeing in all the antecedent work of creation, God is introduced speaking constantly in the *singular* number, the phrase of speech is here *changed,* and God speaks as *consulting,* or deliberating in the *plural* number. And he says, not only, ' let ' us make,' but adds, ' in OUR image, and in OUR like- ' ness.' To imagine this to be done without *some peculiar reason,* is to dream, rather than to inquire into the sense of scripture. And it is not enough to prove, that a *plural* word may be used in a singular sense, except it be also shewn to be so in *this place,* seeing the proper import of it is otherwise. Nor can such an expression, concerning God, be used *honoris gratia,* seeing it is no honour to him to be spoken as *many Gods*; for his glory is, that he is *one only.* It hath, therefore, another respect, *viz.* to the *persons* in the *unity* of the same nature.

§ 13. The foundation of our design from this place being thus established, we may safely build upon it; and that which hence we intend to prove, is, that in the framing and producing of the things which concern mankind, there were peculiar internal PERSONAL *transactions* between the Father, Son, and Spirit. The scheme of speech here used is *(in genere deliberativo)* by way of *consultation ;* but as this cannot directly and properly be ascribed to God, an *anthropopathy* must be allowed in the words. The mutual distinct actings, and concurrence of the several persons in the Trinity, is expressed by way of *deliberation,* because *we* can no otherwise determine, or act. And this was *peculiar* in the work of the creation of man, because of an especial designation of him to the glory of God, as *Three in One.* This, therefore, I have only laid down and proved, as the general principle which we proceed upon. Man was peculiarly created to the glory of the Trinity; hence, in all things concerning him, there is not only an intimation of those *distinct subsistences,* but also of their *distinct actings,* with respect to him. And as his *creation* was eminently the effect of special

counsel

counsel, much more shall we find this fully expressed, with respect to his *restoration* by the Son of God.

§ 14. The same truth is farther revealed and confirmed, Prov. viii. 22—31. 'The Lord possessed me in 'the beginning of his way, before his works of old,' &c. It is *Wisdom* that speaks, and is spoken of. This we believe to be *He*, who is the wisdom of God, even his eternal Son. This the *Arians*, &c. will not grant, although they are not agreed *what* it is that is intended. A *property*, say some, of the Divine nature; the *exercise of Divine wisdom* in making the world, say others; the wisdom that is in the law, say the Jews; or, as some of them, the wisdom that was given to Solomon; and of their mind have been some of late.

The constant use of the verb (קנה) is either to *acquire* and *obtain*, or to *possess* and *enjoy*. That which any one hath, which is with him, which belongs to him, and is his own, he is (קנה) *the possessor* of it. So is the Father said to *possess wisdom*; because it was his, with him, even his eternal Word or Son. No more is intended hereby, but what the apostle more clearly declares, John i. 1, 2. (εν αρχη ο λογος ην προς τον Θεον) *in the beginning the Word was with God*.

It is an *intelligent person* that is here intended; for all sorts of *personal properties* are ascribed to it, as almost every verse in the whole chapter shews. For instance, *personal authority* and power are assumed by it, [ver. 15, 16.] 'By me kings reign, and princes decree justice; by 'me princes rule, and nobles, even the judges of the 'earth.' *Personal promises*, upon duties to be performed towards it, due to God himself, [ver. 17.] 'I love them 'that love me, and those that seek me early shall find me;' which is our unalienable respect to God. *Personal actions*, [ver. 20, 21.] 'I lead in the way of righteousness, in 'the midst of the paths of judgement; that I may cause 'them that love me to inherit substance, and I will fill 'their treasures;' [ver. 30, 31.] 'I was daily his delight, 'rejoicing always before him, and my delights were with 'the sons of men.' *Personal properties*, as *eternity*, [ver. 23.]

23.] 'I was set up from everlasting, from the beginning, or ever the earth was,' [ver. 24, 25.] *Wisdom,* [ver. 14.] Counsel is mine, and *sound wisdom,* I have understanding and *strength.*—Again, the things here spoken of wisdom are, all of them, or at least the principal, expressly elsewhere attributed to the Son, [John i. 2, 3, &c. Col. i. 15—17.]—Moreover, the *relation* of this wisdom that speaks to God, declares it to be his eternal Word or Son, 'I was daily his delight, rejoicing before him;' as he did in whom his soul is always well pleased. And lastly, as we shall farther see, they are the *eternal transactions* of the Father and Son that are here described, which are capable of no other fair and solid interpretation.

§ 15. It is not my design to plead here at large, the eternal existence of the Son of God, antecedent to his incarnation; but because the faith thereof is the foundation of what I shall farther offer, concerning the *origin* of his priesthood, the testimonies produced to that purpose must be vindicated from the exceptions of the professed adversaries of that fundamental truth.

ENIEDINUS (who may be deemed the Goliah of the Antitrinitarian cause) contends, "that *wisdom* is personified by a prosopopeia." This prosopopeia, or fiction of a person, is of great use to the *Antitrinitarians.* By this one engine they presume they can despoil the Holy Ghost of his deity and personality. Whatever is spoken of *him* in the scripture, they say, it is by a prosopopeia; those things being assigned to a *quality,* or an accident, which really belong to a person only. But as to what concerns the Holy Spirit, I have elsewhere taken this engine out of their hands, and cast it to the ground; so that none of them alive will erect it again. Here they make use of it against the *deity* of Christ; as they do also on other occasions.—I acknowledge there is such a scheme of speech used by *rhetoricians* and *orators,* whereof some examples occur in scripture. *That* is sometimes ascribed to a *thing,* which is, indeed, proper only to a *person*; or a person who is dead, or absent, may be introduced as present and speaking. But yet QUINTILIAN, the great master of the

oratorial art, denies, that by this figure, speech can be
ascribed to that which never had it, (Nam certe sermo
fingi non potest, ut non *personæ* sermo fingatur,) "If
you feign speech, you must feign it to be the speech of
a *person*;" or one endowed with the power of speaking.
A prosopopeia is a figure quite distinct from all sorts of
allegories, pure, mixed; *apologues*, *fables*, *parables*; wherein, when the scheme is evident, any thing may be introduced speaking, like the *trees* in the discourse of *Jotham*,
[Judg. ix.] The instance of mercy and peace looking
down from heaven, and kissing each other, is a *mixed
figure*, the foundation of which is a *metonymy* of the cause
for the effect; or rather of the adjunct for the cause,
and the *prosopopeia*, which is evident. But that a *person*
should be introduced speaking in a continued discourse,
ascribing to himself all *personal properties*, absolute and
relative; all sorts of *personal actions*, and those the very
same which, in sundry other places, are ascribed to *one
certain person*, (as all things here mentioned are to the
Son of God) who yet is no person, never was a person,
nor representeth any person, without the least intimation
of any *figure* therein, or any thing inconsistent with the
nature of things and persons treated of, and that, in a discourse *didactical* and *prophetical*, is such an enormous
monstrous fiction, as nothing, in any author, much less
in the Old or New Testament, will give the least countenance to.

There are, in the scripture allegories, apologues, parables; but all of them so plainly and professedly such,
and so unavoidably requiring a figurative exposition from
the nature of the things themselves (as where stones are
said to hear, and trees to speak) that there is no danger
of any mistake about them, nor difference concerning their
figurative acceptation. And the only safe *rule* of ascribing a figurative sense, is, *when the nature of things will not
bear that which is proper*; as where the Lord Jesus calls
himself a *door*, and a *vine*; and says, that *bread* is his
body. But to make allegories of such discourses as this,
founded on the feigning of persons, is a ready way to

turn the whole bible into an allegory, which may be done with equal eafe and probability of truth, as this paffage. Befides, there is a *prophetical fcheme* in the words. It is here declared, not only what Wifdom then *did*, but efpecially what it fhould do in the *days of the gofpel*; for the manner of the prophets is to exprefs things future, as prefent or paft, becaufe of the certainty of their accomplifhment. And thefe things they fpeak of the coming of Chrift in the flefh. [See I. Pet. i. 11, 12.]

But utterly to remove this pretence of *profopopeias* and figures, it need only to be obferved, which none will deny, that the wifdom that fpeaks here, [chap. viii.] is the fame that fpeaks chap. i. 20—23. And if wifdom there be not a *perfon*, and a divine perfon, there feems to me to be none in heaven; for to whom, or what elfe can thefe words be afcribed, which wifdom fpeaks? " Turn ye at my reproof; behold I will pour out my fpirit unto you, I will make known my words unto you; becaufe I called, and ye refufed; I have ftretched out my hand, and man regarded; but ye have fet at nought all my counfel, and would have none of my reproof; I alfo will laugh at your calamity, I will mock when your fear cometh.—Then fhall they call upon me, but I will not anfwer; they fhall feek me early, but they fhall not find me?" If thefe things exprefs not a *perfon*, a *Divine Perfon*, the fcripture gives us no due apprehenfion of any thing whatever. Who is it that " pours out the Holy Spirit?" Who is he that " men fin againft," in refufing to be obedient? Who is it that in their " diftrefs they call upon," and feek early in their trouble? The whole fcripture declares to whom, and to whom alone, thefe things belong, and may be afcribed.—This being the whole of what the enemies of the SACRED TRINITY have to object to our application of this difcourfe to the *eternal Word*, or *Son of God*; and having removed their objections, we may now proceed,

§ 16. To the improvement of this teftimony to our prefent defign. And we find here fully expreffed " A *perfonal tranfaction* before the creation of the world, between the Father and the Son, acting mutually by their one fpirit,

rit, concerning the state and condition of mankind, with respect to Divine love and favour." For the *Wisdom*, or *Word* of God, having declared his eternal existence with the Father, and distinction from him, manifests withal his joint creation of all things; especially his presence with God, when he made " The highest part of dusts of the habitable world ;" that is, " the first Adam," as JARCHI interprets it, and that not improbably. Then he declares, that he was (אצלו) *by him, with him, before him*, (προς τον Θεον, John, i. 1, 2.) And he was with him, (אמון *nutritus) One brought up with him*, of the *masculine* gender, though it refers to the *feminine* (חכמה) *wisdom*, because a *person* is intended.

But in what sense is this spoken of the Son, with respect to the Father? The foundation of the *allusion* lies in the eternal mutual love that is between the Father and the Son, to which is added the consideration of the natural dependence of the Son on the Father; compared to the love of a Father to the Son, and the dependence of a Son on his Father. Therefore, most translations, with respect to this allusion, supply *as* to the words, " *As* one brought up." Again, (אמון, *alumnus) one brought up*, is always so with respect to some special end or purpose; or to some work and service, which is principally here intended. It is with respect to the work that he had to accomplish, that he is called *alumnus patris*, one brought up of the Father. And this was no other but the work of redemption, and the salvation of mankind, the counsel whereof was then between the Father and the Son. In the carrying on of that work, the Lord Christ every where commits himself and his undertaking to the care, love, assistance, and faithfulness of the Father, whose especial grace was the original thereof, [Psal. xxii. 9, 11, 19, 20. Isa. l. 7—9.] And in answer to this the Father promiseth him to stand by him, and carry him through the whole of it; because it was to be accomplished in such a *nature*, as stood in need of help. Wherefore, with respect to this work, he is said to be " *before him*," as one whom

whom he would take care of, and stand by, with love and faithfulness in the prosecution of the arduous work.

§ 17. With respect hereunto, he adds, '*And was delights every day,*' [ver. 30.] There are ineffable mutual delights and joys between the persons of the sacred Trinity, arising from that infinite satisfaction and complacency, which they have in each other from their respective *in-being,* by the participation of the same nature, wherein no small part of the blessedness of God doth consist. And by this word, that peculiar delight which a Father hath in a Son, is expressed. Jer. xxxi. 20. (שעשעים לי) *a pleasant child,* a *child of delights.* But the delights here intended, have respect to the works of God *ad extra* ; as a fruit of that eternal satisfaction, which ariseth from the counsel of God, concerning the sons of men. This the next verse [31.] makes manifest; ' rejoicing in the ha-
' bitable part of his earth, and my delights with the sons
' of men.' For after he had declared the presence of wisdom with God before the first creation, which is a notation of eternity, and its co-operation with him therein, he descends to manifest the special design of God and Wisdom with respect to the children of men. And here such an undertaking, on the part of the Son, is intimated, as that the Father undertakes the care of him, and his protection, when he was to be humbled into the ' form of a
' servant,' in the prospect whereof he delighted in him continually. So he expresseth it, Isa. xlii. 1—7. ' Be-
' hold, my servant whom I uphold, mine elect, in whom
' my soul delighteth,' &c. This is the delight of the Father, and his presence with the Son in his work, an eternal prospect of which is here represented. In answer to it, the Son delights in him whose delight he was, ' re-
' joicing with exaltation,' with an *outward expression* of inward delight; the natural overflowings of an abounding joy. And what this delight of the Son is, in answering the delight of the Father in him, with respect to the work he had to do, the Psalmist declares, Psal. xl. 7, 8. ' Then
' I said, lo I come, in the volume of thy book it is written
' of me, I delight to do thy will, O my God; yea, thy
' law

' law is within my heart.' This (מגלה ספר) *volume of the book*, which our apoftle calls (κηφαλιδα βιβλιϗ) the *beginning*, or the *head of the book*, [Heb. x. 7.] is no other but the *counfel of God* concerning the falvation of the elect by Jefus Chrift, enrolled as it were in the *book of life*, and thence tranfcribed into the beginning of the *book of truth*, in the firft promife given to Adam after the fall. This counfel being eftablifhed between Father and Son, the Son with refpect thereto ' rejoiceth continually before ' God,' on the account of that delight which he had to do and accomplifh his will, and in our nature to anfwer the law of mediation, which was prefcribed to him.

§. 18. For this being declared to be the mutual frame of God and his Wifdom towards one another, Wifdom proceeds to manifeft with what refpect towards outward things it was, that they were fo mutually affected, [ver. 31.] ' Rejoicing in the habitable parts of his earth, and ' my delights were with the fons of men.' That the things here fpoken of were tranfacted in eternity, or before the creation, is evident in the context. The *counfels*, therefore, of *God* and *Wifdom*, with refpect to the fons of men, are here expreffed. The *Word* was now ordained, even before the foundation of the world, to the work of mediation and redemption, [I. Pet. i. 20.] And many of the fons of men were chofen in him, to grace and glory, [Ephef. i. 4.] and the bringing of them to that glory, whereto they were chofen, was committed to him, as the captain of their falvation. This work, and the contemplation thereof, he now *delights* in, becaufe of that eternity of Divine glory, which was to enfue thereon.

And thefe things are revealed for our confolation, and the ftrengthening of our faith; for if there were fuch mutual delights between the Father and the Son, in the Divine counfel, concerning the work of our redemption; and if the Son fo rejoiced in the profpect of his own undertaking to that end, we need not doubt, but that he will powerfully and effectually accomplifh it; for all the difficulties of it lay open and naked under his eye, yet he *rejoiced* in the thoughts of his engagements to remove and
con-

conquer them. He now saw the law of God established and fulfilled, the justice of God satisfied, his glory repaired, Satan under his feet, and his works destroyed. Here we place the first spring of the *priesthood* of Christ, which is expressed by the *mutual delight* of the Father and Son. It was founded on *love and grace*, though in its exercise it respects *holiness* and *justice* also.

§ 19. The same truth also seems to be expressed, Psal. ii. 7. ' I will declare the decree the Lord hath said unto ' me, Thou art my Son, this day have I begotten thee.' From this place the *ancient doctors*[*] constantly acknowledge, that the Messiah was to be the Son of God; or rather, that the Son of God was to be the Messiah. Hence was the inquiry of the high priest, Matt. xxvi. 63. ' I ' adjure thee by the living God, that thou tell us whether ' thou be the Christ, the Son of God.' According to the faith of their church, he takes it for granted, that *the Christ* and *the Son of God* was the same. The same confession, on the same principle, Nathaniel made, John i. 49. ' Thou art the *Son of God*, thou art the *king of Israel*.' And Peter's confession, [Matt. xvi. 16. John vi. 69.] ' Thou art *that Christ* the *Son of the living God*,' was nothing but a due application of the faith of the *Judaical* church to the person of our Saviour, which faith of their's was principally built on this testimony, where God expressly calls the *Messiah* his *Son*. There is, therefore, an illustrious testimony in these words, given to the eternal *pre-existence* of the Lord Christ, in his Divine nature, before his incarnation. And this causeth the adversaries of that sacred truth, to turn themselves into all shapes, to avoid the force of it.

What ENIEDINUS says, " That none of these things belong to Jesus Christ," is above the rate of ordinary confidence. *All the apostles* do not only jointly, and with one accord, apply the things here spoken to the Lord Je-

---

[*] So MAIMONIDES, JARCHI, and KIMCHI confess. The words of JARCHI are plain and remarkable: " Our Masters expounded this psalm concerning the king Messiah."

sus,

sus, but also give a clear exposition of the words, as a *ground* of that application; a thing seldom done by the sacred writers, Acts iv. 24—28. 'They lifted up their 'voice to God with one accord, and said, Lord, thou art 'God, which hast made heaven and earth, and the sea, 'and all that in them is; who, by the mouth of thy ser-'vant David hast said, Why did the Heathen rage, and 'the people imagine vain things? The kings of the 'earth stood up, and the rulers were gathered together 'against the Lord, and against his Christ. For of a truth 'against thy holy child Jesus, whom thou hast anointed, 'both *Herod* and *Pontius Pilate*, with the Gentiles and the 'people of Israel, were gathered together to do whatsoever 'thy hand and thy counsel determined before to be done.' In *their* judgement, *Herod* and *Pontius Pilate*, with the *Romans*, the great rulers over the world, were the kings and rulers intended in this psalm. And so also the (גוים) *Heathen*, they took to be the *Gentiles*, who adhered to Pilate in the execution of his Gentile power; and the (לאמים) *people* mentioned to be the *people of Israel.*—It appears, therefore, that there were *eternal* transactions between the Father and the Son, concerning the redemption of mankind, by his interposition and mediation.

§ 20. (II.) Our next inquiry relates to those *eternal transactions*, which may be considered under the notion of a COVENANT between the Father and the Son. I shall, therefore, *first*, manifest the existence of such a covenant; and then, *secondly*, insist on that part of it, which refers to the Redeemer's priesthood.

We must distinguish between God's covenant *to men*, *concerning Christ*, and that made *with his Son, concerning men*. The *former* is commonly termed the *covenant of grace*; which hath subsisted, under various forms of external administration, ever since the fall, and shall continue in full force to the consummation of all things. The *latter*, which is now the subject of inquiry, is the *personal compact*, which the holy scriptures represent to have taken place between the Father and the Son, before all worlds.

§ 21. Before we proceed, it may be proper to consider briefly the *name* and *nature* of a covenant in general. The Hebrews call a "covenant" (ברית) *berith*, the Greeks (συνθηκη, and the Latins *fœdus*.) Solemn covenants, especially between God and his people, were confirmed by sacrifice. [See Psal. l. 5.] which appears highly probable from what is recorded of Adam and Eve being cloathed with skins; and is abundantly clear from the history of Noah and Abraham, [Gen. ix. 15.] Whereby we learn, that no covenant could take place between God and man, after the entrance of sin, but in virtue of that sacrifice of our High Priest, which these represented. Hence some derive the Latin word *(fœdus* a *feriendo)* from *striking*; and also a custom which prevailed among the idolatrous Heathens, who, in making a covenant *cut a beast in pieces*, laying one half over against another, and so passing between them; which farther denoted an imprecation, as it were, upon themselves, that they might be so *cut in pieces*, if they stood not to the covenant terms.—The Greek word (συνθηκη) is constantly used in all good authors, for a solemn covenant between nations and persons; but the *Septuagint* translators, observing that *berith* in the Hebrew, was of a larger signification, have rendered it constantly by another Greek word (διαθηκη).

The word *berith* is variously used in the Old Testament; nor are learned men agreed about its derivation. However, all covenants are either between the conqueror and the conquered—or between enemies in equal power—or between those who were never at variance; and the end of all is mutual peace and security. Hence Job v. 23. 'Thy covenant shall be with the stones of the field;' that is, *metonymically*, thou shalt have no hurt from them; because peace and concord are the *end* of covenants. The law, written on the two tables of stone, was called a 'covenant,' [Exod. xxxiv.] by a *synechdoche*; for no mere precept, or even promise, can be a covenant *properly so called*. Again, the term is used for an *absolute promise*, Isa. lix. 21. 'As for me, this is my *covenant* with them, 'saith the Lord; my Spirit that is upon thee, and my 'words,

'words, which I have put into thy mouth, shall not de-
'part out of thy mouth,' &c. And God also calls the
appointment of day and night his *covenant*, [Jer. xxxiii.
20.] Hence it appears that the word is used in *various
senses*, which must be sought from the connection; seeing
there is no precept, or promise of God, but many be so
called. And it is worthy our notice, that though no outward signs ever belonged to the *essence* of a covenant,
God never made a covenant with men, but he always
gave them a token, and visible pledge thereof. And whosoever is interested in the covenant itself, hath an undoubted right to the Divinely-appointed token.

§. 22. An absolute complete covenant is, "a voluntary agreement between distinct persons, about the disposal of things in their power, to their mutual concern and
advantage." *Distinct persons* are required in a covenant;
for it is a mutual compact; it must be *voluntary*, with respect to the terms, this being the foundation of all solemn
covenants; and the matter of it must be of things in the
power of them who covenant.

§ 23. As all these things concur in every equal compact, so there is an especial kind of covenant depending
solely on the *personal undertakings and services of one party*,
in order to the common ends of the covenant, or the mutual satisfaction of the covenanters. And such covenants
have —A *proposal* of service,—a *promise* of reward, and
—an *acceptance* of the proposal, with a restipulation of
obedience out of respect to the reward; and this indispensably introduceth an inequality and subordination in
the covenanters, as to the common end of the covenant;
however, on other accounts they may be equal. For he
who prescribes the duties which are required in the covenant, and giveth the promise of either assistance in them,
or a reward upon them, is, in that respect, and so far,
superior to him who observeth his prescriptions, and
trusteth to his promises. Of this nature is that Divine
transaction that was between the Father and the Son about
the redemption of mankind. There was in it, a prescription

scription of personal services, with a promise of reward; comprehending also the other conditions of a complete covenant before laid down.

§ 24. The eternal transactions before-mentioned were *federal* transactions; this is what the scripture intends, where God, that is, the Father, is called by the Son *his God*; and where he says, that he will be unto him a God and Father. For this expression of being *a God* to any one is declarative of a covenant, and is the word whereby God constantly declares his covenant relation to any, [Jer. xxxi. 33. and xxxii. 38. Hof. ii. 23.] For God declaring that he will be A GOD to any, engageth himself to the exercise of his holy properties, which belong to him as God, for their good. And this is not without an engagement of obedience from them. Now, this declaration the scripture abounds in, Psal. xvi. 2. ' Thou hast ' said unto the Lord, thou art my Lord;' these are the words of the Son to the Father, as is evident from ver. 9 —11. Psal. xxii. 1. ' My God, my God.' Psal. xl. 8. ' I delight to do thy will, O my God.' Psal. xlv. 7. ' God, thy God, hath anointed thee.' Mich. v. 4. ' He ' shall stand and feed in the strength of the Lord, in the ' majesty of the name of the Lord his God.' John xx. 17. ' I ascend to my Father, and your Father; to my God, ' and to your God.' Rev. iii. 12. ' I will make him a ' pillar in the temple of my God; and I will write upon ' him the name of my God, and the name of the city of ' my God.' All which expressions argue both a *covenant*, and a *subordination* therein. And on *this account* it is, that our Saviour says his ' Father is greater than he,' John xiv. 28. This place, I confess, the ancients expound of his *human nature* only, but the inferiority of the human nature to the Father is a thing so unquestionable, as needed no solemn attestation; and the mention of it is no way suited to the design of the place. But our Saviour speaks with respect to the *covenant engagement* that was between the Father and himself, as to the work which he had to do.

§ 25. Again, the same important truth is proposed, Zech. vi. 13. (ועצת שלום יהיה בין שניהם) *the counsel* about *peace-making* between God and man, was *between them both*; that is, the two persons spoken of, the *Lord Jehovah*, and *He* who was to be the (צמח) *branch*. And this was not spoken of him absolutely as a man; for so there was not properly (עצה) *a counsel* between God and him; 'For who hath 'known the mind of the Lord, or who hath been his ' *counsellor ?*' [Rom. xi. 34.] And besides, the Son, in his human nature, was merely the *servant* of the Father, to do his will, [Isa. xlii. 1.] But God takes this counsel with him, as he was his *eternal wisdom*, with respect to his future incarnation.

Hereunto regard is also had to his names, *wonderful, counsellor*, &c. for these titles do not absolutely denote properties of the Divine nature, though they are such Divine titles and attributes, as cannot be ascribed to any, but to him who is God. There is in them a respect to the work which he had to do, as he was to be a *child born and given unto us*. And on the same account he is called the *everlasting Father*; a name not proper to the person of the Son, with a mere respect to his *personality*; there is, therefore, a regard in it to the work he had to do, which was, to be a *father to all the elect of God*.

On the same account, God speaking of him, says, ' *my companion*, and *the man my fellow*,' [Zech. xiii. 7.] with whom he had *sweetened*, and rejoiced in *secret counsel*, [as Psal. lv. 14. Prov. viii. 30, 31.]

Particularly, *the will* of the Father and Son concurred in this matter, which was necessary, that the covenant might be *voluntary*, and of choice. The *original* of the whole is referred to the *will of the Father* constantly. Hence our Lord Jesus Christ, on all occasions, declared solemnly, that he came to do the *will of the Father*; ' Lo, ' I come to do *thy will*, O God, [Psal. xl. 7. Heb. x. 5—10.] For in the agreement, the Prescriber and Promiser, whose will, in all things, is to be attended to, is the Father; and his will was *naturally* at perfect liberty from engaging in that way of salvation, which he accomplished

plished by Christ. He was at liberty to have left all mankind under sin and the curse, as he did all the angels that fell. He was at liberty to have utterly destroyed the race of mankind that sprang from Adam in his fallen state; either in the root of them, or in the branches when multiplied (as he almost did in the flood) and have created another race of them to his glory. And hence the acting of his will herein is expressed by *grace*; which is *free*, or else it is not grace; and it is said to proceed from love, acting by choice, all arguing the highest liberty in the will of the Father, [John iii. 16. Ephes. i. 6.] Now, he both *sent* his Son and *sealed* him, and gave him *commands*, which are all acts of choice, proceeding from sovereignty. Let none, then, once imagine, that this work of entering into covenant about the salvation of mankind was *absolutely necessary* to God, or that it was required by virtue of any of the *essential properties* of his nature. God was herein *absolutely free*, as he was also in his making all things of nothing. And this we maintain in perfect consistency with the *necessity* of *satisfaction*, on supposition of this covenant. The *will of the Son* also is distinctly concerned, to demonstrate, that the things he underwent in his human nature, were just and equal; and to manifest, that those very acts, which he had in command from his Father, were no less the acts of his *own* will. Wherefore, as it is said, that the *Father* loved us, and gave his Son to die for us; so also it is said, that the *Son* loved us, and gave himself for us, and washed us in his blood. And whatever is expressed in scripture, concerning the *will of the human nature* of Christ, it is but a representation of the *will of the Son of God*, when he engaged into this work from eternity. Whereas, therefore, he had a sovereign and absolute power over his *own human nature* when assumed, whatever he submitted to was no injury to him, nor injustice in God to lay it on him.

§ 26. If it be objected, that the *will* is a natural property, and therefore, in the Divine essence, it is but one; and how, then, can it be said, that the will of the Father, and the will of the Son, did concur distinctly in the

making

making of this covenant? We reply, that this difficulty may be solved from what hath been already declared. For, if they *subsist* distinctly; if such is the distinction of the persons in the unity of the Divine essence, that they act in natural and *essential* acts *reciprocally* one towards another, as in understanding, love, and the like; what impropriety to suppose that they *act* distinctly in those works, which are of *external* operation? The will of God, as to the peculiar actings of the Father in this matter, is the will of the Father; and the will of God, with regard to the peculiar actings of the Son, is the will of the Son; not by a distinction of sundry wills, but by a distinct application of the same will to its *distinct acts*, in the persons of the Father and Son. And in this respect, the covenant whereof we treat, differeth from a *pure decree*; and by virtue of it, were all believers saved from the foundation of the world.

§ 27. Moreover, a covenant must be about the disposal of things in the *power of them that enter into it*, otherwise it is null or fraudulent. To do good to mankind, to bring them to the enjoyment of himself, was absolutely in the *power of the Father*. And it was in the *power of the Son* to assume human nature, which becoming thereby peculiarly his own, he might dispose of it to what end he pleased, still preserving the indissoluble union. Again, some things are made lawful or good, or suited to the honour, or satisfaction and complacency of them that make the covenant, by virtue of somewhat arising from the covenant itself. Such was the *penal suffering* of the human nature of Christ, under the sentence and curse of the law. This, absolutely considered, without respect to the *ends of* the covenant, would neither have been good in itself, nor have had any tendency to the glory of God. For what excellency of the nature of God could have been *demonstrated* in the *penal sufferings* of one absolutely, and in all respects, innocent? Nay, it was utterly impossible, that an innocent person, considered absolutely as such, should suffer pœnally, under the sentence and curse of the law; for the law denounceth punishment to no such person.

son. Guilt and punishment are related, and where the one is not (real, or supposed, or imputed) the other cannot be. But now, in the terms of this covenant, leading to the limitations and use of these sufferings, they are made *good*, and tend to the glory of God. So the pardoning and saving of sinners absolutely could have had no tendency to the glory of God; for what *evidence of righteousness* would there have been herein, that the great Ruler of all the world should pass by the offences of men without animadverting upon them? What justice would have appeared, or what demonstration of the *holiness* of the nature of God would there have been therein? Besides, it was impossible, seeing ' it is the judgement of God, that ' they who commit sin, are worthy of death.' But, through the terms and conditions of this covenant, this is rendered righteous, holy, and good, and eminently conducing to the glory of God.

§ 28. The *matter* of this covenant in general is the saving of sinners, by ways and means suited to the manifestation of the Divine glory. To declare this design of God, is the principle design of the whole scripture.

§ 29. The *end*, both of the covenant, and the disposal of all things thereby, was the *special glory* both of the one and the other. God doth *all things for himself*. He can have no *ultimate end* in any thing but himself alone, unless there should be any thing better than himself, or above himself. But yet, in himself, he is not capable of any accession of glory, by any thing he doth, or intendeth; his end thereof must be, not the *obtaining* of glory *to himself*, but the *manifestation* of the glory that is *in himself*. And those properties of the Divine nature, which are peculiarly engaged in it, are *wisdom, justice*, and *grace*. That the covenant sprang from these *properties* of the Divine nature, that the execution of it is the work and effect of them all, and that it is designed to manifest and glorify God by them to eternity, the scripture fully declares.

The *peculiar honour of the Son* was two-fold, *viz.* what he had conjunct with the Father, as he is of the *same nature*

nature with him, over all, God blessed for ever; and likewise, as the Mediator of the covenant of grace, that peculiar *glorious exaltation*, which, in his human nature, he received upon the accomplishment of the terms and conditions of this covenant.

§ 30. This covenant had also its *conditions and limitations*, as it had a respect to a prescription of personal obedience and promises of reward. The *promises* made to the Son were various; such as all necessary assistance in his arduous work, as the incarnate Mediator, and the glory which was to ensue upon the accomplishment of it; and particularly the *acceptance* of his work with God. There was, indeed, in the nature of the things themselves, a *proportion* between the obedience of Christ the mediator, and the salvation of believers; but this is not the next foundation of *merit*, though an indispensable condition; for there must not only be a *proportion*, but a *relation* also between the things, whereof the one is the merit of the other. And the relation in this case is not natural, or necessary, arising from the nature of the things themselves, but arose from a *compact* between the Father and the Son to this purpose, and the promises wherewith it was confirmed. Suppose, then, a proportion in *distributive justice*, between the obedience of Christ, and the salvation of believers; then add the respect and relation that they have one to another, by virtue of this *covenant*, and in particular, that our salvation is engaged by promise to Christ, and it gives us the true nature of his merit.

The *conditions required*, or *prescriptions* made to the undertaker, in this covenant, were—that he should *assume* the nature of those whom he was to bring to God;—that in his nature assumed, he should be the *servant of the Father*, and yield universal obedience to him, both according to the *general law of God* obliging all mankind, and according to the *special law of the church* under which he was, and, moreover, according to the *singular law* of that compact, [Isa. xlii. 1. chap. xlix. 5. Phil. ii. 6—11.] and, that he should make *atonement for sin*, by means of our nature assumed.

assumed. And thus we are come to the well-head of salvation. Here lieth the immediate sacred foundation of the *priesthood* of Christ, and of the sacrifice of himself, which, in the discharge of that office, he offered to God.

§ 31. And when God came to reveal and represent to his church this counsel of his will, he did it by the institution of *priesthood and sacrifices*; for the priesthood and sacrifices of the law were not the *original exemplar* of these things, but a *transcript* of what was done in heaven itself, in counsel and covenant, as well as a type of what should be afterwards accomplished on the earth. And the very names of *priests* and *sacrifices* were but improperly ascribed to them who were so called, being only obscure representations of what was past, and types of what was to come.

EXERCIT. 2.

THE NECESSITY OF THE PRIESTHOOD OF CHRIST.

§ 1. *The subject proposed.* § 2. *The righteousness of God, what; as resident in the Divine nature.* § 3. *As to its exercise.* § 4. *What this pre-supposeth.* § 5. *That the righteousness of God necessarily requires the punishment of sin.* § 6. *The objection that mercy prevents the exercise of justice, answered.* § 7. *That sin cannot be pardoned without satisfaction, argued from the holiness of God.* § 8. *The foregoing branches of the argument recapitulated.* § 9, 10. *That justice and mercy are properties of the Divine nature, and not mere external acts.* § 11, 12. *The objection, That Christ could not endure the penalty due to us, answered fwered.* § 13—15. *Other objections answered.* § 16, 17. *Additional arguments, in confirmation of the general thesis.*

§ 1. ON this supposition, that God in his infinite grace and love would save sinners by the interposition of his Son, there was something in the manner of it indispensable and necessary, *viz.* that he should do it by undergoing the *punishment* that was due to them, who should be saved, or offer himself a *sacrifice, to make atonement and reconciliation for them.*

This being a matter of great importance, and strenuously opposed by the *Socinians,* and the defence of it deserted by some otherwise adhering to sound doctrine in the main of our cause, I shall the more particularly insist upon it.

§ 2. Whereas we assert the *necessity of the priesthood* of Christ to depend on the *righteousness* of God, it is requisite, that something be premised concerning it. The righteousness of God is taken two ways, *viz. absolutely* in itself, as it is resident in the Divine nature; and—with respect to *its exercise,* or the actings of God, in a manner suitable to that holy property of his nature. In the first acceptation, it is nothing but the *universal rectitude* of the Divine nature, whereby it is necessary to God, to do all things rightly, justly, equally, answerably to his own wisdom, goodness, holiness, and right of dominion, [Zeph. iii. 5.] 'The just Lord in the midst thereof; he 'will do no iniquity, morning by morning doth he bring 'his judgement to light.' I say, it is the *essential,* natural readiness and disposition of the holy nature of God, to do all things justly and decently, according to the rules of his wisdom, and the nature of things, with their relation one to another. And this *virtue* of the Divine nature considered absolutely, doth not consist in a *habitude* of mind (πρὸς ἕτερον) *with respect to another,* as all *justice* in men doth, but is the infinite essential rectitude of God in his being. Hence it so presides over all the works of God that there is none of them, though proceeding immediately from mercy and goodness on the one hand, or from severity or faithfulness on the other, but that God is said to be *righteous* therein, and they are all represented as acts of righteousness in him. And this, not only because they are his acts and works, who can do no evil, but also because they proceed from, and are suited to that holy absolute universal rectitude of his nature, wherein true righteousness doth consist.

For between the consideration of this righteousness of God, and the actual exercise of it towards his creatures, there must be interposed a consideration of the *right* of God, or that which we call *Jus Domini*, a right, power, and liberty of rule or government. For it is not enough, that any one *be righteous* to enable him to act righteously, with respect to others, but moreover he must have a *right* so to act; and this right in God is supreme and sovereign, arising naturally and necessarily from the relation of all things to himself; being all placed in an universal, indispensable, and absolutely unchangeable dependence on him, according to their natures and capacities.

The right of God, therefore, to rule over us, is wholly of another kind and nature, than any thing is or can be among the sons of men; for it is a sovereign right to deal with us, and act towards us, according to the infinite, eternal rectitude of his nature. And as he hath a right so to do, so he cannot do otherwise, supposing the state and condition wherein we are made and placed, with the nature of our relation to, and dependence on God; for God can act no otherwise towards us but according to what the essential rectitude of his nature doth direct and require; which is the foundation of what we plead in the case before us, concerning the necessity of the priesthood.

§ 3. Again, the righteousness of God may be considered with respect to its *exercise*, which supposeth the right of God before declared. For, suppose the creation of all things, and it is as natural and essential to God to be the ruler over them, as it is to be God. Now, the exercise of the righteousness of God, in pursuit of his right

right of rule, is either *abfolute* and antecedent, or *refpective* and confequential. In the *former* refpect it is exercifed in his laws and promifes; in virtue of the *latter*, he diftributes rewards and punifhments to his creatures according to their work. And one part of this confifts in the punifhing of fin, as it is a tranfgreffion of his law; and this is that wherein, at prefent, we are concerned; for we fay, that the righteoufnefs of God, as he is the fupreme ruler of the world, doth require, *neceffarily*, that fin be punifhed, or the tranfgreffion of that law, which is the inftrument of his rule, be avenged.

§ 4. The exercife of this righteoufnefs in God pre-fuppofeth—the creation of *intelligent* rational creatures in a moral dependence on himfelf, capable of being ruled by a law, in order to his glory and their own bleffednefs;—the nature of the *law* given to thofe creatures, as the means and inftrument of their moral orderly dependence on God, which order the breach of that law would difturb;—the eternal, natural, unchangeable *right* that God hath to govern thefe creatures, according to the tenor of that law;—the *fin* of thefe creatures, which was deftructive of all that order of things, which enfued on the creation, and the giving of the law; for it was deftructive of the principal end of the creation, and of the dependence of the creatures upon God; and was *introductory* of a ftate of things utterly oppofite to the univerfal rectitude of the Divine nature.

We fay, then, that upon a fuppofition of all thefe *antecedaneous free acts*, and of the neceffary continuance of God's righteoufnefs of rule and judgement, it was *neceffary* that the finning creature fhould be punifhed according to the fentence of the law.

Hence the neceffity and fpecial nature of the priefthood of Chrift. Defigned it was in *grace*, as we have before proved, on fuppofition that God would fave finners, but it was this *juftice* that made it *neceffary*, and determined its nature. For this was that, which indifpenfably required the *punifhment of fin*, and, therefore, was it *neceffary*, that he who would fave finners fhould undergo

for

for them the punishment that was due to them. But because this could not be done by men *suffering or enduring punishment*, which is a thing in its own nature indifferent, the will and obedience of Christ, in the manner of undergoing it, was also required. This made his priesthood *necessary*; whereby, whilst he underwent the punishment due to our sins, ' he offered himself an acceptable sacrifice,' for their expiation.

§ 5. What is now distinctly proposed to confirmation, is, " That the justice, or righteousness of God, as exercised in the rule and government of his rational creatures, did indispensably and necessarily require, that sin committed should be punished ;" whence ariseth the *special nature* of the priesthood of Christ. But we shall premise a few observations, which tend to the right explication of the truth.

1. There are some attributes, as the *wisdom* and *power* of God, which do not find, but produce the objects of their first actings *ad extra*. These, therefore, in these actings, must needs be absolutely and every way *free*, being limited and directed only by the sovereign will and pleasure of God. But there are properties of the Divine nature, which cannot act according to their nature, without a supposition of an antecedent object, and that qualified in such, or such a manner. Such is his *vindictive* justice, and *pardoning* mercy; for if there be no *sinners*, none can be punished or pardoned.

2. The rule of God's acting from his *vindictive* justice, is not a mere *free act of his will*, but the natural dominion and rule which he hath over sinning creatures, in answer to the rectitude and holiness of his own nature. Neither does he punish sin as he can ; that is, to the utmost of his power, but as the rule of his government, and the order of things in the universe disposed to his glory, do require.

3. This *justice* exerted itself in one signal act *antecedent* to the sin of man ; namely, in the *prescription* of a *pœnal law*; that is in the annexing of the pœnalty of death, to the transgression of the law. This God did not merely because

cause *he would do so,* nor because he *could do so*; but because the order of all things, with respect to their dependence upon himself, as the supreme Ruler of all, did so require. For had God only given men a law of the rule of their dependence on, and subjection to him, and not inseparably annexed a *penalty* to its transgression, it was possible, that man, by sin, might have cast off all his moral dependence on God, and set himself at liberty from his rule. And having broken and disannulled the sole law of his dependence, what should we have had more to do with him? But this case was obviated by the *justice of God*, in pre-disposing the order of punishment, to succeed in the room of the order of obedience, if that were broken. And that this provision should be made, the nature of God indispensably required.

4. This justice of God, I say, *required a punishment* of sin, as a punishment; but the way and degree, the time, season and manner of it, belong to his sovereign will and wisdom; and I say not that God punisheth sin *necessarily,* as the sun gives out light and heat, or as the fire burns, or as heavy things tend downward by necessity of nature; he doth it *freely,* exerting his power by a free act of his will. For the *necessity* asserted doth only exclude an *antecedent indifference* upon all the suppositions laid down. It denies, that on these respects it is *absolutely indifferent* with God, whether sin be punished, or no. Such an indifference, I say, is opposite to the nature, law, truth, and rule of God; and, therefore, such a necessity as excludes it, must herein be asserted. But herein God is a *free agent,* and acts freely in what he doth. Suppose the determination of his will, and the Divine nature *necessarily* requireth an acting suitable to itself. It is altogether free to God, whether he will speak to any of his creatures or no; but supposing the determination of his will, that he will so speak, it is absolutely necessary, that he speak *truly*; for truth is an essential property of his nature; whence he is God, *that cannot lie.* It was absolutely free to God, whether he would create this world or no; but on supposition that he would create it, he could not but create

it omnipotently and wisely; for so his nature doth require, because he is essentially omnipotent, and infinitely wise. So there was no absolute necessity in the nature of God, that he should punish sin; but on supposition that he would create man, and would permit him to sin, it was necessary that his sin should be avenged; for this his *righteousness* and *dominion* over his creatures did require.

§ 6. It is objected, " That on the same supposition, it will be no less necessary that God should *pardon sin*, than that he should punish it; for *mercy* is no less an essential property of his nature, than *justice*." But those by whom the substitution of the Son of God to answer Divine justice is denied, can give no tolerable account, why *all* are not *condemned*, seeing God is infinitely righteous; or, *all* are not *pardoned*, seeing he is infinitely merciful. But the truth is, there is not the same *reason* of the actual exercise of justice and mercy. For upon the entrance of sin, as it respects the rule of God, the *first* thing that respects it, is *justice*, the province of which is, to preserve all things in their dependence on God, which without the punishment of sin, cannot be done. But God is not obliged to the *exercise of mercy*, nor doth the forbearance of such an exercise any way intrench upon the holiness of his nature, or the glory of his rule. It is true, mercy is no less an essential property of God, than justice; but neither the law, nor the state and order of things wherein they were created, nor their dependence on God, as the supreme Governor of the whole creation, raise any *natural respect*, or obligation between mercy and its object. God, therefore, can execute the punishment that his justice requireth, without the least impeachment of his mercy; for no act of justice is contrary to mercy. But absolutely to pardon, where the interest of justice is to punish, is contrary to the nature of God.

But, moreover, we deny that *sin* and *misery* do constitute the proper object of mercy. It is required, that every thing contrary to the nature of God in sin, and
the

the sinner, be taken out of the way, or there is no proper object for mercy. Such is the *guilt* of sin unsatisfied for. And Socinus himself acknowledgeth, that it is contrary to the nature of God to pardon *impenitent* sinners. And even mercy itself, on the account of an *antecedent* reconciliation, will be *justly* exercised.

§ 7. That it is necessary sin should be punished, or not be *absolutely pardoned*, without respect to satisfaction given to the rectoral *justice of God*, appears from the consideration of his *holy nature*. God, the ruler of the world, is of so *holy a nature*, as that he cannot but hate and punish every sin, and, therefore, so to do belongs to his absolute perfection; for what is the purity and holiness of God, but that universal perfection of his nature, which is accompanied with a displeasure against sin, and a hatred of it, whence he will punish it according to its desert? Heb. i. 13. 'Thou art of purer eyes than to behold 'evil, and canst not look on iniquity.' Not to be able to behold iniquity, expresseth the most inconceivable detestation of it. 'He cannot;' that is, because of the holiness of his nature, to which such an action would be contrary, 'look upon;' that is, to pass by, spare, or connive at iniquity; for that is the rule of what God can do, or cannot do. He can do every thing that is not contrary to himself; that is, the essential properties of his nature. He can do nothing that is contrary to, or inconsistent with his truth, holiness, or righteousness.

Hence this holiness of God is sometimes expressed by *jealousy*, where he would instruct men in his severity, in the punishing of sin, [Exod. xx. 5.] For the nature of jealousy is *not to spare*, [Prov. vi. 34.] nothing but the executing of vengeance will satisfy it. And this is that which God intended in the revelation of himself, which he made by the proclamation of his name before Moses, [Exod. xxxiv. 7.] 'That will by no means clear the 'guilty;' namely, for whom no atonement is made. And it is to instruct us herein, that this holiness of God is expressed by *fire*, [Heb. xii. 29.] 'Our God is a con-'suming fire.' Devouring fire and everlasting burnings,

[Isa.

[Ifa. xxxiii. 14.] If we may not learn thence, that as eventually *fire* will burn any combustible thing that is put into it, so the holiness of God requires, that all sin be as assuredly punished, we know not what to learn from it. If the *punishing* of sin depend upon a *mere free act* of the will of God, which might, or might not be without any disadvantage to his nature, there is no reason why his *holiness* and righteousness should be so often mentioned as those which induce him thereto, and indispensably require it.

Again, God in the scripture is proposed to us as the *supreme Judge* of all, acting in rewards and punishments according to his own righteousness, or what the *rectitude* and holy properties of his own nature require. That God should have any *external* rule or law in his government of the world, is absolutely and infinitely impossible. But *his* law and rule is the *holiness* and *righteousness* of his nature.

§ 8. The whole of what hath been thus far pleaded, may be reduced to the ensuing heads:

1. God is *naturally* and *necessarily* the *supreme Governor* of his rational creatures, with respect to their utmost end, which is his own glory. Upon the supposition of *his being* and *their's*, an imagination to the contrary would imply all sorts of contradictions.

2. The law of obedience to such creatures ariseth naturally and necessarily from the nature of God, and their own; for this original law is nothing but that respect, which a finite dependent creature hath upon an absolute, infinitely wise, holy, and good Creator, suitable to the principles of the nature with which it is endowed; therefore, it is indispensably necessary.

3. The annexing of a *penalty* to the transgression of this law, was nothing but what the *righteousness* of God, as the supreme Ruler of his creatures, did make necessary; as that, without which, the glory and holiness of his rule could not be preserved upon the entrance of sin.

4. The *institution* of *punishment* answereth to the sanction of the law, is an act of *justice* in God, and neces-

necessary to him, as the supreme Governor of the universe.

§ 9. SOCINUS contends,* that the *righteousness* we here plead for is *contrary* to that *mercy*, whereby God forgiveth sins; and therefore, that they cannot be *properties* of his *nature*, but only *external acts* of his will and power. But we reply, that absolutely and essentially, they are the same; nor are their effects *contrary* to each other, though *divers*. To punish, where punishment is deserved, is not contrary to mercy; but to punish, where punishment is not deserved, is cruelty. And yet, to punish without desert, is more opposite *to justice itself*, than to mercy. And so it is where punishment *exceeds* guilt, or where proceedings are not according to an equal standard. Nor is 'to *spare*' by mercy, contrary to justice; for if to *spare* and *pardon* be not for the good of the whole, for the preservation of order, and the end of rule, it is not mercy to pardon or spare, but *facility*, *remissness* in government, or foolish pity. Secure those things in rule and government, which justice takes care of and provides for, and then to *spare in mercy*, is in no way contrary to it. If these things be not provided for, to spare is not an act of mercy, but a defect in justice. And if these things were not so, it would be impossible that any one could be *just* and *merciful* also; yea, or do any act either of justice or mercy; for if he punish, he is unmerciful; that is, wicked, if punishment be contrary to mercy; and if he spare, he is not just, if sparing be opposite to justice. And on this supposition, upon an alike act of the will of God, sin might have been made to be *virtue*, and obedience sin; and so it might have been the duty of man to have hated God, and to have opposed him to the utmost of his power. For all the merely free acts of God's will might have been otherwise, and contrary to what they are. And if you say it could not be so in this case, because the nature of God, and his righteousness required it should be otherwise, you grant all that is contended for.

* De Jesu Christo Servatore, Lib. I. Cap. i. Lib. III. Cap. i.

Moreover, actually *to pardon* is no way opposite to justice, where satisfaction is made; nor is *to punish* opposite to mercy, where the law of obtaining an interest in that satisfaction is not observed. And all that God declares in the scripture, concerning his justice and mercy, with the exercise of them towards sinners, is grounded on the supposition of the interposition and satisfaction of Christ; where that is not, as in the case of the *angels* that sinned, no mention is made of mercy more or less, but only of judgement, according to their desert.

§ 10. That justice and mercy are *properties of the Divine nature*, contrary to the *Socinian* creed, we may even argue from the light of nature; as not only teaching us by the conduct of right reason, that there is a singular *perfection* in these things, which must, therefore, be found in him, who is so the author of all goodness and limited perfections to all others, as to contain essentially and eminently all goodness and perfection in himself; but also, it is not difficult to evince the actual consent of all mankind who acknowledge a Deity, to this principle, *That God is just and merciful*, with that justice and mercy which have respect to the sins and offences of men. When God shewed to Moses his glory, and made a declaration of himself by his name, he did it not by calling over the *free acts* of his will, or shewing what he would or could do if he pleased; but described his *nature* to him by the essential properties of it, that the people might know *who* and *what* he was with whom they had to do, [Exod. xxxiv. 6, 7.] And yet among them is that *mercy* reckoned, which is exerted in the pardoning of iniquity, transgression, and sin. The same is to be said concerning *justice*; for this vindictive justice is nothing but the absolute rectitude of the nature of God, with respect to some outward objects, *viz.* sin and sinners. Had there never, indeed, been any sin or sinners, God could not, in any *outward acts* have exercised either vindictive justice, or sparing mercy; but yet he had been notwithstanding eternally *just* and *merciful*. To say that God may forego this right or remit of it, is to say, that he may, at his pleasure, cease to be our

Lord and God; for the same nature of God, which necessarily requireth our obedience, doth indispensably require the punishment of our disobedience.

§ 11. SOCINUS and CRELLIUS object, "That Christ neither did, nor could undergo the penalty due to us, because that was *eternal death.*" But we reply,

1. That Christ underwent the punishment, which, in the justice or judgement of God, was due to sin.

That the justice of God did require, that sin should be punished with a meet and due recompence of reward, we have proved already; and to satisfy this justice it was that Christ suffered; and, therefore, he suffered what justice required. We should have undergone no more, but what, in the *justice of God* was due to sin. This Christ underwent, and therefore he underwent what we should have undergone. Nor can it be supposed, that in the justice of God there might be two sorts of *penalties* due to sin, one of one kind, and another of another. If it be said, that because it was undergone by *another*, it was not the same; I grant it was *payment*, which our suffering would never have been; it was *satisfaction*, which we, by undergoing any penalty, could not make; but yet he suffered the *same penalty* which we should have done. In short, the Lord Christ underwent that punishment, which was due to our sins; and the justice of God required no other.

2. That which was due to sin was, all of it, comprehended in the *curse of the law*; for in the curse, God threatened the breach of the law with all that punishment which was justly due to it; for the curse of the law is nothing but an *expression of that punishment* which is due to the breach of it, delivered in a way of threatening. But now Jesus Christ underwent the *curse of the law*, by which I know not what to understand, but that very punishment which the transgressors of the law should have undergone. Hence our apostle says, 'That he was made 'a curse for us,' [Gal. iii. 13.] because he underwent the penal sentence of the law. And there were not two kinds of punishment contained in the curse of the law; one

that

that the sinner himself should undergo, another that should fall on the Mediator; for neither the law, nor its curse had any respect to a Mediator. The interposition of a Mediator depends on other principles and reasons than any the law was acquainted with. It was, therefore, the *same punishment*, in the kind of it, which was due to us, that the Lord Christ was to undergo.

3. It is said expressly, that God, 'caused all *our ini-quities* to meet on *him*,' [Isa. liii. 6.] or hath laid on him the iniquities of us all, that he 'bare our sins;' [ver. 10.] Or, 'bore our sins in his own body on the 'tree,' [I. Pet. ii. 24.] whereby he who 'knew no sin, 'was made sin for us,' [II. Cor. v. 21.]

4. Christ *suffered in our stead*; for he was our (ἀντίψυχος) *substitute*. [See Rom. v. 6—8.] When one would substitute himself in the room of another, who was obnoxious to punishment, he that was so substituted was always to undergo that very penalty, whether by loss of limb, liberty, or life, that the other should have undergone. And in like manner, if the Lord Christ suffered *in our stead*, as our SUBSTITUTE, he suffered what we should have done.

§ 12. It is still objected, "That the punishment which we should have undergone, was *death eternal.*"

Death, as *eternal*, was in the punishment due to our sin; not directly, but *consequentially*; and that *a natura subjecti*, not *a natura causæ*; for that the punishment of sin should be *eternal*, arose not from the nature and order of *all things, viz.* of God, the law, and the sinner; but from the nature and *condition of the sinner only.* This was such, as that it could no otherwise undergo a punishment proportionable to the demerit of sin, but by an *eternal continuance* under it. This, therefore, was not a necessary consequent of *guilt absolutely,* but of guilt with respect to *such a subject.* And if it be said, "That the admission of one to suffer for another, who could discharge the debt in much less time than the offender could, is not the same that the *law* required;" we answer, that it is true the *law* requires no such thing as *one to suffer for*

for another, nor abfolutely confidered, doth admit of it; but the fubftitution was from God's gracioufly difpenfing with the law, as the fupreme Lord and Ruler over all. The law takes notice *only of offenders*, nor doth it include any fuppofition, that the offenders muft fuffer, ' or a mediator' in their ftead. But, notwithftanding, it is infeparable from the law, that this *kind of punifhment* is due to the tranfgreffion of it; and by God's *gracious fubftitution* of Chrift in the room of finners, there was no relaxation made of the law, as to the punifhment it required.

§ 13. It is yet farther pleaded, "That if *the fame* be paid in a ftrict fenfe, then deliverance would have followed *ipfo facto*; for the releafe immediately follows the payment of the fame." Howfoever we allow of that expreffion of "paying the fame," it is only *fuffering the fame* for which we contend. Chrift underwent the fame punifhment that the law required, but that his fo doing fhould be a payment for us, depended on God's *fovereign difpenfation*; yet fo, that when it was paid, it was the *fame* which was due for us. This *payment*, therefore, as fuch, and the deliverance that enfued thereon, depended on a previous *compact* and agreement, as muft all fatisfaction of one for another. Deliverance, therefore, doth not *naturally* follow on this fatisfaction, and therefore was not to enfue *ipfo facto*, but *(jure fœderis)* in the way and order difpofed in that *covenant*. The actual deliverance of all the perfons for whom Chrift fuffered, to enfue *ipfo facto* upon his fuffering, was abfolutely impoffible; for moft of them *were not* when he fuffered. And that the whole of the time, way, and manner of his deliverance dependeth on *compact*, is evident from them who were delivered actually from the penalty, long before the actual fufferings of Chrift, merely upon the account of his fufferings, which fhould afterwards enfue. *Deliverance* is no *end* of punifhment confidered merely as fuch, none is punifhed properly *that he may* be delivered: however, the ceffation of punifhment may be called a deliverance. *Mere deliverance* was not the whole end of Chrift's fufferings for us; but fuch a deliverance as is attended with a ftate and condition of superadded blessedness. And the duties of faith, repentance, and obedience, which are prescribed to us, are not enjoyed only, or principally, with respect to deliverance from punishment, but with respect to the attaining of those other ends of the mediation of Christ, in a new spiritual life here, and eternal life hereafter. And with respect to *those ends* may they justly be required of us, though Christ suffered and paid *the same* which we ought. No deliverance *ipso facto*, upon a supposition of suffering or paying the same, was necessary; but only the *actual discharge of him* who made the payment, as an *Undertaker* for others. Accordingly, Christ, immediately on his sufferings as our surety, was discharged.

§ 14. But it may be farther objected, "That it is impossible to reconcile the *freeness* of remission, with the *full payment* of the very same that was in the obligation." To say, that God *freely remitted our sins*, abrogating the law, and the curse of it, requiring no punishment, no satisfaction, neither from ourselves, nor from the Mediator, hath at first view an appearance of *royal grace and clemency*, until being examined, it is found utterly inconsistent with the *truth* and *holiness* of God; and in reality, is a conceit that hath no countenance in scripture. But to say, that God required the execution of the sentence and curse of the law, in the undergoing of the punishment due to sin; but yet, out of his love and infinite grace, sent his Son to undergo it for us, (so, to comply with his *holiness*, to satisfy his *justice*, and fulfil his truth and law, that he might freely pardon sinners) this the scripture *every where declares*; and is demonstrably consistent with all the perfections of the Divine nature. Wherefore the absolute freedom of pardon to us is absolutely consistent with Christ suffering the *same penalty* which was due to our sins.

§ 15. And whereas it is pleaded, "That *satisfaction* and *remission* must respect the *same person*;" the scripture is clear, that *satisfaction* was made by Christ, and remission is made to us; that he suffered, the just for the unjust, that we may go free. Now, God is said to do that
freely

freely for us, which he doth of grace; and whatever he doth of grace, is done for us *freely*. Thus the love and grace of God, in sending Jesus Christ to die for us, were free, and therein lay the foundation of *free* remission for us. This *constitution* of the Redeemer suffering the *same punishment* which was due to our sins, as the *surety* and Mediator of the new covenant, was *free*, and of mere grace, depending on the compact or covenant between the Father and Son before explained. The *imputation of our sin to him*, or the making him to be sin for us, by his own voluntary choice and consent, was in like manner *free*. The constitution of the new covenant, and therein of the way to partake of the benefits procured by the sufferings of Christ, was also *free*, and of grace. The communication of the Holy Spirit to us, enabling us to believe, and to fulfil the condition of the covenant, is absolutely *free*. And there is nothing here inconsistent with Christ suffering the *same* that we should have done, or his paying the same debt which we owed, in the sense before explained.

§ 16. In confirmation of our *general thesis*, besides what hath been insisted on, we may plead the *common suffrage* of mankind in this matter. For what all men have a presumption of, is not free, but *necessary*; proceeding from a principle, which knows only what *is*, and not what may be, or may not be. Of the latter there can be no common or innate persuasion among men: such are all the *free acts* of the will of God; they *might be*, or *might not be*, otherwise were they not free acts. If, therefore, God's punishing of sin were merely an effect of a free act of his will, without respect to any essential property of his nature, there could never have been any *general presumption* of it in the minds of men. But this there is, *viz.* that God is *righteous*, with that kind of righteousness which requires that sin be punished. Hence our apostle, speaking of the generality of the Heathen, affirms, that they *knew* it ' was the judgement of God, that *they who committed sin were worthy of death*,' [Rom. i. 32.] That such punishment is due to sin, they were sufficiently convinced

vinced of by the testimonies of their own consciences, [Rom. ii. 14, 15.] and whereas conscience is nothing but the judgement which a man maketh concerning himself and his actions, with respect to the superior judgement of God; a sense of the *eternal righteousness* of God was there included.

And this sense of *avenging justice* they expressed in all their *sacrifices*, wherein they attempted to make some atonement for the guilt of sin. What was the voice of nature in those actings, wherein it offered violence to its own in-bred principles and inclinations? It was this alone; the Governor over all is just and righteous, and we are guilty; he will not suffer us to live, vengeance will overtake us, if some way or other be not found out to appease him, to satisfy his justice, and to avert his judgement, [Mich. vi. 6, 7.]

§ 17. Again, it is *necessary* that God should do every thing that is requisite to his own glory; this the perfection of his nature requires. It is *necessary*, therefore, that nothing fall out in the universe, which should absolutely impeach the glory of God, or contradict his design of its manifestation. Now, suppose that God should let sin go unpunished, where would be the glory of his righteousness, as he is the supreme Ruler? For to *omit* what justice requireth, is no less a disparagement to it, than to do what it forbids, [Prov. xvii. 15.] And where would be the glory of his holiness? Where would be that *fear and reverence* which is due to him? Where that sense of his terror? Where that sacred awe of him, which ought to be in the hearts and thoughts of men, if once he were looked on to be such a God, such a Governor, to whom it is a matter of *mere choice* and liberty, whether he will inflict punishment on sin or no, as being not concerned in point of righteousness or holiness so to do? Nothing can tend more than such a persuasion to ingenerate an apprehension in men, that 'God is altogether such a one as themselves,' [Psal. l. 21.]

Thus having investigated the *original* of the priesthood of Christ, and demonstrated the *necessity* of it, we should proceed to handle the *nature* of this office, were it not fully done in the expository part of the work, to which the reader is referred.

Exercit. 3.

OF THE KINGDOM, OR LORDSHIP OF CHRIST.*

§ 1. *The grant of dominion to the Messiah foretold in the Old Testament.* § 2. *Asserted in the New.* § 3. *This is a spring of comfort to the Church.* § 4. *Of terror to the wicked.* § 5. *Christ the heir and Lord of all persons, and all things.* 6. (I.) *Persons. First, Angels; and especially,* 1. *Good angels.* § 7. *The original right of this grant.* § 8. *Its gracious ends.* § 9. 2. *Bad angels.* § 10. *Secondly, all mankind.* § 11. 1. *The elect.* § 12. 2. *The reprobate.* § 13—18. (II.) *Things. First, spiritual things.* § 19. *Secondly, ecclesiastical.* § 20. *Thirdly, political.* § 21. *Fourthly, the residue of the creation.*

§ 1. THE grant of *dominion* in general to the Messiah is intimated in the first promise of him, [Gen. iii. 15.] His *victory* over Satan was to be attended with *rule, power,* and *dominion,* [Psal. lxviii. 18. Isa. liii. 12.] This was confirmed in the renewal of that promise to *Abraham,* [Gen. xxii. 17, 18.] for in him it was, that Abraham was to be heir of the world, [Rom. iv. 13.] As also to *Judah,* whose seed was to enjoy the *scepter* and *law-giver,* until HE came, who was to be *Lord* of all, [Gen. xlix. 10.] *Baalam* also saw the star of Jacob, with a *scepter* for *rule,* [Numb. xxiv. 17—19.]

* In the original work, this discourse forms a *digression* on chap. i. 1, 2. See vol. ii, p. 17. of this abridgement.

This kingdom was fully revealed to *David*, and is expressed by him Pſal. ii. throughout. [See alſo Pſal. xlv. 3—8. Pſal. lxxxix. 19—24, and clxxii. 6—9. Pſal. cx. 1—3.] And the ſame important ſubject is diſplayed in all the following prophets. [See Iſa. xi. 1, 2, and ix. 6, 7, and liii. 12. and lxiii. 1—3. Jer. xxiii. 5, 6. Dan. vii. 13, 14, &c.]

§ 2. As this was foretold in the *Old Teſtament*, ſo the accompliſhment of it is expreſſly aſſerted in the *New*. Upon his birth he is proclaimed to be 'Chriſt the *Lord*,' [Luke ii. 11.] And the firſt inquiry after him is, where is he that is born *King?* [Matt. ii. 2, 6.] And this teſtimony doth he give concerning himſelf; namely, that *all judgement* was his, and therefore all honour was due to him, [John. v. 22, 23.] and that all things were delivered unto him, or given into his hand, [Matt. xi. 15.] yea, *all power* in heaven or earth, [Matt. xxviii. 18. Him who was crucified, did God make both *Lord and Chriſt*, [Acts ii. 36.] exalting him at his right hand, to be a *prince and a ſaviour*, [Acts v. 31.] He is highly exalted, having a name given him above every name, [Phil. ii. 9—11.] being ſet at the right hand of God in heavenly places far above, &c. [Epheſ. i. 20—22.] where he reigns for ever, [I. Cor. xv. 25.] being the *king of kings*, and *Lord of Lords*, [Rev. xix. 16.] for he is Lord of quick and dead, [Rom. xiv. 7—9.]

§ 3. And this is the ſpring of the church's glory, *comfort*, and aſſurance. He is our head, huſband, and elder brother, who is gloriouſly veſted with all this power. Our neareſt relation, our beſt friend, is thus exalted to an abiding, an *everlaſting rule* and dominion over the whole creation of God. And it is but a little while before he will diſpel all thoſe clouds and ſhades, which at preſent interpoſe themſelves, and eclipſe his glory and majeſty from them that love him. He, who in the days of his fleſh was reviled, reproached, perſecuted, and crucified for our ſakes, that ſame Jeſus is thus exalted, and made a '*prince* and a ſaviour,' having a name given him above every name, &c. for though he was *dead*, yet he is *alive*, and lives for ever, and hath the keys of hell and death.

§ 4. The consideration of it is also suited to strike *terror* into the hearts of ungodly men that oppose him in the world. Whom is it they despise? Against whom do they magnify themselves, and lift up their horns on high? Whose ordinances, laws, and institutions do they contemn? Whose gospel do they refuse obedience to? Whose people and servants do they revile and persecute? Is it not *He*, are they not *his*, who hath all power in heaven and earth committed to him? in whose hands are the lives, the souls, all the concernments of his enemies? *Cæsar* thought he had spoken with *terror*, when, threatening with death one who stood in his way, he told him, " Young man, he speaks it, to whom it is as easy to do it." He speaks to his adversaries, who stand in the way of his interest, to deal no more so proudly, who can, in a moment, speak them into ruin, and that eternal. [See Rev. vi. 14—17.]

§ 5. He is Lord, or heir ($\pi\alpha\nu|\omega\nu$, Heb. i. 2.) *of all*; that is, *of all persons*, and *of all things*.

(I.) *Persons*, or rational subsistences, both *angels* and *men*; for it is evident, that he is exempted, who hath subjected all things unto him, [I. Cor. xv. 27.]

(II.) *Things*; which are either *spiritual, ecclesiastical, political*, or *natural*.

§ 6. (I.) Persons. Those persons assigned as part of the inheritance of Christ, are,

First, the *angels*, and especially

1. The *good* angels. This *pre-eminence* above them is asserted by the apostle in chap. i. 4. And as he is exalted above them, so, by way of grant, and by the authority of God the Father, they are made *subject* unto him. [See I. Pet. iii. 22. Ephes. i. 22. Psal. viii. 6. I. Cor. xv. 27.] and, to evidence the universality of this subjection, they adore and worship him; the highest act of obedience, and most absolute subjection. This they have in *command*, [Heb. i. 6.] ' Let all the angels of ' God worship him,' [Psal. xcvii. 7. השתחוו] *worship him*

him with proftration, felf-abafement, and all poffible fubjection to him. Their *practice* anfwers the command, [Rev. v. 11—14.] all the angels round about his throne fall down and afcribe bleffing, and honour, and glory, and power unto him, as we are taught to do in our deepeft acknowledgement of the majefty and authority of God, [Matt. vi. 13.] and as to *outward obedience*, they are in all things ready to receive his commands, [Rev. i. 1.] And for this purpofe they always attend his throne, [Ifa vi. 1, 2. 'I faw the Lord upon his throne, and 'about it ftood the feraphims;' this Ifaiah fpake of him when he faw his glory, [John xii. 39, 40.] He was upon his *throne*, when he fpake with the church in the wildernefs, [Acts vii. 38.] that is, in mount Sinai, where the angels attending him, ready to receive his commands, were twenty thoufands, even thoufands of angels, [Pfal. lxviii. 19. Ephef. iv. 8.] or thoufand thoufands, and ten thoufand times ten thoufand, as another prophet expreffeth it, [Dan. vii. 10.] and fo attended fhall he come to judgement, [II. Thef. i. 7.] when he fhall be revealed from heaven with the angels of his power; which was foretold concerning him from the beginning of the world, [Jude 14, 15.]

§ 7. Thus his Lordfhip over angels is *univerfal* and abfolute, and their fubjection to him is anfwerable thereunto. The *original right* and equity of this grant, with the ends of it, are now only to be intimated.

1. The radical *fundamental* equity of this grant lies in his *Divine nature*, and his creation of angels, over whom, as Mediator, he is made Lord. Unto the general affertion of his being made heir of all the apoftle, [chap i. 2.] fubjoins that general reafon, manifefting the *rife* of its equity in the will of God that it fhould be fo: ' By ' whom alfo he made the worlds;' which reafon is particularly applicable to every part of his inheritance, and is efpecially pleaded in reference to angels, [Col. i. 15, 16.] ' Who is the image of the invifible God, the firft-born of ' every creature;' that is, the heir and Lord of them all ; and the reafon is, " becaufe by him were all things created

that

that are in heaven, and that are in earth, vifible and invifible; whether thrones, or dominions, or principalities, or powers, all things were created by him, and for him." This creating of thofe heavenly powers is the foundation of his heirfhip, or lordfhip over them.—This is the *firſt foundation* of the equity of this grant of all power over the angels unto the Lord Chriſt; in his Divine nature he made them, and in that refpect they were before, *his own*; as on the fame account when he came into the world, he is faid to come, [John i. 11. εις τα ιδια) *to his own*, or the things he had made.

2. It is founded in that *eſtabliſhment* in the condition of their creation, which they received by his interpofition to recover what was loft by fin; and to preferve the untainted part of the creation from ruin. In their own *right*, in the *rule* of their obedience, and the *example* of thofe of their number and fociety, who apoftatized from God, they found themfelves in a ftate not abfolutely impregnable: their *confirmation*, which was alfo attended with that exaltation, which they received by their *new relation* to God, in and through him, they received by his means; God *gathering* up all things to a *confiſtency*, and permanency in him, [Ephef. i. 10.] And hence alfo it became *equal*, that the *rule* and power over them fhould be committed to him, by whom they were—although not like us *recovered* from ruin, yet—*preſerved* from all danger of ruin. So that in their fubjection unto him confifts their *principal* honour, and *all* their fafety.

§ 8. And as this act of God in appointing Chriſt Lord of Angels hath thefe equitable foundations, fo it hath alfo fundry *glorious ends*.

1. It was an *addition* to that glory that was *ſet before him*, in his undertaking to redeem finners. A *kingdom* was of old promifed unto him, and to render it exceedingly glorious, the rule and fcepter of it is extended not only to his redeemed ones, but to the holy angels alfo; and the fovereignty over them is granted him as a part of his reward, [Phil. ii. 8—11. Ephef. i. 20, 21.]

2. God hereby *gathers up* his whole family, at first distinguished by the law of their creation into *two special kinds*, and then differenced and set at variance by sin, into *one body*, under one head, reducing them that originally were *twain*, into *one entire family*, [Ephes. i. 10.] ' In the
' fulness of time he gathered together in one all things in
' Christ, both which are in heaven, and in earth, even in
' him.' Before this, the angels had no immediate created head, for themselves are called (אלהים) Gods, [Psal. xcvii. 7. I. Cor. viii. 5.] whoever is the head must be (אלהי אלהים) the *God of Gods*, or *Lord of Lords*, which Christ alone is; and in him, or under him, as one head, is the *whole family* of God united.

3. The *church* militant on the earth, whose conduct into eternal glory is committed unto Christ, stands in need of the *ministry of angels*; and, therefore, hath God granted rule and power over them unto him, that nothing might be wanting to enable him to save, unto the uttermost, them that came to God by him. They are all of them his *servants*, ' the fellow servants of them that have the testi-
' mony of Jesus.' And as some men do wilfully cast themselves, by their religious adoration of angels, under the curse of Canaan, to be the ' servants of servants,' [Gen. viii. 25.] so it is the great honour and privilege of true believers, that in their worship of Christ they are admitted into the society of an innumerable company of angels, [Heb. xii. 22. Rev. v. 11, 13.] for they are not ashamed to esteem them their fellow-servants, whom their Lord and king is not ashamed to call his brethren. And herein consists our communion with them, that we have one common head and Lord.

§ 9. 2. There is another sort of *angels*, who by sin left their primitive station, and fell off from God, of whom, their sin, fall, malice, wrath, business, craft in evil, and final judgement, the scripture treateth at large. These belong not, indeed, to the *possession* of Christ, as he is the heir, but they belong to his *dominion*, as he is the Lord. Though he be not a king and head unto them, yet

yet he is a *judge* and *ruler* over them. All things being given into his hand, they also are subjected to his power.

(1.) This right, as before, is founded in his Divine nature, by virtue whereof he is *fit* for this dominion. He *made* these angels also ; and, therefore, as God, hath an absolute dominion over them. The creatures cannot cast off the dominion of the Creator by rebellion ; though they may lose their *moral* relation to God, as *obedient creatures*, yet their *natural* relation cannot be dissolved. God will be God still, be his creatures ever so wicked ; and if they obey not his will, they shall bear his justice. And this dominion of Christ over fallen angels, as God, makes the grant of rule over them to him, as Mediator, just and equal.

(2.) The immediate and peculiar foundation of his right to rule over the fallen angels, rendering the special grant of it equal and righteous, is *lawful conquest*. This gives a special right, [Gen. xlviii. 22.] Now, that Christ should conquer fallen angels, was promised from the foundation of the world, [Gen. iii. 15.] The seed of the woman, the Messiah, was to break the serpent's head, despoil him of his power, and bring him into subjection ; which he performed accordingly, [Col. ii. 15.] ' He spoiled principalities and powers,' divested fallen angels of all that title they had got to the world, by the sin of man ; triumphing over them as captives, to be disposed at his pleasure. He stilled, or made to cease, as to his power, this enemy (מתנקם) *and self-avenger*, leading captivity captive, breaking in pieces the head over the large earth, [Psal. cx. 6.] binding the strong man armed, and spoiling his goods. And the scripture of the New Testament is full of instances, as to his executing his power and authority over evil angels ; they take up a good part of the historical books of it. Man having sinned by the instigation of Satan, he was, by the just judgement of God, delivered up to his power, [Heb. ii. 14.] The Lord Christ undertaking to recover lost man from under his power, by destroying his works, [I. John iii. 8.] and to bring them again into favour with God, Satan, with all his might sets himself to oppose him in his work; and failing in his enterprize, being utterly conquered, he became absolutely subjected unto him, trodden under his feet, and the *prey* he had taken delivered from him. They are subjected unto him as to their present actings and future condition; he now rules them, and will hereafter finally judge them. Wherein he suffers them in his holiness and wisdom to act in temptations, seductions, and persecutions, he binds and limits their rage and malicious actings, disposing all events to his own holy and righteous ends, and keeping them under chains for the judgement of the great day, when, for the full manifestation of his dominion over them, he will cause the meanest of his servants to set their feet on the neck of these conquered kings.

(3.) The *ends* of this Lordship of Christ are various; as—his *own glory*, [Psal. cx. 1.] the *church's safety*, [Mat. xvi. 18. Rev. xii. 7—9.] the exercising of his *wrath* and vengeance upon his stubborn enemies.

§ 10. *Secondly, All mankind* (the second sort of intellectual creatures) belong to the lordship and dominion of Christ. All mankind was in the power of God, as one mass out of which all individuals are made, [Rom. ix. 21.] some to honour, some to dishonour; the (το αυτο φυραμα) *the same lump*, not denoting the same substance, but one *common condition*; and the *making* of individuals is not by temporal creation, but eternal designation. So that all mankind made out of nothing, and out of the same condition, are destined to *several ends* for the glory of God; the *elect*, or vessels from the common mass, unto honour; and *reprobates*, or vessels from the common mass, unto dishonour: to both is the lordship of Christ extended, and to each of them respectively. He is Lord over *all flesh*, [John xvii. 2.] both living and dead, [Rom. xiv. 9. Phil. ii. 9, 10.] particularly,

§ 11. 1. He is Lord over *all the elect*; and, besides the general foundation of the equity of his authority and power in his Divine nature, and creation of all things, the grant of the Father to him as *Mediator* to be their Lord,

Lord, is founded in other special acts both of Father and Son; for they were given to him from eternity in design and by compact, that they should be his peculiar portion, and he their Saviour, [John xvii. 2.] Of the (πασης σαρκος) *all flesh,* over which he hath authority, there is (παν ο δεδωκε) an *universality* of them, whom the Father *gave* him in a special manner; of whom he says, ' Thine they were, and thou gavest them me,' [ver. 6.] They are a portion given him to save, of which he takes the care, as Jacob did of the sheep of Laban, when he served him for a wife; this was an act of the will of the Father in the *eternal covenant* of the Mediator. His *grant* is strengthened by *redemption,* purchase, and acquisition. These thus given him of the Father, and redeemed by him, are of two sorts:

(1.) Such as are *actually called* to faith in him and union with him. These are further become *his,* upon many other special accounts: they are his in all relations of subjection; his children, servants, brethren, disciples, his house, his spouse. He stands towards them in all relations of authority; is their father, master, elder brother, teacher, king, lord, ruler, judge, husband; ruling in them by his spirit and grace, over them by his laws in his word, preserving them by his power, chastening them in his care and love, feeding them out of his stores, trying them and delivering them in his wisdom, bearing with their miscarriages in his patience, and taking them for his portion and inheritance; in his Providence raising them at the last day, taking them to himself in glory, every way avouching them to be his, and himself to be their Lord and master.

(2.) Some of them are always *uncalled,* until the whole number of them be completed. But *before* this happy event they belong, on the former accounts, to his lot, care, and rule, [John x. 16.] they are already his sheep by grant and purchase, though not yet so by grace and holiness; they are not yet his by present obediential subjection, but they are his by eternal designation, and real acquisition. Now the power that the Lord Jesus hath

over

over this sort of mankind is universal, unlimited, absolute, and exclusive of all other power over them, as to the things peculiarly belonging to his kingdom. He is their king, judge, and law-giver; and in things of God, purely spiritual and evangelical, other they have none. It is true, he takes them not *out of the world*, and therefore as to (τα βιωτικα) *the things of this life*, they are subject to the laws and rulers of the world; but as to the things of God, he is the *only Law-giver*, who is able to kill and make alive.

§ 12. 2. His dominion extends also to the *reprobates* and finally impenitent. They are not exempted from that ' *all flesh*,' which he hath power over; nor from those ' *quick and dead*,' over whom he is Lord, [Rom. xiv. 9.] nor from that ' *world*' which he shall judge, [Acts xvii. 31.] And there are two special grounds that are peculiar to this grant and authority over them:

(1.) His *interposition* upon the entrance of sin against the immediate execution of the curse. This fixed the world under a dispensation of forbearance and patience, of goodness and mercy. That God, who spared not the angels when they sinned, but immediately cast them into chains of darkness, should place sinners of the race of Adam under a dispensation of forbearance and goodness; that he should spare them with much long suffering during their pilgrimage on the earth, and fill their hearts with food and gladness, with all those fruits of kindness which the womb of Providence is still bringing forth for their advantage, is *thus far* on account of the Lord Christ, *viz.* that though these things, as relating to reprobates, are no part of his especial purchase as mediator of the everlasting covenant of grace, yet they are a necessary consequent of his interposition against the immediate execution of the whole curse upon the first entrance of sin, and of his undertaking for his elect.

(2.) He makes a *conquest* over them; it was promised that he should do so, [Gen. iii. 15.] and though the work itself seems to us long and irksome, though the ways of accomplishing it be unto us obscure, oftentimes invisible,

sible, yet he hath undertaken it, and will not give it over until they are every one brought to be his footstool, [Pf. cx. 1. I. Cor. xv. 25.] And the dominion granted on these grounds is — *Sovereign and absolute*; they are in his hand, as the Egyptians were in Joseph's, when he had purchased both their persons and estates to be at his arbitrary disposal; and he deals with them as Joseph did with those, so far as any of the ends of his rule and lordship are concerned in them. And—*Judiciary*, [John v. 22, 23.] as he hath power over their persons, so he hath regard to their *sins*; and this power he variously exerciseth over them, even in this world, before he gloriously exerts it in their eternal ruin: for he enlightens them by those heavenly sparks of truth and reason, which he leaves unextinguished in their own minds, [John i. 9.]. Strives with them by his spirit, [Gen. vi. 3.] secretly exciting their consciences to rebuke, bridle, and afflict them, [Rom. ii. 14, 15.] And on some of them he acts by the power and authority of his word, whereby he quickens their consciences, galls their minds and affections, restrains their lusts, bounds their conversations, aggravates their sins, (in a scripture sense) hardens their hearts, and finally judges their souls.

And thus Christ is Lord over *persons*; angels and men.

§ 13. (II.) THINGS. The second part of the heirship and dominion of Christ consisteth in his lordship over *all things* besides, which, added to the former, comprize the whole creation of God. And, in speaking of 'things,' we shall consider,

FIRST, *spiritual* things; which are also of two sorts: —*temporal*, and *eternal*.

First, *temporal*, or such as in *this life* we are made partakers of. And this may be reduced to two heads; for they are all of them either *grace* or *gifts*, and Christ is Lord of them all.

1. Grace;—pardon of sin—the regenerating of the person of a dead sinner—preservation in a condition of acceptance with God, and holy obedience to the end— adoption, with all the privileges that flow from it. All
the

the stores of this grace and mercy that are in heaven for sinners, are given into his hand, and resigned up to his sovereign disposal, [Col. i. 19.] 'It pleased the Father that in him should all fulness dwell.' All the grace and mercy that are in the heart of God as a father to bestow upon his children, are all given into the hand of Christ, and are his, or part of his inheritance. In particular,

(1.) All *pardoning grace* for the acceptance of our persons, and the forgiveness of our sins ; he is the Lord of it; [Acts v. 31.] He is made a prince and a saviour to give repentance and the forgiveness of sins ; nor doth any one receive it but out of his stores. And what is the dominion of ten thousand worlds, in comparison of this inheritance? Surely he shall be my *God* and *King* who hath all forgiveness at his disposal.

(2.) All *regenerating*, quickening, sanctifying, assisting, persevering grace is his ; [John v. 21.] He *quickeneth* whom he will ; he walks among dead souls, and says to whom he pleaseth, Live ; and he sanctifieth by his Spirit whom he pleaseth. All the living waters of saving grace are committed to him, and he invites men unto them freely, [Cant. v. 1. Isa. lv. 1. John iv. 14. Rev. xxi.] All grace actually assisting us in any duty, is his also, for without him we can do nothing; [John xv. 5.] it is he alone that gives out suitable help at the time of need, [Heb. iv. 16.] and all the gracious privileges whereof we are made partakers in our adoption are his also, [John i. 12.] No man was ever quickened, purified, or strengthened, but by him ; nor can one dream of any grace to be obtained but out of his treasures—his *unsearchable riches*— and exceeding excellency ; which being communicated by him to all the subjects of his kingdom, make every one of them richer than all the potentates of the earth who have no interest in him.

§ 14. The *special foundation* of all this trust is in an eminent manner expressed Isa. liii. 10—12. His suffering and purchase make it just and righteous that he should enjoy this part of his inheritance.

The

"The Father says unto him, "Seest thou these poor
"wretched creatures, that lie perishing in their blood,
"and under the curse? They had once my image glo-
"riously enstamped upon them, and were every way meet
"for my service; but behold the misery that is come
"upon them by their sin and rebellion: sentence is gone
"forth against them upon their sin; and they want no-
"thing to shut them up under everlasting ruin, but the
"execution of it. Wilt thou undertake to be their Sa-
"viour and Deliverer, to save them from their sins, and
"the wrath to come? Wilt thou make thy soul an
"offering for their sins; and lay down thy life a ransom
"for them? Hast thou love enough to wash them in
"thine own blood, in a nature to be taken of them, be-
"ing obedient therein unto death, even the death of the
"cross?" Whereunto he replies: "I am content to
"do thy will, and will undertake this work, and that
"with joy and delight. Lo, I come for that purpose,
"my delight is with the sons of men, [Psal. xl. 8. Prov.
"viii. 3.] What they have taken, I will pay. What is
"due from them, let it be required at my hand. I am
"ready to undergo wrath and curse for them, and to
"pour out my soul unto death."—"It shall be" (saith
the Father) "as thou hast spoken, and thou shalt see of
"the travail of thy soul, and be satisfied. And I will
"give thee for a covenant and a leader unto them, and
"thou shalt be the captain of their salvation. To this
"end take into thy power and disposal all the treasures
"of heaven, all mercy and grace, to give out to them
"for whom thou hast undertaken. Behold, here are un-
"searchable hidden treasures, not of many generations,
"but laid up from eternity; take all these riches into
"thy power, and at thy disposal shall they be for
"ever."

§ 15. 2. All *gifts* that are bestowed on any of the sons of men, whereby they are differenced from, or made useful to others, belong also to the inheritance and kingdom of Christ. These are either *natural* or *spiritual*.

(1.)

(1.) *Natural gifts* are special endowments on the persons or minds of men, in relation to things appertaining to this life; as wisdom, learning, skill in arts and sciences. I call them "natural," in respect of the objects about which they are exercised, which are (τα βιωʃικα) *things of this life*, as also in respect of their end and use. They are not always so, as to their rise and spring; but may be immediately infused, as wisdom was into Solomon, for civil government; and skill for all manner of mechanical operations, into Bezaleel, [Exod. xxxi. 2, 3, 6.] But how far these gifts are educed in an ordinary course of Providence, out of their hidden seeds and principles in nature, in a just connection of causes and effects, and so fall under a certain law of acquisition, or what there may be of the interposition of the Spirit of God, in an especial manner, immediately conferring them on any, falls not under our present consideration. Nor yet can we insist on their use, which is such, that they are the great instrument in the hand of God, for the preservation of human society, and to keep the course of man's life and pilgrimage from being wholly brutish. I design only to shew, that even they also belong (though more remotely) to the lordship of Jesus Christ.

The very use of men's reason, and their natural faculties, as to any good end or purpose, is continued to them upon the account of his interposition, bringing the world thereby under a dispensation of patience and forbearance.

He is endued with power and authority to use them in whatsoever hand they lie, whether of his friends or enemies, to the especial ends of his glory, in doing good to his church. And, indeed, in the efficacy of his Spirit and power upon these gifts of the mind—exciting, disposing, and enabling men to various actings and operations by them; controlling, over-ruling, entangling each other, and themselves in whom they are—his wisdom and care, in reference to the government, chastisement, and deliverance of his church, are most conspicuous,

(2.)

(2.) *Spiritual gifts*, which principally come under that denomination, are of two sorts; extraordinary and ordinary. The *former* are immediate endowments, exceeding the whole system of nature, in the exercise whereof they are mere instruments of him who bestows them. Such, of old, were the gifts of miracles, tongues, healing, prediction, and infallible inspiration, given out by the Lord Christ to such as he was pleased to use in his gospel service, in an extraordinary manner. The *latter* sort are furnitures of the mind, enabling men to comprehend spiritual things, and the management of them for spiritual ends and purposes. Such are wisdom, knowledge, prudence, utterance, aptness to teach; in general, abilities to manage the things of Christ and the gospel to their own proper ends. And as they are the spring and foundation of office, so they are the great and only means of the church's edification. And there is no member but hath its gift; which is the talent given, or rather lent, to trade with. Now, of all these, Christ is the only Lord; they belong to his kingdom, [Psal. lxviii. 18.] when he ascended on high, he took, or received gifts for men; he took them into his own power and disposal, being given him of his Father, as Peter declares, [Acts ii. 33.] adding, that he received *the Spirit*, by whom all these gifts are wrought. And this investiture, with power over all gifts, he makes the ground of that apostle's mission, [Matt. xxviii. 18.] this he had as a fruit of his suffering, as a part of his purchase, and it is a choice part of his lordship and kingdom.

§ 16. The *end* also, why all these gifts are given into his power and disposal, is evident.

1. The *propagation* of his gospel, and consequently the setting up of his kingdom in the world, depends upon them. These are the arms that he furnished his messengers with, when he sent them forth to subdue the world to himself; and by these they prevailed. By that Spirit of wisdom and knowledge, prayer and utterance, wherewith they were endowed, attended when needful, with the extraordinary gifts before-mentioned, did they accomplish

plish the amazing work committed to their charge. Now, the Lord Christ having a right to a kingdom and inheritance given him, which was actually under the possession of his adversary, it was necessary, that all those arms wherewith he was to make a conquest of it, should be given to his disposal, [II. Cor. x. 4.] These were the weapons which, through God, were so mighty to cast down the strong-holds of sin and Satan. These are the slings and stones before which the Goliah of earth and hell did fall. This was that power from above, which he promised his apostles to furnish them with, when they should address themselves to the conquest of the world, [Acts i. 8.] With these weapons, this furniture for their warfare, a few persons, despised in the eyes of the world, went from Judea to the ends of the earth, subduing all things before them, to the obedience of their Lord and Master. And,

2. By these the church is *edified*; and to that end doth he continue to bestow them to the end of the world, [I. Cor. xii. 7, 13, 14. Ephes. iv. 8—13. Rom. xii. 6 —8.] And for any to hinder their growth or exercise is, what in them lies to pull down the church of Christ, and to set themselves against the testimony which he gives in the world, that he is yet alive, and that he takes care of his disciples, being present with them, according to his promise.

3. And by these means and ways is *God glorified* in him and by him; which is the great end of his Lordship over all the gifts of the Spirit.

§ 17. That we may a little, by the way, look into our special concernment in these things, their order and subserviency one to another may be briefly considered; for as *natural gifts* are the foundation of spiritual, and lie in an especial subordination to them; so are *spiritual gifts* enlivened, made effectual and durable by *grace*. The principal end of Christ's bestowing gifts is, the erection of a ministry in his church, for the ends before-mentioned; and where *all these*, in their order and mutual subserviency to one another, are received by any, there and there alone, is a competent furniture for the work of the ministry received; and where any of them, as to their *whole kind*, are wanting, there is a glaring *defect* in the person, if not a nullity as to the office. *Natural gifts* and endowments of mind are so necessary a foundation for any man that looks towards the work of the ministry, that without some competent measure of them, it is folly and madness to entertain thoughts of any progress. Unless unto these *spiritual gifts* are superadded, the other will be never of any use for the edification of the church, as having, in their own nature and series, no special tendency to that end. Nor will these superadded spiritual gifts enable any man to discharge his duty unto all well-pleasing before God, unless they are also quickened and seasoned by *grace:* and where there is an intercession of this series and order, the defect will quickly appear. Thus we see many of excellent natural endowments in their first setting forth in the world, and in their endeavours on that single stock, promising great usefulness and excellency in their way; who, when they come to engage in the service of the gospel, evidence themselves to be altogether unfurnished for the employment they undertake; yea, and to have lost what before they seemed to have received. Having gone to the utmost length and bounds that gifts merely natural could carry them, and not receiving superadded spiritual gifts, they faint in the way, wither, and become utterly useless. And this, for the most part, falleth out, when men have either abused their natural gifts to the service of their lusts, and in opposition to the simplicity of the gospel; or, when they set upon spiritual things, and pretend to the service of Christ, merely in their *own strength,* without dependance on him for abilities and furniture; or, when they have some fixed *corrupt end* to accomplish by a pretence of the ministry, without regard to the glory of Christ, or compassion to the souls of men; to which the Lord Christ will not prostitute the gifts of his Spirit. And sundry other causes of this failure may be assigned. It is no otherwise, as to the next degree in this order, in reference to spiritual gifts and saving grace. When these gifts, in the

the good pleasure of their sovereign dispenser, are superadded to the natural endowments above-mentioned, they carry on those who receive them cheerfully, comfortably, and usefully in their progress. The former are increased, heightened, strengthened, and perfected by the latter, towards that special end, whereunto themselves are designed;—the glory of Christ in the work of the gospel. But if these also are not in due season *quickened* by saving grace; if the heart be not moistened and made fruitful thereby, even they also will wither and decay. Sin and the world, in process of time, will devour them, whereof we have daily experience in this world. And this is the order wherein the great Lord of all these gifts hath laid them in a subserviency, one kind to another, and all of them to his glory.

§ 18. *Secondly*, To close our considerations of this part of the Lordship of Christ, there remains only, that we shew him to be the Lord of all *spiritual eternal things*, which in one word, we call *glory*. He is himself the ' Lord of ' glory,' [I. Cor. ii. 8.] and the Judge of all, in the discharge of which office, he gives out glory as a reward to his followers, [Matt. xxv. 32, &c. Rom. xiv. 10.] Glory is the reward that he will give at the last day as a crown, [II. Tim. iv. 8. John xvii. 2.] And, that he might be *Lord* of it, he hath *purchased* it, [Heb. ix. 12.] taken actual *possession* of it in his own person; and also as the *forerunner*, in behalf of those on whom he will bestow it, [Heb. vi. 20.] And this is a short view of the Lordship of Christ, as to things *spiritual*.

§ 19. SECONDLY, *Ecclesiastical things*, or things that concern church institutions, rule, and power, belong also to his dominion: he is the only Head, Lord, Ruler, and Law-giver of his church. There was a church state ever since God created man on the earth, and there is the same reason of it in all its alterations, as to its relation to the Lord Christ. Whatever changes it underwent, still Christ was the Lord of it, and of all its concernments. But, by way of instance and eminence, we may consider the *Mo-saical* church state under the Old Testament, and the

Evangelical church state under the New. Christ is Lord of both.

1. He was Lord of the Old Testament church state, and he exercised his power and Lordship towards it.—Its *institution* and erection, he made, framed, set up, and appointed that church state, and all the worship of God therein observed. He it was who at first appeared unto Moses, who gave them the law on mount Sinai, and continued with them in the wilderness; by prescribing to it a *complete rule* of worship and obedience. And the same power he exercised by way of *reformation*, when it was decayed; and by way of *amotion*, or taking down and *removal* of what he himself had set up, because it was so framed, as to continue *only for a season*, [Heb. ix. 10. Deut. xviii. 16—18. Hag. ii. 6, 7. Isa. lxv. 17, 18. II. Pet. iii. 13.] which part of his power and Lordship is abundantly proved against the Jews in the exposition.

2. Of the New Testament *evangelical* church state also he is the only Lord and Ruler; yea, this is his proper kingdom, on which all other parts of his dominion do depend; for he is given to be Head over all things to the church, [Ephes. i. 22.] For, he is the *foundation* of this church state, [I. Cor. iii. 11.] the whole design and plat-form of it being laid in him, and built upon him. And he *erects* this church state upon himself, [Matt. xvi. 18.] 'I will build my church;' the Spirit and Word whereby it is done being from him alone, and ordered by his wisdom, power, and care. And he gives *laws* and *rules* of worship and obedience to it, when so built by and upon himself, [Heb. iii. 2—6.] And, finally, he is the everlasting, constant, abiding *Head*, Ruler, King, and Governor of it, [Ephes. i. 22. Col. ii. 19. Heb. iii. 6.]

§ 20. THIRDLY, He is Lord also of *political things*; of all the *governments* of the world that are set up and exercised for the good of mankind, and the preservation of society, according to rules of equity and righteousness. He alone is the *absolute potentate*; the highest on the earth are in subordination to him. That he is *designed*

unto,

unto, [Pſal. lxxxix. 27.] and accordingly he is *made* Lord of lords, and King of kings, [Rev. xvii. 14. and xix. 16. I. Tim. vi. 15.] and he *exerciſeth dominion* anſwerable to his title; and hath hence a *right* to ſend his goſpel into all nations of the world, attended with the worſhip by him preſcribed, [Matt. xxviii. 18. Pſal. ii. 9—12.] which none of the rulers or governors of the world have any *right* to refuſe or oppoſe, but upon their utmoſt peril. And *all kingdoms* ſhall at length be brought into a *profeſſed ſubjection* to him and his goſpel, and have all their rule diſpoſed of to the increſt of his church and ſaints, [Dan. vii. 27. Iſa. lx. 12. Rev. xix. 16—19.]

§ 21. FOURTHLY, The laſt branch of this dominion of Chriſt conſiſts in the *reſidue* of the *creation* of God; heaven and earth, ſea and land, wind, trees, and fruits of the earth, and the creatures of ſenſe. As they are all ununder his feet, [Pſal. viii. 7, 8. Epheſ. i. 22. 1. Cor. xv. 27.] ſo the *exerciſe* of his power ſeverally over them is well known from the goſpel hiſtory. And thus we have *glanced* at this Lordſhip of Chriſt, in ſome of the general parts of it; and how ſmall a portion of his glorious-power are we able to declare, or even to comprehend!

APPEN-

APPENDIX;

CONTAINING

TWO LETTERS,

THE ONE TO

Dr. PRIESTLEY,

AND THE OTHER TO

Mr. DAVID LEVI,

RESPECTING THIS WORK.

BY THE EDITOR.

"SEARCH THE SCRIPTURES; FOR IN THEM YE THINK YE
"HAVE ETERNAL LIFE; AND THEY ARE THEY WHICH
"TESTIFY OF ME."——JESUS.

A

LETTER

TO

Dr. PRIESTLEY.

Concerning the DATA *requisite for a rational investigation of disputed points in theology, and the* OPINIONS *of fallible men, as a guide for the purpose of interpreting the holy scriptures.*

.

§ 1. *Introduction. The Writer's motive.* § 2. *Success in our inquiries after truth depends on method as well as industry and perseverance.* § 3. *Some common principles requisite as* DATA. *Dr. P.'s what. Requested to be explicit on this head.* § 4. *His appeal from scripture to historical evidence of early* OPINIONS *unjustifiable. Not a good guide, because,* 1. *Not calculated to lessen the difficulty, as it pretends, but rather increases it.* § 5. 2. *The precariousness and insufficiency of it appears from constant experience.* § 6. 3. *It has been solidly refuted long ago, by Protestants in the Popish controversy; and to revive it tends to superstition.* § 7. 4. *It is plainly reproved by Jesus Christ.* § 8. 5. *Highly unthcological in its just consequences.* § 9. 6. *Also illogical, the conclusion being gratuitously*

Vol. I.   Y y

tuitoufly affumed. § 10. 7. *If we have no better guide than this, we are left a prey to perpetual fcepticifm, it being infufficient from its very nature to fettle the mind.* § 11. *Divine revelation the only true data, becaufe this alone affords objective certainty.* § 12. *The objection, That a diverfity of opinion ftill obtains among thofe who are agreed in their data and method of inquiry, anfwered.* § 13. *The plan of Dr.* OWEN *in this work. His reafoning not eafily confuted.* § 14. *This Epiftle to the Hebrews utterly overthrows Dr. P.'s grand argument, taken from the hiftorical evidence of early opinions concerning Chrift.*

REV. and DEAR SIR,

§ 1. TO a gentleman who has claimed, for a number of years, and in various kinds of refearches, the laudable pretenfion of impartially inquiring after truth, no other apology is requifite, in foliciting his attention for a few minutes, than the folemn avowal of a fimilar motive and defign, in profecution of the fame important end.

But though I flatter myfelf that, for the reafon now mentioned, no farther apology is neceffary for making an epiftolary addrefs to you, yet it may be expected, by yourfelf and the public, that I affign my reafon for doing it in the prefent form. It is not with a view to folicit any public notice of it from your pen; this is neither defired nor deprecated; but it comes principally to requeft a greater favour—a candid, unprejudiced attention to the contents of the volumes to which this letter is joined, of which I beg your friendly acceptance.

Indeed, when I confider the religious fentiments contained in thefe volumes, the quantity of reading though fo much abridged, and your various other engagements, I can hardly expect your compliance; but on the other hand, when I reflect on your art in improving time, and quick difpatch in perufing larger works, in connection with your known candour, and my author's unqueftionable

tionable character for erudition and piety, I am not without hope that my request will be complied with.

§ 2. Having thus, dear Sir, explained my chief reason for addressing you in this way, I shall take the liberty of suggesting a few things of another nature; and particularly of testifying in how commendable a light I view your persevering industry in a professed search after religious truth. And yet I must observe, what you well know, that success in obtaining the object of our pursuit, very much depends on the *mode* of inquiry: if this be not happily chosen, the more persevering we are the farther we recede from the desired mark. Two philosophers, or divines, may be equally industrious and persevering, perhaps (at least in a sense) equally sincere, in making lovely truth the end of their studious toil, but if nevertheless they disagree in their data and method of investigation, the farther they advance the more remote may be their conclusions.

§ 3. Hence then arises the necessity, among disputants, of fixing on some *common principles*, which may be called DATA. Without this there can be little or no hope of bringing any disputed point to a fair issue. Without this, when closely urged, they will be for ever shifting sides, and running from the spot to which they ought to be confined, as their skill in sophistry may tempt, or the life of their cause require.

Considering the matter in this light, while occasionally attending to the motions of the controversial war in which you have been so long engaged, I have been induced to pause and put the question—What are the *data* of these polemic champions, on which to stand and from which to argue? Is not this the reason that they are so seldom brought to a *close encounter*, and are seen hectoring one another at a distance, spending so much time and breath in the fruitless (not to say *impertinent*) work of estimating the abilities and qualifications of each other? I have sometimes wished to know, in particular, but have yet to learn, what those *common principles* are on which you build your differing system. How far, for instance, you can travel in company

pany with a *Calvinist* in the high road that leads to the temple of truth, and where precisely is the spot on which you must stop and say—I can go no farther, here I must leave you, our road now parts? It would gratify my curiosity much, and perhaps assist my inquiry, to meet with a candid, unequivocal solution of such difficulties. For I am hitherto of opinion, that if there be not some infallible *objective certainty* on which we may depend as a foundation, Christian theology is but an empty name.

§ 4. Though I have sought in vain for your polemical *data*—whether it is revelation or something else, and if the former, whether the whole of the common canon or only a part, and if a part, what it is, and where is the line of difference—though I have been unsuccessful in *this* inquiry, I am furnished with better means of information respecting your *method* of investigating the points of difference, as it is laid before the public in your various writings, and which is briefly summed up by yourself in the following words: " Christians are not agreed in the interpretation of *scripture language*; but as all men are agreed with respect to the nature of *historical evidence*, I thought that we might perhaps better determine by *history* what was the faith of Christians in early times, independently of any aid from the scripture; and it appeared to be no unnatural presumption, that whatever *that* should appear to be, such was the doctrine of the apostles, from whom their faith was derived; and that by this means we should be possessed of a *pretty good guide* for discovering the true sense of the scriptures."*

Now after having thought, dear Sir, pretty deliberately, on the method here proposed, viewed it in different lights, and endeavoured to trace its genuine consequences, it always, and in various respects, appears to me a ' *very bad* ' *guide*,' for several reasons. For,

1. The proposed method is not calculated to *lessen* the difficulty, which it pretends to remove, but rather *increases* it; since men will no less differ about historical

* Defences of Unitar. for 1788 and 1789, p. 83.

evidence than the meaning of scripture. It increases the toil without improving the fruit. By avoiding a visionary Scylla we are driven on a real Charybdis.

'*Christians are not agreed in the interpretation of scripture.*' True; and what is there almost in the whole compass of literature, where mathematical demonstration is wanting, in the interpretation of which men are all agreed? One well observes: " So wild and extravagant have been the notions of a great part of philosophers, both ancient and modern, that it is hard to determine, whether they have been more distant in their sentiments from truth, or from one another; or have not exceeded the fancies of the most fabulous writers, even poets and mythologists.'* And yet, notwithstanding all their jars and blunders, we cannot justly say that there is no *true system* of nature. But what should we say of a reformer in philosophy, who should propose to rectify our notions of the *system of the universe* by setting before us a train of ' historical evidence,' of what was the ' opinion' of the ancients about it? While he urged their *opinions*, had we not a right to demand rather the *principles* and arguments? If it be said that the case is not parallel, because THALES, PYTHAGORAS, ARISTOTLE, &c. were *fallible* teachers, but that Matthew, John, Paul, &c. were *infallible*; this does not alter the case; it is sufficient for my purpose that the '*opinion*' formed of the one or the other is *fallible*. And therefore the opinion of EBION is no more to be confided in than that of CALVIN. And there were false opinions concerning Christ in the apostolic age as well as in the present. Had you taken therefore the *other* side of the question the impropriety would have been all one; for the fault lies in the *very nature* of the medium of proof.

' *But all men are agreed with respect to the nature of histo-*
' *rical evidence.*' By no means; for if I mistake not fact lies directly against it. Christian Protestants, almost unanimously, echo the maxim of CHILLINGWORTH.—
" That the *Bible alone* (as opposed to tradition and histo-

* ROWNING's Compend. Syst. Introd.

tical

rical evidence, &c.) is the religion of Protestants, and a
safe way to salvation" and divine truth. But let me not
misunderstand the position, which is somewhat equivocal;
for the words—' with respect to the nature of historical
' evidence'—may refer either to *fact* or to *right*; either,
what it is that actually constitutes the evidence, so that
all are agreed about the *real meaning* of testimonies of the
ancients, and the *quantum* of evidence they contain for
and against, supposing their opinion to be in its own nature admissible and of moment; or what *influence* such
evidence ought to have towards finally determining our
judgement in favour of the controverted point. But it
does not appear to me that the position is admissible in
either sense. Not the *former*; for daily stubborn facts
prove, that what one admits as ' historical evidence,' another does not; whom yet charity compels us to regard
as intelligent, learned, pious, and impartial. They are
as much divided in their judgements about the meaning
of the ancient fathers, as about the sense of the apostles.
Not to mention the incomparable disadvantage of this
new method of interpreting scripture, arising from its inevitable tediousness, supposing all the necessary materials
at hand. Not the *latter*; for the rational inquirer will
deem it quite unsatisfactory to infer, that because a party
of men had *heard the apostles*, or their immediate successors, therefore the opinions they formed in religious
matters were *just*. This he can no more admit than if
one should say, That the Unitarian hypothesis must needs
be true, because the Unitarians have read the writings of
the apostles: or, because all the Christian societies in
England, in the year one thousand seven hundred and
ninety, have in use the same version of the Bible, therefore their religious opinions must be the same. Nay, we
cannot safely conclude concerning the major part of those
in England this day, who may be stiled *sworn adherents* to
Calvinistic doctrines, that therefore their religious opinions
are *Calvinistic*. In short, that all men are *not agreed*,
' with respect to the nature of historical evidence,' any
how understood, is but too palpably evident in the storms

of

of furious difputations, and the din of paper wars. Hence I conclude, that the method you propofe is not calculated to leffen the difficulty, but rather to increafe it.

§ 5. 2. The precarioufnefs and infufficiency of it appears from *experience*. As a fpecimen of the truth of this remark, let one fact fuffice *inftar omnium*. It refpects a writer of the prefent day—a writer of erudition, of extenfive learning and knowlege, and who can boaft of an intimate acquaintance with the recondite treafures of ecclefiaftical antiquity, and who can alfo boaft of being ' much at home' in the learned languages. Dr. HORSLEY, then Archdeacon of *St. Albans*, now Bifhop of *St. David's*, took upon him (in 1786) to eftablifh as a fact—" The decline of Calvinifm amounting almoft to a *total extinction* of it among our Englifh diffenters; who no long time fince, were generally Calvinifts."* He adds; " I believe however that the truth is, and is pretty notorious, that *Calvinifm is gone* among the diffenters of the prefent times."† And again ; " I confider it as the reproach of the diffenters of the prefent day, that a *genuine Calvinift is hardly to be found*; except in a fect, confpicuous only for the encouragement, which the leaders of it feem to give to a diforderly fanaticifm."‡ Were not the writer already known, one might be induced, on perufing this account, to exclaim, Did this extraordinary declaration proceed from fome " ιδιωτης" of the eighteenth century? Did the writer refide in fome remote corner of the world, taking his information at fecond hand from incompetent vouchers? Was the ' religious opinion' of which he gives an account fo remote from his own, that he could hardly be thought fufficiently interefted in it to make a due inquiry? Nothing lefs. Confeffedly fenfible and learned, near the metropolis at the time, himfelf a Calvinift, and while he laments the decline of Calvinifm,

---

* Tracts in Controverfy with Dr. PRIESTLEY, p. 386.
† Ibid. p. 397.
‡ Ibid. p. 400.

he utters the above declaration; nay, he undertakes *professedly* to establish it as a fact. You know, Sir, too well the state of the *real* fact to need a comment; and the use I think we should make of this and similar mistakes that we so often meet with, is, That we should be peculiarly circumspect in admitting 'historical evidence' for the state of religious opinions, whether in later or in earlier times. To illustrate this matter we will suppose a case; *viz.* that some ages hence there will appear a learned *collector* of the state of religious opinions in the eighteenth century; and that the ravages of time will destroy all monuments of counter-evidence to invalidate the above assertion; how could the historical collector choose but admit for fact, though nothing in reality be less so? What! might the historian say, shall I tax the veracity, or impeach the knowledge of such a writer, and a writer so advantageously circumstanced for all necessary information, as to hesitate in my conclusion? The application is *in promptu.* And it is a matter that we must not forget, that the late Dr. WORTHINGTON, and other eminent characters now living, assure us, that the world *grows better*, and therefore that the ancients are *less entitled* to our credit and confidence than the moderns. Again,

§ 6. 3. The attempt to " determine by *history* what was the faith of Christians in early times, independently of any aid from the scripture, that we may thereby gather what was the doctrines of the apostles," has been long ago *solidly refuted*, and justly exploded by the great CHILLINGWORTH, and other eminent Protestants, in their controversy with the Papists. There is no admitting of it but at the expence of one of the noblest principles, and strongest pillars of the reformation from popery—" That the scripture is the *only rule* whereby to judge of controversies;" and it appears to me that the revival of it into a rule would directly tend to restore the popish privilege of rendering blind obedience to our spiritual guides. For every attempt to explain scripture by scripture principles, would be checked as wrong and dangerous, while the unlearned, that is, the body of the Christian church, would

would be called upon to embrace, on the word of a few learned, and every Chriftian church on the *ipfe dixit* of its paftor, however unqualified to make a fair report, to fubmit to the *opinions* of the ancient church for their guide; which leads at once to impofition and impofture on the one hand, and to blind obedience, fuperftition, and an abject deference to human authority in matters of confcience on the other. Befides,

§ 7. 4. The above method of proceeding is plainly *reproved by Jefus Chrift* in the New Teftament. For it is the fame principle muft give it life as was adopted by the *Jewifh doctors*, which taught them to appeal, on every occafion, from revealed evidence to human traditions, or a pretended *oral law*; the fayings and *opinions of their ancients*, which they reckoned a *good guide* for the right underftanding of the Mofaic writings. But this pretended guide, inftead of being honoured and recommended, is by our Lord oppofed and reproved, [Matt. xv. Mark vii. &c.] Nor does it make any difference, in the prefent argument, whether the human traditions and opinions be *written* or *unwritten*.

§ 8. 5. The fcheme propofed is, moreover, highly *untheological* in its confequence; for it is inconfiftent not only with human fallibility, but alfo with free agency and accountablenefs. In phyficks, indeed, we may often with certainty infer the caufe from the effect; but in ethicks and religion, where the *morality* of an act, or the *truth* of an opinion, is in debate, it is abfurd to fay, that becaufe a fallible creature acts or thinks in this or that manner, he *therefore ought* to do fo; nay, it is fo untheological that it ftrikes at the root of all religion, natural and revealed. For if men confeffedly imperfect and uninfpired are not always *liable to err*, they are not *free*, and therefore not accountable. Therefore the ' opinions' of fuch perfons, though they lived in the apoftolic age, and fuppofing them to be exactly afcertained, can be no fafe medium of proof. They are utterly incapable of affording us any objective certainty, any more than ours to thofe who fhall come after us. Their *antiquity* makes no difference, becaufe that does not alter their *nature*; nor does it much matter, for the same reason, whether they are few or many. Wherefore without better *materials*, whether orthodox or heterodox, the controversial warrior will do little execution on a reflecting judicious mind, though he should charge his ' *cannon*' with them, together with his ' small arms.'

§ 9. 6. I shall venture a step farther, and profess to you, dear Sir, that the method you propose for settling our opinions, appears to me *illogical*; as teaching us to infer the truth of the premises from the fact of the conclusion. In other words, it makes the conclusions of men, who were fallible and fickle as ourselves, and which they pretended to draw from the premises of Revelation, to be a safer guide by which to form our judgement, than Revelation compared with itself, the premises from which they professedly inferred their conclusion; that is, we are led by it to assume a fallible conclusion, and from the gratuitous assumption to pronounce upon the truth of the premises.

§ 10. 7. Once more; if we have no better guide than this, we are exposed as a prey to perpetual *scepticism*, it being insufficient from its very nature to settle the mind. If this guide leads any one to the temple of truth, it is by accident, and not because it was ever designed for that end; we cannot, therefore, put any *confidence* in it while we are following its footsteps; the event would always appear dubious, and the prospect of success would never be sufficient to counter-balance the toil. In short, it directly tends (supposing the sole motive of the inquirer to be the love of truth) it directly tends to retard the pace of industry, and to clip the wing of genius; and, therefore, can be no genuine friend to free inquiry.

I think, Sir, that thus far I have stood on firm ground in my reasoning; there is no theological truth to be found, in which we may put any confidence, without some *data*, some first principles of this Divine science, possessed of *objective certainty*; but the *foundation* you have chosen for your polemical building is an *uncertain* one, and the *guide* you recommend is, in my apprehension, a " *very bad*" one;

one; seeing it is so far from lessening our difficulties, as Christians and theologians, that it considerably increases them;—it is found to be insufficient from the experience of all ages, and undeniable facts;—it is what our most eminent reformers from Popery, and Protestant polemicks, have solidly refuted in their opposition to blind obedience, church authority over conscience and arbitrary power;— it is reproved and condemned, in its principle, by our Lord himself;—is untheological, as incompatible with the moral state of man in this life of fallibility and imperfection;—is contrary to the rules of just reasoning, by gratuitously assuming the conclusion of the practical syllogism included in it;—and, finally, is deserving of a charge of no small magnitude, its being of a sceptical tendency. What weight my arguments have in opposition to the *fundamental principles* of your controversial and historical writings against the orthodox faith, is left to your candid examination, and the verdict of the impartial public.

§ 11. Having shown the necessity of *some* principles, as *data* peculiar to the science of which we treat, and endeavoured to shew the insufficiency of what you substitute for that purpose, it may naturally be expected, that I should be explicit in avowing what is it that I judge deserving of that important claim; and this I very willingly do, but with the greatest brevity; seeing it would seem impertinent to *defend in form*, what you have not *in form attacked*. My *data* then are, DIVINE REVELATION, and that *only*, and the *whole* of it. And it appears to me, on the maturest reflection, that if *Divine revelation self-compared* doth not answer that purpose, nothing else will; and that whatever else is set up for that purpose, is demonstrably fallacious. " The *positive evidence* of scripture (as I have observed elsewhere) holds the same rank in theology, as *experimented evidence* does in reference to any hypothesis in philosophy. As, in the latter case, there is no disputing in favour of a system *against facts*, phenomena, and experiments; so, in the former case, no reasoning can be valid in opposition to *positive evidence*, or express discernible authority."* Common sense, right reason, the opinions of the good and great, &c. have their use, and an important use, in their proper places; but they are no *data* in Christianity. As to the order of investigation, *preceding* revelations, and Divinely-authenticated facts, are the only safe *rule* by which we ought to examine any *particular part* of scripture. Every *foregoing* dispensation of religion, and indeed, every revealed fact is, I may say, a torch lighted in heaven, to illuminate those that follow, until we come to the "sealing of prophecy," or the end of the canon; and every succeeding one, to the last, reflects a still more abundant light on all that went before. Wherefore, let all that revere the authority of heaven, all the friends of revelation and rational inquiry, attend more to *this light* that shineth in a dark place, and not (I mean as the principal, and only safe means) not to the false lights of human opinions (early or late) in the church, by following which we expose ourselves to wandering and danger every step of our road, while in pursuit of truth and happiness.

§ 12. If it be objected, That a *diversity* of opinions still obtains among those, who are agreed in their *data*, and method of inquiry, I would briefly reply in the following particulars:

1. To urge this objection is the same as to urge that men do not form their opinions *mechanically*, but freely; and that some of them reason *falsely*. But what then? Shall I depreciate and reject a rule, concluding it is not a good one, because I know not how to use it?

2. The objection implies, as far as it has any force, that men are not *accountable* for their mistakes, nor liable to make any, provided their *means* are sufficient; which amounts to little less than self-contradiction. It is much the same as to object against an experiment—an accurate experiment—in philosophy, because the consequences, which the learned draw from it, are various.

* Antipedob. Examined. Chap. III. § 2.

3. While

3. While men are free and accountable, it is no less necessary, that the *disposition* of the mind be right, than that the principle be well chosen. Free inquiry of itself will never insure success, without a *right use* of that freedom. This is the only way, that I know of, to avoid bad consequences, and any other, short of this, must prove abortive.

But let us not forget, that the *good disposition* which we need for this purpose, is not only to be cultivated by the use of means, but also is to be received, in the habits of it, from the Divine favour, as a matter of gospel promise. If there is any thing of a spiritual nature promised in the word of God, there is the promise of a *Divine influence* to be obtained by *asking* for it; that is, importunate seeking in God's appointed way. [See Luke xi. 1—13. Jam. i. 5—8.] And this is so far from being inconsistent with moral agency in this our state of trial for eternity, that the *trial* eminently consists, with respect to those to whom the promise is given, in their submitting, or not submitting, to its gracious import. In short, for 'the heart to be established with *grace*,' [Heb. xiii. 9.] is the best preparative for using our freedom well, and the best preservative in the line of truth. And if after all, our pretensions to sincerity and teachableness, the love of truth and impartiality in seeking it, are equal, and yet our sentiments differ, there is no remedy in *this* world; to our common Master we stand or fall; our own judgement of ourselves, as well as that of our fellow-creatures concerning us, must be equally submitted to the Judge of the whole earth. 'Every way of man is *right in his own eyes*; but the Lord pondereth the heart,' [Prov. xxi. 2.]

I must confess, dear Sir, that I was much grieved, when I perused the following sentence, which you not only suffered to drop from your pen, but to be published to the world: "If, to your *arguments* you can even add *miracles*, the doctrine you propose (*i. e.* personal distinctions in the Deity) could not be received."

ceived."* What a reflection upon the Christian church; and upon millions of the most distinguished pious characters in every age! But though the expressions are strong, and your conviction such as they represent it to be, yet you must allow, that it is *possible* you may be in a mistake; for such have been the *convictions* of many persons in favour of an *erroneous sentiment*, as to stand firm against *actual miracles*, repeated miracles, performed in proof of a contrary sentiment. Your own observation will justify and illustrate this remark: "The prejudices of some persons against the clearest and most important truths may be so strong (as we see in the case of the Scribes and Pharisees of our Saviour's time) that *no evidence will convince them*." †

§ 13. If you condescend, Sir, to peruse these volumes, you will find that the Author, who, for depth of erudition, and extent of knowledge, proper for an accomplished divine, has been excelled by few, if any; you will find, that he undertakes no less a task than to demonstrate, that this Epistle to the Hebrews teaches doctrines and facts, which utterly overthrow the opinions you espouse concerning the person and priesthood of Christ. His foundation is not laid upon the *surface*; he first demonstrates the canonical authority of the epistle, before he proceeds to investigate the contents of it; and the latter he does in the light of *preceding revelations*, and a very enlarged acquaintance with Judaism, both ancient and modern, in its pure and corrupted state. His exposition, reasoning, and doctrines, are all along founded on the *general scope* of the passage he is upon; and it will not be easy for any one to convict him of mistake, without shewing, that he has mistaken the *main design* of the epistle itself, which, in my opinion, would be a Herculean task.

§ 14. Before I conclude, I have one remark to make, which, I presume, is not altogether unworthy your atten-

---

* Defences of Unitar. for 1788 and 1789, p. 176.

† Sermon on the proper conduct of Dissenters, with respect to the Test Act, p. 10.

tion.

tion. It is this: If the *Nazarenes* and *Ebionites* were what you have reprefented them to be—Jewifh Chriftians, who held the mere humanity of Chrift, and who may be traced to the very age of the apoftles—the plain inference is, that this Epiftle to the Hebrews was intended, by the Author of it, and by him who is Head over all things to the church, as an *antidote* to counteract fuch an opinion in the moft direct manner: and were the hiftorical evidence of the pofitions you have advanced, Sir, concerning the perfon and offices of the Meffiah, a thoufand times more clear than it is, or is likely to be, the irrefragable conclufion is—that the writer of this epiftle, and all who embraced his doctrine, were *difpleafed* with them, in that very thing for which you feem to *carefs* them. And if any of the Nazarenes themfelves *fubmitted* to what it plainly inculcates, they muft have *abandoned* the fentiments you afcribe to them; or if they did not, their obftinate refufal ftands condemned by it in every page.

But "Paul often reafons inconclufively;" a bold charge! and a charge deftitute of proof. Now, fuppofing, without granting, that "he wrote as any other perfon of his turn of mind and thinking, and in his fituation, would have written without any particular infpiration." It is but reafonable to fay, that the number of his converts, and of the churches founded by him, was very confiderable; and that they imbibed his fentiments to a great degree, at leaft, appear from his writings addreffed to many of them; now, upon what principle of reafon and equity can we gather, that *Ebion* and his adherents, holding contrary opinions, deferve the honour of being better qualified to rectify our judgements concerning points of the greateft importance in Chriftianity, in preference to Paul, and the churches founded by him? Were the *Nazarenes* infallible? or did *Ebion* ever reafon inconclufively? Was the church at Jerufalem infallible? or were their paftors *more conclufive* reafoners than Paul? If they were, upon what principle; if not, why impeach *his* apoftolic teaching in particular (in which we may
pre-

presume he sometimes *reasoned)* and degrade his abilities? The truth is, St. Paul was a wise master-builder, who laid the foundation of many churches, and edified them in the most holy faith, by his preaching and his pen. 'From Jerusalem, and round about unto Illiricum, he *fully preached* the gospel of Christ; he was sent by Christ himself to *open men's eyes*, and to turn them from darkness to light, through mighty signs and wonders, *by the power of the Spirit* of God; he was an apostle (not of men, *neither by man*, but by Jesus Christ, and God the Father) and certified his converts, that the gospel he preached was not after man; for he saith, " I neither received it of *man*, neither was I taught it, but by the revelation of Jesus Christ."

Upon the whole, for any one to prefer a few obscure accounts of a few obscure persons, to the accounts we have of the commission, authority, principles, and reasonings of this Man of God, by which to form our judgements concerning true Christianity, appears to me, like a person who should prefer a heterogeneous mixture of *iron and clay*, to pure gold; and then, to make his wisdom appear more consummate, that he should, after having once made the choice, rummage all the musty scraps of antiquity for something that may help to stamp a current value on it, and to depreciate what has been thus renounced. In reality, the Nazarenes were *ignorant* of the true nature of the gospel; whatever *instructions* they were favoured with, they had made little *proficiency* in the school of Christ; else why should they be so tenacious of what *all the apostles* laboured to dispossess them of? Why attempt to build again, what they had unanimously, and by Divine direction, been pulling down?—I forbear enlarging; but disinterested observers of what is going on among us, will be ready to exclaim—" Surely we may congratulate the *humility* (if we cannot the wisdom) of the eighteenth century, so famous for many other interesting and memorable exploits, while we behold its " most rational divines," after struggling for liberty, and improving science, commencing, with no small complacency,

cency, the obsequious disciples of these obscure, ignorant, anti-apostolic Nazarenes and Ebionites."*

Wishing

* The following passage, from a late learned and acute *Reviewer*, of the " History of Corruption," &c. appears to me so just, and so much to the purpose, that I cannot forbear transcribing it : " But an indifferent reader may, perhaps, stop the disputants in this career of controversy, and ask them, of what importance it is to the main object of the debate between them, to know what the opinions of these Nazarenes were; especially as it is a point agreed upon between both, that these Nazarenes, whatever their principles of faith might have been, were ignorant and bigotted observers of the Mosaic law, which both the Orthodox and Heretics acknowledge to have been abrogated by the death of Christ? Do *they* stand so high in the scale of authority, that we should appeal to them in the decision which respected the nature and person of Jesus Christ? What is gained on the one hand, and what is lost on the other, by settling this dispute, supposing it capable of being settled at all?—A very proper question ! and the answer we shall make to it is this: That though the believers in the pre-existence of Christ have a thousand testimonies to appeal to, in proof of their faith, yet this seems to be the *last resort* of the Socinian, when he is called on to produce authority for his principles in the primitive ages. Deprive the Socinian of this *twig of antiquity*, and he is ready to make the same lamentable outcry, that was made by Micah in old times: " You have taken away my gods, in whom I trusted, and what have I more?"

" The argument drawn out in form is the following: The first Christians were called Nazarenes. Those who afterwards went by that name, were their genuine followers; but those succeeding Nazarenes did not believe that Jesus Christ had a pre-existent nature; *therefore*, it was not a doctrine believed by the first Christians, because the later Nazarenes transmitted their opinions (at least on *this* head) in their original purity, without the adulterations of those who were afterwards called Orthodox.

" There are many things in this argument which may be doubted, and some which may be denied. If the Nazarenes were the members of the original church of Christ, and the genuine followers of the apostles, how came they so far to counteract the design of the Christian institution, as to mix with the ordinances of the gospel, the abrogated ceremonies of the Mosaic law? Was such conduct, in any respect, authorized by the New Testament? Was it not in direct opposition, both to the conduct and instructions of the apostle Paul? We know what *such* a Nazarene as Toland would say on this subject; but what would Dr. PRIESTLEY say?—If the Nazarenes were people of such low and carnal sentiments, so weak in their understandings, and so superstitious

Wishing that you may possess an abundant measure of the Divine teaching, promised in the sacred oracles, to lead you into all truth—that you may have peace in believing—that you may be found in Christ Jesus, not having your own righteousness, which is of the law—and finally, that you may be replenished

titious in their practices, can we deem them fit authorities to be appealed to, in contradiction to the concurrent testimony of the most eminent lights of the primitive church; If, in points of practice, in which the laws delivered for their direction were so clear and definite, they still pertinaciously adhered to old and exploded customs, which the gospel had rendered totally useless, is it a matter of any surprise, that they should have fallen into some errors of faith, and maintained, with an obstinacy peculiar to their race, some of the false prejudices of the Jews, relating to the nature and qualifications of the Messiah?

"For our part, we are ready to confess, that if the Nazarenes were, with the Ebionites, given up to the Socinians, who are so eager to claim them as their elder brethren, we do not perceive the very great advantage they would gain by such an acquisition.

"Dr. PRIESTLEY is not always careful to keep clear of *gratuitous* assertion. It is a compendious method of argument; but unless it comes from an *oracle*, we have a right to admit, or reject it, just as we please. '*No* person, says he, can, I think, reflect upon this subject with proper seriousness, without thinking it a little remarkable, that the Jewish Christians, in so early an age as they are spoken of, should be acknowledged to believe nothing either of the divinity, or even of the pre-existence of Christ, if either of those doctrines had been taught them by the apostles.' On the same mode of reasoning, and with equal propriety, we might say,—It is a little extraordinary, that the Jewish Christians should have continued such adherents to the rituals of the Mosaic law, if they *had* been explicitly taught, that they were abrogated by the death of Christ. Can we suppose any who owned the truth of the gospel, to have remained ignorant of the grand design of its promulgation, if that design had been properly delineated and explained? Or could they have persevered in an obstinate resistance to it, if it had been enforced by proper authority?—These were the standards of *ancient simplicity!*—at least simplicity of *Christian doctrine*; though the veil of Moses was over their faces, and the yoke of the old law fettered their necks!"

MONTH. REV. Vol. lxix. p. 219, &c.

with

plenished with the spirit of power, and of love, and of a sound mind.

I am, Reverend Sir,

Your most obedient

humble Servant,

EDWARD WILLIAMS.

Oswestry, Feb. 1790.

A LETTER

TO

Mr. DAVID LEVI;

Recommending this Work to his candid and attentive Perusal.

DEAR SIR,

WHAT I observed to your late antagonist, Dr. PRIESTLEY, in my preceding letter to him, respecting my principal motive in addressing him in the manner I have done, is applicable also in general to the present address. It is not intended to provoke your polemic pen, but to solicit a favour. Since you profess a sincere love of truth, and an openness to conviction, your *candid and attentive perusal* of the volumes herewith sent you, is amicably requested.

The Epistle here commented upon was *originally designed* for your nation, the Hebrews; not only for the edification of those who had embraced the gospel, but also for the conviction of such as continued to reject it. This being

being its primary defignation, and it being, as I firmly believe, Divinely revealed, I can no lefs than importunately and affectionately recommend it to you and your friends, as an inftrument chofen by infinite Wifdom, admirably calculated, when rightly underftood, to fubferve your beft and everlafting intereft.

The Writer of it was a Hebrew of the Hebrews; in the former part of his life zealous for the law, in your view of its import: he was a ftrict Pharifee, and no fmall proficient in the learning of the Jews, as well as their religion. Nor did he embrace the Chriftian faith, which I venture to call the accomplifhment and *perfection* of the Jewifh, but upon the cleareft evidence and ftrongeft conviction that the mind of man, in matters of this nature, is, perhaps, capable of. He was well qualified to form an eftimate of both; and the refult was, upon the moft deliberate review, that he counted all things but lofs for the excellency of the knowledge of Chrift Jefus, his Lord. This, it is true, brought upon him the odium of his countrymen, as if he were an apoftate from the religion of their forefathers; whereas, in reality, no man, after his embracing the gofpel, better underftood wherein the life and glory of that religion confifted. No man had a higher veneration for the Divine authority of the Hebrew Scriptures, and the exalted character of Mofes. What he before thought to be quite inconfiftent—the legiflation of Mofes, and the Meffiahfhip of Jefus Chrift—appeared now, as indeed they are, perfectly reconcileable.

His writings in general, as well as this epiftle, are characterifed not only by a depth, compactnefs, and force of argument, but alfo by an admirable fpirit of *benevolence*. So powerfully did this Divine principle operate in his virtuous and holy mind, that it breaks forth into language inimitably ftrong and pathetic. [See Rom. ix. 1—5.] Left any fhould imagine that his adherence to the Chriftian caufe was the effect of bigotry; that he was only a violent party man, he declares in the moft folemn terms, that for the love he bore to his brethren, his kinfmen according to the flefh, he could even fubmit, were that available, to the same treatment from the Christian church, as he had received from the Jewish.

The subject of this Epistle is peculiarly interesting. It treats of a religious controversy of great magnitude; indeed, I may say, the greatest controversy that ever existed in the church of God, and in which you and your brethren are concerned in a direct and immediate manner. This is another reason that induces me to solicit your attention to this work, in your professed capacity of an impartial inquirer.

But there is reason to fear that we are very liable to mistake the true nature of this controversy; and while we labour under that mistake, it is no wonder that our prejudices are strengthened in favour of our own tenets, right or wrong, while affronted truth, indignant, eludes our disappointed grasp. Though the question—Whether Jesus Christ be the true Messiah—be to Jews and Christians, if properly weighed, infinitely momentous; yet, in my apprehension, it is a question too complicated, or not sufficiently radical, for an accurate inquirer to begin with. If I may presume to offer my thoughts on this important subject, the *previous* question ought to be—not whether any part of the Old Testament ought to be attacked and renounced, as if not given by Divine authority, but—*What is the* TRUE IMPORT *of the Old Testament system?* Was it given with a *subordinate* design; with a view to introduce a dispensation of a more *spiritual* form, or was it not? Are the Messiah's kingdom, and its grand blessings, as represented in the ancient promises, and by the spirit of prophecy, of a temporary and perishing, or of a *permanent and eternal* nature? Before we can, therefore, properly agitate the question about the *person* of the Messiah, we ought, as regular investigators and controvertists, for the sake of lessening the labour, to come to a previous issue concerning—*What kind of a Messiah* the ancient records hold forth? What is the nature of the *work* there assigned for him? Do his offices relate only to this transitory life, or do they respect redemption from moral evil

and

and everlasting misery? If the former, you are in the right; but if the latter, we bid fair for being so.

I may here observe, that you stand, in a sense, the representative of your English brethren, while publishing and defending *that sense* of the Old Testament writings which this epistle undertakes to prove is the *wrong* sense of them. St. Paul's *interpretation* of the holy scripture, and *your's*, are diametrically opposite. This consideration also, in connection with my idea of Paul's knowledge, disposition, and abilities, induces me to call your closest attention to his different method of explaining the sacred oracles. And may the God of all grace lead you into all truth! By the knowledge of his merciful and sovereign pleasure in his various dispensations, may you effectually learn wherein consists the true kingdom of God!

With respect to the *Exposition* of this epistle, by the learned and pious Dr. OWEN, together with the *Exercitations*, they contain, in my opinion, a full reply to every thing of moment contained in your late publications in favour of Judaism. Without reflecting on what others have done, I am inclined to think, that this work enters more into the merits of the cause, than any thing you seem to be acquainted with, as far as I can judge from your writings. Will you excuse me if I here add—that I am satisfied, from the idea I have of the general tendency of this work, and a truly religious character, that were your progenitor Abraham on the land of the living, to peruse it, he would subjoin his *hearty amen*.

When I consider your notion of the Messiah's kingdom, and of the *unanimity* of his subjects, I am aware of your being ready to object to *every* proposal from a Christian, be it what it may, as in your first letters: " To convert a nation, such as the Jews to Christianity, the professors thereof ought to be *unanimous*, in what the work of salvation consists; otherwise, they might be deterred therefrom, by reason of the difficulty attending the making a proper choice of that which is right."* That

---

* Letters to Dr. PRIESTLEY, p. 72.

is, if there be any force in the objection, you will be right in rejecting Christianity, because Christians differ in their judgement about the particulars of their religion. But how unreasonable, how preposterous the requisition! Do any Christians differ about Jesus being the Messiah? No: give us then the meeting *thus far* before you object to less general differences. If you expect such unanimity among uninspired men in the present state, before you grant them leave to recommend their religion to their fellow-men, as of Divine original, you must suppose them to be mere machines, that do not act by free choice. On this principle it is impossible that there ever should be unanimity among men. For just with the same reason may every individual object, of whatever religion, Christian, Jewish, Mahometan, or Heathen. It is the same as to say, I will never embrace truth until all who profess it act a worthy part; I will never aim at being truly religious until all others are so first; I will have nothing to do with *any truth* but what acts mechanically on all who *profess* it, producing in them an uniform good effect whether they will or no!—But, dear Sir, you seem to expect among the subjects of King Messiah, what will never be in this world, and which God has never promised. That those of the same general denomination are not " agreed among themselves" in some particulars, is so far from being a characteristic mark of a false religion, that it is in reality, no more than the natural, and in the present imperfect state, the unavoidable result of human freedom. It is acknowledged by yourself, that " conscience ought to be free;" that is, I presume, in every state, under the reign of the Messiah not excepted. Men, in the present state, are fallible and accountable; consequently no mere profession of the sublimest truths conceivable can ensure unanimity. Modern Judaism is either *right* or *wrong*, notwithstanding the petty jars among its professors; and the same is true of Christianity.

Reflecting farther on your views of religion, liberty of conscience, and charity, I can easily conceive how uninteresting must appear to you, any attempt at conversion, whe-

whether by Jews or Christians. "We do not, say you, think ourselves bound, as the Christians, to *propagate* our religion," not even " by *arguments.*" Singular and frigid sentiment! and not less singular the ground on which it stands ; for concerning mankind, who are not Jews, you observe : " If they do but keep the *law of nature;* that is, the *seven precepts* of the sons of Noah, or Noachides, we maintain, that they thereby perform all that God requires of them, and will certainly *by this service,* render themselves acceptable to him."* These you call the *pious* of the nations of the world, who will be partakers of *eternal life!* The seven precepts are these : " *First,* Not to commit idolatry. *Second,* Not to blaspheme. *Third,* To appoint and constitute just and upright judges ; that justice may be maintained, and impartially administered to all. *Fourth,* Not to commit incest. *Fifth,* Not to commit murder. *Sixth,* Not to rob, or steal, &c. *Seventh,* Not to eat a member of a living creature." Alas! alas! if Noah and his sons had *no better* ground of hope of *eternal life,* than arose from their performance of *this service,* they could no more have quieted the accusations of conscience, or abated the horrors of an eternal existence with a holy and just God, than they could avert the stroke of death, or suspend the laws of nature! Is *this* your view of religion, and the Divine dispensations The absurdity is almost unparalleled, and wants a name. Blessed be God for the gospel!

" If you are really in earnest," say you to Dr. PRIEST-LEY, " and wish to convert the Jews, to what you call Christianity, I think you must produce more substantial proofs in support of your hypothesis, than what you have yet done. And, if I might presume to offer my opinion in so weighty a cause, I think that the fairest method, and that which is the likeliest to lead to conviction on either side is, to take a review of *all the prophecies* concerning the Messiah, from Moses to Malachi, and compare them with the acts of Jesus, recorded in the New

* Ut supra, p. 12.

Testament, to see whether or no they have been fulfilled in his person."* I must confess, that this method, as far as it goes (for it includes *only* the prophetic part of the ancient oracles) appears to me, under the limitations before observed, a good one; and doubt not but that it meets with the approbation of all liberal Christians. Nay, Jesus himself recommends it: " Search the Scriptures, for they are they that testify of me." And as you announce such a design, it may be of service to you, to weigh very carefully what Dr. OWEN has done this way in the Exercitations; and if you should think him not sufficiently minute in the abridgement, you would do well to consult the original edition. But excuse me, dear Sir, if on this occasion I drop a monitory hint, *viz.* that you *deal fairly*, and draw no conclusions which are not justified by a thorough knowledge of the subject, and a comprehensive view of it. Without this we cannot be said to *investigate* the meaning of Scripture, but to trifle with it to our own ruin. Happy were it for us all, if nothing but the clear evidence of truth, arising from an acquaintance sufficiently extensive with any controverted subject, determined our choice. The happy effects would be, more humility (that valuable though old-fashioned virtue) more moderation, and less premature triumph in disputants, more industry in seeking, and peace in enjoying truth.

But to what end is it to *examine prophecies*, while you examine them by the following standard? " *We hold the perpetuity* of the law of Moses, and to which nothing is to be added or diminished by any succeeding prophet whatever."† If this were granted you as an *axiom* (but which I call a *fundamental error)* you would make quick work with all the prophecies as well as the gospel. But while you hold this opinion, you hold what I think can never be proved, what the law neither requires nor intends, what is highly affronting to God himself, and destructive to the souls of men. Were Moses upon earth, he would, perhaps, be the first to contradict your interpretation of

---

* Ibid. p. 90. † Second Letters, p. 56.

his words. We maintain with Paul, what is, I think, demonstrated in the following Epistle and Exposition, that it is not by a *different authority* from that which enacted the law, that it is repealed: and surely it must be absurd to contend (while his own declarations do not oblige) that a local, ceremonial institution cannot be abrogated by the supreme Lawgiver. That the " apostles inculcated the *abolishment* of the Mosaical dispensation," is very true; and it is equally true, that it was at first given with that design. And has not Providence incontestably confirmed their doctrine? Has it not rendered the observance of the Mosaic law absolutely impossible? If we hold with the apostles, " that the law of Moses cannot effect the justification of mankind," it is, because we believe and prove that it was never given for that end, never effected for that purpose, and is, in its own nature, incapable of it We do not reject the law, nor did the apostles, as if it were not holy, just, and good in its *proper place*; it is good as a schoolmaster, but not as a saviour; as a mirror of the Divine will, and the rule of human obedience, for the time, and to the end of its appointment. And we confidently add, that the Mosaic law is more truly and effectually honoured by every true Christian, than by any Jew in the world: for if the grand end of it, in its covenant form, be answered in the life and death of Christ, and if the ceremonial part of it be *repealed* by the united voice of the gospel, and of Providence (both which we maintain to be facts) our conduct must be more honourable to the law and the Law-giver, than your's can be. And obstinately to adhere to a *repealed* law, is but a slender proof of respect to the legislative authority. Besides, the apostles were taught this very doctrine from the words of Jeremiah, [chap. xxxi. 31—34.] and other prophetic testimonies, as well as from the nature of the Jewish œconomy and Divine direction. That " God never contradicts himself," we readily believe, which is a strong reason, among others, obliging us to receive Jesus as the Christ of God; for we think that if he is not the *Messiah*, we have nothing left us but a heap of contradictions, as

the venerable author here recommended to you abundantly
shews. On your supposition, we think, neither promises,
prophecies, sacrifices, characteristic notes of the Messiah,
or his principal offices—to save from sin and misery—have
any meaning; and we apprehend that your interpretation
must be at every step subversive of itself.

You, indeed, frankly acknowledge, that " if Christ's
divinity is false, and he did not come to suffer for the *redemption* of mankind, as Christians hold—he came for
nothing."* When we hear such language, we cannot
help inquiring, What *better work* have you for *your* expected Messiah? Or in what *better manner* can you conceive of a redemption to be brought to men, than that
which is exhibited in the New Testament? Is there
any enemy worse than *sin*, or any better method of deliverance from it, than what we maintain? If *motives* are
required, what can we desire, or even conceive of, more
forcible and engaging? And that the Mediator of the new
covenant does not authorize *external force* to procure uniformity of sentiments and worship, is so far from being a
defect, that it must appear to every considerate mind perfectly consistent with all just views of human nature, man's
designation in this state of trial, and the Divine perfections. If men act a part unworthy of the best means,
while they profess an adherence to them, this no more
argues the deficiency of those means, than it would argue
the badness of the seventh command, and the Mosaic le-
gislation, because a professed Jew commits adultery. As
to the insinuation, that the New Testament recommends
our going after *other Gods*—because the *divinity* of Christ,
as you justly contend, is taught by the apostles; or, that
he is God manifest in the flesh—as if the apostles and their
followers taught *another* God than the God of Abraham, is
a calumny that must be answered for before him, who
says, " Thou shalt not bear false witness against thy neighbour."

* Second Letters, p. 12.

You are pleafed to fay, that you are "*a Jew by choice, and not becaufe* you are born a Jew." And I am happy to fay, that I am a *Chriftian* by *choice*, and not becaufe I was born a Chriftian. But one of us muft be certainly *wrong* with refpect to the point of difference, which, if there be any truth in religion at all, is a point of infinite importance. While our views of religion are fo directly oppofite, *both* of us cannot have *clear evidence* that we are right. How dear your religion is to you I cannot tell, but this I can fay, that, according to my habitual feelings, I would not exchange for ten thoufand worlds, were they at my difpofal. I would not exchange my *prefent peace of mind*, which is the pure effect of the religion I embrace, as held forth in the New Teftament, independent of the *eternal weight of glory* it exhibits to be enjoyed hereafter, for all the advantages that your moft fanguine hopes can imagine, as attending the appearance of another Meffiah. And my fatisfaction is derived as well from the *Old* Teftament as the *New*; the writings of Mofes, as well as thofe of Paul; for the mercy of God, through the Mediator and his atoning facrifice, explicit or implied, fhines in every page; in both I find pardon, peace, righteoufnefs, and life; grace reigning through righteoufnefs, unto eternal life by Jefus Chrift, whom God hath fet forth a propitiation for fin, in order to *declare his righteoufnefs*, that he might be *juft*, and the *juftifier* of him who believeth in Jefus. And Dr. OWEN undertakes, in this performance, to demonftrate, that for any of Adam's race to be pardoned and made happy with God for ever, without fuch a provifion, is utterly inconfiftent (even taking the Old Teftament only for our *data)* utterly inconfiftent with all juft apprehenfions of the attributes of Jehovah; and we defy all the world fairly to difprove his conclufion. But alas! what a light and infignificant thing is the *demonftration* of a Chriftian in the fcales of a Jew! I can eafily conceive, that the human mind (fuch is the darknefs and degeneracy of our fallen nature)

Letters, p. 91.

is capable of admitting the bare *opinions* of friends to be of greater weight and authority than the *demonstrations* of others. Hence we may learn to adore the *sovereignty of Divine grace* in every instance of a cordial submission to the truth of God. If men hear not Moses and the prophets, in their testimony for Jesus, neither will they be persuaded though one rose from the dead—*as he has actually done.*

Dear Sir, my heart's desire and prayer to God for Israel is, that they might be saved; may the God of Abraham, of Isaac, and of Jacob, the God and Father of our Lord Jesus Christ, by his effectual grace, bring you to know his eternal truth! How differently would you then judge of the evil and demerit of sin, and of the need of a real atoning sacrifice to secure the honour of the Divine government! How infinitely desireable would then appear, a Saviour from the power and love of iniquity, and from a fatal security under its dominion and deceitfulness! With what concern would you then regard the folly of that interpretation of the lively oracles which confines the work of the promised Messiah to this short life, the life of a mere mortal, and a small spot of this globe! Seriously reflect, dear Sir, how unworthy of God, how inadequate to the real wants of an immortal mind, and how inconsistent with the whole tenour of Divine revelation, as well as absolutely contrary to the clearest passages, must such an interpretation be.

I am, Dear Sir,

Your sincere wellwisher,

EDWARD WILLIAMS.

Oswestry, Feb. 1790.

www.ingramcontent.com/pod-product-compliance
Lightning Source LLC
Chambersburg PA
CBHW032044220426
43664CB00008B/846